Human Relationships

Human Relationships

4th Edition

Steve Duck

SAGE Publications
Los Angeles · London · New Delhi · Singapore

First published 2007

Apart from any fair dealing for the purposes of research or private study, or criticism or review, as permitted under the Copyright, Designs and Patents Act, 1988, this publication may be reproduced, stored or transmitted in any form, or by any means, only with the prior permission in writing of the publishers, or in the case of reprographic reproduction, in accordance with the terms of licences issued by the Copyright Licensing Agency. Enquiries concerning reproduction outside those terms should be sent to the publishers.

 SAGE Publications Ltd
1 Oliver's Yard
55 City Road
London EC1Y 1SP

SAGE Publications Inc.
2455 Teller Road
Thousand Oaks, California 91320

SAGE Publications India Pvt Ltd
B 1/I 1 Mohan Cooperative Industrial Area
Mathura Road, New Delhi 110 044
India

SAGE Publications Asia-Pacific Pte Ltd
33 Pekin Street #02-01
Far East Square
Singapore 048763

British Library Cataloguing in Publication data

A catalogue record for this book is available from the British Library

ISBN 978-1-4129-2998-1
ISBN 978-1-4129-2999-8 (pbk)

Library of Congress Control Number: 2006929060

Typeset by C&M Digitals (P) Ltd, Chennai, India
Printed in Great Britain by The Alden Press, Witney
Printed on paper from sustainable resources

Contents

Preface

In the 20 years since *Human Relationships* was first published, there has indeed been the huge increase in the number of courses on relationships in such disciplines as communication studies, family studies, sociology, and personality and developmental psychology that I had hoped for. A consequence is that there have been not only substantial advances in theory, scope and methods, but also diversity in the ways in which the subject matter is taught. All of these make the original 1986 version of this book gratifyingly dated and also impel revision of the Third Edition that was published in 1998. For example, there has been substantial attention to attachment theory, sociobiology, evolutionary theory, and culture but there is also corresponding attention to the practical and qualitative effects of conduct of everyday life in the routine behaviours of relationships — how people carry them out. The blending of these elements, characterized by the connection of predisposing qualities to the actual performances of daily life, is one of the main changes that characterize this Fourth Edition.

The attention to relationship performance gives the book a broad appeal to those disciplines concerned with interactions, while the inclusion of evolutionary and attachment perspectives will attract readers whose main interest is in factors that predetermine certain behaviours (such as biological predispositions, acquired personality proclivities, styles of interaction acquired in early experience and more distant influences such as cultural norms). Of course all of these things have importance in the study of relationships, and this book will not be imperialist in claiming that there is only one interesting way to look at relationships. It does, however, argue against those who say that there is only one such way. This edition thus blends the established UK emphasis on discourse with the more traditional US focus on experimental perspectives, stressing the ways in which the predisposing aspects of psychology, such as personality, evolutionary and socio-biological components of psychological dispositions are given their real and enacted form in the interactions of everyday life among networks of real people.

Another necessary increase in attention is given both to the dark side of relationships — the things that are clearly bad about relationships such as jealousy and stalking — and to the smaller everyday management of difficulties in relating, the perpetually recurrent crises in all relating that require us to balance rewards and the inevitable costs that stem from the essentially dualist and dialogical nature of relationships in practical life. This type of management is an inescapable challenge of relationship conduct since they are always changing and so we must constantly adjust as part of the natural process of the maintenance and evolution of relationships (and, indeed, of our own changing life circumstances, as we progress through the life cycle). The routine management of the difficulties of relationships now takes up an entirely new chapter in this edition (Chapter 7 'The Management of Relationship Difficulty').

All relationships are networked experiences and in everyday life that makes them difficult as well as beneficial. Particularly the sociologists have demonstrated how naïve it is to see relationships as occurring only as emotional events between two partners on their own. For one thing most partners get introduced by mutual friends — which brings networks right into the very beginning of relationships — but the advice and critique of outsiders is also perpetually available whenever two or three are gathered together. The modern cult of celebrity brings the relationships of film and pop stars and politicians into public scrutiny and even ordinary folk are criticized for their relational behaviour by others on TV and in the newspapers. Bosses and co-workers freely comment on romances at the office, and friends, parents and other relatives are even asked their opinions about the suitability of partners and to make assessments of the behaviour that occurs in relationships. When Hillary Clinton forgave Bill for his affair with Monica, most people didn't say 'Okay, that's their private business', they had TV phone-ins devoted to comments from people who didn't actually know any of the participants involved nor any of the details of their behavior or relationship circumstances. Yet nobody said that the callers were in any way wrong to voice their opinions on the matter. In addition to the growth in theory and research, this recognition of a shift in balance from the dyadic to the culturally contextual is taken into account in this Fourth Edition.

Furthermore, there has been a significant growth in relational technology: cell phones, the Internet, IM, texting, facebook/myspace, online dating. The fact that relationships and roles bleed across boundaries between previously segmented parts of life is now a major feature of living and one cannot ignore the fact that such boundary crossing is important, not only to student readers, but also in the greater world. The new Chapter 6 ('Technology and the Boundaries of Relationships: It's all Geek to me') now covers these developments, arguing that technological change is in fact a *relational* change because electronic technology is essentially used as *relational* technology and that relational space is now effectively ubiquitous.

Also, the Fourth Edition highlights the places where applications and practical implications of relationship research can be found. Increased recognition of the role of relationships is now standard in health sciences (relationships as sources of health and of additional anxiety and discomfort for the chronically sick), legal disciplines, where relationships in jury decision-making, law enforcement and criminality are recognized, and in business, where management and marketing both now attend to relationships. Beyond these cases however, the Fourth Edition offers an emphasis on the broader application of research. Each chapter now contains examples and exercises where the principles discussed in the chapter can be applied in the real world that students know and live in. The field has now reached the state of maturity where its practical usefulness can also be demonstrated in a world dominated by a corporate mentality, which requires answers about the practical value of the academy. Thus, the students who read this book not only will learn about relationships, but will begin to think about them in a way which can be applied broadly, once they leave college — but they are encouraged to understand and illuminate their own lives even before that.

To this end the Fourth Edition contains a number of new pedagogical devices to aid student learning and reflection about their experiences, while also assisting the instructor in using the material to best effect and making dry theory come alive. Each chapter contains a set of boxes, sometimes more than one of each. One of these is a '**Try this out**' box that indicates ways in which the students can employ the concepts used in the chapter to inform and understand their own life as it happens to them (i.e. not just a vague expectation that '… this is how social psychology explains your life at the theoretical level' but actual cases drawn from their own experience to use in understanding concepts explored in detail in the chapter). Students will be encouraged and directed to refer to the usual dry theoretical concepts discussed in each chapter by directly applying them to their own daily experience and will be directed to consider how and why their experiences differ from those of their classmates. This in itself will make class activity more rewarding for the instructor as well as for the students themselves since a variety of perspectives will predictably emerge and provide fodder for contemplation (those elusive times that instructors know, and desperately seek, as 'teachable moments').

Frequent '**Look out for this in the media**' boxes provide the students with culturally critical guidance on TV or film examples illustrating the specific concepts developed in the chapter. Students will be steered to discover examples of a concept as presented by TV and other media. In many cases recent films are suggested as illustrators of examples of concepts in the chapter and in some cases specific scenes are identified either for student or instructor viewing or use in class.

Each chapter has one or more '**Listen in on your own life**' boxes to encourage and attune students to attend carefully to their own conversations directly and astutely, so gleaning evidence to illustrate items discussed in each chapter, often with specific suggestions about what to listen out for in ways they will not have imagined using before. Similar but more demanding '**Keep a journal**' boxes focus the students on issues for class discussion and they are guided to record and report on their observations about experiences in their daily life that would help to illustrate the chapter concepts and which otherwise they might not learn to notice. At the end of each chapter, '**Self questions**' present the students with a number of questions that invite them to reflect on their own performance of relationships. Questions are of the form 'Am I doing ...?', 'How do I ...?', 'What do I see my friends and others doing ...?' and are directed in each case to demonstrate the topic of the chapter. In at least one case the questions are intended to make the students reflect very carefully on much broader but taken-for-granted social/cultural issues such as the nature of childhood, relating difficulty, and the spilling over from one role or relational performance boundary to another when they use their mobile phones or send a text message.

At the end of each chapter '**Practical matters**' boxes direct readers to some much wider issues. These are chosen to have practical application in the broader social/cultural world beyond the academic or personal experiences and may guide students in career or family choices later in their life outside of their course requirements while nevertheless offering ideas that could be useful for longer study as final projects or undergraduate degree dissertations.

Chapter summaries are provided in fuller detail in this edition. These, already present in the Third Edition, are expanded in the Fourth Edition to offer improved guides for study and revision, while new **Focus points** at the start of each chapter steer the students to the main concepts that will be reviewed in the chapter and so help to point them in the right direction when taking notes as they read the chapters in the first place.

Acknowledgements

In addition to all those people whom I acknowledged in the previous editions, for this Fourth Edition I am particularly grateful to Dan Kirkpatrick for careful reading and commentary on specific material. Several of my recent students discussed topics in this book and gave me good ideas, among them Walter Carl, Yanrong Chang, Dani Chornet, Robin Crumm, Megan Foley, Maria Garcia-Pastor, Masahiro Masuda, David McMahan, Stephanie Rollie, Erin Sahlstein, Mike Searcy, Jill Tyler, Lise VanderVoort-Valentine, Alaina Winters, and Brendan Young. My deep thanks and appreciation once again go to Joanna, Ben, and Gabriel for their tolerance of my abstraction and focus on the book when they had other things on their minds, and also to Julia T. Wood for her constant encouragement, good advice and email enlightenment.

Thank you all.

Steve Duck, *Iowa City*

Publisher's Acknowledgements

The author and publisher would like to thank the following for permission to use copyrighted material:

Chapter 2
Figure 2.1 simplified diagram from page 163 of
Bartholomew, K. (1990). Avoidance of Intimacy: An attachment perspective. *Journal of Social and Personal Relationships, 7,* 147–178. London: SAGE.

Chapter 3
Figure 3.1 modified from page 119 of
Duck, S.W. (1994). *Meaningful relationships: Talking, sense and relating.* Thousand Oaks, CA: SAGE.

Table 3.1 reproduced from pages 7–8 of
Douglas, W. (1987). Affinity testing in initial interaction. *Journal of Social and Personal Relationships, 4,* 3–16. London: SAGE.

Figure 3.2 modified from Duck (1982: 16) 'A topography of relationship disengagement and dissolution', in S. W. Duck (Ed.), *Personal Relationships 4: Dissolving Personal Relationships.* London: Academic Press. Reprinted with permission from Elsevier.

Figure 3.3 modified from Duck (1984: 169) 'A perspective on the repair of relationships: repair of what when?' in Duck, S. W. (ed.), *Personal Relationships 5: Repairing Personal Relationships.* London: Academic Press. Reprinted with permission from Elsevier.

Chapter 7
Diagram from page 226 of Duck, S. W., Foley, M. K., & Kirkpatrick, C. D. (2006) Relating difficulty in a triangular world. In C. D. Kirkpatrick, S. W. Duck & M. K. Foley (Eds.), *Relating difficulty: Processes of constructing and managing difficult interaction.* (pp. 225–232). Mahwah, NJ: Lawrence Erlbaum and Associates. Reprinted with permission from Lawrence Erlbaum and Associates.

Every effort has been made to trace the copyright holders but if any have been inadvertently overlooked the publisher will be pleased to make the necessary arrangement at the first opportunity.

1

Meaning and Relationships in a Biological and Cultural Context

Focus points for note taking when reading this chapter:

- How far is our relating determined by biology and how far is it created by our culture?
- How does culture interact with biology in our relationship activity?
- Everyday conduct is partly verbal and partly nonverbal: consider carefully the role of language and nonverbal body language in your relationships with other people.
- How does NVC [Nonverbal communication] 'work' such things as power, gender and identity into a relationship?
- How do NVC and language convey our sense of ourselves, our attitudes towards others and our sense of ease (or not) in a relational situation?
- How does our communication send both relational and content messages?

When those of us from a Western culture first think about human relationships we tend to assume that they are results of the emotions that two people have for one another. You like someone, so you become friends; you love someone, so you become romantically attached, or, stated differently, we are friends with someone because we like them; we get romantic because we love someone. These assumptions don't place much emphasis on biology or culture, though we live our lives both as biologically animal and as culturally situated individuals. Our emotions might therefore have a biological basis, even if they are expressed in a culturally understandable way. Floyd (2004) for example, points out that many communication processes and outcomes have physiological markers, and that heart rate changes when we experience not only anger, but sexual arousal and love; that parts of the endocrine system regulate hormone production that can be tied to family conflict or marital depression; and that galvanic skin responses and pupillometry have been used to assess liking, preference, and aversion to both things and people. At a contrasting level of analysis, Manusov & Milstein (2005) recently analysed the vast media frame through which the historically important 1993 handshake on the White House lawn between Yassir Arafat and Yitzhak Rabin was interpreted. The handshake was seen as 'sending a signal' to various political groups about the reception that their views would receive from the powerful figures who played a major part in the interaction.

This simple pairing of examples brings up the fact that the analysis of relationships is available at many different levels, from the microbiological analysis of chemical changes wrought by sexual desire or depression and individual endocrine performance effects on a pair's marital interaction to the oppressive cultural machinery that has historically directed women to a place of relational inferiority, treating them as the property of fathers and husbands for centuries, for example. Yet even now we do not think it odd that parents have the sort of relational power that allows them to take their children to a vacation spot of the parents' choosing without the children being consulted, that children may be denied their choice of playmates by disapproving parents, and that some marriage ceremonies still ask 'Who giveth this woman to be married to this man?' The media may debate the 'rightness' of same-sex marriages and we may feel horror when a paedophile is convicted at the same time as we share with our friends mildly amused joking references to Michael Jackson who was acquitted of such charges. So even if relationships are based on biology it is clear that immediate individual psychological and social communicative processes combine with distant societal and sociological forces to influence our ways of looking at them in a living society where people do not satisfy themselves merely by passing around self-rating questionnaires or the contents of their catheters but actually talk to one another in a social context.

CONTEXTS FOR ANALYSING RELATIONSHIPS

The mystery that a book about human relationships must confront therefore is that there is simultaneously far too much to be said and far too little known about the nature of relationships, far too much that is commonsense and far too little that is understood about the reasons why relationship processes are either common or sense, and far too much that is personally important about the everyday practical consequences of understanding relationships for it to be left only to science, even if that could be restricted to one sort of science (from the physiological to the sociological).

In brief, then, both of these above levels, the physical/physiological and the media frames in a culture, affect human relationships and the ways in which behaviour in them is created and then understood. Accordingly, we must not allow our first thoughts about human relationships to overlook either the biological or the many contexts that create and modify expression and interpretation of personal preferences. Even if desire has a physical basis, real life practical constraints limit our ability to act on our emotions and 'Why can't we do it in the road' even with our spouse. Culture constrains expression of biologically-based desire. This book explores research on relationships with an emphatically contextual lens and teaches that even individual liking is not just individualistic and desire is only infrequently the simple origin of actual relational behaviour. Biology and culture, personal meaning systems created in early childhood, communication, 'audiences' for the performance of our relational behaviour, and nonverbal communication which goes beyond – and modifies the meaning of – the felt emotion and the spoken word modify relationships. Other contexts (the papers or TV, for instance) both facilitate and limit this apparently most private of areas – *personal* relationships. Human relationships are not simply created by liking or attitudes about another person. They are based on many other features which a rich field of research has uncovered in the last 25 years.

Biology: the animal background

Since human beings tend not to think of themselves primarily as animals, we assume that when it comes to mating, there may be more at work than simple individual biochemistry. All the same we understand that in the animal world there are dark forces at work which limit the opportunities for mating success. Darwin (1859) observed that most organisms reproduce very rapidly, and that even slowly reproducing animals such as elephants could cover the globe in a few centuries if there were not other factors that limited their reproductive success. One of the things which influences success is competition within a species (the stags with the strongest muscles mate more frequently than other stags). Another factor is the availability of the resources that the animal needs to survive, such as their specific foods and habitats. A third element that limits reproductive success results from competition for the same resources: for example, if elephants and goldfish both need water, the fact that elephants can drain the pond makes life difficult for the goldfish.

As we look around at the people on our bus, can we see such relational principles essentially still at work, even if they have been modified by thousands of years of social civilization? Yes, say Kenrick & Trost (2000) who point to a sociobiological basis for human mate selection. In competition with other members of the species, those human beings who possess particularly attractive characteristics will be at an advantage in the selection of reproductive mates. Likewise, those people who command more resources than others (the strong versus the weak or the wealthy versus the poor) will be at a reproductive advantage. Finally, those humans who are able to brush aside the competing attractions of competitors for attention will be more likely to secure the attachment of their beloved. A large amount of research has been accumulated to demonstrate that human beings are subject to their biological impulses in ways that many people fail to recognize or take into account sufficiently. For example, dominance hierarchies evident in human relationships where some people are on top and some occupy a lower position, can be related to animal dominance hierarchies, and are based on reproductive characteristics such as strength and testosterone. Buss & Dedden (1990) suggested from an evolutionary perspective that even the way in which humans comment negatively about other individuals reflects evolutionary concerns. They found a tendency for women to derogate other women in terms of their looseness, implying that men would not be able to know whether any resultant offspring was theirs (i.e. the suggestion is that the competitors are genetically unreliable because they sleep around); the corresponding tendency for men is a derogation of the reproductive abilities of competitors, such that women could not rely on rewarding reproductive activity (i.e. the suggestion is that competitors have limited apparatus and relevant skills). Similar sociobiological and evolutionary claims have been made to explain tendencies towards rape, jealousy and spouse abuse ('mate retention' as they call it) which Shackelford, Goetz, Buss, Euler & Hoier (2005: 447) describe as 'designed to solve several adaptive problems such as deterring a partner's infidelity and preventing defection from the mating relationship'. In short, the emphasis on biological explanations for human relational behaviour has a substantial basis.

Culture: the large overlay

Although one cannot deny the relevance of such work, you might feel that in an evolved social world, the biological impulses are not crudely animalistic but are shaped by membership of organized and 'civilized' society. Thus, although our biological bases cannot be denied neither should they be allowed to obscure the ways in which our distinction from the apes has brought us TV, the police, and the rituals of Valentine's Day. Atop an undoubted biological base is constructed a superstructure of social conventions that also has to be given due weight in any full analysis of human relationships.

On a personal note, the first lectures I ever attended as an undergraduate were from Niko Tinbergen, who won a Nobel Prize for his work on animal ethology, and I won a Distinction in an exam on animal behaviour at Oxford. My general drift has since been towards the social and away from the biological, and this book will reflect that. I do not deny that biological factors play out in relationships, but I choose to focus on the socially developed forms of influence, and in particular I attend most specifically to the social psychological and communicative aspects of human behaviour that make relationships more than the pheromones or biological resources from which they undoubtedly draw.

For me it is less important that human relationships are sourced from biological urges than that the presentation of such urges takes a socially modified form. The Chinese, Arabs and Canadians manifest desire differently, although they share animal biology with one another. What, I therefore ask, makes human relationships specific to a culture and how can we explain the fact that humans driven by the same stirrings in their loins and the same micro chemicals surging through their veins, nevertheless manifest a staggering range of marriage ceremonies? Even between such similar cultures as the USA and UK the styles of relating are noticeably different in certain respects, such as the degree of initial 'openness' in conversations with strangers.

Daily practices and everyday experience

Start by looking at things we tend not to notice: the cycles of daily life, that differ between cultures (which organize themselves around different sorts of time frames, different religious festivals, even different arrangements for 'the week' some starting it on Sunday some on Saturday). Begin by thinking about the humdrum activities in our own culture and the structures of social experience that bring people together whether they like one another or not (Wood & Duck, 2006) and also ask whether your relational behaviour might be influenced by subtleties of the calendar. Okay, not subtleties – we all get bombarded with information about birthdays, and the necessity of acknowledging anniversaries – but what about things like day of the week? Are Wednesdays good for relationships? Alberts, Yoshimura, Rabby & Loschiavo (2005) say no. In a study of daily reports of individuals' relational activities, it became clear that Wednesdays are actually bad for relationships, confirming Duck, Rutt, Hurst & Strejc (1991) who showed a tendency for greater conflict on Wednesdays. Perlman & Serbin (1984) likewise showed that days of the week are not relationally neutral, and that people experience greater loneliness on the weekend than they do on other days, even if the number of interactions that they have are actually the same on all of these days. People expect more 'action' on weekends, and are more disappointed when it doesn't happen then than they are on other days of the week.

Let's assume that relationships are not experienced as the same all the time, on all days, at any point in the calendar. This might not seem like a particularly important observation at this moment, because it feels like common sense, but when you read further into the book and find that researchers are reporting about relationships as if the calendar did not exist, then we may want to return to this observation. We all knew already that relationships are variable, and that even when we are reading research that acts as if a relationship is the same through all time, we know that our own relationships are not like this. When we read research, however convincing the statistics, we need to connect it with our everyday experience, and ask whether it fits. When it does not, then either we are learning something exciting, or the researchers got it wrong.

Uncertainty and practicality

So far we have three such contexts: biology, culture, and everyday life variation. A fourth is uncertainty: we may be very confident that a date will go well *before* it happens, but afterwards, we might end up sobbing on the bed. Things don't always work out as we hoped. This is something to bear in mind when we discuss research based on questionnaires which assess only people's guesses about hypothetical scenarios. In every imaginary scenario things always go well, there are no problems, just roses, bluebirds and sunsets, and nobody changes their mind. Surprisingly, researchers very often base sweeping conclusions on such imaginary reports (Dragon & Duck, 2005), and although there will be many examples pointed out to you during the course of this book, you should keep an eye out for it when reading research for yourself.

LISTEN TO YOUR OWN CONVERSATIONS

Pick two days and a couple of hours randomly selected in the future (next Thursday 10.00 am–1.00 pm and Friday 6.00 pm–9.00 pm, for example) and then when those times come, keep an informal record of the people you happen to be talking with and the subjects of conversation and also the ways you felt about it. Identify similarities and differences between the different times. Are there any major patterns? Do you talk with particular people about particular sorts of things? Is it harder or easier to list the topics covered with friends than with strangers? Does time of day appear to make any difference or no difference to the topics and styles of conversations?

Some relationships are composed by circumstances over which partners have little emotional control. The workplace, the living place, and the social environment are all made out of passages, offices, rooms, buildings that are close to buildings, rooms, offices, and passages where other people live and work. These environmental contexts shape our relationships, influence the kinds of people we meet, and constrain or facilitate relationships: we are likely to know people we meet a lot, yet even those we love deeply may never be real partners if we live in different countries. The fact is that relationships are conducted at a distance as a feature of modern life (Sahlstein, 2004) and email, instant messaging, and mobile phones have all affected, for large parts of our population anyway, the ways in which relationships are conducted and conceptualized (see Chapter 6). Such movements in society are part of what we need to explore in understanding human relationships: changes in the way that relationships get done are important, because changes in the way we *do* things can result in changes in the way we *experience* things (Duck, in press SAGE CA, see refs).

Society also contains blueprints that shape our thoughts about relationships and how to do them. For example, we all know what a 'mother' or a 'friend' is, but we would not understand relationships of obligation that are familiar in Japan such as *amae* where each partner identifies with the self-interest of the partner and sees a direct connection between outcomes for other and self. Also we probably wouldn't assume that a relationship like 'wife of a brother' could be more important in some cultures than 'sister' or that it may be impolite to address an older brother by his first name – rather the *title* 'brother' should be used. We may also not appreciate that in a society which stresses individualism we assume that relationships are formed from individual preference whereas other cultures (e.g., Colombia) emphasize that relationships are based on the interconnectedness of persons in networks who do exercise *palanca* (or 'leverage'/favours) on one another's behalf as a part of everyday life (Fitch, 1998). Some cultures look at relationships in terms of the good that accrues to the family overall rather than to the individual (Gaines & Ickes, 2000), so two people might get married because it would be good for the families, not because they fall in love in the way our Western culture expects.

KEEP A JOURNAL OR KEEP/READ A BLOG

Do the same exercise as the above one (p. 6) over a longer period of time and take special note of relationally relevant interactions. Record whether you thought they would be important before they happened and whether they turned out to be so. What does a relational blog look like, whether yours or someone else's? How does it match up with the sorts of things you read in research reports about relationships?

Although we are often amused by these 'odd' (from our perspective) ways of relating, we simply do not realize how much of our own relating is influenced by our own culture because our own culture is usually taken for granted as the 'normal' way to do things, just as the people from other cultures do about their own practices (Fitch, 2003). As you read this book you should tune up your ability to notice what is hidden in your daily relational experience. Let's start here with the media as an unnoticed force on your relationships.

We might not ponder the ways in which views of relationships are shaped by ideological influences such as media, yet magazines and TV shows regularly depict 'the right way' to have marriages, conduct romances, or be friends (Duck & McMahan, forthcoming). Magazines run quizzes like '10 ways to improve your marriage', 'Intimacy: the five steps'. This constant 'below-radar' barrage shapes expectations about relationship conduct. Duran & Prusank (1997), for example, looked at the advice about 'relationships' contained in men's and women's magazines and found that there was a great deal of it and it concerned a large range of relationships (e.g. marriage, dating, friendship), relational issues (e.g. conflict, sexual relations, initiating relationships), and advice-laden presentations of how they *should* be conducted. Duran & Prusank concluded:

> Given the various configurations of relationships and the ambiguity they generate, it is logical to assume that men and women are turning to the media as one source of information concerning relational issues. Researchers interested in the study of interpersonal dynamics cannot ignore the influence of media messages which overtly and covertly make their way into the public consciousness and serve to (re)shape and (re)frame relationships. (1997: 186)

You may feel that these are just magazine articles and are interesting but do not really influence anyone – but if they do not have any effect then why do people keep reading them and why do people compare their relationship experiences with the magazines' recommendations and buy millions of self-help books that tell them how to do relating or how to win friends and influence people? Can you honestly say that you have never read such an article nor been influenced by the portrayal of relationships in films and TV or compared your way of doing relating with the way other people in such sources do relating? It will be worthwhile for you to discus this matter with your classmates and see the extent to which there is conformity concerning the ways in which relationships could be conducted. Think of the number of times other people have commented about whether someone should have treated a friend the way they did. Consider how many times someone has given you advice about the sorts of ways to carry on with your relationships. All these things feel normal and usual, but in fact as the rest of this book will show, they are the places where an ideology about relationships is put into effect, the place where cultural stereotypes of relating are enacted in everyday life. They are where we are influenced by social norms concerning the emotions that (we may have assumed at first) are purely personal experiences.

CLASS EXERCISE

Collect examples from the media that present standards for relationships. Look for quizzes about the number of times that people have sex or the number of feelings that they express or the way in which they talk to one another. But don't overlook reports about paedophilia or child pornography and the implicit condemnation contained in such reports. Discuss the results in class.

Quality and appropriateness in relationships

These notions suggest that there is a *right* way to do relating and that it can be articulated and written down, as Montgomery (1988) points out: any reference to 'quality' is also a reference to social norms and ideologies that prefer one way of doing things over another. Few of us would immediately recognize this as a means of social control, yet the idea of 'quality' prepares the ground for a kind of social influence that sets a standard for other people to use in commenting on the ways in which we conduct relationships: 'It's not right', 'He should not treat friends that way', 'She was disloyal to her parents', 'He betrayed her; true friends don't do that'. Comment and criticism based on social expectations are also available to every one of us as we conduct our own relationships ('I felt like hugging him but it would have looked bad'). The Little Person Inside Our Heads tells us when we are doing something that we would find hard to justify to other people, even if that 'something' is the conduct of personal relationships. These feelings arise because sociological context, structural factors and social forces are ever-present ways in which we decide what is 'appropriate' in human relationships (Goodwin & Cramer, 2002); politeness rules encourage us often to conceal our true emotions in public ('be nice even if you don't really feel it'); we may exaggerate or misrepresent expression of our interest in someone or our relational feelings about them, as when we smile at boring strangers at parties or kiss embarrassing relatives at family gatherings. Furthermore, even the highly positive expression, 'I love you', can be judged inappropriate if it comes from the 'wrong person' or at the 'wrong time'. Thus, it is clear that *having* (or *expressing*) emotions is not all that we need to understand in learning about human relationships: we need to think more about contexts and what limits the social legitimacy of indicating emotions in public places. (Is it OK to hold hands in the street? Not in China.)

But there is a deeper aspect of contexts for relationships. Wood (1995) observes that women assume a disproportionate share of responsibilities for home-making in marriage and child care in parent–child relationships. She indicates that if we explain such observations only in terms of individual attitudes and values then we mistake the degree to which attitudes are constructed by cultural views of 'a woman's place', views represented in literature, TV shows, talk, use of language and even Internet games (where women are often depicted as objects to be chased while men get on with the really important business of decapitating fighting lizards). Foley (2006b) points out that many social organizations, such as the priesthood or the police, reinforce particular views of relationships – e.g., by telling battered women that they should 'tough it out' because marriage is a relationship that 'requires that women obey their husbands'. For this reason, many battered women stay in abusive relationships because they receive no support from cultural institutions which take the view that a wife's duty is to oblige her husband, come what may (J. West, 1995).

Communication as a context for 'quality'

Obvious, too, but often overlooked, is that language is the medium through which many relationship activities are conducted. We talk, write, call, text, or email friends, lovers, parents, children, neighbours, or colleagues – and obviously use language to do that, even if the SMS (Short Message Service [Texting])/MTMF language is special (Chan & Cheng, 2004). Language, however, is not a neutral medium but provides a formative context for discussion of relationships. Think what is implied by metaphors to describe relationships: 'bonding' or 'couple' (Baxter, 1992). 'Bonds' and 'couple' are both metaphors implying ties, connection – chains, even.

We should reflect on ways in which language structures our thinking about relationships along culturally normative lines. Magazines, norms, friends, and 'others' all shape our views of acceptable relationship practices but do not need to explicate cultural norms ('Be loyal to your friends'). The terms in which they tell stories about friends can play into cultural norms anyway. For example, friends' stories about their behaviour can point out loyalty, and hence adherence to that norm of friendship. Furthermore in ways that we will explore later, everyday talk serves to present our opinions of the ways in which the world *should* be viewed. Communication, language, and all that is culturally encoded within it are thus crucial bases for establishing conduct for human relationships and their quality.

Although it might appear, then, as insignificant activity, nevertheless as we gossip with friends so we select descriptions of behaviour that record approval or disapproval as compared to cultural norms ('Sure, I'll help you. What are friends for?'), or decide whether a person was being good or bad ('He's so reliable', 'No he's just boringly predictable'). In such subtle ways as selection of what to include in a story or the ways to gossip about others' behaviour, people reinforce social norms, and their language embodies norms for us. Language thus *structures* meanings about human relationships as well as reporting them (Duck, 1994). For example, we are used to explaining relationships in terms of emotion, love and attraction, but language also loads in metaphors that set up context and 'take a view' about the ways in which people are *supposed* to progress in *building* a relationship (Allan, 1993). The way in which we describe the development of a relationship is a story imposed on a number of occurrences perceived within a particular culture as a *reasonable* path (Baxter, 1992). By describing relationships in particular ways, cultures provide contexts for individuals not only to view the way relationships are *supposed to* develop, but also to speak with culturally-shared vocabularies for representing relationship growth. 'We fell in love' is a commonly accepted explanation for romantic involvement in most Western cultures; 'It is a good match for both families' is more acceptable in many other parts of the world.

What we should not overlook are the subtler influences on relationship conduct that are created by contexts of talk that enact social norms or invite moral judgements about relational behaviour. Indeed, on the day I was writing this, a politician running for the leadership of a UK political party withdrew from the contest because of newspaper revelations of an affair with a 'rent boy' and TV commentators were unrestrained in offering viewers a context for judging the behaviour!

The conduct of relationships will ultimately be judged by social communities rather than by partners alone (Simmel, 1950). Relationship partners often articulate that behaviour may be judged by others (e.g., 'What will the neighbours think?' and 'What do we tell the kids?' are common thoughts in couples considering divorce – see Chapter 4). Muraco (2005) even showed that heterosexual college students evaluate friendship behaviours in context and see them more positively when the persons are described as heterosexual rather than as gay – even when the behaviour is identical. J. West (1995) notes that when we talk of relationships breaking up our cultural reference point is placed within a powerful language of 'failure' that makes partners think carefully about their relational skills. Many people stay in painful relationships because they do not want other people to think them failures.

Thus we have to recognize that even relationship behaviours do not mean much without being placed in some larger conceptual contexts. Attempts to focus explanations for relationship processes only on the inside of the relationship or the individual partners' choices and emotions are incomplete and limiting because they overlook important social, sociological, and cultural contexts that 'prefer' certain sorts of relationships and regard other forms negatively (Goodwin & Cramer, 2002; VanderVoort & Duck, 2004). Whenever we talk about relationship quality or assess relationships as 'good' or 'bad' or partners as 'skilled' or 'unskilled' or evaluate people as 'good friends' or see divorce as a relational failure rather than a bold or realistic move then we are essentially backing into an ideology that sets a standard and also has set criteria for 'quality' (Montgomery, 1988).

This book looks at relationships therefore not just as individual emotions but as illustrating ways in which an individual's social cognition reflects social context through communication and the practicalities of membership of a society. We start examining human relationships by looking at language and talk, since these are broad public contexts for relating, but we must not overlook NVC (nonverbal communication), a biologically based system for expressing emotion in ways that modify the meaning of talk (e.g., ever seen anyone say they are interested while nevertheless yawning?).

COMMUNICATIVE CONTEXTS FOR DOING RELATIONSHIPS

Two scholars once wrote that 'We converse our way through life' (Berger & Kellner, 1964), and in the case of everyday relationships, you cannot get away from that fact. If you were to sit and list the things that you do with friends, then top of the list would surely have to be 'talking' (Wood & Duck, 2006). Talk composes relationships – whether they are starting, getting better, disintegrating, or just carrying on. Everyday talk creates intimacy (Wood, 2006), pulls families together (Bruess & Hoefs, 2006), enacts friendship (Metts, 2006) and 'does' social support (Foley, 2006a). Talk changes relationships, expresses emotion, handles conflict, and indicates affection, but it also shares attitudes and 'does identity' (Mokros, 2006). Talk declares love, desires, goals and relational fantasies. We talk to handle conflicts, disputes and irritations, to get out of relationships, and deal with daily hassles (Kirkpatrick, Duck & Foley, 2006). We talk to exact revenge (Foster & Rosnow, 2006), deal with in-laws (Morr-Serewicz, 2006) and to forgive (Waldron & Kelley, 2005).

In carrying out these activities we *choose* the words to use and even casual talk selects descriptive preferences or registers a decision to stay silent (Nicholson, 2006). Silences and words both report our *assessment* of the world and attempt to persuade others to endorse that view (Carl & Duck, 2004). Relationships are persuasive and they provide context for other considerations, such as whether you *should* do a favour for your friend. In everyday communication, we are influenced by things friends say and we rarely do something without considering the relational consequences.

There is more to human relationships than talk, though. It is the broader context of *communication* as a whole that is the basis for relating, including not only talk but 'paralanguage' (such as sarcastic tones of voice that communicate feelings) that modifies a communication (for example the facial expression or posture that we adopt) – something said with a wink can carry different meaning if attention is paid only to 'the content' of the speech. Indeed an important claim is that every spoken message contains not one but two elements (Watzlawick, Beavin & Jackson, 1967): the *content* and a *message about the relationship* between speaker and listener. You cannot utter a word without also simultaneously indicating how you *feel* about the other person.

Communication is thus not merely the passing of messages between persons but the whole processes by which meaning and identity are managed (Antaki & Widdicombe, 1998). Additionally, relationships are managed by such things as politeness and 'face work' (that is, attending to whether someone loses face from the way in which you treat them – García-Pastor, 2005). This context includes NVC (i.e., nonverbal communication), silent messages of touch, smiles, warm and tender eyes, and bodily postures that convey culturally accepted messages of invitation, approval or rejection as well as subtleties of the conversational text itself. For example, talk shapes interactions towards power usages and Antaki, Barnes & Leudar (2005) indicate that therapist talk serves to reformulate what the client has said, adding an overlay of interpretation. Whenever we summarize what someone has said (whether intentionally or not), we add a commentary that frames what the person said, and we can thereby indicate our (dis)agreement with it.

SILENT LANGUAGE: NONVERBAL COMMUNICATION

Bodies talk. Whenever we sit, stand, walk, position ourselves next to someone, or look at someone else, we give off messages, some of which we may not have intended to make obvious (Guerrero & Floyd, 2006). Equally, we can learn that someone dislikes us without a single word being said, that he or she is deliberately lying to us (Searcy, Duck & Blanck, 2005), or that a person finds us sexually attractive or appealing (Keeley & Hart, 1994). Also, through usage of spacing (closeness or distance, for example), messages of intimacy or dislike can be conveyed in a given culture, just as they are by words. From the nonverbal accompaniments of speech, human beings deduce overtones about relationship messages, as when a sensitive comment is made more comforting by a tender touch or supportive embrace. The study of NVC covers an enormous amount of material on which many books and journals are available (See 'Further reading' listed at the end of the chapter), so coverage here is skimpy. You need to know some key terms however: *Proxemics* – the nonverbal messages conveyed by being close or distant from someone and by general space usage; *Kinesics* – the messages conveyed by the way in which someone moves around or the postures which a person adopts; *Chronemics* – the messages conveyed by ways in which time is used, for example by hesitancy in speech or by a person showing up 'fashionably late'; *Haptics* – the messages of touch; *Eye contact* – the messages (usually liking, or honesty) conveyed by looking someone else in the eye. Eye contact is also used not only to convey emotional messages, but also to regulate social interaction and an interaction is not supposed to begin until you have 'caught someone's eye'.

Much of this sort of communication in relationships – whether spatial, paralinguistic (i.e. conveyed in the tone or style of the words) or based on gestures and facial expressions – is familiar to us, even if the terms used in research are abstruse. Yet just as kids may be able to ride a bicycle without being able to explain balance or the physics of motion, so we may be unaware of the rules and meanings that underlie familiar behaviours.

Nonverbal communication (NVC) is made up of, for instance, the spacing between people when we interact, the gestures, eye movements and facial expressions that provide context for, but also supplement, our speech, and a range of other cues (Keeley & Hart, 1994; Riggio & Feldman, 2005). It can be quite explicit and inter-cultural: Captain Cook (famous for revealing Australia and New Zealand to the European world) noted in 1774 that when he first met the Maoris, 'One fellow showed us his backside in such a manner that it was not necessary to have an interpreter' (Hughes, 1991: 258).

We never speak without adding to the message by powerful body language. Guerrero & Floyd (2006) show its relational relevance such that close proximity, touch, and gaze, along with reduced verbal fluency, longer times between the end of one person's speech and another's starting, and more silence distinguish romantic relationships from friendships. Nodding and vocal interest are more prevalent in friendships than in romantic relationships. There are even relational differences between the ways in which bodies are 'arranged' in complementary ways ('postural congruence' occurs when two people adopt the same posture – for example both leaning on a wall or both resting elbows on a table with head on hands); postural congruence occurs more in same-sex than in opposite-sex dyads. More than this, women display more direct body orientation and gaze, but men engage in more forward lean and postural congruence.

Yet it is important to recognize that such findings about relationships emerge against the background of the profound importance of nonverbal communication in general interactions and the inappropriateness that is indicated when nonverbal behaviour mismatches the words spoken. Research has long told us that in such cases we are more influenced by nonverbal than verbal components of messages (Argyle, Salter, Nicholson, Williams & Burgess, 1970). NVC serves to indicate messages of liking, feeling, attitudes about others, and attitudes about relationships; NVC also regulates interactions, making them smooth and relaxed or awkward and formal. Of course, the two are connected and the more we like someone the more relaxed the interaction becomes, so we signal liking not only by direct and single cues (e.g., lots of eye contact when we like someone), but also by sequences and the tone of interaction.

Are there social rules about space?

A large number of messages about status and liking are structured into interactions and a great deal of influence on social encounters is exerted by space and its management ('proxemics'). These factors position people both literally and metaphorically in relationship to one another. Space carries forceful messages about relationships and is a powerful ingredient in the mix of nonverbal and verbal indicators of liking.

Space even gets into our talk about relationships. For example, we talk about being 'close' to someone. 'Close' is a word that literally refers to space and yet we use it metaphorically to apply to relationships, almost unthinkingly. We can even talk about 'growing apart' when we mean that our liking for someone is decreasing or our relationship with them is getting more difficult. In fact *spatial metaphors* run through much of our thinking about relationships and there is a reason for that: space influences the way in which we relate to others and it communicates messages of power, liking, and attitudes towards others. There is a rich array of metaphorical statements about power and position that are made in spatial terminology. For example, we talk of people being 'high and mighty', 'head and shoulders above the rest', 'the tops', 'way above the competition', 'the greatest'. Good experiences are 'highs'. We have *high* moral principles and are *above* doing anything mean such as showing *low* cunning.

Spatial metaphors also refer to 'inferiority' (derived from the Latin *inferus*, meaning 'below' or 'lower'): people are of low status, lowly, lowdown no-goods, beneath (rather than above) contempt. A bad experience is a 'downer', and we feel low. In doing something bad, we may stoop *low*, or let others *down*. When we assert ourselves, on the other hand, we stand *up* for ourselves. Our language equates spatial position with moral, social or relational position and 'up' is 'good' (Lakoff & Johnson, 1980).

Powerful social rules govern actual rather than metaphorical use of space in social situations, too. These work through posture, gesture, orientation (i.e., the way our body is facing) and various other subtleties like eye movements, but are so powerful that the very discussion of NVC is hard to do and we rarely refer directly to someone's nonverbal behaviour: to do so is rude or aggressive ('Wipe that smile off your face', 'Look at me when I'm talking to you'). The rarity of such comments emphasizes that the competent use of NVC is a prerequisite to relating to other people.

The rule system for competent NVC makes six basic assumptions: (1) the use of nonverbal cues is identifiable and recognizable; (2) the operation of nonverbal cues is systematic, even if occasionally ambiguous; (3) we translate feelings and intentions into nonverbal messages (i.e., we *'encode'*); (4) observers can interpret it (or *'decode'*); (5) whether we intend it, observers decode our behaviour as relationally relevant, even attending to signals that we thought successfully concealed; (6) NVC is judged in cultural context, such that a behaviour appropriate (or meaningful) in one culture may not be appropriate (or may carry another meaning) in another cultural context. For instance, the placing of the thumb and forefinger together as a circle means 'Perfect!' in the USA but is a crude sexual insult in Sicily, and US troops occupying Iraq have been trained on the cultural differences in

American and Iraqi nonverbal communication (see e.g. http://news.bbc.
co.uk/2/hi/technology/4729262.stm.)

Nonverbal communication is not only systematic in the above ways but also
serves five functions for us (Patterson, 1992). These functions are to: (1) provide
information about ourselves, especially our feelings or relational attitudes; (2) regulate interaction (e.g., by enabling us to see when someone has said all that they
intend to say and it is our turn to talk); (3) express emotional closeness in relationships; (4) attempt social control (e.g. by dominating others); (5) engage in ser-
vice-task function (i.e., to depersonalize certain contacts that would otherwise be
'intimate'. For example, think of the parts of your body that physicians can touch
but which other people may not – unless they are remarkably close friends). Also
some parts of the body can be touched in private but not in public (Davis, 1983),
or in an informal setting like a bedroom but not, say, when you are in church.

TRY THIS OUT

Pair off and start a conversation. After about a minute or so the
instructor will give you a signal and you must now hold both your
partner's hands and continue the conversation; after a second signal
you should place both your hands on the other person's shoulder, one
on each, and continue; and finally both hands on the waist of the
other person.

Points to discuss: How it felt; how it changed; what factors made
a difference (sex of partners, whether and how well you know them,
depth of relationship if any). If you feel uneasy, what do you feel
uneasy *about*, given that this is a class exercise, not an event occurring outside of class? How might you feel when you see your partner
outside class now?

Territories in space

Let us begin with a large context for behaviour: the space in which it occurs. At first
sight 'territory' may seem irrelevant to everyday human relationships, even though
animals and governments use the concept a lot. Some birds attack invaders that
come into their 'patch', dogs mark out territorial boundaries with body products,
and governments put up their flags on their territory. Yet humans use space, too, in
a systematic way that has territorial and relational overtones (i.e., we use space as if
it is invisibly 'attached' to us or under our control). This occurs both in fixed settings,
like offices, and in dynamic settings, during conversations.

Within the general study of 'proxemics', Hall (1966) differentiated space into *intimate* (i.e., direct contact to around 18 inches [46 cm] away from another person – obviously someone we know and like); *personal* (around 18 inches [46 cm] to about 4 feet [1.4 m] apart usually used when talking to casual friends or acquaintances); *social* (around 4 feet [1.4 m] to around 12 feet [4.2 m] apart – usually used for business transactions and impersonal encounters), or *public* (more than 12 feet [4.2m] apart – how a speaker at public events stands away from the audience).

As long as we can breathe comfortably and basic biological needs are met (e.g., we are not too hot/cold) then sociocultural and relational rules for distribution of space will be followed. In different relational contexts we are comfortable with different distances; imagine talking to friends, to a teacher, and going to a lecture – you would not sit as close to a teacher giving a lecture as you would to a friend telling a story. Another thing is that as we get to know someone better so we indicate this by holding conversations at smaller distances from each other. The more intimate we become emotionally, the more intimate we get spatially; we get closer in two senses and will more often touch people we know very well.

In relational settings the use of different sorts of space conveys different messages. Knapp & Hall (2002) distinguish four different types: Primary territories (always ours, central to our lives) such as our house, car, body, wallets and purses, or items claimed temporarily for our primary or sole use, such as cutlery in a restaurant, or a hotel bed); Secondary territories (not central to our lives, nor exclusive to our use, such as TVs in common rooms); Public territories (available for temporary occupancy by anyone – park benches or bus seats); Personal space refers to that space legitimately claimed or occupied by a person for the time being.

In the course of everyday interaction, entry into our spaces by other people sends different signals, depending on the space and the kind and duration of the entry. For example, if someone else sits on the same park bench, that is not a violation of our personal space, even though we might resent them using it. On the other hand, if someone sleeps in our hotel bed uninvited, then that is an invasion of our rights. We can therefore differentiate these entries into our personal space as either *Violation* (unwarranted encroachment into personal space, such as sitting in your assigned seat on a plane or putting their hand down your shirt), *Invasion* (longer-term violation of space, such as when the younger sibling moves into your bedroom after you leave for college), and *Contamination* (defilement of personal space, such as you would feel after a burglary or if someone throws up on your living room carpet). We can attempt to prevent such entries and violations by the use of 'markers' which stake a claim to the space (for example by hanging a coat over the back of a chair we wish to use in the library, or by putting up a 'No trespassing' sign). You might like to consider whether the gift of an engagement ring sends the same kind of (relational) message.

LOOK OUT FOR THIS IN THE MEDIA

With reference to news items specifically, how do people designate territory as theirs? Think not only about such things as national flags or name tags on desks or furniture arrangements, but look at ways in which two people claim property through nonverbal means in news stories. Discussion of relevant news stories reported by class members should generate at least 40 minutes of discussion if they have done their observations properly.

Claiming space is claiming power

Space rules carry information about status, ownership, and the relationship between participants. Human beings decorate their rooms, houses, cars, other possessions, and themselves in a way that indicates these things. For instance, furniture in offices is arranged in ways that indicate who owns what, who is superior to whom, and how much of the space is 'public'. Desks and tables are arranged to show power relationships between people, in addition to any reasons to do with lighting or ease of communication. For example, bosses usually make you sit across the desk from them as a distancing device to indicate their power and importance. By contrast, therapists tend to sit with nothing but a low table in between clients and themselves. This reduces physical and psychological barriers, promoting a context for informal and relaxed interaction.

Chang (2002) noted that in a Chinese courtroom, the defendant is placed on a low stool in the centre of the room, a position of inferiority consistent with the presumption in Chinese courts that defendants are guilty and there to be punished, not to be tried for guilt or innocence. We also use furniture in this way to make implicit statements about relative power in a relationship. For example, receptionists' desks are usually placed in your path and so communicate the receptionist's power to restrict your entry further into the office. It is *physically* possible to break the rules, but is a *social* offence. For example, moving your chair round the barrier so that you sit next to the boss, moving round to the other side of the table, opening a door marked 'Private', or sitting on a receptionist's desk, all violate a social rule. Such violations would most probably lead to comment, discomfort or possibly to the other person becoming angry. Someone who habitually violates such rules in conducting relationships will be seen as difficult to deal with (and they may have Nonverbal Learning Disability: http://www.nldontheweb.org).

Symbolic decoration of territory also indicates ownership and affirms control and power. The most obvious example is clothing: physically, I could put my hand in your pocket, but socially … it could be a big mistake. The placing of posters or decorations on a wall can also indicate that the person claims that space and also states identity: a person putting Eminem on the wall claims a different identity from someone posting George Bush and Tony Blair shaking hands. Furthermore, if we observe an empty seat with a coat hanging over the back, we know it is a meaningful symbol laying claim to the space: the coat owner is indicating that he or she will return and is 'keeping' the chair. You might like to consider whether the same sort of principle is implicit in *relational* 'decoration' such as wedding rings.

A further way of claiming space is through *self extension*. Placing your feet on a coffee table, sprawling across an empty bench, and leaning across a doorway are all ways of claiming control over the space. Claiming space is claiming power, ownership, and, above all, status. As people are promoted in an organization, so this is symbolically recognized by larger offices, longer desks, taller chairs, and wider blotter pads. Space is a metaphor for status.

Most often spatial claims are *horizontal*: the floor space allocated to a person. Status claims, however, can be vertical too, as in 'higher' or 'lower' status. Kings, queens, judges and professors sit on raised platforms. Equally, temporary changes in status can be acknowledged by height changes as when a scoring footballer jumps up in the air or is lifted up in triumph by team mates. More subtly, persons sometimes bow or curtsy (thus reducing their height) when they are introduced to someone of much higher status, and in Ancient China persons introduced to the emperor had to reduce their height by hurling themselves to the floor and banging their foreheads on the ground. Nowadays, only Assistant Professors seeking tenure do this.

TRY THIS OUT

Divide the class into threes. The class instructor will now leave for five minutes. Each group of three should be instructed to set off a part of the classroom as their own, using any method they can think of. When the instructor returns, it must be clear which bits of the classroom 'belong' to each group. Discuss the ways in which people have done this exercise and what it teaches us about nonverbal communication and 'territorial markers' that people use.

Space and conversation

Space matters not only statically but in the dynamic flow of social encounters (Guerrero & Floyd, 2006). To lean across someone's desk more than about half way is a threat to them personally. To lean beside someone with your hand on the wall beside his or her shoulder at a party is to 'claim' the person: you are telling other people to 'Keep out'. The other person in these circumstances can obviously escape physically by brushing past, but to do so would be rude and violate a social rule about the relational 'meaning' of space. Likewise, invasion of someone's space by touching them can be a statement about intimacy, as can moving closer, crossing over the table to sit next to one another rather than opposite, though these may also be seen just as invasive. Guerrero & Andersen (1991) showed that the level of public touch between partners was actually curvilinear – lower for couples at early or late/stable stages of relationships, highest for those at middle or developing stages. They also found that public touch increased primarily in the hand and waist areas during intermediate stages of relationships. In short, dynamic use of space carries relational messages that affect the tone of an interaction and show degree of (dis)liking or hostility/friendliness.

Nonverbal systems of meaning

You may be starting to see a problem. What exactly is *the* meaning of space in social encounters? At some times, our physical closeness indicates intimacy (e.g., when we sit next to people whom we like), but at other times it can indicate personal threat and cause a rise in blood pressure (Floyd, 2004). The two kinds of meaning are attached to eye movements as well. Gazing at a person's eyes is usually, but not always, an indication of intense liking; we look at people more often if we like them. In the West, eye contact (i.e., when two people look one another in the eye) indicates interest, liking, and acceptance (Keeley & Hart, 1994), but in the East inferiors may not look superiors in the eye because it is regarded as disrespectful or challenging. Pupil size marginally increases when we see someone or something we like (Walker & Trimboli, 1989). Yet, as with proximity, staring and gazing can be threatening also. An intense stare can be used as a threatening cue both in animals and in humans. The stare is a stimulus to flight, and drivers who are stared at when they stop at traffic lights will accelerate away faster from the junction when the lights go green (Ellsworth, Carlsmith & Henson, 1972). Like physical closeness, eye contact thus can indicate threat or dominance, as well as liking.

How do people decide the intended meaning, then? The interpretation of space rules is learned within a specific culture. The cultural system guides us not only on the interpretation of individual cues but on how to put different cues together and make sense of the whole context. This happens because the verbal–nonverbal communication system is a *system* of parts (like space, eye contact, touch) that provides a context to help us to decode people's meaning but also is a system within a cultural system of meaning that 'explains' how they work together (Guerrero & Floyd, 2006). Individual cues like proximity hardly ever happen in isolation and we can learn the full relational message by attending to the *system* of cues, not just to one. We work out relational meaning from eye-contact-plus-context or from proximity-plus-words. When someone stares and smiles, then we know we are favoured; if someone stares and frowns, then we are in trouble.

If we add two positive messages together, what do we get? Does eye contact plus closeness take the intimacy level beyond what people can bear? Argyle & Dean (1965) proposed an equilibrium model, namely, that the appropriate intimacy level of an interaction is held steady by balancing proximity and eye contact. As proximity increases so eye contact will decrease (unless the two are lovers where the two cues are 'appropriate' together); that way, the total level of signalling for intimacy will stay about right. If proximity decreases then eye contact should increase to maintain the equilibrium. This works with other signals for intimacy, too. For example, as an interviewer's questions become more personal, so the interviewee reduces eye contact when giving answers (Carr & Dabbs, 1974).

Nonverbal signals as interaction regulators

NVC serves another important function and *regulates* social behaviour. There are social rules about speakers' turn-taking, for instance, and interactions do not run smoothly if one or both partners violate(s) the rule. Think briefly whether you could state precisely what the rules of social behaviour are. (You could even try to list them for yourself before reading on and then check your list against mine.) These behaviours are termed 'social skills' and the teaching of such behaviours is called 'Social Skills Training,' or SST for short.

Interactions have to be started, sustained, and ended in culturally appropriate ways, and this is usually managed by nonverbal means. Two nonverbal signals are generally used to start typical interactions: one is eye contact (in this case, 'catching someone's eye'); the other is orientation (i.e., we need to face the right way and have our body oriented openly towards the other person). It is inappropriate, rude, and extremely difficult to open up a conversation without looking at the person and having them look back. It is also hard to continue an interaction when one is wrongly oriented.

TRY THIS OUT

Have a conversation with someone outside of class, someone you know well. Before you respond to anything they say or before you make any spontaneous contribution to the conversation at all, count silently to three, then speak normally. With a different person try responding immediately and as often as possible. What do these disruptions of the chronemics of talk do to the conversations and what do people say about your performance?

A person can decline to engage in conversation merely by refusing to establish eye contact or orientation. Busy waiters and bartenders do it all the time. However, eye contact conjoins with other cues to regulate interactions in other ways also (Guerrero & Floyd, 2006). Eye contact, gaze, looking, and eye movements are associated with 'floor-sharing' (i.e., turn-taking in conversation) and with power and dominance of interactions. Speakers look at listeners less than listeners look at speakers, but speakers start to signal that they have come to the end of their 'speech' by looking at the listener and re-establishing eye contact; this lets the listener 'take over the floor', if desired (Kendon, 1967). Socially anxious people tend to avert their eyes too frequently and so disrupt the flow of the interaction by breaking the rules (Patterson, 1988). High power, on the other hand, is associated with high levels of looking at a listener whilst you are talking whereas less powerful or less expert people tend to look only when listening (Dovidio, Ellyson, Keating, Heltman & Brown, 1988).

Our conversations are regulated also by other factors, some to do with the general rewardingness that is expected in social encounters (Burgoon, Coker & Coker, 1986), and some to do with the general rules about turn-taking (Cappella, 1991). We alter speech patterns and conversational turns as a result of the 'reinforcements' that we receive. Reinforcements here are nonverbal cues that reinforce, encourage or lead us to increase behaviours. Several forms of reinforcement for speaking are available, especially smiling, nodding, and gazing at other persons (Gatewood & Rosenwein, 1981). The same nonverbal cues will encourage and reinforce quite subtle parts of behaviour. One can influence the production of plural nouns, use of abstract concepts, or particular kinds of topic, each of which can be reinforced and increased by specific nonverbal encouragements from a listener (Argyle, 1967).

However, there are also social expectations about amount of gaze, and people who do not gaze enough are violating such an expectation. Without such reinforcements, speakers will often stop, under the impression that the listener is bored, is becoming less involved in the conversation or else, perhaps, wants to intervene (Coker & Burgoon, 1987). One way of 'taking the floor' (or getting a word in edgeways) is to stop being reinforcing and to signal one's disinterest. The listener sends a strong signal by this: 'Please stop talking. It's my turn now'.

Does nonverbal communication show how we really feel?

An important role of nonverbal communication is to convey attitudes (Guerrero & Floyd, 2006; Keeley & Hart, 1994). These may be attitudes about self (e.g., conceited, diffident, mousey, shy, humble); attitudes towards the other person (e.g., dominant, submissive, attracted, disliking, hostile, aggressive); or attitudes about the interaction (e.g., affability, comfortableness, relaxation, intimacy, nervousness).

We tend to assume nervousness and anxiety just from the presence or absence of certain nonverbal behaviours. This is not surprising, given that increased body movement tends to occur in association with speech dysfluencies or errors

(Hadar, 1989). Several studies find that such cues are the ones used by police or customs officers in detecting criminality or smuggling (Searcy et al., 2005). However, there are many reasons for nervousness apart from criminality (such as embarrassment, low self-esteem, shyness) and such nonverbal cues do not necessarily indicate anxiety, deceit, and the like. In a provocative paper, Stiff & Miller (1984) looked at the behaviours that people show when they lie and the behaviours that people use to determine when someone else is lying to them. The crucial behaviours that we use are response latency (i.e., the time the person takes before starting to answer a question) and speech errors (i.e., interruptions to the flow of speech). Facial expressions are generally less useful for detecting deception, but they do indicate nervousness. Obviously this is very relevant to relationships – particularly beginning ones – since people who appear shy or nervous may be unfairly distrusted or disliked (Bradshaw, 2006).

One feature of real lying is that it must be *learned*. In order to understand what lying is, we have to be told what the truth is and what it means to lie. Therefore lying involves some concentration ('cognitive load'): we are emotionally involved, so we experience stress. In fact, lying as normally understood (i.e., saying something that is deliberately false) seems to be quite rare in close relationships, and deception is most commonly practised in relationships in the form of *withholding* of information. Indeed, L. West (1994) has shown that deception between relational partners most commonly involves withholding a thought or feeling, either positive or negative, with the intention of maintaining the current level of relational intimacy or sparing a partner's feelings. Naturally enough, what is omitted cannot be accompanied by nonverbal cues, though hesitancy in speech can indicate that something else is being omitted.

If we are talking to someone we know, then they may be acquainted with us well enough to spot behaviours that give us away, so we pay close attention to our behaviour and try hard to control anything that might 'give us away' or 'leak' true feelings. The whole experience is therefore arousing for us. In a clever study looking at these factors Greene, O'Hair, Cody & Yen (1985) had subjects lie (about where they had been on holiday) to a confederate of the experimenter. That was the easy part; many people can lie that they have been to Puerto Rico, especially if you have been told in advance that the question will be asked. The difficult part – which the subjects were not actually expecting – was what to do when the confederate became intensely interested in the trip and asked all sorts of details about it. Greene et al. (1985) found that subjects can control leakage of the fact that they are lying up until the point when they suddenly have to think hard and carefully about what they are saying.

[Un]Skillful use of nonverbal cues

Poor social skills could take two forms: poor encoding or poor decoding. *Encoding* refers to the ability to put feelings into practice, to 'do what we mean' (e.g., to act assertively if we want to assert, to look friendly if we feel friendly). Conversely, *decoding* refers to the ability to work out what other people mean, by observing their nonverbal communication and correctly working out their intent. Some people are inept at this. For example, sometimes you may read in the papers that a fight began in a bar because someone was staring 'provocatively' at someone else. Perhaps, one person really was staring inappropriately (poor encoding) or perhaps the other just thought he or she was doing so (which would be poor decoding on this thinker's part) or perhaps alcohol caused their respective social psychological judgements to decline in validity.

People with poor social skills

The list of people who show social skills deficits is well established. At the extreme end, patients with schizophrenia are very poor at decoding nonverbal signals (Hooley & Hiller, 2001), as are some violent prisoners (Howells, 1981); and depressed patients (Gotlib & Hooley, 1988), particularly when describing themselves (Segrin, 2000).

Some shy, lonely, or psychologically disturbed or depressed people have poor NVC and seem nervous, embarrassed, or socially incompetent when their NVC communicates negative attitudes about themselves or their feelings towards the encounter (Bradshaw, 2006). Persistently lonely people have poorly adapted eye movement, smiles, gestures, and nods (Guerrero & Floyd, 2006), but this is often because they have essentially disengaged from the social world and stopped trying. Other people who have poor social skills are depressives and schizophrenics (Segrin, 2006), children who are unpopular at school (Asher & Parker, 1989) or who become bullies or victims of bullying (Boulton & Smith, 1996; Smith, Bowers, Binney & Cowie, 1993). Such skill deficits not only are symptoms of their problems but may be partial causes (or, perhaps, may exacerbate and increase their problems). Also, partners in distressed marriages – especially the husbands – are poor at decoding one another's meaning and/or poor at encoding their own feelings, often communicating feelings as negative ones when they are not intended to be negative (Noller & Gallois, 1988).

By contrast, those who are successful in their careers are better at social skills than those who are failures (Argyle, 1987), and physicians can improve their success in healing patients by improving their social skills (Hays & DiMatteo, 1984). Clearly, then, such socially skilled communication is of great significance. Although nonverbal behaviour usually occurs in the context of verbal behaviour also, it has been found that nonverbal cues exert 4.3 times more effect than does verbal behaviour on the impressions formed of a speaker (Argyle et al., 1970) and the dominance of NVC is widely accepted. It is important, however, to pay attention to the context in which the cues are shown and which provides 'relational meaning' for people. For these reasons, correction of social skills problems is often attempted in training programmes (Duck, 1991). Such social skills training brings about improved social functioning in relationships and also improves the person's feelings about himself or herself (Dunkel-Schetter & Skokan, 1990). On the other hand, Caplan (2005) showed that people with poor social skills could make good use of Internet interactions though this does little to improve their face-to-face abilities.

You have probably been noticing as you have read this section, that the whole idea of 'skill' and including such words as 'correction' and 'improvement' in the discussion of behaviour plays into the social norms about 'quality' in social behavior that were identified earlier in this chapter. You could discuss this in class. Why is one form of physical behaviour preferred over another?

We have plenty of evidence, now, that NVC provides an important context for relationships and represents a significant context for relational communication. NVC affects the way in which other behaviours and styles are interpreted, provides a context for comprehending emotions, sincerity, dominance, and feelings towards someone else, and has a significant impact on relational feelings and conduct. NVC not only conveys important relational meanings but also serves to control and moderate the conduct of relationships. Having established this basic context for relationships we can now go on to language itself and the context that it provides for the conduct of relationships.

SPEAKING UP FOR YOURSELF: USING WORDS

It ain't what you say: the role of language and paralanguage

Some people think (and write) that communication is just about the sending of a verbal message from one person to another, but this is simplistic. Ever since Bartlett (1932) it has been known that the message that people 'receive' is not necessarily the one that was 'sent' and unless you are a person who has never been misunderstood, you'll know exactly what I mean. You may even have said 'I love you' to someone and found out too late that the sending of a message is not received the way you intended it, even when the other person hears it the way you meant it.

Communication involves a lot of other complex processes that are often overlooked. Messages are often complex and multi-layered – as for example in jokes or irony or sarcasm where the face value of the message is not the only way it can be interpreted. 'Yeah I really like your choice in music' can mean the opposite of what the words appear to say, for example. Second there is not always a message sent but there can be one received anyway. For example, I might blush and 'leak' to you that I am embarrassed when I did not intend you to know that. Or a person may brush up against another one's arm (no message intended, just the result of crowd jostling) but the other person could honestly believe that he or she had been assaulted or that you were trying to be familiar or intimate (message received). Obviously if the message sent was the same as the message received there could be no argument about such things but there are plenty of familiar cases where there *can* be an argument about whether there was a message and if so what it meant. If communication was simply about the sending of messages then we'd all know whether it had happened and what the right interpretation of the message was. What we need to think about, then, is how such ambiguity happens and also why and when it does not – what 'straightens it out' for us?

We already have learned that 'communication' has both a content level and a relational component. Whenever I make a statement, it contains claims to be speaking facts but it also addresses your social 'face' in some way. A polite statement 'I'm sorry I am blocking your way' contains both a factual claim and a recognition that the other person has a right not to be obstructed. If I speak politely it is because I recognize your rights to be treated as a dignified human being. If I speak discourteously it is because I either do not recognize or else choose to ignore your rights to be treated nicely, and obviously you and I could argue about which of the two interpretations is right in the circumstances. In some situations we might even get into a fight about it: 'You always treat me disrespectfully. Who do you think you are?'

Originally stated by Watzlawick et al. (1967), this claim actually does not go far enough. In fact communication is all about relationships and it cannot occur at all unless there is a relationship between the speaker and the audience, even if the two people are 'strangers' to one another. They share a similar cultural background but also recognize the ways in which their common society acknowledges strangers. You know how to treat strangers in your society. People in China know how to do it in theirs. In Japan there are 211 different forms of address that can be used to speak to another person and I have no doubt that strangers can be addressed in at least 30 of those ways, so you have to pick your stranger address terms pretty carefully if you do not want to be rude. Being rude is a form of communication: it recognizes that the content in a statement is not all that the statement communicates.

Paralanguage

The ways in which we *use* words are just as important as the words themselves. If I *shout* 'Fire!!', then it means more than just 'I can see pretty dancing flames': it means there is an emergency. I will therefore look at the structure, use, and form of language since they carry messages over and above the meaning of the actual words spoken. Researchers use the term *paralanguage* to refer to features of speech like accent, speed, volume, error-rate and tone of voice. Rather like NVC, however, paralanguage has meanings in relationships but also occurs within a system of meanings that serves to clarify what is intended. For instance, persons who shout 'Fire!' in an emergency probably also have some accompanying NVC that indicates at least urgency and possibly even panic and so distinguishes them from someone shouting it out as a joke. Also notice that the way a person does the shouting could convey messages about their credibility. Someone who screams 'Fire!' while looking distraught is likely to be believed; someone who shouts 'Yoo … oo … oo … hooo! Fi … i … re!' may be disregarded.

These observations create two issues. How do people use language so that it conveys messages for (and about) speakers? How does language interface with NVC to affect human relationships? We might ask how accent, speed, volume, error-rate, tone of voice, and 'speech style' affect the relational impact of messages. We shall see that *power* is indicated by a communication's tone and shall learn how to structure messages to maximize their persuasiveness (see Chapter 5). Language style conveys more information than is contained in the sentence. For example, different actors can give different character to the same passage of Shakespeare just by speaking it differently. Thus a 'message' is more than the content of speech and is significantly embossed by a number of elements of speech not contained in the content alone (Wood, 2006).

Amount of speech

A measure of leadership in small group discussions is the amount of speech that a person contributes: the more often someone 'holds the floor' (by speaking) the more will observers assume that the person was leading the group's activities. In Stang's (1973) study, subjects listened to tape-recorded group discussions which had been arranged so that one person spoke 50 per cent of the time, another person 33 per cent of the time, and a third spoke only 17 per cent of the time. The most talkative person was seen as the leader, irrespective of the content of what was said, and the second most frequent contributor was rated the most popular. This is further confirmed and extended by Palmer (1990) who showed that man-agement of 'floor time' is used as an important indication of someone's control of, and contribution to, the conversation.

Amount of speech is also affected by communication apprehension and social anxiety (Ayres, 1989), with highly anxious males talking less (and also using smaller amounts of reinforcing head nods) than less anxious subjects. Anxious people tend to withdraw from interpersonal interaction somewhat and to say very little. When they do speak, however, it is probably planned out and hangs together well because they have thought about it and it is important to them! Thus there is some truth to the common belief that fluency means something about expertise, mastery, compe-tence, and truthfulness. From a person's verbal fluency, we deduce information about the kind of person that he or she is, how that feels inside, and whether anxiety is felt in the present setting. The other side to this belief is the assumption that persons' views of themselves, the kind of person they (think they) are, actually do affect fluency. Competent people simply do speak fluently: they know what they are doing and their fluency is a signal of that. Hence we are likely to deduce a per-son's competence from the *appearance* that they are composed and self-possessed, whether or not that is how they feel inside (Duck & McMahan, forthcoming).

Rules about speech

How does language change as a result of the situation or relationship in which the conversation takes place, and what are the influences of language and 'speech style' on social impressions that observers form? Where a linguist would be interested in the grammatical rules in a given society (the so-called *langue*), a social psychologist, communication scholar, or sociolinguist is more likely to be concerned with the ways in which people actually use the language (the *parole*). Social uses of language do not always follow the strict rules of grammar (e.g., on the radio this morning I heard an interviewee say 'I reckon there's lotsa workers as thinks the same like what I does' – and yet everyone could have a stab at knowing roughly what he meant to convey by this).

Language is 'situated' in various ways according to the goals of the interactants. As people's goals change, so does their speech. In a social setting, conversation is frequent and almost any topic of conversation is permissible in a chat with close friends. By contrast, when concentration is required, it seems perfectly natural that people converse less and speech acts will decline or that speech will be specifically task-oriented. Similarly, competent university lectures are supposed to contain information about the course, and competent professors do not normally just show holiday slides and talk about their vacation.

Just as in nonverbal communication, a significant aspect of verbal communication is an appreciation of the social rules that apply. Speakers in a conversation must be polite and recognize when it is appropriate to raise particular topics and when it is not. They must know when to match their speech acts to the rules, since evaluation of their competence depends upon it. Daly & Vangelisti (2003) indicate that especially competent conversationalists are excellent at picking up social cues of appropriateness, sensing the hidden messages in others' speech, and noting unspoken power dynamics in conversational settings.

Such sensitivity can apply to goals of the actors. In task-oriented discussions, people are happy with a language system containing technical jargon-based forms. By contrast, a conversation between friends is usually not task-oriented but socio-emotionally oriented. Because it is focused on feelings, 'atmosphere', and informality, a different speech style is appropriate – one where grammatical rules may be broken and where the transfer of information is less significant than is the aim of keeping people happy and relaxed. Of course, such 'atmosphere' is important in human relationships, and 'atmosphere' is another word for context, the underlying theme of this chapter.

Most cultures have two forms of language code available, a so-called *high form* and a *low form*. The high form is planned, formal, careful, precise, complex, full of jargon, and a little pompous. It appears in educational settings, religion, courtrooms, and on official notices: for instance, 'I was proceeding in a northeasterly direction towards my domestic establishment' and 'Kindly extinguish all illumination prior to vacating the premises'. The low form is informal, casual, direct and simple. It is the most familiar form of everyday speech. For example, 'I was going home' and 'Kill the lights when you go'.

The two forms are used in different settings in appropriate ways. However, there are occasions when this causes difficulties and we deliberately break the rules to communicate a social message, like a joke or a distancing from someone. An example of the conveyance of social messages through use of codes is use of a high form in a casual setting to deflate someone, for instance, when your mother says 'Ms Weinstock, kindly clean your room'. This calculated misjudgement of the circumstances conveys a social message over and above the grammatical content. In a formal setting, however, if the message form is made inappropriate to the form of the encounter (e.g., informal language in a formal setting) the social result is negative (e.g., a judge called by his or her first name by a witness might fine the witness for contempt of court).

Movie experience: Watch *My Cousin Vinny* with particular reference to the way in which power is handled in the courtroom by the judge and the would-be lawyer.

One other message is conveyed by differences in use of high and low forms of code, and that is knowledge and hence power. Powerful and knowledgeable persons use jargon-based high code, while the rest use low code translations. One reason why do-it-yourself car repairers are usually 'one down' when going to buy spare parts is because they do not know the proper terminology. Asking for 'one-of-those-round-things-with-the-bent-bit-at-one-end' is a betrayal of low status in such situations. Use of technical terms is a way of claiming status, particularly if it is done deliberately to someone who does not know the terminology. Car mechanics could perfectly well talk about 'round-things-with-the-bent-bit-at-one-end', but they instead talk about 'channeled CJ47s' and so on. Social scientists could write about chatting and conversation, but instead they write about 'socially situated speech acts' and 'interacts' (Knapp & Vangelisti, 2004).

More about content

The content of speech carries two important social messages, one of which is *power* and the other is *relationship* between speaker and listener. Brown (1965) refers to these dimensions as *status* and *solidarity*. These two dimensions are very similar to two 'messages' conveyed by nonverbal cues also: dominance and liking.

Relationships between speaker and listener
In some languages (e.g., French, German, Spanish), there are two words that can be translated as 'you' in English, and in times gone by there were also two choices

in English (thee/thou, ye/you). The so-called V-form (*vos* in Latin, *vous* in French, *Sie* in German, *usted* in Spanish) is actually plural, just as ye/you used to be in English, where the T-form (*tu*, *du*, thee/thou) is actually singular. Where the two forms still coexist, intimate friends and relatives are addressed with one pronoun (*tu*, *du*) and the other is used for people whom one does not know or whom one treats with respect (*vous*, *Sie*, *usted*). Thus the French say *tu* when talking to a friend, to someone younger, or to a person of lower status, but use *vous* for talking to a stranger, to an elder, or a parent-in-law. Use of the T-form therefore conveys messages of solidarity and intimacy, while the V-form conveys messages of formality, respect, and distance. Brown (1965) also notes that a status norm has evolved in countries which still use the two forms of address. The choice of just one single word (*tu* or *vous*) tells everyone about the speaker's status and familiarity relative to the other person and communicates something about the closeness of relationship between speaker and addressee. The V-form is used to address a person superior in status. The T-form is reserved for those of lower status. Persons who are of equal status both use the T-form to each other if they are close personally, but the V-form if they are not. German and French each contain special verbs (*dusagen*; *tutoyer*) to describe the switch from one form to another (i.e, to indicate that it is acceptable to be more intimate). The form of address carries a message about the power relationship between the speakers. The message can be a personal one ('I am superior to you'), a solidarity one ('We are equals'), or a political one ('All persons are equal; there is no hierarchical structure in society'). During the French Revolution, the peasant revolutionaries purposely addressed the toppled aristocrats as *tu* in order to reinforce by language the political changes that had taken place. It was meant to stress the new-found equality.

The early Quakers also decided to adopt the style of calling everyone 'thou' in order to indicate the equality of all people. This T-form pronoun had previously been reserved for use only to close intimates, lower or equal status family members, and 'inferiors' like servants, children and pet animals. This style caused considerable amounts of abuse to be heaped on Quakers; indeed, in 1714 Thomas Ellwood found that it led to trouble between himself and his father, who evidently felt disrespected: 'But whenever I had occasion to speak to my father … my language did [offend him]: for I [did] not say YOU to him but THEE or THOU, as the occasion required, and then he would be sure to fall on me with his fists!' 'Thou' was also used as an insult indicating moral distance or inferiority when two persons were otherwise socially equal. At the trial of Sir Walter Raleigh for treason, the prosecutor (Sir Edward Coke) berated Raleigh with the words 'All that Lord Cobham did was by Thy instigation, Thou viper; for I 'thou' Thee, Thou traitor' (Hughes, 1991: 98)

Our culture also knowingly distinguishes respectful forms and informal ones. Do you call your professor 'Professor Surname', or 'Chris'? What do colleagues call the same person? Do you call your father by a title (Dad, Father, Pop, or even

Sir) or by his first name? What does he call you? Whenever I discuss this with my students in class it is obvious that the difference is a very real one. Those people who use a title would feel uncomfortable using a first name and vice versa, but I make them choose either to call me 'Steve' – or else to use 'Professor Duck' but then to quack at the end of the sentence. (Actually 'Duck' is a Viking surname derived from the nickname for a hunchback.) Mamali (1996) notes that political control can also be achieved by names and titles, since in some formerly Soviet countries it was the custom to address a person by his or her communist party title, thus subtly reinforcing the remembrance of the party and its control over social life.

TRY THIS OUT

Try calling some of your professors by their first names without per-mission and see what reaction you get. More interestingly, see how it feels to you personally. If you really want an experience then try call-ing them 'Mac'.

Speech style, power, and relationships

Speech style can also represent a relationship of speaker to audience in terms of whether the speech is powerful or powerless (Lakoff, 1973). Powerless speech uses a high proportion of: *intensifiers* (very, extremely, absolutely, totally, really); *empty adjec-tives and adverbs* (wonderful, incredibly, amazingly); *deferential forms* (would you please? may I?); *tag questions* (isn't it? don't you?); *hedges* or *lack of commitment* (I sup-pose, I guess, maybe, it was … like); *hypercorrect grammar* ('To whom is it that you wish to speak?'); overuse of *gestures* during speech (suggesting lack of significance in the speech itself); *intonational patterns* that seem to 'fuss' and 'whine'; *lack of persever-ance* during interruptions, and *acquiescence in simultaneous speech*. Note that since many of these forms are 'polite' in our culture, polite speech can seem powerless.

Using language to relate to other people

Content and types of talk

You already know that you do some types of talk with some people and not others. Goldsmith & Baxter (1996) discovered that everyday relating 'appears to be dominated by six kinds of talk event: gossip, making plans, joking around, catching up, small talk, and recapping the day's events'. The types of talk have a taxonomy of types of talk arranged on three dimensions: formal/goal directed; important/deep/involving; and positive valence. Changes in speech are not simply strategies by which people change their relationships but are in fact ways in which they embody the nature of the relationship and even the small talk of everyday relating is making the relationship (Duck & Pond, 1989). Thus instead of seeing communication as something that is used by people in a relationship merely to achieve some desired goal or express a cognitive state or attitude, Goldsmith & Baxter see it instead as 'an *embodiment* of a particular kind of relationship constructed jointly by the parties' (1996: 89; emphasis added).

The advantage of such a way of looking at the connection of communication to relationships is that it notes the ways in which communication *is* relational and is not simply an instrument for making relationships. Communication generally, both verbal and nonverbal, involves relational activity – my whole point in this chapter – and the use of language is relational in and of itself.

A familiar example of talk shows the relationship between the speaker and audience: the profanity that is found in everyday speech (some estimates indicate that 13 per cent of everyday talk is profane; Winters & Duck, 2001). Most of us probably think that when someone curses they are simply being vulgar or inappropriate. People tend to swear when they are angry or have very strong feelings about something and the use of cursing or swearing words is a strong way to indicate emotion. However, such a view of swearing is limited (Hughes, 1991). The sorts of swearing that have taken place over the course of history, the sorts of slurs that are chosen for people, and the history of changes in the uses of such words show that swearing is not only relational and but also subtly about power. It involves social structure, hierarchy, rights, social position, the marginalization of groups, and the evaluation of attitudes. Let's think a bit about that and connect it to the topic of this chapter and the evaluation of ways of viewing the world (which is what 'context' is about).

Speech is persuasive and endorses (cultural) visions of the world (Carl & Duck, 2004), that is to say it proposes and embodies ways of seeing the world. Words are not idly chosen but express personality, attitudes and a person's view of the world and their self-identity within the culture. The same is true of swearing and cursing, which represent ways of seeing other people, ways of categorizing or denigrating other people and ways of enforcing interpretations of central features of life. Try to recall the last time you called someone a 'blackguard' (which your fifteenth-century ancestors would have felt to be a personal insult). How recently did you wish 'a pox on you' to someone, which your seventeeth-century ancestors would have found deeply offensive?

Hughes (1991) traces the changes in profanity that have taken place through history. Those words which we use as swear words – 'the F-word' for example – were once regarded as simple descriptions of activity and were ordinary language words without vulgar overtones. Instead, in fifteenth-century England the words that people used to belittle one another were to do with social position: a 'blackguard' was the lowest kitchen servant who washed the blackened pans, a 'villain' was a lowly member of the feudal system; a 'bastard' was an illegitimate child without legal rights; and like their modern counterparts, our ancestors often called one another the names of lowly regarded farm animals like 'pigs'. Hughes (1991) indicates that such words then were used as relational insults, conveying messages of status discrimination or implying that the other person was inferior. In much the same way modern swearing applies names that refer to parts of the body that are particularly unappealing. You can probably think of several examples of such names associated with nasty bodily functions, and even 'the pits' (as applied to a place of little value) is short for 'armpits'.

As Hughes has documented, then, many swear words convey relational position, but are moulded by a culture's concerns at that moment. When disease was especially disfiguring (as was smallpox), our culture used many disease-based terms as curses ('A plague on both your houses' in *Romeo and Juliet,* for example). Many of our profane phrases these days involve associating the target with morally debased activity (e.g., incest is alleged by use of the term 'motherfucker') and hence with morally tainted evaluation. The use of such terms in everyday life functions rather like gossip in that it comments negatively on moral character and social status. The implicit message of such a label is an invitation for the person to adjust their behaviour by taking a morally better pathway, so profanity makes moral judgements in a context of relationships.

LISTEN TO YOUR OWN CONVERSATIONS

Do you ever swear, use nicknames? How many of the swear words or derogatory nicknames imply some kind of relational commentary? Hatred and rejection for others are conveyed by nicknames just as are endearment and closeness. Whereas a lover may be 'Honey', 'Sweetie' or 'Sugar' – all metaphors to do with consumption of food, obviously – many nicknames of rejection are associated with the opposite end of the alimentary canal, such as 'he's a shit', 'an arsehole' or even a 'septic' (septic tank = Yank, in Cockney rhyming slang) which was current in Second World War Europe.

Do you ever gossip? Bergmann (1993) shows the relational force of gossip. It serves as a form of relational control – we gossip about other people's relational activity ('I hear they're having an affair') or their treatment of one another ('He is really mean to her'). Such comments act out a social control of others' behaviour by moralizing about it and supporting a view of what is 'right' in relationships, so gossip structures our social world. Listen out for use of gossip as social control.

Structure of talk

One aspect of language is the way in which it can be used to indicate the relationship between the speaker and the listener. We are all sensitive to the relational messages conveyed by different forms of speech, and we change them as relationships develop. Processes of growth in a relationship are managed through communication; we can indicate to a partner and to the world at large that we have grown closer simply by subtly changing the way in which we address the person. As Knobloch & Haunani Solomon observe, 'A question fundamental to the study of interpersonal communication and close relationships is how the characteristics that people associate with the relationships are evident in their conversation' (2003: 482). Not only does communication require the sorts of coordinated behaviour between people that I was discussing in the preceding sections, but it also requires that people present their dyadic understandings about the relationship through their talk. To start talking of 'us' is to claim that a relationship exists or is coming into existence; to encourage greater intimacy in language is simultaneously to instigate greater intimacy in relationship.

Such internal features of speech convey messages of connectedness that are evident to outsiders as signals of the relationship between two speakers. Planalp & Benson (1992), Planalp (1993) and Planalp & Garvin-Doxas (1994) have shown that judges can discriminate between conversations of friends and of acquaintances on the basis of the coherence and internal structure of the conversation. There are systematically observable differences in the conversations of friends and acquaintances (typically evidence of mutual knowledge), and that the level of accuracy in discriminating such conversations is about 80 per cent. From Knobloch & Haunani Solomon's recent (2003) confirmation of the importance of this element of intimate speech it is clear that there are structured aspects of speech, forms and contents of language, and features of conversations that give off cues to everyone that a conversation is between intimates and not simple acquaintances. Thus language not only indicates amount of relaxation and competency in an interaction but it also shows degrees of relationship. For one thing, the speech of friends usually includes reference to 'taken for granted' aspect of their relationship, such as their mutual knowledge of one another or their common understanding of specific events or places. For instance, if we hear a conversation between two people swapping their names and addresses we'd be likely to assume that the people are not friends but have just met; if we hear them discussing 'Joe's new date' we are likely to assume that they know one another and have mutual friends.

Equally, partners develop private languages to personalize their relationship (Hopper, Knapp & Scott, 1981) and there are eight types (nicknames for the partners; expressions of affection and terms of endearment; labels for other people outside of the relationship; confrontations; requests and routines; sexual references and euphemisms; sexual invitations; teasing insults). Even long-term married partners use nicknames for one another (Bruess & Pearson, 1993), such as 'sweet pea' and 'pussycat' and it turns out that greater marital satisfaction is associated with greater numbers of such 'personal idioms' in the relationship. Couples without children use the most nicknames and those later in life use the fewest. Also, brothers and sisters routinely use such personal idioms, especially nicknames, to insult one another, rattle one another's cages, and make reference to alleged parental favouritism (Nicholson, 2006). The use of such idioms thus serves to create either coherence or conflict between relational partners but simultaneously serves to exclude other people and so to draw boundaries around the relationship by using language that other people do not understand. In short, language conveys degrees of intimacy, is a powerful developer and definer of relationships, and is used to indicate many privacies in relationships. It conveys relational messages by its structure as well as by its content.

Since there are public and private languages, both high and low forms, informal and formal styles and so on, you might have thought of a rather good question: what messages are conveyed by 'switching' between styles during a single conversation? What relational messages are conveyed, for example, by a switch from high to low forms of speech? Low form is typically associated with informal, friendly settings while a high form goes with formality and emotional distance. A switch from low to high is a distancing strategy that shows disapproval, aloofness, dislike, and hostility. By contrast, a high–low switch is an affiliative strategy that indicates liking, approval, and a desire to become more friendly. For most of his career, Giles (e.g., Giles, Taylor & Bourhis, 1973) has been showing that we 'accommodate' our language (whether language style, speech style, accent, code or content) to our interaction partner if we feel attracted. We play down the distinctiveness of our own individual style of speaking and accommodate, or move towards, that of the other person ('convergence'). For instance, parents frequently accommodate and talk 'baby talk' to young children whereas adults adopt the code form preferred by the powerful actor in a given setting (e.g., they talk formally to their boss but informally to their peers). Also, speakers often adapt their speech to be more similar to that of their conversational partner, particularly when they wish to relax that person or ingratiate themselves (Giles et al., 1973). Such 'convergence' can involve speech rate, silences, choice of language (where the speakers are bilingual), regional accents, or vocal intensity and loudness (Giles & Powesland, 1975). The higher prestige language is usually adopted in a bilingual community as long as partners like one another (Giles, 1978). Divergence is equally powerful (Bourhis & Giles, 1977). When speakers dislike their partner or the ethnic group from which he or she comes, they will adopt extremely different speech styles, occasionally refusing to speak in the partner's adopted language (e.g., persisting in speaking Welsh to disliked English weekend-holidaymakers in Wales).

Language itself indirectly and directly conveys important *relational* messages. However, it does not do it on its own in the course of normal everyday interactions. It is a part of a system. We can be both verbally close and nonverbally intimate, for instance, and this could be important in indicating relational intimacy – yet it could be problematic if the two 'channels' (verbal and nonverbal) do not match up, as we'll see below.

KEEP A JOURNAL

Listen out for two samples of talk, one where you can tell that one person is a stranger to the other and one where you can tell that the persons are friends. Make some notes on the differences.

Listen to some everyday conversation and see if you can find evidence both for and against the idea that such conversation is implicitly persuasive and all about the alignment of people's rhetorical visions and world views.

PUTTING VERBAL AND NONVERBAL TOGETHER

So far, I have been looking at the components of communication separately as linguistic and nonverbal forms; but obviously, in real life they occur together most of the time. In relationships especially, they most often go together and amplify one another. When we say angry things, we usually look angry; when we say 'I love you', we usually look as if we mean it. Thus NVC can *complement* verbal messages. However, verbal and nonverbal messages can also be put together in conflicting or complementary ways. Use of NVC can help in learning and children learn better about addition and subtraction when told by both speech and gestures about the plus and minus signs (Singer & Goldin-Meadow, 2005). This might explain why people gesture vigorously when they are on the telephone and the person at the other end of the line cannot see any of it! However, researchers have been interested for a long time in looking at the inconsistencies between the two channels (verbal and nonverbal). For instance when I say nice things but frown, or when I shout 'I'm NOT ANGRY', how do observers interpret such inconsistencies? Do you have examples of this from your everyday life as a student?

Facial messages are long established as the most powerful components of such contradictions (Zaidel & Mehrabian, 1969). They are seen as conveying the real messages and as giving the true evaluation of the *person*. Words, on the other hand, are assumed to relate to the person's *acts* or *deeds*. 'Well done' said with a scowl, for instance, indicates grudging praise for someone who is disliked. Young children have particular difficulty with such inconsistent messages and tend to treat all such messages as negative, whichever channel conveyed the negativity (Bugental, Kaswan & Love, 1970). For adults, the human relationships in which communication occurs normally give people very strong cues about the overall 'meaning' of the inconsistency. While the NV channel is still seen as the more important ('Actions speak louder than words', after all), the most likely thing is that an observer will actually work out the 'true meaning' from the context built into the relationship.

SOMETHING TO TRY WITH NONVERBAL AND VERBAL BEHAVIOUR

Pair up with another student and take it in turns to say the following with a happy expression, a sad expression and no expression. After you have done the nonverbal part, repeat the exercise using only your voice modulation to convey the different tones to the speech.

'I'm too tired for this.'
'I thought the movie was poor.'
'I like the colour of your shirt.'
'You are my favourite person.'

Discuss what it feels like to do this exercise in the various modes. Which is harder, the nonverbal or the verbal? What do you think might be the reasons?

SUMMARY

This chapter has begun our investigation of human relationships by looking at some of its biological and cultural bases as evident in everyday life nonverbal behaviour, verbal behaviour and the way in which these two systems interact together. We looked at nonverbal behaviour as an indicator of relational state and also as a regulator of interpersonal interaction. We also looked at the messages which are sent by the tone and quality of speech, as well as by its content, noting that relationship messages are always contained in speech, whatever its content otherwise. Language and nonverbal communication (even down at the level of usage of space) both convey implicit as well as explicit messages about power, control, liking, many of them based in cultural expectations and norms. Every time we speak we convey social messages about how much we like someone and what we think is our relationship to them – not just by explicitly saying so in the content of our talk but also by the style of the language and the accompanying nonverbal communications. Identity management is achieved by both verbal and nonverbal means, and the form of speech is as important as minute movements of face, eyes, and body that make up the whole nonverbal system. These fundamental building blocks thus create the basis for all human relationships before we even get to the topic of emotion.

You should now be in a better state to begin understanding the way in which relationships work in terms of basic mechanisms and you should now be more inclined to look out for people's behaviour at the nonverbal level and also for some of the subtleties of their speech patterns. You should now be aware of the way in which speech sends relational messages all the time, and more attuned to seeing the way in which the media and the conversations that you have in every-day life work within those frameworks to construct your relationships and your understanding of them.

SELF QUESTIONS

What are your particular styles of nonverbal communication? Can you identify the use of power in the forms of speech that someone uses? What sorts of nonverbal invasion do you find particularly offensive?

Pay attention to the behaviour of people in elevators (lifts) where space is confined and close physical proximity is unavoidable. How do they deal with this? Look at the way in which people use lack of eye contact in order to remain comfortable in a confined space. What happens if you face towards other people in an elevator instead of turning to face the door?

If you find someone's comments offensive then can you now analyse what it is they are saying (or more importantly *how* they are saying it) that makes their comments aversive?

What is on the desk or walls of your room that shows: (a) it is your space; (b) who you are?

What other markers can you find in the world to indicate people's claims on a territory or claims to an identity? Take another look at graffiti.

FURTHER READING

Antaki, C. (2004). Conversation analysis. In S. Becker, & A. Bryman, (Eds.), *Understanding Research Methods for Social Policy and Practice* (pp. 313–317). London: Policy Press.
Antaki, C. & Widdicombe, S. (Eds.) (1998). *Identities in talk*. London: Sage.

(Continued)

(Continued)

Guerrero, L.K., & Floyd, K. (2006). *Nonverbal communication in relationships*. Mahwah, NJ: Lawrence Erlbaum and Associates.

Journal of Nonverbal Behavior

Keeley, M., & Hart, A. (1994). Nonverbal behaviors in dyadic interaction. In S.W. Duck (Ed.), *Dynamics of relationships* [*Understanding relationships 4*]. Thousand Oaks, CA: SAGE.

Knapp, M.L., & Hall, J.A. (2002). *Nonverbal communication in human interaction* (5th edn). New York: Holt Rinehart and Winston, Inc.

Manusov, V., & Patterson, M.L. (2006). *Handbook of nonverbal communication*. Thousand Oaks, CA: SAGE.

Remland, M.S. (2004). *Nonverbal communication in everyday life* (2nd edn). Boston, MA: Houghton Mifflin.

Spitzberg, B.H., & Cupach, W.R. (2002). Interpersonal skills. In M.L. Knapp & J.A. Daly (Eds.), *Handbook of interpersonal communication* (3rd edn). pp. 564–611. Thousand Oaks, CA: *SAGE*.

PRACTICAL MATTERS

- Social skills training may be used effectively to improve performance in a variety of practical settings and involves training in NVC and sequencing of people's conversational style, or attentiveness to the relational implications of actions and words.
- Argyle (1967, 1975, 1983) reported on lengthy programmes of research to make people's nonverbal behaviour more appropriate to the situation.
- General 'pepping up' of depressives' responsivity in social encounters is shown to contribute to patient recovery (Dunkel-Schetter & Skokan, 1990).
- Lonely and shy people can be trained to adopt new styles of social behaviour that enhance the skill of their performance (Jones, Hansson & Cutrona, 1984). Such training can also be directed at conversational turn-taking or topic management and general interpersonal communication competence (Spitzberg & Cupach, 2002).
- Nonassertive persons benefit from training related to posture as well as to other behaviours more obviously related to request-making (Wilkinson & Canter, 1982).
- Managers can be trained to use their powers in more effective ways by attending carefully to the speech patterns of employees (Lovaglia & Lucas, 2006).

2

Attachment and Emotion

It requires no great insight to realize that [some people] are deeply distrustful of close relationships and terrified of allowing themselves to rely on anyone else, in some cases in order to avoid the pain of being rejected and in others to avoid being subjected to pressure to become someone else's caretaker. (Bowlby, 1979: 138)

Focus points for note taking when reading this chapter:

- How far is any of our relating a result of our previous/early/childhood experiences rather than just to do with the present experiences we are having in the relationship in question?
- What sorts of childhood influences can affect later human relationship in adult life?
- What is the relative effect of our own infancy versus the later experiences that we get as young children or adolescents?
- How much of our relationship skills/tendencies do we learn from what happens to us, what we observe happening to others, or our comparison of our own experiences and those of siblings/other children?
- Where do we learn what 'emotion' is and how to express it? (Remember culture and biology from Chapter 1 and now add 'experiences in early life' as you take notes.)
- Are emotions pure experiences or are they felt in relation to other people/cultures/contexts?
- What is the role of language in emotional experience and expression?
- How are our emotional experiences influenced by what we do in day-to-day life routines?

Childhood provides us with a variety of experiences, where we learn to read and write, and also to understand other people and ourselves. Nowadays we think of childhood and children warmly and we expect good things to flavour the experience. Yet Tuchman points out that 'Of all the characteristics in which the medieval age differs from the modern, none is so striking as the comparative absence of interest in children. Emotion in relation to them rarely appears in art or literature or documentary evidence' (1978: 49). In those medieval times, Philip of Novara (thirteenth century) regarded children as 'so dirty and annoying in infancy and so naughty and capricious, that it is hardly worth nurturing them through child-hood' and Tuchman concludes that

> On the whole, babies and young children appear to have been left to survive or die without great concern in the first five or six years. What psychological effect this may have had on character, and possibly on history, can only be conjectured. Possibly the relative emotional blankness of a medieval infancy may account for the casual attitude towards life and suffering of the medieval man. (1978: 52)

We must recognize, then, that our modern view of childhood and of the parent–child relationship is not an inherent condition of humanity, but one nurtured within a particular cultural, historical, and intellectual context (Duck, in press SAGE CA, see refs). The things we attribute to childhood and the results we expect from it (either in terms of parent–child or sibling relationships or the longer-term effects of childhood) are relative. In interpreting research on 'the effects' of childhood we must recognize that childhood has been variously understood through history and across cultures.

Even in modern times, we emerge from the long years of childhood and adolescence with mixed experiences. We probably had both fights and alliances/cooperation with brothers and sisters (Nicholson, 2006), went through both put downs and encouragement by (different?) teachers, had varied experiences of parents on good and bad days, observed mixed experiences of our caretakers' long-term partnership, which may have ranged from same-sex parental caring (Suter, 2006) to other configurations including blended families (Baxter, Braithwaite, Bryant & Wagner, 2004), single-parent upbringing or shared custody with one parent absent most of the time (Rollie, 2006), and possibly experience of parental divorce (Barber & Demo, 2006). These mixed observations of long-term partnership and how it 'works', mixed experiences of peers – from bullying to close friendships – doubtless combined with ice cream, birthday parties, and relentless teasing. Childhood experiences can scar us for life or give wonderful opportunities for growth, and we may derive strength, shyness, ambition, depression, hope, enjoyment, despair, and preparation for ultimate success or failure in life. Nobody comes out of childhood without some experiences that they wish had never happened, but much of it can be positive too.

My point? Well, actually I have several. We learn in childhood from experiences which occurred to us directly; we learn also from things that we merely observe; we learn from a multiplicity of sources, whether parents, siblings, teachers, peers, or even the Internet. 'Childhood' is a richly textured, full, and varied experience given these sources and contexts, so it is surprising that much research tends to focus on uniform influences. As you look around the world at the people here, it seems more likely that there is no universal experience of childhood, and no universal lesson learned there about human relationships nor only one source for the outcomes. But as you read the scientific literature, you will find that this is not the apparently shared perception, and researchers routinely prefer to identify major key persistent themes in childhood experience that have huge influence on later relationships.

So what should we make of childhood from the point of view of human relationships? How might childhood predispose us towards relationships as an adult? There are lots of possibilities here: first, our own direct treatment by other people as infants could 'set' us to expect that treatment from everyone else for evermore; second, our indirect observation of lots of other people's relationships could channel the way we think about relationships of our own; third, the experiences we have of *particular* kinds of people (teachers, parents, men, authority figures, and so on) could influence future experience of, say, powerful women, tall males, or friendship in general; fourth, *broad* motivations could be 'set' in childhood, such as sociability, shyness, tendencies to possessiveness in relationships, or pursuit of intimacy versus other goals like career; fifth, childhood adversity specifically, such as early death of a parent, could affect one's later sense of the reliability of deep attachments (indeed the experience of parental divorce affects the likelihood of one's own divorce although there is substantial variation in responses; Barber & Demo, 2006); sixth, a person's experiences of relationships at school, such as bullying, could form a pattern affecting interpretation of other people's motives or our own skills in relationships. Jones (2005) indicates that individual beliefs about personal relationships may affect the way in which we understand the emotional states of other people, especially their emotional states towards us as inferred from their statements and meanings carried by their behaviours towards us.

KEEP A JOURNAL

During one day write down anything that comes up and reminds you of a childhood experience. How often does it happen (of course you were primed to think about it on this occasion)? How often do people treat you in ways that remind you of the treatment that you received (or specifically resisted) when you were a child?

EFFECTS OF CHILDHOOD ON LATER RELATIONSHIPS 1: ATTACHMENT

One predominant explanation for effects of childhood on other relationships has emerged in the social psychological literature, and is based on people's *relational* experience of caretaking when they were infants. Bowlby (1969/1982) proposed that patterns in infant behaviour are reflections of infants' treatment by their 'caretakers' – a term covering parents or people primarily responsible for the child's upbringing, although in Bowlby's era, this was normally assumed to be 'the Mother' (hence the following pronouns). Working in children's hospitals, Bowlby noticed different reactions in different infants to both their mother's absence and her return. Some got distressed when she went away and some did not. Equally, some reacted positively to her reappearance and some seemed quite indifferent to it. So Bowlby noticed two infant responses: different kinds of distress when the caretaker went away and different sorts of responses when she returned. This is an important observation, but he had the insight that the infant reactions to the behaviour of the caretaker might be connected to her behaviour style. He observed that some mothers responded consistently positively to the infant whether at reconnection or other times (consistently responsive to infant signals, showing warmth), some were indifferent and inconsistent (generally inept and showing broad insensitivity to infants' needs), and some seemed uninvolved and distant ('rejecting' and averse to physical contact, showing emotional distance and general rigidity in care-giving). Bowlby concluded that the way in which the mothers treated their children was connected with the infants' anxiety levels and hence their responses to separation and belief in the likely security/reliability of any reconnection.

Bowlby described the infant responses as *attachment styles* or ways of connecting to other people. Some infants learned to trust their caretaker and some did not; some saw her as reliable and some did not; some acquired a sense of security from her and some learned to be anxious and unsafe in her presence as well as during her absence. Bowlby regarded these styles as enduring 'working models' that the infant developed about relationships on the basis of this first relationship with the caretaker. He did not regard such infant experiences as finally and irrevocably determining later interaction with everyone else as the person matured, but he did raise the possibility that these early experiences were formative and influential. He found such patterns to be stable across infancy (tested up to 3.5 years) and ended up proposing three working model/personality types:

- *securely attached*: an infant who welcomes a caretaker's return and seeks proximity to the caregiver;
- *anxious-resistant/ambivalent* infants are ambivalent at caretaker's return and can't be comforted on reunion after absence;
- *avoidant* infants avoid proximity and show no interest in the returning caretaker; they perform blank stares or body turns or movement away from their caretaker.

For our purposes this idea gains greater importance if early learned behaviours transfer to later life romantic relationships with other adults. Hazan & Shaver (1987) suggested that adult styles of loving represent processes similar to, and based on, those found in attachments between infants and their parents. *Secure attachment* develops into a general sense of confidence and security in later intimacy. By contrast, *anxious/ambivalent attachment* develops into dependency, lack of

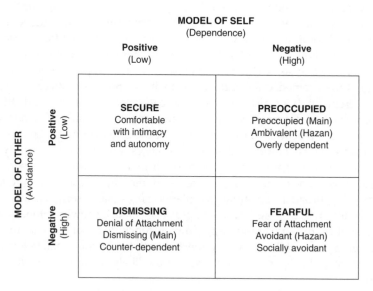

Figure 2.1   Styles for adult attachment

confidence in later relationships, and a sense of lack of appreciation by others. Finally, *avoidant attachment* develops into later general lack of acceptance of others, avoidance of closeness and discomfort in intimate situations.

Although such styles may come loosely from memories of childhood social experience, some theories have developed these ideas into a more structured framework, suggesting that there are two major dimensions on which a person's approach to relationships in later life can be mapped. Bartholomew (1990) proposed a four-way model (Figure 2.1) based on two dimensions: in childhood we learn our own social value (*model of self*) and what makes other people tick (*model of others*, broadly speaking, whether they should be approached because they are rewarding or avoided because they are painful to be with).

Bartholomew (1990; 1993) extends Hazan & Shaver's (1987) three-part system to a four-part one by distinguishing 'avoidant' into two: a *fearful avoidant style* when the person feels a desire to obtain social contact but is fearful of its consequences; and a *dismissive avoidant style*, when the person defensively denies the need for social contact. People who are fearfully avoidant regard themselves as undeserving of the love of others, whereas dismissively avoidant people view themselves positively but just do not regard other people as necessary or desirable. Before we get too much further you might like to try a quick and superficial classification of yourself on the basis of the above categories.

Researchers have used the Shaver and Hazan model and the Bartholomew models with equal enthusiasm and the research indicating the effects of early experience on later life, whether on direct relationship experiences or such indirectly relevant variables as alcoholism and violence, is one of the impressive growths of the last 20 years. Later work on relationships has found this to be a very rich source of information about relationships and a single listing of all the relevant articles with 'attachment' in the title would probably fill the rest this book. Some examples are Feeney, Noller & Roberts (2000) who noted that not all people fit an attachment category 'stably' over time, but that there are noticeable connections between attachment style and stress, coping, relationship quality, relationship stability, and emotional experience (especially of anger, sadness, and anxiety and the experience of control of emotion). Broadly speaking, secure attachment style is associated with more positive outcomes in all of these variables than is an anxious style. Rowe & Carnelley (2005) found that attachment networks (i.e. friendship or romantic relationship networks) differed in content and structure in accordance with global attachment style. By using a hierarchical (bull's-eye) mapping method the authors showed that secure individuals included a higher number of secure relationships in their networks and placed them closer to their core sense of self than they did with their insecure relationships. Anders & Tucker (2000) showed that securely attached persons report larger and more satisfying social support networks than anxious or avoidant persons. The authors suggested interpersonal communication competence – something close to social skills discussed in Chapter 1 – as a possible mediator of these associations and found that poor interpersonal communication led to smaller social support networks and also to lower levels of satisfaction especially in the anxious and avoidant people, and especially in those who lacked assertiveness or used lower levels of self-disclosure. Perhaps attachment style is associated with specific forms of instrumental/communication deficit or skill, and that this in turn affects people's relative failure or success at later relationships.

Banse (2004) found that marital satisfaction could be predicted by the individual's attachment, the partner's attachment, and the interaction between them. Once again it is secure attachment that was related to higher, and insecure attachment to lower, marital satisfaction. In an interesting variation on the usual styles of research however, Banse looked at the ways in which the two partners' individual attachment styles interacted with one another, finding that the positive effects of secure and the negative effects of insecure attachment styles are either amplified or attenuated depending on the attachment of the spouse (Secures create better relational environments). Cohen (2004) showed that attachment style even relates to people's reactions if their favourite TV soap characters were taken off the air! Anxious-ambivalents foresaw the most negative personal reactions to such disasters. The author discusses the results as evidence of the similarity between parasocial relationships and close social relationships. It might be worth you thinking a little bit more carefully about why attachment theory would have any connection whatsoever with something like this. Perhaps there's something about the nature of 'relationships' as conceived by attachment theory, which makes these findings understandable.

EFFECTS OF CHILDHOOD ON LATER RELATIONSHIPS 2: EXPERIENCES AND OBSERVATIONS

Other relevant learning in childhood may affect parenting. Some parents recall their own childhood with strong repugnance (or strong affection) and so avoid (or reproduce) the opportunity for their own children to experience childhood similarly. Some parents believe that experiences that they loathed as children must at all costs be prevented from happening to their own children (Putallaz, Costanzo & Klein, 1993). I even know one couple who between them had two such awful childhoods that they agreed upon marriage never to have children themselves – and Rholes, Simpson & Friedman (2006) found that 'avoidant' attachment style predicts lower willingness to become a parent and more negative expectations of how it will turn out. Other people may believe that one of the best things about their own childhood was (… you name it) and so they want to make very sure indeed that it happens to their own children, too (Putallaz et al., 1993).

In the everyday context of parent–child interaction, parents no doubt communicate ideologies of relating that influence (but do not determine) a child's experiences of relationships and of social reality. For example, Doucet & Aseltine (2003) linked parental disruption and childhood family conflict with the quality of the children's later marriages as adults. Although parental divorce during childhood was not significantly related to the quality of marital relationships in young adulthood, childhood family conflict was strongly related to measures of later marital quality. There are wide ranges of childhood adversities that have persistent effects on emotional development during the rest of the life course, but these derive from the interaction of the parents with one another, rather than with the child alone. Also a person's adolescence may moderate any earlier effects in childhood. Individuals are evidently engaged in lifelong learning about relationships!

Kitzmann & Cohen (2003) likewise indicated that children's *perceptions* of parental conflict showed strong associations with dimensions of their own friendship quality and this suggests that the resolution quality of parents' conflict – rather than conflict intensity, conflict frequency, or children's conflict-related distress – is associated with the quality of the child's close friendships. It is through observation of their parents' conflict resolution that children learn something about 'how to be intimate'.

Children also learn from their experiences with other children, too, and Qualter & Munn (2005) conclude that children's representations of their social reality are critical features in what they ultimately get out of social life meaning, in essence, that the way a child thinks about other children may be derived from specific behavioural experiences with them and that these get internalized. A child can derive a sense of his or her value from experiences of interaction with other children as well as from their experiences with adults. Hence, we might conclude that beliefs about value of self to peers might be different from sense of value of self to caretakers/adults.

The force of early learning shapes perception of others and expectancies about emotion, sets various triggers and comfort zones, and leaves a significant amount of imprints that guide us all in later life, but does so in a variety of ways. Whether attachment theory is right in detail, the broad assumption that early life 'sets' the framework for later relationships seems undeniable, though in these broad terms the claim has rarely been denied. The advances made by Attachment Theory come in the form of specific predictions about particular types of personality style and their relationship to later romance and interpersonal dealings, but we should not overlook other influences and possibilities, too.

LOOK OUT FOR THIS IN THE MEDIA

Find news stories about killers that 'explain' their murders in terms of their childhood experiences.

Watch the film *Shine* paying particular attention to family dynamics as portrayed there.

Life at home and school

Parental style of control in a family can affect the child directly and also can provide a model for the child's subsequent social relationships. Ladd, LeSieur & Profilet (1993) show that parents often structure their children's play in ways that expose the children selectively to experiences of control over their own relationships: for example some parents forbid a child to play with particular other children, or parents may 'hang around' and make specific suggestions about games or roles when the child plays with others. Pettit & Mize (1993) looked at indirect ways in which parents influence children's styles of relating behaviour. For instance, parents 'teach' children tacitly through their own interaction style as well as explicitly by verbal comments about how to 'do' social relationships. Children learn about relationships from stories in books and on TV as well (Duck, in press SAGE CA, see refs).

This approach to parental teaching of relationships is in distinction to old work (Baumrind, 1972) that identified three styles of parental treatment of children and then presumed that such styles 'produced' children with different social characteristics. *Authoritarian parents* control and evaluate the behaviour of a child using absolute standards of behaviour. They stress obedience and punishment – often physical punishment but also withdrawal of love or psychological blackmail.

Secondly, *permissive parents* relate to the child's behaviour in non-punitive and accepting ways, often consulting the child about its behaviour, offering rationales for the standards used, and relying on reason rather than punishment. Finally, an *authoritative style* is based on direction of the child through reason but not on the basis of equality nor, necessarily, of acceptance of what the child is doing. Such a parent exercises firm control, but does so by communication rather than by physical force. This style of parenting is more successful in 'producing' children who are independent, cooperative, friendly and achievement-oriented, and is generally recommended by family therapists.

The idea that there is a direct one-way effect has been challenged (Lollis & Kuczynski, 1997) and relatively recently attention has been paid to broader frames for the experiencing of other people. Kramer & Baron (1995) considered the inter-generational linkages created by parents' experiences with their siblings as frames for the ways in which they evaluate relationships between their own children. If my own experience of 'being an older brother' is that 'younger brothers are favourites' then I may attend more carefully to my elder son in order to ensure that he does not suffer the disadvantages that go with the role. Kramer & Baron (1995) reported that mothers who claimed negative sibling histories were most likely to have children who interacted positively with one another as a result of the mother's selective child-rearing practices, such as less differentiated treatment of siblings. Of course children learn a lot from siblings (Dunn, 1997), not only from interacting with them but also from seeing others interact with them. For instance, a child could acquire a negative view of self from seeing parents consistently treat a sibling in a more favourable manner (Nicholson, 2006).

What is going on here? It should not surprise us that parents use their own past experience in order to structure their approach to parenting. Humans typically use their past interpretation or thoughts about events as guides for the future (Duck, 1994), but this does not mean that they do so without adding their own spin, fantasies, hopes, or good ideas when they can. Furthermore, it should not surprise us to find that the two persons in a relationship influence *each other*, even if one of them (the child) seems on the face of it to have less formal power than the other (the parent). Neither children nor romantic partners simply experience relationships as 'recipients' or as 'creators' but as both, working together interactively to make their relationship work. Children can often control parents (e.g., by being demanding or uncooperative and hence requiring a parent to attend).

Research has moved away from the simple idea that parents just imprint their kids and the kids respond, instead emphasizing the constructive/interpretative role of the child rather that seeing it as a receptacle for parents to put ideas into (Pettit & Clawson, 1996). Children have several different paths to the achievement of peer competence, whether they adapt to parental style (Baumrind, 1972), observe siblings and peers (Dunn, 1996; Nicholson, 2006), follow explicit parental advice (Pettit & Mize, 1993), or experience the benefits (or costs) of parental memories of childhood (Putallaz et al., 1993), or parental management of the social environment (Pettit & Clawson, 1996). This is an instance of a more general trend to credit all relational partners with their own interpretative frameworks that mean that relating is never just the activity of one person upon another, but instead is two constructive persons working together reciprocally (Carl & Duck, 2004).

INTERPRETING EMOTIONS

Given this background, can we blend a personal style of approach to other people into the social and cultural context for interpreting emotions generally? Are our abilities to feel emotions directed by childhood experience? What other things may (also) come into play in the emotions of relationships? Some researchers have already connected emotion to broader styles and Ryan, La Guardia, Solky-Butzel, Chirkov & Kim (2005) conducted three studies on people's willingness to rely on others for emotional support. Those people who show more emotional reliance generally also experience greater well-being although this varies significantly across different relationships, cultural groups, and sex. People also showed systematic variations in emotional characteristics that were connected to need satisfaction within specific relationships. Feeney (2004) examined a typology of hurtful events in couple relationships and distinguished between hurtful comments and hurt feelings, since previous research has developed a typology of hurtful speech acts, but utterances are only one source of hurt. Some people have argued that the central theme of hurtful events is relational in nature and is specifically derived from a relational devaluation, whereas Feeney talks of a sense of rejection.

Although we usually think of emotions as feelings that happen to us or which we experience, recent theory is taking the view that many of our feelings in relationships are contextually and situationally driven rather than being 'pure feelings'. For example, Feeney (2005) looked at perceptions of the appraisals specifically involved in hurtful events in couple relationships. She suggested that hurt feelings are elicited by relational transgressions that generally imply relational devaluation and that evoke a sense of personal injury by threatening positive mental models of self and/or others: 'It seems that hurt feelings generally reflect a complex set of perceptions about the value of the self, the partner, and the relationship [and] … [u]npacking the complex experience of "hurt feelings" is thus an important goal for researchers and clinicians' (2005: 270). In short, specific events trigger emotions but do so partly because they imply devaluation of both self and the relationship.

When events rub up against personal styles of thinking about one's value to another person, then emotions of a very striking quality are created. The emotions, however, come from both the events themselves and the preexistence of a relational context in which to judge them, and so the personal response to such things is guided in part by one's sense of self, but only in part. Feeney's paper raises the question: what are the major events that count as hurtful in romantic relationships? Such a question of course, conceals some issues about the way in which emotions are understood in a particular culture and the value which is given to certain kinds of relationships. In Britain and Australia it is much more common and acceptable to tease and 'put down' friends as a part of friendship than it is in the USA, for example. Therefore, what may be treated as 'hurtful' in the USA may not be so regarded in the UK or Australia.

The feelings that we have in relationships are partly the result of context in many different ways and particularly as a result of how we feel or expect to be treated in relationships, but a further context for the practical conduct of relationship is the use of language. Metts & Planalp (2002) consider at length the ways in which expression of emotion functions in everyday life not merely as a revelation of an inner state, but as a 'speech act' that is intended to bring about a result or alter something in the social context. Thus, 'I'm very angry with you' is not simply a declaration, but rather it is an accusation that is intended to generate a confession, an apology, or an expression of regret from the other person.

We can recognize the force of language in expression of emotions (e.g., in expression of anger, hurt, or declarations of love), but communication is also something that takes place directly *about* relationships as well as *in* relationships. Not only do people talk about how their relationship is going (Carl, 2006a; Wood, 2006), but they may talk in order to express deeper emotion in a relationship or to start and continue a relationship in the first place (Sprecher & Duck, 1993). Partners also often show relationship awareness and convey their thoughts about the relationship to one another directly in talk (Acitelli, 1988; 1993). Finally emotion may be both generated and discussed during conflict or daily hassles (Alberts et al., 2005), or in confronting various relationship challenges, such as dealing with long-distance relationships or temporary separation (Sahlstein, 2006b).

Sanderson, Rahm & Beigbeder (2005) examined individuals' focus on intimacy and whether that might lead them to interacting in distinct ways that lead to different levels of relationship satisfaction. Patterns of interaction (e.g., time spent, social support exchange, self-disclosure), as well as good perceptions of one's friend's goals connect well to high satisfaction at least in part because people with these characteristics interact in their close friendships in distinct ways. Intimacy is connected to satisfaction through close attention to the 'stuff' that happens in life, and also individuals with a strong focus on intimacy goals handle conflict in more constructive ways in both romance and friendship, a finding similar for both sexes. However, people's willingness to express emotion or to do things, such as comforting someone else, that follow from such emotions, are judged in a social context – as Burleson, Holmstrom & Gilstrap (2005) indicate 'Guys can't say that to guys' and some forms of male expression of distress or of comfort and compassion are evidently limited by the masculine roles and whether the emotions are seen as suitable for expression by males.

LISTEN IN ON YOUR OWN LIFE

- Do you talk to other people about the emotional quality of your relationships?
- Are you more likely to talk to women or men about these things?
- Why does it make sense to discuss your own personal feelings with someone else in the first place?
- Discuss these matters in class

Emotions are often represented as the stuff of which the peaks and troughs of life are made, as when, for example, we feel exhilarated, depressed, shy, lonely, jealous or in love. Those selected emotions are particularly powerful (for example, love and jealousy – which some countries accept as legitimate excuses and legal justifi-cations for 'crimes of passion'). However, the emotional experiences that create and sustain relationships are not necessarily so consistently dramatic and are certainly not limited to turbulent emotions, but might be found in social anxiety about a date or in fear of bullying by a boss or in sexual harassment. Clearly in daily relation-ships we experience regret, disappointment, sadness, guilt, anxiety, contentment, joy, satisfaction, irritation, admiration, disgust – and most important, and most of the time, not very much at all except a sense that things are pretty much where they were last time we checked. What is true of relationships is one simple fact: they are not composed of universally strong or universally positive experiences but are rather humdrum (Wood & Duck, 2006). Most of what we do in daily life is to *man-age*. We manage and balance our own feelings as against those of a partner; we manage the good and the bad things in a relationship that generate positive and negative emotions, we handle daily 'stuff' (Duck, Foley & Kirkpatrick, 2006b). The present chapter next explores some of the emotions that we instantly – and perhaps superficially – think of as 'relational'; the following chapter relates them to actual experiences of living relatively mundane daily life in human relationships. My point is that to focus only on dramatic emotional upheavals and to use them as the focus of research on emotions in relationships is unbalanced. It is important to understand that strong emotions may be relatively rare experiences in the daily conduct of human relationships and that a focus on such things takes our attention away from the huge amount of routine relational and emotional work that we do at other times and in rather trivial ways (Duck, in press SAGE CA, see refs).

Secondly, it is important to recognize that the topic of 'emotion' is in any case one surrounded by much controversy. Our automatic approach is to represent emotion as a strong, internal, individual feeling of some kind. We may even think about how people represent emotions to other people and we may recognize that whatever they are, emotions are not just internal subconscious disturbances that never get out into the real world, but may be revealed in the course of confession about relational transgressions (Afifi, Falato & Weiner, 2001) and in any case are often interpersonal conversational experiences as much as they are internal psychological events. Indeed, as cheating lovers may well find, jealousy can be expressed in some intriguing, and occasionally fatal, ways. All the same, just as we saw in Chapter 1, the feelings about other people occur, or come into being, as part of contexts that are outside of the individual per se, such as the culture, society, family and workplace. Therefore the exploration of emotion in relationships should not stop short at the point where the feeling is felt, nor rest satisfied with explanations in terms of the cognitive or social structures that 'produce' it. Rather, we must understand the ways in which emotions have impact on relationships in their everyday working contexts and vice versa (Dutton & Ragins, 2007 have a book on positive relationships at work; Harden Fritz & Omdahl, 2006, have one on difficult relationships at work, and Kirkpatrick et al., 2006, have one about relating difficulty anywhere). Such a goal will entail us understanding the ways in which human beings have been socialized to *express* (or limit their expression of) emotions about relationships and relational partners within a particular social and relational context. Foster & Campbell (2005) discuss the adversity of being in a secret relationship and the problems associated with decisions to reveal or conceal it, finding that secrecy and the desire to maintain secrecy about a relationship tend to increase negative feelings and to decrease satisfaction with the relationship itself. It is evidently a painful thing to feel something strongly, but to be constrained by social norms not to tell people about it. The goal of maintaining social respectability, then, in these cases can conflict with other relational goals and the intensity of a positive feature is balanced by an intense sense of oppression in not being able to declare it openly in a way that is accepted by other people (cf. Lannutti, 2005).

The intention to conduct relationships appropriately will also entail us realizing the extent to which emotions are exacerbated by contexts for expression and the ways in which a culture judges emotions as appropriate to a given context or set of circumstances. For instance, one interesting and recurrent observation in jury trials is that defendants who appear calm and collected when told about a spouse's death are often catapulted into first place as prime suspects because that sort of emotional (non)reaction is not regarded as 'appropriate' to the receiving of tragic news (Searcy et al., 2005).

Labelling and expressing feelings

The emotions that are expressed in a given society are a mixture of apparently universal human feelings and cultural prescriptions that define the form and appropriateness of the expression of those emotions. For example, we assume that all humans experience fear and joy; indeed Darwin did some work not only suggesting that such emotions are common to all societies and to some animal species also, but that there is a certain amount of 'cross-species' recognition of major emotional expressions (Guerrero & Floyd, 2006). Some societies, however, place very strong emphasis on such emotions as 'shame' while others recognize it but give it little weight. Some societies expect grief to be borne with quiet, stoic dignity and reserve, others expect loud wailing expressions accompanied by energetic physical demonstrations of distress (Duck, in press SAGE CA, see refs). There is some discussion by scholars on whether communication of emotion *is* the emotion (for example, some argue that we can never know more than the *expression* of emotion; also some people make themselves feel angry just by shouting), or whether communication is a component of emotion (some people feel worse when they express anxiety than when they do not), or whether emotional expression is simply the externalizing of some inner state that is ascribed as a result of socially accepted labels. For example, Schachter & Singer (1962) showed that people who were emotionally aroused could be enticed to describe their feelings as either anger or joy depending on the label that fitted their social surroundings best (for example, whether people around them were laughing or hostile). In other words, the 'emotion' they were feeling was steered towards the label presented by the behaviour of other people in a social setting and was not simply felt as a pure emotion. This analysis was even applied to the emotion of love by Berscheid & Hatfield (1974) and held some currency for a while as researchers showed that high arousal led to descriptions of 'appropriate' emotions if people were presented with the right cues to pin their feelings upon (arousal in the presence of an attractive person was labelled 'attraction' but without such a stimulus was labelled as 'anxiety', for example, so be careful who you sit next to during an exam). The discussion of emotion is thus complicated by some important cultural contexts for emotion and is not simply a question of looking at the feelings that people 'naturally' have.

First, the strong social imperatives about the need for, and means of, communication of emotion spoil some people's relationships and relationship problems such as shyness often show up as culturally unusual or inappropriate ways of communicating feeling (Bradshaw, 2006). Second, when we report or describe emotions, we frequently edit our accounts of them so that they make sense to other people, not just to ourselves. Therefore we use culturally accepted language, reference points, and narrative form for describing emotions (Acitelli, Duck & West, 2000). Typically these describe emotions and relational behaviours in ways that are accepted in our culture as valid ones (for example, our culture accepts that someone 'falls in love' rather than 'gets bitten by the love god's mosquito').

Usually our language for describing emotions in relationships also means that we summarize them as future-oriented, enduring or continuous states rather than momentary or fleeting micromomentary feelings (Duck & Sants, 1983). For instance, we are more likely to say 'I am in love with you', or 'I will love you for ever', or 'I am friends with you' rather than 'I felt a twinge of love for you at the particular moment when you looked at me' or 'I felt friendship towards you just for the moment when you shared that secret with me'. This characteristic of language – that it labels and stabilizes or perpetuates an appearance that life is made up of 'states' and transitions between states – is crucial to the conduct of relationships, which we also tend to describe as continuous states rather than turbulent, or at least variable, experiences (Duck, 1994). All the same, much of our emotional life is devoted to the long-term organization of the variabilities and inconsistencies of daily experience or the creation of uniform labels for muddled and diversiform experiences (Duck, 2006).

The summary of emotions and translation of them into state language in this way make it hard to pinpoint the true initial causes of emotions or love and friendship. Perhaps we can explain it as 'love at first sight' but usually we prefer to look back over a whole range of experiences and events to 'explain' emotional states. We would feel foolish saying that we loved someone only during a particular few seconds a week or only when we thought of it or merely for the shape of the nose. Our culture prefers to believe that it takes time to fall in love, and that love is a complete emotion constructed from many cues and causes all rolled together over periods of time, particularly due to something uplifting, like expanding one's awareness by including the other's perspectives as part of one's self (Aron & Aron, 1997). Yet considerations of the role of language and communication in relation to love are becoming more common. Beall & Sternberg (1995) noted that the depiction of love draws on a large arsenal of social expectations such as those created in novels concerning the ways in which love should proceed (see Chapter 1 on 'quality' of relationships and emotions). Prusank, Duran & DeLillo (1993) have documented the ways in which popular magazines influence and also reflect people's experiences of romance and marriage in providing guidelines and advice about the ways in which relationships 'should' be conducted. Interestingly, but in line with my arguments here about cultural context, such advice about relationships has changed over the last 50 years, from an assumption that there is only one correct way to do relationships, a way agreed by all experts, to the more recent view that freedom to be oneself, however that works, is most significant and so supersedes joint relational maintenance as the primary concern in life.

Rephrasing the above in a more technical way, statements about social emotions use dispositional or continuous language to provide 'summary affect statements' about our partner and these are socially appropriate to the culture in which we happen to find ourselves. They summarize our feelings about someone using culturally approved terminology and culturally accepted explanations for the basis of relationships, just as the discussion of attachment theory runs the risk of representing a person's approach to all relationships as only one sort of thing. They are not simple descriptions of short-term personal emotional peaks or troughs; instead they reverberate to social norms. They emphasize implicit continuity in relationships and prepare partners and others to expect a certain shape to the future – a future that still has the relationship in it! In fact, much of the construction of relationships is based on various ways of manipulating our expectations about the future in this way, since relationships involve unfinished business that continues throughout the life of the relationship itself (Duck, 1990; 1994). Much of the basis of emotion is founded in the organization of routines of behaviour that make up the day-to-day conduct of this unfinished business where disruption to routines causes annoyance, change to routines occurs as a result of falling in love, and continuous conduct of routines reassures us about the relationship's significance to our partner as well as to ourselves (Duck, 2006; Wood, 2006). In short, social emotions are not just fleeting physiological experiences but are organized, long-term behavioural creations that find their form and shape in the behaviour and routines of everyday conduct of relationships, expressed in ways that carry symbolic force in a given society (Fitch, 2003).

As a matter of fact there is some evidence that the symbolic values of emotion and relationships have changed somewhat through history, even in our own culture. In a fascinating report, Contarello & Volpato (1991) have explored both the similarities and the differences in literary descriptions of friendship over the last 1000 years. They found that friendship has always involved intimacy, respect, and mutual help, plus the likelihood of the friend confronting one's own weaknesses honestly. By contrast, in the passage from the sixteenth to the seventeenth century, friendship went through a profound change, with conflict emerging as a common element. Also although all the texts examined in this study were written by female authors, female friendship was hardly ever mentioned in the early texts! Werking (2000) gives close discussion to another often overlooked relationship, cross-sex platonic relationships. Although Harry (*When Harry met Sally*) felt that 'Men and women can never be friends; the sex thing always gets in the way', West, Anderson & Duck (1995) and Werking (2000) discuss at length the fact that such friendships are increasingly commonplace. Yet cross-sex friends always face cultural constraints on the relationship, must contend with disbelief that their friendship is not really a secret sexual one, and have to battle scepticism that there really is 'just' friendship. Indeed for many reasons, cross-sex friendship is one of the hottest and understudied of relationships in the research literature (Werking, 2000; West et al., 1995; Wood & Duck, 1995) and has now been extended to 'hook-ups' (Paul, 2006) and FWBRs – Friends With Benefits (Hughes, Morrison & Asada, 2005), partly because it points up so clearly the fact that relationships are not the result of pure emotion but take on a life (and form of life) that is shaped by response to the prevailing practices and opinion on the street.

LISTEN TO YOUR OWN CONVERSATIONS

... on hook-ups, FWBRs and the double standard.

Check out what people are saying these days about hook-ups, friends with benefits, and Internet dating. Listen out for ways in which people describe these relationships as judged differently according to whether men's or women's involvement is being described. Make a note of any differences that you observe, and discuss them with your classmates and friends.

POSITIVE EMOTION: LOVE

Love is blamed for a lot of things from the Trojan War to various crimes of passion that appear in the tabloid newspapers. It is called 'a temporary insanity' (Bierce, *The Devil's Dictionary*. He went on to add that it is 'curable by marriage'). So what is it? 'It is difficult, if not impossible, to answer the question "What is love?" because any answer must reflect its time period and place and in particular the functions that romantic love serves there' (Beall & Sternberg, 1995: 417). In attempting to answer the question, however, several lines of work have been developed. Their focus has been almost exclusively on heterosexual romantic love but Huston & Schwartz (1995) and Peplau & Spalding (2000) have extended the discussion to exploration of homosexual love in different compositions of gendered groups. More recently, Lannutti (2005) has placed the issue in the context of legally recognized same-sex marriage and the role of such an institution in the understanding of the possibilities offered by people feeling specific emotions. Clearly the recognition of possible forms of relationship between pairs of people who are in love depends on the norms existing in a particular society and what it assumes may be allowed to matter. All in all, the research suggests the brilliance of James's (1890) observation that the worst thing that can happen to anyone is to go through life without getting noticed by anybody else when you wish to be acknowledged (and in this case without it being possible for your strong emotions for another person to be formally recognized as permissible). Indeed Mak & Marshall (2004) suggest that mattering to other people helps us to locate ourselves and gives a sense of purpose. Since love is the ultimate form of mattering, we should attend to it carefully here.

LOOK OUT FOR THIS IN THE MEDIA

Look out for ways in which the media celebrate length of relationship and treat it as 'success'.

Love is a juicier topic than friendship, and could be seen as the primary relational emotion especially given the emphasis that our culture places on long-term partnerships as an ultimate measure of relational 'success'. If we were Contarello & Volpato, mentioned above, we'd immediately note that love was not 'big' in marriages in the twelfth century. It was not even expected to be there – at least not in the sense that we expect it to be the basis of marriage nowadays. Marriage, especially between noble persons, was politically arranged and served the needs of strengthening the ties between different groups, families, or 'houses'. Tuchman indicates that: 'Although the free consent of marriage partners was theoretically required by the church, and the "I will" declaration was considered to be the doctrinal essence of the marriage contract made before a priest, practical politics overlooked this requirement, sometimes with unhappy results' (1978: 47) If the partners liked each other then that was a bonus, but all that was *necessary* was loyalty, with fidelity. Nowadays we do things differently, and, in America and the UK, we have a divorce rate at 50 per cent!

Also important is the fact that the 'experience' of love is tied in important ways to the manner in which it may be expressed in a given society. Kovecses (1991) notes that we communicate about love in many different ways, using some very obscure and some very complex metaphors and cultural meaning systems. For example, love is often likened to food or eating ('sugar', 'honey', 'feast your eyes upon…', 'good enough to eat…') but also to consumption of other types ('all aflame with passion…', 'burning desire', 's/he sets my heart on fire'). The extensive system of meaning and communication through metaphors and other linguistic devices shows us, through Kovecses' analysis, the power of the system of description. This perhaps points to common threads of experience for us all in trying to understand and communicate our feelings of love to other people. For instance, we can readily understand and sympathize with someone who claims to be displaced (for example, 'head over heels in love' – rather a curious phrase when you think that the head normally is over the heels anyway) or distracted (for example, 'I'm mad with love for you', 'They are nuts about each other').

Does such a finding of regular and systematic use of specifically vivid metaphors about love indicate that we typically experience it in culturally 'agreed' ways? Marston, Hecht & Robers (1987) looked at the subjective experience of love and the ways in which people communicate about it. From interviews and questionnaire data they found that there are essentially six ways in which people communicate about love. The subjective experience of love has at least three components: 1) relational labels/constructs, like commitment and security; 2) physiological labels, such as feelings of nervousness and warmth; 3) behaviour and NVC, such as doing things with the other person or ways of looking at one another (Marston et al., 1987). Given that love-smitten subjects conceptualized love in terms of *different mixes* of these elements, rather than in terms of different strengths of the same mix, Marston et al. found evidence for six types of experience of love. These are: *collaborative love* (supportiveness); *active love* (joint activities and 'erratic rhythms' such as changes to the pace of daily routines); *intuitive love* (NVC ability to communicate feelings); *committed love* (togetherness); *traditional romantic love* (future commitment and feeling good); *expressive love* (telling the other person about one's feelings). Hecht, Marston & Larkey (1994) found that people experiencing committed love have higher quality relationships. However, the relationship labels themselves are cultural provisions, as are the criteria for deciding whether a relationship is of high quality: cultures have norms that help individuals decide what is a relationship and whether it is 'good', as we saw in Chapter 1.

Are there different types of love?

Several scholarly approaches to understanding love are based on the idea that we can distinguish different sorts of the same basic emotion. For example, there are some differences (though there are also many similarities) between the ways in which women and men respond to love. For one thing, although men and women report experiencing the same levels of intensity of love (Rubin, 1973), men 'fall in love' at an earlier point in a relationship than women do, whereas women fall out of love sooner than men do (Hatfield & Walster, 1978). This has led to men being called 'FILOs' (First In, Last Out) and women 'LIFOs' (Last In, First Out). On the other hand, women say that they have been infatuated more often than men (on average, 5.6 times for women and 4.5 times for men), but both sexes report being in loving relationships about as often – around 1.25 times (Kephart, 1967).

Such findings raise the possibility that love is not a simple single emotion but a complex mix of many different feelings or types of emotion. Maslow, an early theorist, distinguished B (for being) love, which he saw as positive and implying independence, from D (for dependency) love, which he saw as negative and implying neediness. Another distinction is between passionate love and companionate love (Berscheid & Walster, 1974): passionate love is the steamy sort that Casanova and Don Juan specialized in, whilst companionate love is the kind that kin and long-term marriage partners may have. Companionate love is enhanced by an increased sense of commitment whilst passionate love derives primarily from physiological arousal and excitement.

Is love really just either madly passionate or boringly dispassionate? Is this passionate–companionate dichotomy too simple to account for all the feelings that we can have towards a lover? Another proposal suggests that there are six types of love (Lee, 1973) and that persons can mix the types together in various ways. The six types are labelled with various Latin and Greek words for types of love: *eros*, *ludus*, *storge*, *pragma*, *mania* and *agape*. Each has a typical character and a brief explanation may assist us in working out the nature of love.

Eros (romantic love) focuses upon beauty and physical attractiveness; it is a sensual love that expects to be returned. People who score highly on *eros* typically believe in 'love at first sight' and are particularly sensitive to the physical blemishes of their partner, such as overweight, broken nose, smelly feet or misaligned teeth. They are attracted to partners on the basis of physical attraction, like to kiss and cuddle soon after meeting a new partner, and report a definite genital response (lubrication, erection) to the first kiss.

Ludus (game-playing love) is like a game and is seen as fun, not to be taken seriously. People scoring high on *ludus* typically flirt a lot, keep partners guessing about their level of commitment to them and stop a relationship when it stops being fun. They get over love affairs easily and quickly, enjoy teasing their lovers and will often go out with someone even when they know they do not want to get involved.

Storge (friendship love) is based on caring, not on passion. People scoring high on *storge* typically believe that love grows from friendship, that lovers must share similar interests and enjoy the same activities. For storgic lovers, love grows with respect and concern for the other person. They can put up with long separations without feeling that the relationship is threatened and are not looking for excitement in the relationship, as ludic lovers are.

Pragma (logical, shopping-list love) is practical and based on the belief that a relationship has to work. People scoring high on *pragma* ask themselves whether their lover would make a good parent and they pay thoughtful attention to such things as their partner's future career prospects. Pragmatic lovers take account of their partner's background and characteristics like attitudes, religion, politics and hobbies. Pragmatic lovers are realistic and relatively unromantic.

Mania (possessive, dependent love) is essentially an uncertain and anxious type of love; it is obsessive and possessive and half expects to be thrown aside. Manic lovers get very jealous. People scoring high on *mania* typically believe in becoming ill or doing stupid things to regain their partner's attention if ever the partner ignores them or takes them for granted. They also claim that when the relationship gets into trouble, they develop illnesses like stomach upsets.

Agape (all-giving, selfless love) is selfless and compassionate and generally loves other human beings in an unqualified way, as preached by Gandhi, Buddha and Jesus. In their close relationships, Agapic lovers would claim that they use their strength to help their partner through difficult times and may say that if their partner had a baby with someone else, they would want to help to care for it as if it were their own. Lee (1973) reports that he did not encounter any persons who were perfect examples of agapic lovers, although many people reported brief agapic episodes.

Do such love styles get communicated differently in speech? What about cultural contexts also and how do they modify expressions of the feelings? If there are these types of love, then do men and women experience them to different extents? Yes. Men are erotic and Ludic in their attitudes to love (Hendrick, Hendrick, Foote & Slapion-Foote, 1984), whilst women are pragmatic, manic, and storgic. In other words, men's love is typically passionate and uncommitted, with an element of game-playing coupled with romance. Women's love is typically practical and caring, with an element of possessiveness, a view that could be explained in terms of economic factors and the fact that in the past it has paid women to be practical and to think long term when they have had a choice. This is not to say that women do not base their love on passion or that men do not care about their lovers. The sexes mix their experience of love in different blends. However, the broad differences in love style between men and women are very broad assessments that do not do justice to the subtleties of love style and there are now known to be several other levels of difference that moderate or compli-cate the general rule that men and women are different in their experiences of love. For example there are differences apparent in different types of relationships (Hendrick & Hendrick, 1990) and differences between people in love and those who are not (Hendrick & Hendrick, 1988). Also people report their feelings of love differently in different circumstances or to different audiences (Hendrick & Hendrick, 2000). Thus the broad style of love is a springboard from which a com-plex, multiform compendium of emotions is expressed in talk.

Developing love?

So far, we have explored love as a state of feeling that is expressed and communi-cated but we should also look for expressive change as people fall in love. Aron, Dutton, Aron & Iverson (1989) showed that falling in love is characterized by fre-quent expression of the fact that the other person is like the self, by comment on the other's desirable characteristics, by talk of similarity, and communication of a sense of 'mystery or magic'. By contrast, falling in friendship is reported as due simply to similarity and propinquity, with a little less emphasis on the other's desirable char-acteristics and practically no mention of any magic or mystery. Aron & Aron (1997) further delineate the ways in which the experience of falling in love is also an expe-rience of self-expansion or enrichment of the sense of self by inclusion of the other. In other words, humans are geared towards the expansion of their self through exploration, development of competence, integration of incoherent experiences, or extension of awareness. The development of a relationship with someone who diver-sifies the expansion is deeply satisfying and enriches both persons' sense of self.

Another possibility is that falling in love is a transition between different blends of the types of love. For instance, initial attraction to a possible lover might begin as erotic love, mixed perhaps with *mania* (desire for possession) and *ludus* (game-playing). As the relationship develops, the lovers might express greater feelings of *storge* (friendship) as they develop caring on top of passion. This may lead the partners on to talk about the working of the relationship in the long term, that is, to discuss the partner's potential as a long-term mate, co-parent of the children, and so on – in short, to an assessment of pragmatic concerns. If the partner seems to pass that test, then they might begin to express *pragma* love. All of this would suggest that married couples would score more highly than other couples on *pragma* love, whilst new dates might score more highly on erotic love, that is, views about the 'right type' of love for different sorts of relationship will vary. As the relationship to a partner develops, so the type of love will be communicated differently also (Hendrick & Hendrick, 2000)

All of the above suggests the centrality of the way in which love is communicated. As Marston et al. (1987) found, when I feel love or think about it, I also communicate about it and I may communicate in order to do something about it or to change the relationship (Metts & Planalp, 2002). When I feel it, I may even think of inventive ways to communicate it ('My love is like a red, red rose that's newly sprung in June; My love is like a melody that's sweetly sung in tune…'). But there is something equally important: the way in which we express love may be *coloured by the circumstances of the moment*. If we are on a date then we may be interested in openly conveying lust (if we are feeling lucky) or at least strong positive feelings (something like *eros*). By contrast, if we are discussing marriage, our minds may turn to the roles involved in long-term commitment (something like *pragma*). If we are feeling playful and having a good time, or in a group of friends who can overhear what we are saying, then we may just start teasing (something like *ludus*). These could all be different modes of expression of the same single positive attitude towards a partner rather than different types or styles of emotion. Attitudes do not have a single level of intensity or only one mode of expression. As rhetorical theorists note (Dixson & Duck, 1993), we express our attitudes and make statements in particular forms as a result of the *audience* to whom we are talking and the *situation* where we are speaking. 'The attitude' is thus represented by many different forms of expression and is a somewhat amorphous and protean thing. I suspect that researchers of love ought to look less at the presumed single-minded and enduring aspect of the person who feels the love (as psychologists tend to do when they explore love attitudes or love styles). Instead they should pay more attention to the circumstances and rhetorical/social/interpersonal contexts or situations where love is expressed and communicated in everyday life. Although you can feel love without expressing it to anyone but yourself, the occasions that are most interesting are obviously those where it is not only felt but also expressed. There it carries social and relational consequences and yet is also constrained by social and relational forces without actually changing its nature.

LOOK OUT FOR THIS IN THE MEDIA

Check out recent movies for different types of love style. You can find *eros* in the bar scene in *Top Gun* and *agape* in *The Bodyguard*, for example. See if you can find other more recent examples of all the love styles.

The behaviour of lovers

Aside from the feelings of love which drive us into relationships, there are behavioural and communicative consequences also (Acitelli, 1993; Aron & Aron, 1997). Love is both a felt emotion and an expression of that feeling in the behaviour through which we communicate to partners – and to the outside world – that we love them. Obviously, partners who are married often choose to wear wedding rings to communicate the fact; dates hold hands; partners embrace or put their arms around one another in the street. These NVC indications are slight but well known. They are called 'tie signs' (Goffman, 1959) in that they indicate that two people are 'tied' to one another (like other uses of symbolic spatial, personal, and territorial markers discussed in Chapter 1). Furthermore, lovers sit closer to one another than do 'likers', and they gaze at one another more than do people who are just friends (Rubin, 1973). Obviously also lovers and would-be lovers talk to one another in intimate ways that are 'readable' by outsiders and which occasionally make lovers sensitive about audiences or careful about how they behave in company (Baxter & Widenmann, 1993).

Also Sprecher & Duck (1993) investigated the ways in which first dates are converted into second dates (because at some point they obviously have to be if people continue the relationship, yet this practical aspect of relationship development had almost never been studied before – or, regrettably, since!). As may be expected, talk plays a critical role in the enterprise and is a central mechanism for converting initial attraction into a working form of relationship. Furthermore, as things move even further forward, the partners wind up talking about the relationship itself at some point as it becomes a topic of conversation in its own right (Duck, 1994). Indeed Acitelli (1988, 1993) has shown that such talking is a key way in which people adjust their perceptions of one another, ratify their evaluations, and increase mutual understanding, checking out discrepancies of understanding and generally clearing the way to a better grasp of one another's inner core. The very act of talking about the relationship is a key way in which love is indicated, especially for women (indeed men sometimes assume that something must be *wrong* with the relationship if the partner wants to talk about it!). On the other hand, Caughlin & Afifi (2004: 479) found that 'associations between topic avoidance and relational dissatisfaction were moderated by individuals' motivations for avoidance and by personal and relational characteristics that are conceptually linked to such motivations. These findings are consistent with theoretical arguments that topic avoidance can be benign – and even helpful – in some relational circumstances'. Again, then, we see the connection between the specifics of a relational situation and the particular motivations held by the partners, but the basic message seems to be that *management* of talking about your relationships is important.

One part of love, then, is a direct communicative display of the fact that we love our partner. However, as both Acitelli's and Caughlin & Afifi's work shows in their different ways, some of the cues that are contained in communication are subtle and indirect, and not only reassure the partner but also tell the outside world that the relationship exists and draw subtle boundaries around the relationship, while also being built on the partners' internal working models of what matters. Of course, the sorts of display that we choose on a given occasion are also likely to be influenced by the rhetorical situation, the social context and the interpersonal environments as discussed earlier. Presenting a partner with a ring, doing a really big and inconvenient favour, and disrobing are all, in their own ways, capable of conveying a message of love and fondness through behaviour. Nevertheless, each is appropriate only to a particular set of circumstances or for a particular audience and would be inappropriate in other circumstances or with other audiences, as you can imagine.

For this reason, *loving behaviour* itself develops and changes as love attitudes themselves develop. Developing love is not simply an increasingly powerful attitude but is also a changing constellation of behaviours. As Aron et al. (1989) show, the *experience* of falling in love is usually described in terms only of attitudes and feelings, based on other people's personalities or physical characteristics, similarity to oneself or propinquity. Aron & Aron (1997), however, went on to describe the importance of shared activity – and in particular exciting shared activity – in the process of developing love, especially that which involve is high levels of physical activity (dancing, hiking, bicycling) or newness and exoticness (attending concerts or studying nature).

In addition to the feelings associated with falling in love there are some pleasant consequences and some side effects. There is a strongly reported change in behaviour, as well, such as increased eye contact, physical closeness, and self-disclosure (Hendrick & Hendrick, 2000; Rubin, 1973). Beyond this there is a broader change to the structure of everyday life behaviours. For instance, we gradually pay more attention to a new lover and spend less time with old friends; we start to share more activities and adjust our lifestyles as we let our new lover into our lives; we arrange to spend more time with our partner and less with other people (Milardo & Wellman, 1992; Parks & Adelman, 1983). In short, part of falling in love is an increased binding together of the habits of daily life and a developing routine interdependence (Dainton, 2000), and even close friendships have to be maintained by routines like sending holiday greetings cards (Dindia, Timmerman, Langan, Sahlstein & Quandt, 2004). More than this, a big part of it is extending the range of ways in which love can be expressed and communicated. However, such behaviours frequently create stress or difficulty in ways that confirm the point that daily life is about management of conflicting forces (Baxter & Montgomery, 1996). Baxter, Mazanec, Nicholson, Pittman, Smith & West (1997) show that persons who are withdrawing from interaction with their network of friends in order to facilitate or extend a deep romantic relationship actually experience competing loyalties. The problem is how to distribute a fixed amount of time when different relationships (friends, family, lover) regard it as part of their relational rights to have access to a person's time.

Perhaps for this reason, *people who fall in love frequently* report that it is highly disruptive and that they develop a high level of nervous disorders and skin problems (Kemper & Bologh, 1981). However, when love is going well, people report feeling good both in mind and body (Hendrick & Hendrick, 1988). Disruption to love is more problematic, however. People who have never been in love claim that they have a high number of minor bodily disorders like colds and flu, and people who have recently broken up with a partner suffer similar physical disorders too (Kemper & Bologh, 1981). Those whose partners had broken off with them typically report sleep problems, headaches, and loss of control of emotions. Those who caused the break-up suffered less, except that females reported stomach upsets.

SOME PROBLEMATIC EMOTIONS: JEALOUSY AND SHYNESS

Since we have looked at a positive emotion and yet human relationships are made up of negative ones too, I will briefly consider the emotional experiences of jealousy and shyness. These represent negative emotional contrasts to the positivity of love, although in the case of jealousy or relational obsession, they may be prompted by love of some kind in the first place. Love makes us feel valued by someone else, and we feel jealous when we fear that he or she does not value us or that s/he is spending too much time with someone else. (On a technical point of definition, one is jealous of what is one's own, but envious of that which is other people's. Thus one is jealous – or possessive – of one's own partner, but envious of – covetous of – someone else's).

Jealousy

Positive emotions have long been viewed as resulting in feelings of competency and accordingly the negative ones are often explained in terms of inadequacy – that is, inadequacy relative to other people and their feelings for us. The negative emotions in relationships (like jealousy) are often unpleasant precisely because they affect our self-esteem or our sense of competence as a social performer or partner. However, jealousy, obsession, shyness and loneliness all in their own ways are complex blends of feelings, thoughts and behaviours (in the case of jealousy these are often treated by researchers as if they are coping behaviours).

Jealousy can be broken down into different types. Mazur (1977) distinguished five types:

- *Possessive jealousy* is a response to perceived violation of 'property rights'. For instance, we sometimes feel possessive jealousy if our partner acts in an independent way.

- *Exclusive jealousy* is a response to occasions when we are omitted from a loved one's important experiences or when we are not allowed to share a loved one's private world.
- *Competitive jealousy* is a feeling of inadequacy if our partner is actually better than we are at something where we ourselves wish to excel.
- *Egotistical jealousy* is the feeling that our way is the only way. In short, it is a desire to stay as we are, being uninfluenced to adapt to other people's wishes or needs.
- *Fearful jealousy* is a reaction to the threat of loneliness or rejection.

KEEP A JOURNAL

Record instances of jealousy that you observed in yourself or in other people. What gets said? What kinds of underlying emotions can you now recognize in what you said?

Jealousy can be communicated in different ways and Fleischman, Spitzberg, Andersen & Roesch (2005) even noted that people have a range of different strategies that are used to evoke jealousy in a partner in order to sustain the relationship by regaining the partner's attention and commitment to it, such as appearing to withdraw from the relationship (relational distancing), pretending to flirt with other people (flirtation façade), and discussing the possibilities of relational alternatives. Guerrero, Trost & Yoshimura (2005) looked at the relationship between jealousy-related emotions and communicative responses. Different characteristics of jealousy were considered: anger, fear, sadness, envy, guilt, sexual arousal/passion, positive affect. Various communication acts were noted ('I yelled at him' 'I gave him guilt trips'). The authors wanted to explore how jealousy is communicated and also to show the varied types of communicative behaviours that follow from the simple experience of this specific emotion. The responses cover quite a range but most often contain strong elements of both anger and fear.

In accordance with the view that I am taking here, then, Guerrero et al's (2005) work indicates that a blend of feelings leads to a blend of communicative acts, both of which are given context by particular interpretations or symbolic meanings that we give to the acts that 'cause' jealousy on a given occasion. These will probably direct a person's attention to specific parts of the whole jealousy-evoking event (e.g., to a sense of feeling helpless and fearful and then to angry words). Contexts differ as a result of the degree of relationship intimacy between the relevant parties as well as according to the 'valued resources' that flow through and are controlled by that attachment (i.e., whether the relationship runs through our life fabric or is marginal and peripheral to it); and to the perceived degree of 'intrusion' into that attachment by the third person (whether he or she really threatens it or just slightly unsettles it). The latter is important because no one expects a relationship with someone else to exclude all outsiders in all respects all of the time. We recognize that our partner will need and want other friends too: we cannot have the partner all to ourselves. Rather, we feel jealous when a third party threatens an area that is seen as central to our attachment to a partner (e.g., we would feel jealous if someone else looked like becoming our best friend's best friend), or else when feelings of discontent are brought about by another's evident superiority.

In our society, we usually have labels – 'friendship', 'marriage' and 'engagement' – that help us to mark out our relationships in ways that delineate their status, nature and importance to us and so warn outsiders that our partner is central to our attachment in this way. The labels indicate where the limits of the attachment lie, and the community helps in various ways to enforce the relationship. Thus, to announce an engagement or a marriage is to use a tie sign to tell the community to act as an extra guardian against intrusion or trespass on the relationship by outsiders. To put this another way, interpretations of situations are made on the basis of knowledge of the systematic behaviour of the partner; and also from social and cultural rules and knowledge from which to infer those interpretations of the person, such that the interpretation is based on normative or cultural expressions of meaning, and these meanings can be used to invoke the aid of others in watching over the proper performance of a relationship. In short, feelings of jealousy are not simply internal experiences of fear or anger, but are shaped 'as' jealousy by the relational frameworks within which the fear and anger arise.

Feelings are shaped partly as a result of social context and partly as a result of general social rules about the appropriateness of expressing certain emotions about relationships (Buunk, 1995). We may feel outrage as well as jealousy if someone infringes cultural rules – for example, by committing adultery with our spouse. In Victorian times, husbands were often encouraged to go and shoot their wife's lover(s) and in some countries the claim to have felt overwhelming jealousy is a permissible legal argument against severe sentences in 'crimes of passion'. However, if the relationship between sexual partners has not been formally agreed by society (e.g., if we are living together but are not married) then no rules govern the expression of feelings about the same sexual transgression. We may feel jealous but we will get no social support for feeling outraged.

Further, personal experience of our partner and the ways our lives are intertwined by routines together provide a basis for interpreting the meaning of certain behaviours that may affect our reactions. For instance, if we both agree that flirting with other people is an acceptable behaviour then we should not feel jealous when we catch a partner doing it (Bringle & Boebinger, 1990). In open marriages, for instance, partners feel jealous of their partner only when his or her behaviour violates the agreed rules about sexual conduct in the relationship and not just because the behaviour occurred (Buunk, 1980). 'Swingers' noted that it is acceptable for their partner to have sex with another person so long as he or she does not 'get emotionally involved'.

Such swingers would not feel jealous because the partner had extramarital sex but they would feel jealous if the partner became emotionally involved. Dijkstra, Groothof, Poel, Laverman, Schrier & Buunk (2001) extended this work to homosexuals, asking them whether emotional or physical infidelity was more upsetting, assuming that the two can be separated psychologically. The findings were that homosexuals tended to resemble heterosexuals of the opposite sex: that is to say, heterosexual women and gay men are more upset by emotional infidelity, whereas heterosexual men and lesbian women are more upset by physical infidelity. On the other hand, it now seems true for 'friends with benefits' relationships (Hughes et al., 2005) and hook-ups (Paul, 2006) that the implicit rule is that the sexual activity must be construed as physical and not 'relational' or 'emotional'. Such a categorization apparently relieves the sexual activity of any relational threats it would otherwise create.

LISTEN IN ON YOUR OWN LIFE

When you express jealousy, which of the following things is most likely to be reported as bringing it on:

- A sense of injustice that partly 'legitimates' the feeling?
- A sense that something is wrong with the relationship rather than with just one of the partners?
- Anger and feelings of self-doubt and self-accusation or a feeling of inadequacy?
- A desire to placate or to accommodate to the partner's desires or needs?

Shyness

Shyness is 'a dispositional tendency to experience feelings of anxiety and to exhibit behavioral inhibition in social situations' (Bradshaw, 2006: 17). Shyness is basically therefore embarrassment in advance, created by the belief that our real self will not be able to match up to the image we want to project.

Everyone feels shy from time to time, but some people are likely to feel more shy than others. Also obviously some people feel shy about certain topics (e.g., discussing sex) but not others (e.g., discussing taste in clothes), whereas some people feel shy about speaking in public when they are the focus of social attention, whatever the topic. Some 41 per cent of people believe that they are shy and up to 24 per cent think that it is a serious enough problem for them to do something about it (Duck, 1998). If you are not shy yourself, then two out of the next four people you meet will be and one of them will feel that it requires seeking professional help.

There is one key feature to shyness and it revolves around problems with interpersonal communication (Kelly, 1982). A central problem for many shy people is their unwillingness to communicate (i.e., 'reticence'), characterized by avoidance of, and ineptitude at, social interaction and performance in public or at the centre of attention in a social encounter, whatever the topic. Is the cause deficient communication skills; or anxiety about communication (so-called 'communication apprehension'); or simple avoidance of communication? In other words, is it because the person generally dislikes communication; or becomes paralysingly anxious about it; or just cannot do it well behaviourally? In practical terms there are few differences among the results of these three possible causes (Kelly, 1982), although the first two seem to be attitudinal or cognitive causes whilst the last is a behavioural or communicative problem. Programmes that improve (behavioural) performance actually reduce anxiety also, so we cannot distinguish the behavioural and the attitudinal components readily. What is readily distinguishable is that part of shyness is the experience of dyadic communicative difficulties and that part of it is the communicative difficulties themselves. This raises the intriguing question of whether shyness is a particular sort of social interaction rather than a trait of particular people (Bradshaw, 2006).

Whichever of these possibilities is ultimately correct, a serious problem for shy people is that reticence is evaluated by outsiders as if the shy person felt actually hostile and negative towards people rather than being simply reserved or nervous about them (Burgoon & Koper, 1984). When strangers are asked to assess videotapes of reticent persons talking to other people, the strangers rate the reticents quite negatively. They see reticents as expressing too little intimacy/similarity, being detached and uninvolved in the interaction, and showing too much submissiveness and emotional negativity. They also rated reticents as not credible or somewhat 'shifty'. When the shy persons' friends saw the same videotapes, however, they usually rated the behaviour as more positive. In other words, shy persons' behaviour appears negative to strangers, but their friends had already become used to it and do not read it as hostile, merely quiet and reserved. Once shy people get friends they are seen positively; the problem is that their behaviour is such that strangers probably would not want to become their friends in the first place.

Bradshaw's recent (2006) review of shyness points out that it has different elements and affects the formation of relationships, as well as producing difficulties with both relatively distant 'social' relationships (e.g., talking with strangers, shop assistants, neighbours) and relatively close 'personal' relationships (e.g., problems with self-disclosure, intimacy, friendship, feeling nervous around possible romantic partners). Such difficulties are all ultimately overcome by most shy people, such that they enter stable relationships – well, look around! If 41 per cent of the population is shy and not able to get into relationships, where are they all hanging out? However, the common thread identified by Bradshaw (2006) is that shy people feel uncomfortable being 'themselves' and this is because they anticipate rejection or derogation and therefore do best in those situations where a sense of acceptance is readily available or can be created by others in the setting. This may be one reason why shy people do better online (for example, Ward &

Tracey, 2004 demonstrated that individuals who score more highly on shyness and computer confidence tend to get satisfactory involvement in online relationships. Shyness also differentiated relationship involvement across face-to-face and online relationships with shy people doing better online).

You might like to consider as a result of the above discussion in this chapter how shyness and jealousy might map on to an attachment style. Indeed, you might consider more generally, the ways in which attachment style can be represented in the emotions that humans generally seem to experience. If emotions are things which are communicated in the course of relationships and are deeply embedded in them, then they are likely to be affected by attachment processes, but as we will see in the next chapter, many enduring dispositions of personality are modified by the actual routine behaviours of everyday life. We are therefore faced with the question of whether dispositions or actual practices are more influential in generating relational activity … and feelings.

SUMMARY

This chapter has looked at the way in which development of emotional responses and attitudes towards relationships may be traced back to childhood. We have also looked at some powerful relational emotions including love, jealousy and shyness. The emotions that we have looked at here share a number of features:

1   They occur in relationship to other people, involve expressive and communicative behaviour, and are closely connected to the notion of worth and competence in relationships, based on standards set within particular cultures. Each in its own way is a form of expression that communicates our assumed value and worth to other people in that cultural context. The question is whether Attachment Style produces them or culture or … ?
2   These emotions do not need specific external events to spark them off but can all be rekindled just by thought and by fantasy or imagination about social encounters, past, present, or future. They can be experienced in the absence of other people but are 'about' them, though they take a cultural form of expression.
3   They are sometimes experienced as just hot surges of emotion, but are more often enduring emotional states reported in dispositional *language* (I am in love; I am a shy person) or seen to have possible long-term effects on relationships. They can become ways of social life, enshrined in ways of communicating and expressing ourselves through behaviour, and indeed are sometimes expressed in order to do something to the relationship.
4   They are structured into or impact upon social routines and everyday behaviours. That we feel jealous or shy or in love influences the way we *communicate with other people* in the long term, as well as in the short term. It can affect how we look at them, how we speak to them, and how we deal with them, as well as how we choose to relate to them. In short, personal emotions have dyadic, communicative effects also and are based within the language system with which a person thinks and speaks.

In short, I have been making the case that *social emotions* are essentially dyadic, communicative, and relational ones, and as such occur in a cultural context that adds layers of meaning to them by providing a context in which the 'meanings' of specific behaviours are interpreted and moderated.

You should now be more able to recognize and reflect on the way in which your childhood experiences affect the way in which you experience emotion and you should be more able to understand the ways in which emotion is expressed as part of relational experience. You should also be able to identify ways in which relationships are moderated by emotions but more specifically by the way in which they are articulated and communicated to other people.

SELF QUESTIONS

1 Childhood and relationships

In what ways are our views of childhood like and unlike those of previous generations? That is a broad question, so look at it in these ways:

- Should children be given the vote?
- Would you condemn a parent who took a child on the family holiday without asking the child?
- Do you think children are full of original sin, which has to be ground out them as they become civilized like adults are, or is childhood a natural state of innocence that socialization takes away?
- Do children learn good lessons from trying risky things for themselves?
- Should children call parents by their first names?

When you have completed these exercises, check out the Internet for the reasons given in the 1850s why women and slaves should not be given the vote and see how different or similar are the reasons that you listed in response to the question about children voting above.

2 Advice and cultural exceptions about emotions and relationships

- Have you ever completed a magazine quiz about emotions or relationships, and then compared answers with those given in a key? Do you accept the magazine's assessment?
- What do you think of the primary types of advice that are available in the media concerning emotions and relationships?
- How easily can you find specific advice about handling of emotions in any form of media that you know or have access to? Why is that?
- Take the quiz on jealousy on http://www.romanceclass.com/miscr/LoveQuiz/QZ247 and notice how the advice on your responses is prescriptive, telling you what you should have said.

Class discussion time!

FURTHER READING

Bradshaw, S. (2006). Shyness and difficult relationships: Formation is just the beginning. In C.D. Kirkpatrick, S.W. Duck, & M.K. Foley (Eds.), *Relating difficulty*: *The processes of constructing and managing difficult interaction* (pp. 15–41). Mahwah, NJ: Lawrence Erlbaum and Associates.

Brennan, K.A., & Shaver, P.R. (1998). Attachment styles and personality disorders: Their connections to each other and to parental divorce, parental death, and perceptions of parental caregiving. *Journal of Personality*, 66, 835–878.

Buss, D.M. (2000). *The dangerous passion*: *Why jealousy is as necessary as love and sex*. New York: Free Press.

Metts, S. (2000). Face and facework: Implications for the study of personal relationships. In K. Dindia, & S.W. Duck (Eds.), *Communication and personal relationships* (pp. 72–94). Chichester: Wiley.

Miller, R.S. (1996). *Embarrassment*: *Poise and peril in everyday life*. New York: Guilford.

PRACTICAL MATTERS

- Anger management programmes are available these days, but how would they connect with attachment style?
- Relationships are not static but as you read the research you may discover that typical approaches to studying them (correlational studies, or lab surveys about a typified example) often treat them as if they are. What practical implications follow from the fact that studies treat relationships as dispositional?
- What information from the present chapter would you take forward to a parenting role?

3

Daily Life: The Everyday Conduct and Management of Relationships

People are actors in giving communicative life to the contradictions that organize their social life, but these contradictions in turn affect their communicative action ... praxis focuses on the concrete practices by which social actors produce the future out of the past in their everyday lives (Baxter & Montgomery, 1996: 13–14)

Focus points for note taking when reading this chapter:

- To what extent are relationships practical experiences rather than emotional experiences?
- Do we like people who are like us – or is there more to it?
- Are relationships based in information about other people or other things (too) and if so then what is the relative balance of information versus other things?
- What sorts of information about other people are most relevant to our likelihood of forming a relationship with them?
- Are we 'in' relationships (which might suggest that they are fixed and unchanging things) or do they change? Or both?
- What can we rely on as stable about a relationship we are 'in'? What changes?
- To what extent do outsiders influence what goes on inside a relationship?
- Do relationships break up because people stop liking one another or are there other processes at play (as well)?
- How do ordinary routines of life keep relationships together or stop them staying together?

You might have noticed that so far the chapters have considered some sort of *contextual* variables that are relevant to relationships – biology, culture, personality, childhood. Here I'm trying to look at everyday life pragmatics/praxis as the context, and I mean to draw attention to the things that we do, particularly the things that we *do* in everyday life, perhaps without even noticing. We perform all sorts of actions in our daily lives – going to work, conversing with people in our networks, rearranging furniture or tidying our work area, nurturing children, assisting with homework, or answering parental enquiries, eating meals, having sex, just hanging out. Although I cannot draw out the relational implications of all these things (see Duck, in press SAGE CA, see refs), I want this chapter to make you think about your everyday life and how its little bits and pieces get tied up in the formation, growth, and maintenance of your relationships.

Chapter 2 looked at some emotions, and connected 'feelings' to language, culture, and management of relating and the conduct of daily life. I started to edge us towards thoughts about the connection of emotion to communication and so to the ways that people actually enact emotions in daily life. We do not experience emotions merely on some abstract plane: they hit us in the face as a part of daily life or in response to relational experience (Wood & Duck, 2006). Much of what happens in daily life relating is quite trivial, mundane or routine without huge and tumultuous emotional peaks and troughs, as I already noted in Chapter 2. Relationships are most often carried out through routine talk and meetings, the absence of which is noted and complained of.

The present chapter examines research on the roles of behaviour and communication in building, sustaining, and reifying relationships. This idea may come as a bit of a shock to you if you thought that human relationships were all about psychological states such as feelings. Actually I won't be claiming that those things are irrelevant or unimportant, but only that *expression and management* of emotion and communication in everyday life generally have a far more significant role in the creation of relationships than we may suppose. Consider for example how much importance you give to the chance to simply sit and chat with friends about nothing very much. Fun, isn't it? Losing such jaw-time with friends often leads to strains in the relationship (for example, when a friend finds a new romance and cuts down on time with you in order to be with the new beloved, you might comment on the fact resentfully). When we miss someone, we usually miss *talking* with them as much as anything else, or conversely when we sustain Long Distance Relationships (Sahlstein, 2006b), we do so by chatter on the phone or instant messaging rather than just by feeling a longing, or when we keep relationships going this is done through calls home, or daily babble with people around us, rather than just by the feeling of an emotion of attachment to a person even though relationships are all partly in the mind (Duck, 1980, 1994). In the course of such talk, we do not merely pass the time but we actively *accomplish* many things, such as continuing the relationship's existence, or learning the rules of relating.

LISTEN IN ON YOUR OWN LIFE

How do you keep your relationships going? Write a list of routines, or conscious maintenance strategies. Also listen in on your own conversations, paying attention to ways in which the future or expected future of the relationship shows up in what gets said. Some of this will be obvious (as, for example, when you plan to meet again) but some of it will require you to be more thoughtful and incisive in order to uncover it. By the time you get to the end of this chapter, you should be able to see some of it more obviously and can look back over your notes from this exercise.

As Wood (2006) suggested, relational emotions are often to do with management or organization of daily life routines and expectations. True, we think of relationships as based on emotions and abstractions but we *do* them all the same. Also if we think of relationships only as being based on emotions we miss perhaps the most important point about relationships: they happen in daily life where lots of other things happen too besides emotions – things like gossip, hassles, decisions about our calendars and time organization, manipulation of impressions by others, trivial organization of leisure time, sharing of experiences, reading about other people's relationships in magazines …

It is true that when we are asked about what matters to us most in life and gives it its fullest purpose, the majority of people have always given one simple answer: relationships (Klinger, 1977), meaning most probably the positive ones. However, I doubt if people are really talking about *emotions* in relationships when they answer that way. I'd bet they are talking about the experience of relationships in all its complexity, including the complexities of unusual forms of relationships (e.g. FWBRs – friends with benefits – Hughes et al., 2005, and hook-ups – Paul, 2006) and the complicating issue of whether a relationship is heterosexual or homosexual (Muraco, 2005) and whether legally recognized or not (Haas & Stafford, 2005; Lannutti, 2005; Duck & VanderVoort, 2002). What is more I'd bet that the difficult and negative relationships also matter in the practical conduct of life and in some cases are more powerful forces on our thinking and behaviour than are the loves and friendships that surround us (Kirkpatrick et al., 2006; Wiseman & Duck, 1995). Also important is the handling of little details: it is fine to like someone but where do you find the time to talk to them if you have pressing work to do, or other people competing for your attention and time or other relationships you are also in and which demand your attention? What is sacrificed if you spend time with them and what does it mean if you don't choose to make that sacrifice? How does work spill over into your relational life? What if you had a bad day at work and (how) does that affect your personal relationships with people *un*connected with your work?

Relationships are obvious sources of joy and happiness but good relationships can be hell when they go wrong or get into trouble and cause us pain, or when a partner calls on us to fulfil a relational obligation (like providing support and help) when we don't really care to do it. Relationships must not be stripped out of daily life even though much research work does that. The present chapter shows the important role of relationships as a whole, particularly maintenance and change in relationships, not only in social life but also their effect on our 'sense of being' or sense of self-esteem. One thing you need to notice is that although we think of relationships as stable places where we live, most of our daily experience is in fact varied and unstable and occasionally very difficult (Kirkpatrick et al., 2006). This is true not only because humans are moody and occasionally obnoxious beings (Cunningham, Shamblen, Barbee & Ault, 2005; Davis & Schmidt, 1977), but also because some topics, like relational transgressions or complaints, are painful to discuss (Dailey & Palomares, 2004) and some situations, such as work, present us with a mix of positive and negative experiences pretty much any day (Dutton & Ragins, 2007; Harden Fritz & Omdahl, 2006). For these and other reasons covered below, although we talk about relationships in emotional terms yet we probably spend most of our time dealing with them in practical terms, and their *management* is one of the key balancing acts of the human relational experience.

STARTING RELATIONSHIPS: BIOLOGICAL AND CULTURAL CONTEXTS OF ATTRACTION

Just as we tend to think of relationships in the abstract so we have a number of relatively simplistic ideas about the ways in which they start and finish. The whole notion of a clear start to a relationship is at odds with some of our other experiences of life. When did you start the relationship with your check-out clerk? Does the way you 'started' the relationship with your mother really matter that much? Have you ever had a relationship where you really had to think back quite hard to remember how it started because it just grew out of some relatively frequent contact? Did you and your partner ever disagree about how it started or have you always seen the start of the relationship in identical terms? Doesn't that strike you as remarkable (either way)? Of course, in many cultures, people ask one another out on dates and can pinpoint that time as the start of the relationship, but it may be that the *planning* to ask someone out on a date is the real start, not the date itself. Or perhaps the date itself is not really the start, but the relationship changed form as it grew out of the date (Sprecher & Duck, 1993). Much more likely is the fact that you were introduced by someone else anyway, and it wasn't your free choice that made it all happen. Parks (2006) indicates that the majority of romantic relationships start this way through mutual introduction by members of the social network and Sprecher & Felmlee (2000) noted that network approval for a relationship is associated with its stability and growth, whereas network approval for a breakup is related to its increased likelihood of occurring.

In everyday life we are disproportionately influenced by first impressions as opposed to 'rational choice'. Job applications, interviews, and the whole course of a relationship can be 'set' by the first few moments. In everyday life, we make many snap judgements about people and form instant likes and dislikes. Some of the earliest work in what is now the field of personal relationships was about such initial attraction. Although the major paradigm was concerned with the similarity of attitudes, the basis of the theory used to explain the attractive force of attitudes about it was biological (Byrne, 1971). As discussed by Dragon & Duck (2005: ch. 2), Byrne based his work on the classical conditioning paradigm of Pavlov, whose work was famously concerned with the salivation response of dogs. Although dogs are naturally predisposed to salivate when they see food, they can be conditioned to associate the appearance of food with a bell, and will eventually salivate as soon as they hear the bell and before they see the food. Byrne argued that human beings are naturally predisposed to feel good when their attitudes are validated; that they can be conditioned to associate the occurrence of attitude validation with the person who provides it; and that they will rapidly experience this association as 'liking' and will report that they like the individual who provides reinforcement for their attitudes (Byrne, 1997). This paradigm generated a vast amount of research and an equally vast amount of controversy and criticism (Dragon & Duck, 2005). However, in addition to the sociobiological claims that were discussed in Chapter 1, this approach provides a further biological underpinning for the reasons why we might prefer some people's psychological characteristics to others, as well as emphasizing the importance of initial 'gut' responses to other people at the start of relationships.

TRY THIS OUT: AN EXERCISE ON RELATIONSHIPS

- Think for a moment about the people with whom you are particularly friendly. What do you like about them and how did the relationship get started? How does the relationship with each person differ from those that you have with other people?

(Continued)

(Continued)

- Write out two short lists (say ten items each) giving: (a) the features of a friend that you like (seven items) and those that you dislike (three items); (b) the sort of activities that you perform or topics you talk about almost exclusively with friends (seven items) and those that you do with other people too, but that are 'better' with friends (three items).
- Think about an attractive person you have seen but not really met – one you would like to start a relationship with if you were completely free to do so. Write two short lists (ten items each) giving: (a) what you find attractive about them (seven items) and what you find unattractive about them (three items); (b) seven things you would do or talk about with them if you got to know them and three items you would definitely not talk about or do.

Compare your various lists and try to work out the important differences among them, if any. Consider the differences involved in 'relating' to strangers and friends, and think what it is that changes when strangers gradually turn into acquaintances and friends.

INFORMATION AND ACQUAINTANCE: HOW WE REVEAL THINGS ABOUT OURSELVES

Researchers of initial attraction are usually well aware that they are studying a small part of a broader set of issues (e.g., Byrne, 1997). Often, they are both startled and hurt by critics who effectively say 'This work on strangers is silly because it tells us nothing about marriage'. Work on obstetrics tells us little about senility, but that is not a reason for not doing it. Many real-life examples make initial attraction an obvious and important area of concern. What we must bear in mind, however, is that of course not all attractions lead to relationships (Byrne, 1992) and that when strangers are introduced – even in the laboratory – to have a conversation, the most powerful initial effects of attitude similarity 'wash out' somewhat (Sunnafrank, 1991).

Similar people do not necessarily like one another any more than do dissimilar ones after they have had a brief interaction. Also, dissimilar partners who are able to interact also like their partner more than do dissimilar ones who do not interact. So it is interaction that has a positive effect on liking, and it modifies the effect of dissimilarity on its own. When communication exceeds a 'one-off conversation' and is extended over time and to explicit discussion of attitudinal issues, then again it is the *dissimilar* stranger who gets a better rating (Sunnafrank, 1991), perhaps because they appear stimulating and interesting. All the same, Sunnafrank & Ramirez (2004) have shown that although relational partners may not make irrevocable decisions within the first few moments of interactions, it remains the case that there are rather surprising and enduring effects of initial conversations on longer-term relationships and that these effects are still observable nine weeks later.

This is one reason why shyness (Chapter 2) or the skills in NVC discussed in Chapter 1 can be such important influences on relationship (dis)satisfaction levels because many people who report being lonely or shy feel frustrated when they are unable to carry out their wishes to begin or set up desired relationships. If you can't deal with strangers you won't get friends without some help (perhaps from third parties, matchmakers, or the environmental forces that 'make' us get to know people willy-nilly, as the workplace environment does). This is also a reason why Internet matchmaking sites do so well: they provide opportunities (and also more control over one's own timing and depth of response) to people who are otherwise awkward in social situations; and they establish that the persons on the other end are 'relationally available', though whether genuinely or not is another issue (however in other social settings that availability or willingness to negotiate may not even be presumed in the first place). Also on the Internet, you typically connect with people in your own time, at your convenience, and from a safe place where other people most likely are not looking at you. Shy or unskilled persons are not therefore at any particular disadvantage in such settings.

However, the reasons for lack of relationship development lie outside the person as well as inside biology. There is a myriad of social and cultural reasons why we do not even think of starting to set up relationships with every attractive person we meet, the most significant being: lack of a wish to do so (e.g., already married or engaged, going steady, not enough time, too many commitments); inappropriateness (e.g., differences in status, circumstances not conducive); but many sorts of relationships are unconventional, disapproved or actually forbidden (Duck & VanderVoort, 2002), such as adultery, incest, paedophilia, or teacher–student relationships, and people who are attracted to other people in these circumstances, may just hold off. In addition, there are social pressures for people to be heterosexual (Lannutti, 2005; Muraco, 2005) and these pressures can steer the free exercise of every flush of attraction that we may feel.

All the same, attraction to strangers is the starting point for all relationships that do eventually get going. In everyday real life, one meeting with a person often leads to another. When we know that fact, it probably affects what we do and how we treat those strangers whom we may see again and get to know better. Acquaintance is thus a process with long-term ramifications and is not simply caused by initial attractions in any simple or non-interactive way: relationships do not work like electric motors – which just start and run whenever we press the right switch. That sort of mechanical metaphor, surprisingly, is widely held ('we just clicked'), even though it is an inadequate idea. Of course we have to do something communicatively in the long term to make relationships work: we do not just 'sit there looking pretty' in the hope that the rest is automatic. Instead, relationships are created by the mechanisms through which mutual understanding is developed (Duck, 1994: ch. 4), since this helps people to coordinate their behaviour in a relationship, their roles, and their particular interactions. For instance, Gore, Cross & Morris (2006) showed that coordination of disclosures (and hence of shared meanings) assisted the development of intimacy and other interpersonal relational processes, such as comprehension of how the partners see themselves as individuals and as partners.

Getting to know you: shared meaning

Figure 3.1 helps to guide us through the understanding of the process. As we work through the research on initial attraction, note that the similarity that has been talked about in research and the sorts of similarity that come to mind when we just sit and think about it actually have four layers when you strip things down in terms of social *actions* and conversational connections that take place in the practical world of everyday life. For example, Baxter, Dun & Sahlstein (2001) showed how a sense of destiny in a relationship (Knee, 1998) draws on an implicit theory of compatibility and develops into a sense of growth based on 'hard work' in a relationship. In everyday life these ideas get worked out in practical use of rules in a relationship and its interactions, even in parent–child communication (Muehlhoff, 2006), but they also depend on the systematic unfolding of information about one another and the organization of it into a working model of the other person's meaning system.

Sometimes, we act as if two people *are* similar and that's that (this is 'Commonality' in Figure 3.1). But in the praxis of real life, things are not so simple: even if two people are similar, they must communicate that similarity to one another before it can have an effect ('*Mutuality*' in Figure 3.1). Bochner claims that 'One of the main functions of communication in early, and perhaps even in later, encounters is to foster perceptions of attitude and personality similarity and also to create the impression of being an interesting and stimulating person' (1991: 487). So obviously we talk to one another and in so doing we create the mutuality noted in Figure 3.1, partly perhaps by *making* the pieces click together. We never see the internal states or attitudes of other persons directly so we can only infer them from the sorts of nonverbal and verbal behaviour discussed in Chapter 1 and the cultural rules for interpreting their behaviour discussed in Chapter 2. Because of this, the two people's reading of each other's nonverbal behaviour will be crucial to this inference process and highly significant in acquaintance. Also important will be the ways in which they 'mesh' that behaviour to make the interaction smooth and enjoyable (Burleson, Kunkel, Samter & Werking, 1996).

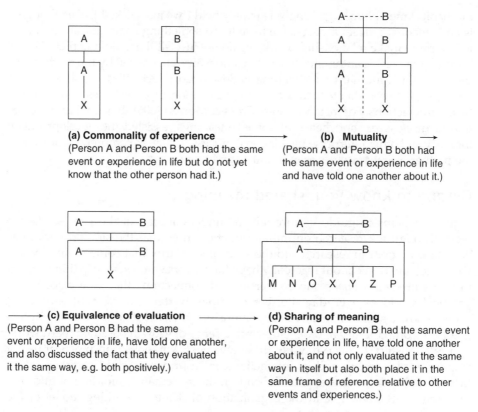

(a) Commonality of experience
(Person A and Person B both had the same event or experience in life but do not yet know that the other person had it.)

(b) Mutuality
(Person A and Person B both had the same event or experience in life and have told one another about it.)

(c) Equivalence of evaluation
(Person A and Person B had the same event or experience in life, have told one another, and also discussed the fact that they evaluated it the same way, e.g. both positively.)

(d) Sharing of meaning
(Person A and Person B had the same event or experience in life, have told one another about it, and not only evaluated it the same way in itself but also both place it in the same frame of reference relative to other events and experiences.)

Figure 3.1   A model of the serial construction of meaning.
(modified from Duck (1994))

Uncertainty reduction

We become acquainted by an extended process of uncertainty reduction that continually shifts its focus and moves on to new, unknown areas. However, the development of relationships is not simplistically equivalent to the revelation of information nor to the decrease of uncertainty. The process of relationship development is created by the interpretation of such things by the partners, not by the acts themselves (Duck, 1994) and it involves the *evaluation* phase noted in Figure 3.1. When we understand a person at a superficial level, we look more deeply and broadly into other parts of his or her make-up. When we know someone's attitudes to romance, for example, we may want to know more about his or her deep personal feelings about parenthood, for instance, but this is not simply because we desire more facts – it is to give us a better framework for understanding what we already know. The process of getting to know someone is the process of framing and understanding the Other at as many levels as we can until we reached a sense of *shared meaning* (Figure 3.1). But it is also a process that continues forever – unfinished business that proceeds right through our lives and the life of the relationship (Duck, 1994), since each new day, every new interaction, and all meetings with the partner are fresh and informative and could change our understanding as time goes by. Therefore, we are continually exploring our partner as we see him or her in the unfolding practical circumstances of life and continually reevaluating the meanings that we share and the extent to which we do so.

Historically the focus on different matters as acquaintance progresses has been called 'filtering'. We can see why: it is as if we have a sequence or series of filters or sieves and when a person passes through one they go on to the next. Our first 'filter' may be physical appearance. If we like the other person's looks then we will want to go on and see what his or her attitudes are like and whether we can relate to them. 'Attitudes' could then be the second filter, and so on. We assess our acquaintances within a progressive series of 'tests': those who pass one test go through to a deeper level of friendship – and on to the next test. At each point we learn more about the person's thinking.

In my own adaptation of this old approach (Duck, 1994), such tests are subtler and subtler comparisons of one's own attitudes, beliefs, and personality compatibility with the partner, as partners seek to enmesh their respective meaning systems. In pursuing this process we start by latching onto the indicators that are available. For instance, we may begin with 'ball park' indications of someone's pattern of thought ('Are they extroverts – or introvert like me?'), and become more and more fine in our 'tuning' as the relationship goes on. What specific values do they hold most dear and are they the same as mine? What little things upset them when they are in a bad mood? What are their deep, deep, deep fears about themselves and what does that tell me about the way they 'tick'? We work through such filters because we wish to understand and create a thorough picture of the partner's mind and personality in as much detail as possible. The tests, or filters, help us to reduce uncertainty and draw our partner's personality in finer and finer detail as the relationship deepens and develops.

Filtering theories are more sophisticated than the 'switch on' models that suggest that relationships are caused by one simple feature, like attitude similarity or physical attractiveness. However, I now realize that filtering theories overemphasize thought and cognition, and they really only propose a more sophisticated sequence of motors to be switched on. Honeycutt (1993) offered an interesting variation on this theme and suggested that when people describe their relationships as moving through stages they are in fact responding to a cultural script that depicts 'stages' as the way to think about relationship development. The apparent 'movement' in relationships is in fact just a perceptual or memory device established by individuals and societies. In other words, rather than being something 'real' in relationships, relationship development is *perceived as if* it followed predigested patterns that are recognized by cultural beliefs or by the processes of cultural contextualization indicated in Chapter 1.

Self-disclosure

One result of such beliefs is that people feel they should reveal personal information about themselves as appropriate to the script for stages. These revelations serve as a sign of growing intimacy and of trust in our partner. 'Self-disclosure' occurs usually by words but occasionally by nonverbal means, as when we let someone sit closer or touch us more than before. We self-disclose when we tell someone how we have been upset by something recently or 'what I am most ashamed of about myself' or 'what I dislike most about my parents'. We self-disclose when we tell secrets or give other people access to private attitudes that we share with very few others. We can also self-disclose nonverbally by 'giving ourselves away', for instance, bursting into tears unexpectedly or suddenly blushing. In most social psychological and communication work, self-disclosure refers to verbal intimacy, particularly the content of messages that are so disclosed. This work assumes two things: (1) that we can tell how intimate others are merely by examining the words they use, the topics they talk about, and the subjects they introduce to a conversation; and (2) that intimacy proceeds by the successive revelation of layers of information about oneself, like peeling the layers off an onion (Altman & Taylor, 1973) or by managing the boundaries of privacy (Petronio, 2002). Such topics have occasionally been listed and rated for intimacy level. For example, Davis & Sloan (1974) put 'How I react to others' praise and criticism of me' at the bottom of their list and 'My feelings about my sexual inadequacy' at the top of their list for very intimate topics.

Remembering the discussion in Chapter 1, you may find this a bit dissatisfying. In life, there are more indicators of intimacy than just words; nonverbal cues as well as the relationship between the partners help to define and communicate intimacy. For this reason, Montgomery (1981) talks of 'open communication' rather than just self-disclosure. She describes it as composed of five elements, some of which occur more often in some types of relationships whilst others appear more frequently in others:

- Negative openness covers openness in showing disagreement or negative feelings about a partner or situation.
- Nonverbal openness relates to a communicator's facial expressions, vocal tone, and bodily postures or movements (see Chapter 1).
- Emotional openness describes the ease with which someone's feelings or moods are expressed and his or her concealment of emotional states.
- Receptive openness is a person's indication of his or her willingness to listen to other people's personal information.
- General-style openness refers to the overall impression that someone creates.

LOOK OUT FOR THIS IN THE MEDIA: USES OF SELF-DISCLOSURE/OPEN COMMUNICATION

Watch out for instances in the media of an attempt by interviewers to obtain a self-disclosure, that is to say something that is revealing personally about the individual who is being interviewed. Consider whether a question is asked directly or whether some indirect method is used to make the persons 'reveal' themselves. Is the same technique used in the case of men as women, whether as interviewers or interviewees?

Even if we look at just the content of speech then we can split openness into different elements, of which topic intimacy is one (Montgomery, 1981). However, intimacy of a topic is not the same as 'intimacy of topic *in a relationship*'. For instance, the relational context for a topic can make it intimate or non-intimate. Thus, the question 'How is your sex life?' looks like a promisingly personal and intimate topic unless it is our physician who asks us about it. In short, even intimate-sounding topics can be discussed non-intimately, or in non-intimate contexts, and there really is no such thing as an absolutely intimate or absolutely non-intimate topic (Spencer, 1994). Other factors that make for intimacy in conversation are, as we have learned before, verbal immediacy, nonverbal accompaniments and relational context. Openness, then, includes both verbal and nonverbal aspects of behaviour and deals as much with the function of a message as with its medium (Montgomery, 1981). When we look at open communication in context, it is appparent that content and topic intimacy alone do not discriminate between high and low open communicators. Obviously open communication is preferred to deception and people form negative impressions of those who lie to them although they will often tend to believe that they may reciprocate by lying in return (Tyler, Feldman & Reichert, 2006). All the same, some topics such as experience in war are so personal and sensitive to the individual that marital disruption can be a result of talking about them even to a spouse (Cohan, Cole & Davila, 2005). This is partly explained by examining more carefully the complex nature of self-disclosure and the way that it works relationally in interaction.

Dindia (1994) indicates that relational self-disclosure is a highly complex and contextualized occurrence. It involves a complicated mixing of intra-personal processes (for example, decisions about one's readiness to discuss a particular topic, beliefs about a partner's likely reaction to the topic itself rather than to one's disclosures about it – i.e., a judgement about the other person not just about the topic itself). Thus work on self-disclosure that treats it as driven only by the 'pure intimacy' of a topic misses the important practical consequences of the fact that we live everyday lives where topics assume intimacy (or not) *in context* and *in relationship*, not in any unattached or pure way.

Spencer (1994) also notes that self-disclosure is not simply a device for revealing information about self but is also a mechanism for giving and receiving advice. If I self-disclose to you that I have a problem about shyness then you can implicitly advise about how to deal with it by self-disclosing one of your most embarrassing experiences and how you overcame it, for instance. You can self-disclose that you have had the same problem and then start to self-disclose some examples of situations where it happened and how you dealt with it, thus subtly presenting me with advice about how to deal with it. In that case, self-disclosure serves a relationship purpose (helping me out) and shows intimacy and loyalty (because you help me) and is not simplistically or only about the successive revelation of layers of yourself.

Various other investigations suggest that self-disclosure is not simply the exposure of information, but rather is a complex self-presentational and self-preservational activity in addition to all else that it does. Caughlin & Afifi (2004) and Caughlin, Afifi, Carpenter-Theune & Miller (2005) have shown that the keeping of secrets is both common and relationally problematic. Of course one could usefully consider what makes something 'a secret' as opposed to merely 'a piece of self that has not yet been disclosed', but the point remains that management of such material holds relational consequences that can be very serious.

Petronio (2002) accordingly offers a more complex analysis based on the fact that topics have particular sorts of meanings within different relational contexts (see above) and on the fact that people experience a tension between a desire for privacy and a demand for openness in relationships, whether psychological or physical openness. Accordingly, couples tend to create rules for regulation of privacy, which are rules that they both find consistent with the nature of their relationship, such as the things that are appropriate and inappropriate for discussion between themselves, or in front of the children, or when talking to third parties about their own relationship. This analysis essentially points out a number of things about self-disclosure, but one of them is that it is not universally a good thing when unrestrained. Another thing is that people have segmented selves, only parts of which they see as suitable for disclosure, the suitability being something that is modified by relational context. Third, it points out that the topic of how to do self-disclosure – and how much of it can be a topic for discussion (often called 'meta-communication' or communication about communication) – can be a matter of personal preference, but also, that its uses can be *interpreted and evaluated*, a position consistent with the model of meaning making offered in Figure 3.1.

THE NATURE OF RELATIONSHIPS: EVERYDAY MANAGEMENT IN A PRATICAL PHYSICAL WORLD

How strategic are we in making acquaintances?

Has it struck you how passive much of the work on self-disclosure has assumed that we are, if it implies that we successively and inevitably reveal information about self in layers, more or less routinely? Do we just sit back, smile, flash a few attitudes around and hope that people will react positively to our successive revelations? No. I believe that we actually spend quite a lot of time *trying* to get other people to like and appreciate us and also to check out how we are doing. We become upset when we fail to create positive feelings in other people; it is a great source of personal distress and dissatisfaction. We must have strategies for making others appreciate us and an awareness of 'how we are doing'. We have already seen (Chapter 2) how Fleischmann et al. (2005) indicated that people use the creation of jealousy to light an established partner's fire, but at earlier points of relationships other strategies are also used to create and test commitment. Douglas (1987) explored the strategies that people use to discover whether another person is interested in developing a relationship ('affinity testing'). These are listed in Table 3.1. In essence, people rarely ask directly whether someone is interested in a relationship or not (well, the person might say 'no' and that would be that!). Because it puts us on the line if we ask directly, there is a preference for indirect strategies that get us the information without us having to ask directly. Or we may ask ambiguously so that if the other person turns us down we can deflect the negative implication of rejection: for example, instead of saying 'Will you go out with me to this movie?', you may say 'This movie is on at the Cineplex, do you like that kind of movie?', which gives the person the chance to treat the question as an invitation (and to reply 'Yes, shall we go together?') or as a straightforward request for information but *not* as an invitation to go and see it together ('Yes, those films are interesting and I also like the ones by the director's son'). To choose to answer just the question itself as precisely asked is also in effect to reject the invitation but to do so without causing offence.

At the start of a relationship we might need to assess the partner's interest in further meetings, such as may be discovered by use of the strategies in Table 3.1. Alternatively we might be in an established relationship and wish to test out the partner's level of commitment. The ways which partners in relationships conduct 'secret tests' of the state of the relationship were studied by Baxter & Wilmot (1984). Baxter & Wilmot argued that partners are often uncertain about the strength of their relationship yet are reluctant to talk about 'the state of the relationship'; they regard it as a taboo topic (as Baxter & Wilmot, 1985, found in a different paper). Our usual solution is to apply direct and indirect tests – secret

Table 3.1   *Strategies of affinity-testing*

Confronting

Actions that required a partner to provide immediate and generally public evidence of his or her liking.

1   I asked her if she liked me.
2   I asked her if I appealed to her.
3   I put my arm around her. It made her say yes or no.

Withdrawing

Actions that required a partner to sustain the interaction.

4   I just turned myself off and just sat there real sedate. I knew if he started jabbering (which he did) then he was interested.
5   I would be silent sometimes to see if he would start the conversation again.
6   We were at a disco and I said, 'Well, I'm leaving'. I wanted him to stop me. You know, to say, 'Are you leaving already?'

Sustaining

Actions designed to maintain the interaction without affecting its apparent intimacy.

7   I kept asking questions. You know, like, 'Where was she from?' 'What music did she like?'
8   I met this girl. I liked her. I asked all these questions. 'What do you do for a living?' 'Where do you live?'
9   I tried to keep him talking. I asked him questions. I told him about me.

Hazing

Actions that required a partner to provide a commodity or service to the actor at some cost to himself or herself.

10   I told him I lived 16 miles away. Sixteen miles from the church I mean. I wanted to see if he would try and back out.
11   I told her I didn't have a ride. She said that was OK. She said she would take me. I told her where I lived; it took about an hour to get there. I told her she couldn't come into my house even if she gave me a ride. I knew that she liked me because she accepted the situation I put her in.
12   I met this guy at a party. He asked me if I wanted to go see a movie. I said OK. When we got there, I told him I didn't want to see it, I wanted to go home. I didn't really. I wanted to see how much he would take.

Diminishing self

Actions that lowered the value of self; either directly by self-deprecation or indirectly by identifying alternative reward sources for a partner.

13   I asked her if she wanted to talk to somebody else. You know, 'Was I keeping her from something?'
14   I told him I wasn't very interesting. Waiting for him to say 'Oh, no'.
15   There were these other guys there. I kept pointing them out to her.

(Continued)

Table 3.1   *(Continued)*

Approaching

Actions that implied increased intimacy to which the only disconfirming partner response is compensatory activity.

16   I would touch his shoulder or move close to see if he would react by staying where he was or moving closer.
17   I moved closer. He didn't move away.
18   I moved closer to her. We were sitting in a bar. You know, at one of those benches. I wanted to see if she would move away.

Offering

Actions that generated conditions favourable for approach by a partner.

19   I waited for him to come out of the restroom. Everyone else had left by that time. If he wanted to ask me out, he could.
20   I helped him carry some things out to his car. I made it to where we were by ourselves so that if he was going to ask me for a date, we would be in a position where he could do it.
21   I knew we would have to play with someone close to us in line. So I stood in front of him. I wanted to see if he would pick me.

Networking

Actions that included third parties, either to acquire or transmit information.

22   I went over and asked his friends about him. I knew his friends would tell him about it. Then, if he came over to me again, I would know he liked me.
23   I told other people there I liked him. I knew it would get back to him. I knew other people would tell him. If he ignored it, I would know he wasn't interested.
24   There was one guy at a party. We chit-chatted and he looked pretty interesting. There were some of my friends there, so I left and, later, I asked them what he had said about me.

Source: Douglas, W. (1987)

tests – as means of discovering how things stand. Such methods involve, for instance, asking third parties whether your partner has ever talked about the relationship to them. Alternatively one might use trial intimacy moves to see how a partner reacts – and so gives away some indication of intimacy. Such moves can take the form of increased physical or emotional intimacy, but might be more subtle. For example, a person might use 'public presentation': inviting the partner to visit parents or talking about your own intentions to have children some day. The real but concealed questions in each case are: how does my partner react, and does he or she accept the increased intimacy or the open commitment? Other methods described by Baxter & Wilmot (1984) are the self-put-down (when you hope the partner will respond to your self-deprecating statement with a supportive, intimate statement) and the jealousy test (when you describe a potential competitor and hope to observe a possessive, committed response by your partner).

Self-disclosure as a strategic relational activity

If we are successful in initially attracting someone to us, what happens to deepen the relationship? Recall that some self-disclosure is a sign of good mental health and influences the course of relationships. A certain amount of intimate disclosure is expected in our culture, whether as an indication that we genuinely trust another person or as an indication that we are psychologically normal and healthy. We are supposed to say a few disclosing and revealing things in order to open out. Women are particularly expected to self-disclose and are often pressed into doing so if they do not do so voluntarily; closed women are asked direct questions that make them open out (Miell, 1984).

Reciprocity of self-disclosure is also expected, at least in the early stages of relationships. If I self-disclose to you, you will self-disclose back. It confirms a desire to develop a relationship since you could have chosen not to reveal the information, especially if it is quite personal. Conversely, we could hold back a relationship, if we wanted, by just not revealing something personal to our partner even if our partner did so to us (Miell, 1987). Self-disclosure is used strategically both to develop relationships and to hold them back or to shape the relationship into one form rather than another (e.g., to keep someone from getting too intimate, too fast, or to protect the relationship from straying on to taboo topics; Baxter & Wilmot, 1985; Miell, 1984). It is also worth noting, however, that reciprocity of self-disclosure wears off as relationships mature. As Wright (1978: 206) puts it, 'Apparently, in the more comfortable and less formal context of deeper friendship, the partners do not feel they owe it to one another, out of politeness or decency, to exchange trust for trust: the trust is already there'. Furthermore, Miell (1984) showed that some people are subtle enough to be able to use self-disclosure to interrogate other people or to find out information. It works like this: I know that there is a norm of reciprocity about self-disclosure; I therefore know that if I self-disclose about some topic in the right kind of circumstances and do it appropriately, then you will feel normative pressure to self-disclose back also; therefore I know that if I self-disclose 'well', you will tell me something personal back again. Thus if I self-disclose appropriately, I can find out things about you because my self-disclosing will tend to open you up and evoke self-disclosure back from you in reciprocation of my own self-disclosing.

This latter approach, however, confirms that in everyday life, self-disclosure is not used in any simple way but is managed actively to do all sorts of things: to project oneself as normal and open, to obey social norms of reciprocity and civility, to reveal oneself (as a sign of intimacy in the relationship), to shape up a relationship, to construct a level of comfort with self, to find out information about other people, to develop relationships (Dindia, 1994; Petronio, 2002), to establish trust or give advice (Spencer, 1994) or to manage and present impressions (West & Duck, 1996) rather than simply to reveal layers of one's personality. For example, people can reveal something personal about themselves in order to show the other person that he or she is trusted to keep things secret, or a person could tell a story about their personal experience or their feelings in a way that is intended not simply to reveal information but to help the other person ('I was very shy myself too when I was your age and I felt so ashamed of the fact that I blushed a lot and was awkward, but I soon learned that I could feel better if …'). In such cases the comment is serving many goals and it would be wrong to see it as *only* a disclosure of private personal feelings or information about self (Spencer, 1994). Likewise a person could say 'My friend is gay and he's really cool', which is both a disclosure of personal information (how I feel about my friend's homosexuality) and an *alignment* with the friend, indicating support and admiration. Thus a disclosure of personal feelings can also be a statement of attitude or even a political statement or the management of the impression that one is open-minded (West & Duck, 1996), but it is additionally in all cases a statement about the relationship too. As I have been suggesting here, then, any statement has to be seen in rhetorical context as something that achieves different purposes and not as an activity with a single purpose or only one possible meaning: the content of disclosure reveals something, but the *act of disclosure itself* reveals something also about a speaker's personal sense of the status and significance of the relationship. Meanings are developed between people in interaction in context and are not absolute things that exist simplistically in the words: they happen when interaction happens, in a context, and between people and they do something to establish and maintain relationships.

ACTIVITY BOX

Pair off in class and each write down one thing about yourself the other person would not know. It can be anything that you feel comfortable telling. Hand them what you wrote and open a discussion on the topic.

What did you learn from the exercise? Was your disclosure less or more intimate than your partner's and what inferences resulted from the exchange? Was any part of your exchange devoted to further disclosure about the topic that went beyond what you had written? What conclusions do you draw?

ESTABLISHING, DEVELOPING AND MAINTAINING RELATIONSHIPS

What is the psychological relationship between initial attraction and long-term liking? Apart from disclosures and release of information, what are the processes by which we convert 'gut attraction' into a working relationship? Note also, of course, that most meetings with strangers do *not* develop into intimate relationships (Delia, 1980) and for that matter neither do lots of relationships with people we know, such as shop assistants, classmates, colleagues at work, or even some distressingly odd family members. Also interesting but so far largely overlooked by mainstream research (but see Hess, 2000, 2002 who deals with disliked others) is the question of how do we actively keep relationships from developing and keep people at arm's length. (If you want a good research project, then try that one. Keeping liked people at arm's length is a tricky task sometimes, and we could expect processes to be quite as delicate as those involved in developing intimacy, the point being that it is difficult to convey that message without giving offence and yet we may like someone without wanting to get intimate.)

In real life, my experience is that we plan to meet people and we share points of contact but also that predictable routines constantly force us together frequently with those we know well. Our real-life encounters are only occasionally unforeseen, unexpected, and accidental and are also predictable, anticipated, and (most often) prearranged or unavoidable (e.g., with roommates). Because meetings are like this, they come from somewhere and we have coded memories about the persons and the relationship in which they arise: stories about where the relationship came from, what it means to us, and where it is going. Miell (1987) has shown that a person's beliefs about the future of the relationship are very often influenced by the last three days of routine experience in the relationship more than they are influenced by the whole history of its long-term idealized past. Duck, Pond & Leatham (1994) have shown that memory for past relational events is influenced very strongly by the *present* state of the relationship. This makes a lot of sense: when relationship problems occur, they occur in the present, the here and now, and all the fond memories of the distant past become degraded or idealized by the insistence of urgent present feelings.

Furthermore, most of the time, daily life is remarkably humdrum, routine, predictable (Wood & Duck, 2006). We take our long-term relationships for granted most of the time and assume that the partner we slept next to will wake up still feeling like a partner tomorrow. Relationships which have major effects on people are of this perpetual but essentially unquestioned and dormant kind: parent–child relationships, marriages, friendships, collegial relationships at work. They are part of the unchallenged and comfortable predictability of lives made up of routine, regular conversation, expectation, and assumptions that most of tomorrow will be based on the mental foundations of today. We do not go through a ritual each breakfast time where we treat each other like strangers and run through a whole range of rewarding techniques to reestablish the relationship and take it to where it was the day before: we behave that mental way only with friends we have not seen for ages. However, we do tend to exchange end of day 'catch-up' Self-report and Other-report with close partners to keep up with the bits of daily life that we did not observe (Alberts et al., 2005).

The remarkable fact about daily life is that continuities exist in our minds and do not have to be worked for, once the relationship is defined and established (Braithwaite & Koenig Kellas, 2006; Metts, 2006). Friendships can feel as if they exist and continue over years and miles without any contact except the occasional 'phone call, Christmas card or letter (Dindia et al., 2004; Sahlstein, 2004). Relationships have their permanence *in the mind*, on the basis of beliefs (Duck & Sants, 1983) and routines of behaviour (Dainton, 2000). Relationships survive distance, climate, revolt, pestilence, and Act of God, as long as both people *think* they last, but more importantly they survive because we *act* as if they do, performing a hundred little daily acts that make them endure. Sigman (1991) referred to relationship endurance through the concept of RCCUs (Relational Continuity Constructional Units) and he specified three types: *prospective units* (those activities or statements that imply that there is a future to the relationship, for example 'See you tomorrow' or planning for joint activity next weekend), *introspective units* (thoughts or symbols that restate the relationship without physical co-presence, such as a photograph of a fiancé on a desk at work), and *retrospective units* (reestablishment of connection once the partners are back in one another's presence after a separation, for example asking someone 'How was your day?' on their return home from work).

KEEP A JOURNAL

Start writing down instances where you observe how you and other people maintain relationships. Note the number of 'relationship artefacts' that people display (photos, wedding rings, even wearing one another's clothes). Record the frequency of 'catch-up' talk and instances of 'future talk' not just the obvious ones like 'See you tomorrow' or 'Talk to you soon' but trying to look for more complicated and subtle ones.

As in the rest of life, so in relationships I think we can easily misunderstand what really goes on if we overlook the importance of 'trivial' behaviour. It does not feel to me as if the world is full of relationships where perfect strangers grasp one another's collars in breathless attempts to shake out the other person's attitudes in a search for reinforcement. Neither do I see people in long-term relationships going round giving grades to partners for their every action and calculating whether the cost–benefit arithmetic works out well enough for them to stay in the relationship for the next ten minutes. Not every encounter is a surprise; not every person a blank slate upon which rapid calculations have to be performed. Not every member of the family has either just fallen in love with you or is about to file for divorce, or is either a young child with a tendency to initiate violent acts or an elderly incontinent who feels lonely. Neither is precisely the same level of feeling felt towards each partner all the time irrespective of mood or circumstances, but rather our feelings about people – even people we love – can vary not only in the long term but even in the course of an interaction, as things turn ugly or else as people warm to one another and become more fond or even passionately aroused.

Relationships are a part of life, and everyday life is a part of all relationships. As those lives change through our ageing, so do the concerns we have and the things we do (such as about dating in later life, Dickson, Hughes & Walker, 2005; or about relationship concerns generally, Bedford & Blieszner, 2000). As days go by, so our feelings and concerns are subject to change or variation. Our friendship needs vary a lot through life as do our opportunities for getting them and our bases for seeking them (Dickens & Perlman, 1981). Also they vary day by day in the face of circumstances (Alberts et al., 2005). In teenage years, the main search is for a group of friends and for sexual partners (Berndt, 1996); later, most people become committed to one partner and their network of friends stabilizes for a while (Notarius, 1996). If we commit to the partner and add children, then our friendship needs are affected by these circumstances and by career developments (Crouter & Helms-Erickson, 2000). When the children leave home, parents often become involved in the community more extensively and start up new friendships in the middle years of life (Adams & Blieszner, 1996). As life develops new demands and new routines so we change friendship 'work'. Our feelings can go up and down as joys and resentments arise, recede and gain resolution. Thus the statements that we make about liking and loving are likely to be *summary statements* (see Chapter 2) that can be more or less accurate reflections of how we felt three days ago or two hours ago or last year, just as any 'average summary' is only a more or less accurate reflection of a specific case.

A consistent element of all life routines consists of such trivial variation, and we apparently waste a lot of time doing seemingly unimportant things. For example, we spend much of our time talking to other people about commonly experienced events including TV programmes (Alberts et al., 2005), gossiping, and giving views of one another (Bergmann, 1993) or advice and support about relationships (Foley, 2006b). Acitelli (1988, 1993) shows that when people talk about relationships they are not only describing and celebrating them, as researchers have previously thought, but also formulating them and perhaps changing their attitudes towards the relationship, or to broader issues and values in society such as the nature of work (Cockburn-Wootten & Zorn, 2006).

Do partners always agree about their relationship?

Discrepancies of interpretation, even between close partners, are an inevitable part of everyday social life (McCarthy, 1983) and tend to lead to *action*, such as conversation to resolve the differences. When researchers find such disagreements, it should surprise them less than it does. Our own and everyone else's cognitive processes are inaccessible to us; if we do not know what other people are thinking, we can depend only on guesswork and we often guess wrongly. Yet Hewes, Graham, Doelger & Pavitt (1985) show that people have sophisticated knowledge about the likely sources of error in information that we have about other people and are able to correct for biases in 'second guessing'. By talking to others in routine ways, we can assess their cognitive processes more and more accurately, but to do so we may have to work through disagreements, during conversation (Muehlhoff, 2006). Second, we seldom discuss our views of relationship openly and explicitly with our partners except when we think something is wrong (Acitelli, 1988, 1993). So we do not get much experience of seeing explicit agreements about our relationships (though they are nice when we get them), and the experiences we do get will emphasize the discords instead.

The *problems* with relationships are more likely to be visible, accessible and familiar than are the smooth parts, since, like a satisfactory digestion and good government, they tend to go unremarked while the opposite does not. More importantly, partners probably each see different events as crucial in the relationship, so there is no good reason to expect partners to be in total agreement about the nature or course of the relationship (McCarthy, 1983), but in any case, people tend to segment and punctuate the flow of experience, including relational events, somewhat differently (Watzlawick et al., 1967). What happens when disagreements are detected is that people talk them through (or at least talk about them), so once again in everyday life, conversation is an important tool for developing and sustaining relationships, but may also cause trouble when discrepancies and conflicts of opinion or interpretation arise (and may create physiological distress as well; Floyd, 2004).

Does it matter what 'outsiders' think?

In real life, relationships take place in a context provided by talk with other people not just by the partners' own thoughts and feelings. The presence of others (and what they know about the relationship) distinguishes between our behaviours in public and secret relationships (Duncombe, Harrison, Allan & Marsden, 2004), but can also affect the things we do in cooperative and competitive, open, trusting and closed, threatening relationships. Much research shows that we are aware of such outside influence on relationships both at the personal level and from such sources as media and social culture (Klein & Johnson, 2000; Milardo & Wellman, 1992; Parks, 2006). Outsiders can affect the course of a relationship by expressing general disapproval or encouragement (Parks & Eggert, 1991), but there are other effects, too. First, as we pull into one new relationship we correspondingly have a little less time for our old friendships (Milardo & Allan, 2000). New friendships disrupt old ones; marital relationships reduce opportunities for 'hanging out' with friends. Second, outsiders, in the shape of the 'surrounding culture', give us clues about the ways to conduct relationships. For instance, Klein & Milardo (1993) show how outsiders are often arbitrators of conflict between members of a couple or give them advice on how they 'ought' to handle it. Equally, motivated by concern over the reactions of other people, we may try to hide affairs and hope that the newspapers or our acquaintances do not find out about them, yet we are happy to publicize marriages in those self-same newspapers and to those acquaintances.

LOOK OUT FOR THIS IN THE MEDIA

Look out for things that the *print* media such as papers and magazines comment on concerning relationships. Look for stories about celebrities, but also other people. Purchase a copy of *People* magazine, *OK*, or *Hello!* How do these illustrate the role of outsiders' opinion about relationships? What are the stories telling us not only about the rich and famous, but about how to do relationships in our lives?

As partners become more involved in a courtship, so this adversely affects their relationships with friends (Baxter et al., 2001; Milardo & Wellman, 1992). Respondents in the later stages of courtship interact with fewer people, relative to persons in the earlier stages of courtship, and see them less often and for shorter periods of time. However, the most noticeable changes in rates of participation occur with intermediate friends rather than close ones. Changes in frequency and duration of interactions subsequently lead to a decrease in the size of network (Milardo & Allan, 2000). In other words, as we see our date more, so we see our casual friends (but not our close friends) less until they finally drop out of our network altogether, if the courtship progresses satisfactorily (Allan, 1998; Milardo & Allan, 2000). Courting partners are thus less of a 'substitute' for close friends than for casual acquaintances. However, emotional commitment to one romantic partner sends ripples through the larger network to which we belong.

Some of the preceding suggestions show that a developing relationship between two people not only has meaning for them but begins to have meaning for *other* people, too, and that affects the way it works. It becomes an 'organization' over and above the feelings that the partners have for one another and begins to carry social obligations, cultural constraints, normative significance, and the shaping hand of expectation (Allan, 1998; McCall, 1988). Whilst social psychologists explore the ways in which feelings for one another pull partners together, and communications scholars explore the ways in which those feelings are expressed and communicated, sociologists are interested in relationships as social units over and above the two members in them (McCall, 1988). In a sociological analysis of friendships, Allan (1993, 1995) points to the ways in which social life in turn structures our choices of partners and creates patterns of activity that help us to express emotions, regulate our feelings in relationships and provide opportunities for relationships to take a particular form. Sex, class position, age, domestic relationships and pre-existing friendships all pattern and constrain an individual's choices and limit freedom in everyday practical life in ways not considered by those who imagine that attraction and friendship choices are the simple result of emotion or of cognitive processes of information management. You will not be allowed to marry the First Lady, even if you love her. Instead our analysis of relationships has to recognize the effects of context on such emotions and processes and hence we need to attend not only to what people *think* but to what they *do* in everyday life, not only in their development but also in their breakup.

TRY THIS OUT

How much freedom of choice do you really have in your relationships and how much pre-sorting is done for you by society and other people? Write down a list of your romantic relationships and main friendships. Make sure you have written down all your major relationships. Then cross off all the people who are the same religion as you, the same socioeconomic group as you, or who have worked in the same place as you before you became friends, or who have lived within 5 miles of you or attended the same school as you at some point in your life before they became connected to you in a relationship, and then delete all those who had friends in common with you before they were your personal friends or partners. How many people are now left on the list?

BREAKUP AND RESURRECTION OF RELATIONSHIPS

So far I have focused on the bright side of relationships but much talk and many routines are also directed towards the less appealing side of relationships: when they break up, need repair, or have to be straightened out. By far the most common experience of negative things in relationships is the management of minor irritations and trivial hassles that arise day to day in relationships of all kinds (Kirkpatrick et al., 2006), and so I will devote another chapter to that (Chapter 7), looking here only at the major catastrophe of relationship breakup. The rosy picture of relational progress drawn so far is thus only part of the truth and Cupach & Spitzberg have devoted several books to the 'dark side' of relationships (Cupach & Spitzberg, 1994; Spitzberg & Cupach, 1998), while the topic of less severe challenges and relating difficulty is starting to get research attention also (Duck & Wood, 1995; Kirkpatrick et al., 2006). For instance why have researchers just focused on love and overlooked needling, bitching, boredom, complaints, harassment, and enemyships (Wiseman, 1986; Wiseman & Duck, 1995)? Why do we know more about romantic relationships than we do about troublesome relationships (Levitt, Silver & Franco, 1996)? Things often go wrong in relationships in all sorts of ways and cause a lot of pain when they do, some of it intentionally hurtful (Feeney, 2004, 2005). Sometimes it is Big Stuff and leads to breakup of the relationship, but most of the time it is relatively trivial and leads to nothing except hurt feelings and the conflicts involved in *managing* the occurrence. How does it happen?

When things go wrong

There are several parts to acquaintance, and so we should expect there to be several parts to its undoing. As Hagestad & Smyer (1982) note, there are three elements that are affected when a relationship breaks up: (1) feelings towards the partner; (2) the role and any status that was associated with it ('being married', 'being engaged', 'having a steady relationship'); (3) the routines that went with the relationship ('We always used to go to a special restaurant for Friday dinner, and now I miss that'). When people's relationships go wrong, they can have trouble adjusting to any of these three elements being changed. Not only this but in line with points made in Chapter 1, there is a definite cultural and media backdrop against which people define relational breakup. If a culture (or the media) use the length, durability, or persistence of a relationship as a measure of its 'success', then short relationships are going to be defined as bad and long ones as good. As already noted, you can read a newspaper any day and find the length of a relationship used as the measure of success. People celebrating their 50th wedding anniversary get to be pictured in the paper, whereas people who have been dating for three weeks do not.

A further important cultural context is so obvious that we do not even think about it. It considers relationships in terms of 'success' and 'failure'. In our culture relationships are regarded as 'successful' if they stick together, and as 'failures' otherwise. This judgement is made even if holding the relationship together hurts the people who stay together (who hate or abuse one another), and even if making the relationship come apart is a brave decision that helps the people to save one another, psychologically (by saving them from a life of mutual nastiness, for example). Therefore, anyone whose relationship ends 'prematurely' and who becomes a single person again as a result, or who remains single or isolated or chooses to be solitary will be regarded in a cultural context of failure and needs to explain and account for their (lack of) relationships in that context.

This highlights the fact that relationships are complex things and their breakup likewise involves different activities and adjustments, but it also is important to note that relationships exist in time and usually take time to fall apart, so that at different times different processes are taking a role in the dissolution. It is also because, like a motor car, a relationship can have accidents for many reasons, whether the 'driver's' fault, mechanical failure or the actions of other road users. Thus, in a relationship, one or both partners might be hopeless at relating; or the structure and mechanics of the relationship may be wrong, even though both partners are socially competent in other settings; or outside influences can upset it (Cupach & Canary, 2000). All of these possibilities have been explored (Fine & Harvey, 2006). However, I am going to focus on my own approach to these issues and refer you elsewhere for details of the other work. One reason for doing this is that my own theory of relationship dissolution is closely tied to my approach to relational repair (Duck, 1984a) as well as to my approach to the development of acquaintance (Duck, 1999) and so provides links between what has gone before here and what follows.

The original model (Duck, 1982) has recently been modified by Rollie & Duck (2006) and so I will run through the basic ideas of the 1982 model and then go on to the newer model which much more strongly emphasizes communication patterns and content to identify the workings of relationship dissolution at different points and is presented in Figure 3.2.

The 1982 model suggested several different phases, each with a characteristic style and concern. The first phase is a breakdown phase where partners (or one partner only) become(s) distressed at the way the relationship is conducted. This generates an *intrapsychic phase* characterized by a brooding focus on the relationship and on the partner. Nothing is said to the partner at this point: the agony is either private or shared only with a diary or with relatively anonymous other persons (bar servers, hairdressers, passengers on the bus) who will not tell the partner about the complaint. Just before exit from this phase, people move up the scale of confidants so that they start to complain to their close friends, but do not yet present their partner with the full extent of their distress or doubts about the future of the relationship.

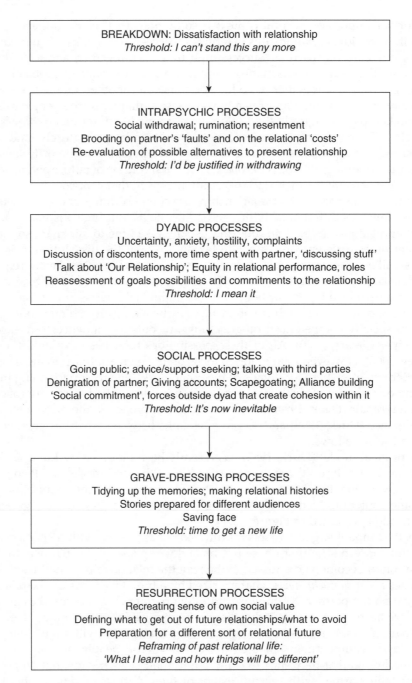

Figure 3.2   Breakdown process model (significantly modified from Duck (1982))

Once we decide to do something about a relational problem we have to deal with the difficulties of facing up to the partner. Implicit – and probably wrongly implicit – in my 1982 model was the belief that partners would tell one another about their feelings and try to do something about them. People often leave relationships without telling their partner, or else by fudging their exits. For instance, they may say 'I'll call you' and then not do it; or 'Let's keep in touch' and never contact the partner; or 'Let's not be lovers but stay as friends' and then have hardly any contact in future (Metts, Cupach & Bejlovec, 1989). However, many partners in formal relationships like marriage will have to face up to their partner, whilst partners in other relationships may or may not do so. The *dyadic phase* is the phase when partners try to confront and talk through their feelings about the relationship and decide how to sort out the future. Assuming that they decide to breakup (and even my 1982 model was quite clear that they may decide *not* to do that), they then move rapidly to a *social phase* when they have to tell other people about their decision and enlist some social support for their side of the debate. It is no good just leaving a relationship: we seek other people to agree with our decision or to prop us up and support what we have done. Other people can support us in ways such as being sympathetic and generally understanding. More important, they can side with our version of events and our version of the partner's and the relationship's faults. ('I always thought he/she was no good', 'I could never understand how you two could get along – you never seemed right for each other'). This is the *grave-dressing* phase: once the relationship is dead we have to bury it 'good and proper' – with a tombstone saying how it was born, what it was like, and why it died. We have to create an account of the relationship's history and, as it were, put that somewhere so that other people can see it and, we hope, accept it. In this phase, people may strategically reinterpret their view of their partner for example by shifting from the view of the person as 'exciting' to being 'dangerously unpredictable' or from being 'attractively reliable' to being 'boring' – exactly the same features of the person are observed, but they are given different *labels* more suited to one's present feelings about the person (Felmlee, 1995).

In breakdown of relationships as elsewhere in life, gossip plays a key role. Here it works in the social and grave-dressing phases and in a dissolving relationship we actively seek the support of members of our social networks and do so by gossiping about our partners (La Gaipa, 1982). In some instances, we look for 'arbitrators' who will help to bring us back together with our partner. In other cases, we just want someone to back up and spread around our own version of the breakup and its causes. A crucial point made by La Gaipa (1982) is that every person who leaves a relationship has to leave with 'social credit' intact for future use: that is, we cannot just get out of a relationship but we have to leave in such a way that we are not disgraced and debarred from future relationships. We must leave with a reputation for having been let down or faced with unreasonable odds or an unreasonable partner. It is socially acceptable to say 'I left because we tried hard to make it work but it wouldn't'. It is not socially acceptable to leave a relationship with the cheery but unpalatable admission: 'Well basically I'm a jilt and I got bored dangling my partner on a string so I just broke the whole thing off when it suited me'. That statement could destroy one's future credit for new relationships.

Accounts often serve the purpose of beginning the 'getting over' activity that is essential to complete the dissolution (Weber, 1983). A large part of this involves selecting an account of dissolution that refers to a fault in the partner or relationship that pre-existed the split or was even present all along (Weber, 1983). This is the 'I always thought she/he was a bit of a risk to get involved with, but I did it anyway, more fool me' story that we have all used from time to time.

However, accounts also serve another purpose: the creation of a publicly acceptable story is essential to getting over the loss of a relationship (McCall, 1982). It is insufficient having a story that we alone accept: others must also endorse it. As McCall (1982) astutely observed, part of the success of good counsellors consists in their ability to construct such stories for persons in distress about relational loss.

The Rollie & Duck (2006) modification of this model emphasizes predominant processes rather than discrete phases, spells out the communicative fall-out of the whole thing and adds an extra process ('*resurrection*') that addresses the ways in which people prepare and launch themselves for new relationships afterwards. As Figure 3.2 shows, the new model can be represented as processes that can overlap or have common features, but which also have different identifiable purposes and consequences for communication, both in terms of topics covered and in terms of the people to whom things are said. For example, in the first two sets of processes I assume that people tend to withdraw from contact with their social network, either to brood alone or to take time to talk things over with a partner, whereas in later processes they actively engage with the network in order to seek support and advice or to 'tell their tale'. In essence, then, this new model looks at the behavioural consequences of breakdown rather than just at how it feels.

Putting it right

The Rollie & Duck (2006) model suggests two ways in which relational breakdown can be 'put right': (1) The partners can sort out the relationship as discussed below; (2) one person can heal the self by getting out of the current relationship and working on a new relational face. If two people wanted to put a relationship right, then they could decide to try and make it 'redevelop'; that is, they could assume that repairing a relationship is just like acquaintance, and go through the same processes in order to regain the previous level of intimacy. This means that we have to assume that breakup of relationships is the reverse of acquaintance, and that to repair it, all we have to do is 'rewind' it. This makes some sense: developing relationships grow in intimacy whereas breaking ones decline in intimacy so perhaps we should just try to rewind the intimacy level.

In other ways, this idea does not work, though. For instance, in acquaintance we get to know more about a person but in breakdown we cannot get to know less, we must just reinterpret what we already know and put it into a different framework, model, or interpretation ('Yes, he's always been kind, but, then, he was always after something').

I think that we need to base our ideas about repair not on our model of acquaintance but on a broader model of breakdown of relationships that takes account of principles governing formation of relationships in general. Research on relationships has begun to help us understand what precisely happens when things go wrong. By emphasizing processes of breakdown of relationships and processes of acquaintance, we have the chance now to see that there are also processes of repair although these tend to have been overlooked. These processes do, however, address different aspects of relationships in trouble. This, I believe, also gives us the chance to be more helpful in putting things right. Bear in mind the model just covered, as you look at Figure 3.3, and you will see that it is based on proposals made earlier.

If the relationship is at the intrapsychic processes of dissolution, for instance, then repair should aim to re-establish liking for the partner rather than to correct behavioural faults in ourselves or our nonverbal behaviour, for instance. These latter may be more suitable if persons are in the breakdown processes instead. Liking for partner can be re-established or aided by means such as keeping a record, mental or physical, of the positive or pleasing behaviour of our partner rather than listing the negatives and dwelling on them in isolation (Bandura, 1977). Other methods involve redirection of attributions, that is, attempting to use more varied, and perhaps more favourable, explanations for the partner's behaviour – in brief, to make greater efforts to understand the reasons that our partner may give for what is happening in the relationship.

At other processes of dissolution, different strategies of repair are appropriate, according to this model. For instance, at the social process, persons outside the relationship have to decide whether it is better for the partners to try to patch everything up or whether it may serve everyone's best interests to help the partners to get out of the relationship. Figure 3.3 thus indicates that the choice of strategies is between pressing the partners to stay together or helping them to save face by backing up their separate versions of the breakup. An extra possibility would be to create a story that is acceptable to both of them, such as 'It was an unworkable relationship ... and that is nobody's fault'.

Essentially, this model proposes only three things: relationships are made up of many parts and processes, some of which 'clock in' at some points in the relationship's life and some at others; relationships can go wrong in a variety of ways; repairing of disrupted relationships will be most effective when it addresses the concerns that are most important to us at the process of dissolution of relationships which we have reached.

DISSOLUTION STATES	PERSON'S CONCERNS	REPAIR FOCUS
1 Breakdown: Dissatisfaction with relationship	*Relationship process; emotional and/or physical satisfaction in relationship*	Concerns over one's value as a partner; Relational process

Threshold: I cant stand this any more

2 Intrapsychic Phase: Dissatisfaction with partner	*Partner's 'faults and inadequacies'; alternative forms of relationship; relationships with alternative partners*	Person's view of partner

Threshold: I'd be justified in withdrawing

3 Dyadic Phase: Confrontation with partner	*Reformulation of relationship: expression of conflict; clearing the air*	Beliefs about optimal form of future relationship

Threshold: I mean it

4 Social Phase: Publication of relationship distress	*Gaining support and assistance from others; having own view of the problem ratified; obtaining intervention to rectify matters or end the relationship*	*Either.* Ways to hold partners together and return to Phase 1 *Or* Ways to save face and move to Phase 5 & Phase 6

Threshold: It's now inevitable

5 Grave-dressing Phase: Getting over it all and tidying up	*Self-justification; marketing of one's own version of the break-up and its causes*	Repair of self and self image; putting the past into a better perspective
6 Resurrection Phase	*Defining self anew, setting new styles for relating in future; defining and rejecting past mistakes and key features of past partners and/or relationships*	Ways to create or affirm a new Relational Self

Figure 3.3   A sketch of the main concerns at different phases of dissolution repair (significantly adapted from Duck (1984: 169))

The ways we change our 'stories' about a relationship provide important psychological data, and they indicate the dynamic nature of the help that outsiders have to give to relationships in trouble. Different parts of the story need to be addressed at different processes of breakdown. Is one and the same kind of intervention appropriate at all stages of a relationship's decline? Probably not. It makes more sense to look for the relative appropriateness of different intervention techniques as those dynamics unfold. There are few 'scripts' for handling breakup of relationships and many intriguing research questions surround the actual processes by which people extricate themselves (or can be helped to extricate themselves) from unwanted relationships. For example, Miller & Parks (1982) look at relationship dissolution as an influence process and show that different strategies for changing attitudes can help in dissolution. It is now a major aim in the personal relationships field to explain dissolution and repair of relationships (Fine & Harvey, 2006).

SUMMARY

This chapter has looked at personal relationships by exploring the ways in which they are *practical*, rather than emotional, matters that start between strangers. It has elaborated the processes (attitude similarity, self-disclosing, and organization of routine behaviours) that are needed to develop and maintain relationships. It has stressed that even though this process is based on acquisition of information from others, it is more involved with the social, dyadic and communicative bonding that is embedded in influential social contexts. The chapter has emphasized the view that relationships are continually developing processes and are not static states begun and defined only by partners' initial psychological make up but are open ended processes that have to be managed. The chapter also has stressed the ways in which outsiders influence the shape and development of partners' feelings and organization of their relationships. The chapter emphasized the creation of relationships; the effects of time and process; the interaction of beliefs with social skills and behaviour; and the role of outsiders' perspectives and influences on the relationship. Decline, dissolution and repair of relationships were considered in tandem with the role of everyday routines and everyday talk.

You should now be in a better position to notice the development and the decline of relationships, and to detect from the talk of other people the processes of relational decline in which they may see themselves. When people are focused on negative reports of their partner's behaviour, for example, they may need help reinterpreting what their partner has been doing. You should also be better able to notice the way in which relationships are maintained by ordinary routine behaviours.

SELF QUESTIONS

- This chapter has identified some issues in the growth and breakdown of relationships and you should now be able to recognize some of the ways in which relationships are built, sustained, or may collapse. How do the issues discussed in this chapter reflect your own personal experience of relationship growth or breakdown? Do the discussions in this chapter apply equally well to friendship as they may to romance?
- When people's relationships breakdown, this chapter has suggested that people do a certain amount of self presentation. Can you identify the sorts of 'self' that a person is projecting in their stories about relationship breakup?
- In what ways did your membership of other groups influence your experience of friendship and/or romance as an adolescent? Does it still happen that way today?

FURTHER READING

Dainton, M. (2000). Maintenance behaviors, expectations for maintenance, and satisfaction: Linking comparison levels to relational maintenance strategies. *Journal of Social and Personal Relationships, 17*(6), 827–842.

Duck, S.W., & Wood, J.T. (Eds.). (1995). *Confronting relationship challenges [Understanding relationship processes 5]*. Newbury Park, CA: SAGE.

Fine, M.A., & Harvey, J.H. (2006). *Handbook of divorce and relationship dissolution.* Mahwah, NJ: Lawrence Erlbaum and Associates.

Petronio, S. (2002). *Boundaries of privacy.* Albany, NY: SUNY Press.

Wood, J.T., & Duck, S.W. (Eds.). (2006). *Composing relationships: Communication in everyday life.* Belmont, CA: Thomson Wadsworth.

PRACTICAL MATTERS

- The breakdown of relationships is one of the major catastrophes of life for most people and it may be due to poor relationship

(Continued)

(Continued)

abilities or to difficulties adjusting to changes in routine and role or to difficulties in self concept, as a result of relationship loss. Practical applications of research into these things must make this distinction first, especially for people called upon to help others in relational distress.

- Poor relationship skills are associated with criminality, violence and aggression, neurosis and depression, illness, shyness, drug and alcohol problems, marital difficulties, divorce, spouse beating, and child abuse (Foley, 2006b; Wood, 2004;). They also create demands on us to provide help, comfort and resources to others or oblige us to be available to others when they are in difficulties, especially in times of illness and stress (Stein, 1993).

- The phenomenon of 'care-giver burnout' has been widely researched (Miller, Stiff & Ellis, 1988) whether in respect of mental health service professionals and counsellors who experience exhaustion from all their caring for others (La Gaipa, 1990) or merely untrained folk who care for sick relatives (Lyons, Langille & Duck, 2006).

- People also give us daily hassles (Kirkpatrick et al., 2006) and present us with binds and dilemmas (Wiseman, 1986) or stretch our loyalties (Baxter et al., 1997). In living practical relational lives, these are variations with which we must be prepared to contend, and considering what we may be letting ourselves in for, there might be a case for never getting into relationships at all!

4

Relationships Within Other Relationships: Social Networks and Families

We humans are social animals down into our very cells. Sociality is not some artificial burden foisted upon natural men and women, as Rousseau (1755/1984) imagined in his famous *Discourse on Inequality*. Nature does not make us noble loners. Instead we are in our most natural state when we are with families, lovers, enemies, friends, acquaintances, fellow workers, leaders, followers, and all the rest who light the constellations of human affiliation. (Parks, 2006: 1)

Focus points for note taking when reading this chapter:

- The earlier parts of the book have looked at the role of emotion, experience, culture, and routine in the internal workings of a relationship. Other *real* people are the direct links of every individual to any broad abstractions like 'society' though.
- What is the role of other people – either as closely connected others or as representatives of 'society' and 'culture' – on the ways in which people behave in relationships?
- What is the effect on our personal relationships of the connections that we have to other people beyond a specific partner?
- What is 'private' about a relationship?
- How are we influenced by other people's views and opinions in our personal relationships?
- In a family, what results follow from the fact that each person has a separate personal relationship to each other person as well as to the larger group as a whole?
- Consider the ways in which children are affected by the relationships of adults, especially their parents and especially when the family is non-traditional in form or goes through a traumatic disruption of some kind.

Chapter 3 began by noting the insistence of this book on the importance of *context* in understanding dyadic personal relationships. The present chapter introduces another context, namely the *other* relationships that we are in. Neither any person nor any couple is an island and all of people's relationships intersect with each other. For example, would you worry about 'coming out' if you didn't believe that anyone *else* would have an opinion about it, that their reactions could be negative, or that you may have to explain yourself to someone who frightens you? Would you really date a person whom all *your friends* had universally condemned beforehand as a dog? Would you argue with your child in public about your sexual habits, or shout at your child's school teacher in the presence of other parents?

It is both an obvious and an overlooked point that a lot of what we do in our personal interactions is done because of the fact that we know that other people (than just the person we are talking to at the moment) can observe and comment on our relationships – and we care what they think (Milardo & Wellman, 1992; Parks, 2006). Even our apparently private relational behaviour is something we might not want to become public (for example, we may not want to confess to relational transgressions, infidelity and affairs; Duncombe et al., 2004) and some families operate with a careful eye on the in-laws (Morr-Serewicz, 2006) or the absent/non-custodial parent of a shared child (Rollie, 2006). Social networks even play a role in relational dissolution also, as we saw in the previous chapter.

So this chapter is about the ways in which our relationships with a specific partner are affected by our embeddedness in other sorts of relationships and processes. This influence takes two forms: in the present chapter, we will look at relationships as influences on other *relationships*; in the next chapter, we will look at relationships as influences on other *processes* (persuasion and moral judgement), but in both cases one set of relationships influences what happens in another set of relationships and the judgements that are made about behaviours in them.

Even in this chapter, where we are limited to the influence on one relationship of other relationships, we can explore social influences on the dyad or look at the complex inter-linkages between sets of relationships that occur in the family (older parents' influences on their adult children intending to marry, young parents' influences on children, or siblings' influences on one another and on their parents, to name only a few). In this chapter, we will do both, but the underlying principle is the same: relationships even when 'close', 'personal' and 'private', are subject to the influence of other relationships, other people and social norms and conventions. Social networks are not simply a convenient academic abstraction, but are lively intersections of people and their habits, actions, and opinions on one another. Also of course an extension of the points made in the preceding chapter is that routine organization of a relationship tends to draw in other people, who therefore and thereby serve a gluing function, such that even the breakup of an organized 'personal' relationship falls out on the social network too and affects its functioning and interconnections, perhaps disrupting its stability or its information-flow patterns.

KEEP A JOURNAL

Keep a record of the number of times during the next week in which any specific dyadic relationship in which you are involved is required to be reorganized (or re-timed to do things in different sequences or patterns than you had expected) as a result of the influence of *third parties* rather than just because you and your partner want personally to make the changes in timing.

ORGANIZING AN EXCLUSIVE RELATIONSHIP WITHIN OTHER RELATIONSHIPS

The tendency is for us all to see relationships as operating in stages or pathways, usually seen to have an emotional parallel, either in the deepening or the broadening of affection or in an emotional or organizational re-connection. In fact, even this belief is a relative one that depends on a culture recognizing differences between emotions, labelling them as progressively connected, and naming them as acceptably intertwined with equally recognizable organizational stepping points for change or status modification in 'the relationship' itself. In other words, we have to recognize differences in relationship 'stages' that we can 'pin on' changes in emotion.

In our culture, this is an easy assumption and the notion of 'progress' in relationships is essentially one with two elements: (1) a moral element (it is 'good' to move towards a particular goal – say a long-term commitment – and 'bad' not to try to do so, or, having tried, to fail to attain long-term stability); (2) a descriptive preference for seeing 'a relationship' as something that changes in important ways over time, usually and primarily in terms of a change in emotions (hence 'falling in love' implies descent into something in increasing depth). Chapter 3, however, also noted that the description of such stages and changes is culturally specific: some cultures (e.g., the USA) see 'dating' as a stage that precedes another form of relationship whose ultimate form and organization is 'marriage' whereas other cultures (e.g., Spain) do not recognize such a stage (Chornet-Roses, 2006). Thus any 'stages' that exist do so partly because they are recognized as such by other people, and when individuals in a couple identify change in relationship status it is because they can meaningfully manifest such change to other people in some evident and physical way that those people recognize as indicating a status change – a ring, a ceremony, a style of intimacy in public, sexual exclusivity, a new child, for example.

The emphasis in research on such stages, however, has most often been on the internal dynamics of the couple – how they feel differently/more deeply about one another, have greater commitment, and so on at each 'stage' – rather than on how they reorganize the relationship or reframe their behaviour with other people. But what is 'an exclusive relationship' if not one that denies *other people* something? 'Exclusivity' in a relationship is thus a reference to the placement of a dyad in a network of other relationships and a statement about the couple in contrast to that network. Making a relationship 'exclusive' is making an adjustment to its organization that ultimately affects the network too, when you think about it.

The social context for organizing relationships

Several centuries ago, marriage was not normally preceded by a 'stage' seen as courtship, as we know it, and as we saw in Chapter 2 even the free consent of marriage partners was overlooked in some political marriages. Nowadays, we expect a certain amount of choice of potential partners in the first place, as discussed in Chapter 3, and we certainly expect freedom of consent to marriage and so we expect to be asked, in front of witnesses – other people who belong to our friendship network and family, most likely – to say whether our consent is indeed freely given. It is part of the ceremony that such a public declaration is made to the network of other people whom we know and have invited to be there to hear us make such a declaration. Their recognition and approval form a necessary part of the relational status change that turns us from a couple of 'lovers' into 'a married couple'.

An interesting development is that we also nowadays expect a certain degree of *continuous* choice about a *developing* relationship – from which we are able at any point to remove ourselves quite easily at least until marriage or a formal civil contract brings in other forces that keep us in place – but even a civil bond can be relatively easily dissolved nowadays. Where there is choice there is also responsibility and so we tend to regard the successful completion of courtship or marriage as a responsibility of the couple. Therefore, modern emphasis falls on successful development of courtship as a pathway to marriage and counts as 'successful' only those marriages that continue until the death of one partner.

The previous chapters have made the point that emotions per se are not the only bases of relationships and this is true of courtship, families and marriages as much as of other sorts of relationships. Despite the romantic novels, where lovers walk off hand in hand into the sunset, such a 'lovers' relationship' has only just started to need work, rather than having reached its point of stability – and the early years of marriage contain significant problems for most couples often in the form of the reapportionment of time and sharing of household responsibilities (Veroff, Young & Coon, 2000). Also all couples are not kept together just by great sex or by the fact that they hold similar attitudes but, as Huston & Schwartz (1995: 95) put it, by the fact that 'they will have something mutually interesting to discuss over breakfast'. Forget, for the purposes of this chapter, that long-term romantic relationships magically result from love. Recent research consistently shows that far more important than gooey love are the ways the relationship is built and made to work through everyday life behaviour including such things as organization of recreation time, socializing, and the disposition of practical aspects of everyday life (Alberts et al., 2005; Emmers-Sommer, 2004; Koenig Kellas, 2005), whose successful management far outweighs any deep feelings that two people may otherwise have for one another. Thus it is important to look at the ways in which partners structure their interaction and patterns of daily life not only for themselves (Chapter 3), but for other people also.

LISTEN IN ON YOUR OWN LIFE

Pick two relationships that matter to you and listen out for ways in which you and your partner (friend/parent/child/lover/whatever) discuss the organization of the relationship or relationship activities or shared routines, duties, or behaviours, as compared to the number of times you talk about emotion. Also note the relative impact of the different sorts of discussion on what happens next.

This structuring is important whether partners are heterosexual or homosexual. As Huston & Schwartz (1995) show, homosexual couples have particular problems in working out structures for their relationships, since their activity is in many cases rooted in a concern to protect the precise nature of the relationship from the public so as to avoid the negative reactions of other social groups. However, when it comes to the interior (nonpublic) conduct of such relationships, that is indistinguishable in most major respects (Haas & Stafford, 2005). Rather, the external network context is the relevant force for recognizing *differences* in relationship 'stages' and it is therefore the network which imposes those differences on different forms of relationships and establishes a context for the public enactment of relationships. However, any *secret* relationship typically may be reported as temporarily exhilarating but as ultimately having a feeling of lower quality (Foster & Campbell, 2005), again reflecting the fact that recognition and/or a reaction by outsiders has important effects on internal emotion on its own.

In understanding the role of social context in the foundation of relationship patterns, however, it is very important to understand that the expressed reactions of others (outsiders) are a force on all relationships (Klein & Milardo, 1993; Parks, 2006). We *all* care about the responses of other people to our relationship and are influenced by the social context in which it occurs (Milardo & Allan, 2000) and most of us also recognize that if marriages are not made in heaven, then we have to do most of the work on them ourselves but not just in the couple or the dyad (Allen & Walker, 2000). Milardo & Allan (2000) note that while we think of 'society at large' as providing the context for long-term commitment, the norms of society are actually directly enforced and sustained by the intricate styles of dyadic/interpersonal connection that individuals form with one another face to face, with family, or with networks of acquaintances.

Parks (2006) takes this point further and indicates that such structural interdependence affects the flow of information (the people with whom you choose to talk about particular topics, for example) and the sanctioning of individuals' behaviour (by the neighbours or in-laws, for instance) in ways that reinforce norms of conduct for relationships, including the stories and narratives about their formation, stabilities and dissolution. Indeed, the effects of such social norms even on *sequences* of hearing/announcing news may not be something that is obvious until it is pointed out, but you are perfectly familiar with the way in which this works. In fact, it is so 'obvious' that you take it for granted that you will tell certain people things *before* other people in a way that reflects intimacy or status and that some people would have a right to feel insulted if they hear something after someone who is lower down in the pecking order relationally. If your parents are the last people to know that you are intending to get married, they have a right to feel affronted. If you get to hear an important piece of news about someone in your network, you're pretty sure to contact other network members straightaway in order to make sure that they know about it too. It's a perfectly human response, but it points out the role of networks and also demonstrates the rules within which those networks affect the way in which we run our *personal* life.

Who makes a relationship work?

The cultural emphasis on the emotions as bases for relationships tends to help us overlook the fact that much of a relationship is conducted in *organizational talk* about apportionment of time, arrangement of the demands of work relative to home/social life, or reorganizing one's own marriage in light of strains in the parental empty nest (Veroff et al., 2000). Talk not only serves these instrumental purposes to organize relational action but is used in social settings to conduct arguments, to divide work, to plan holidays and to create an imagined future (Duck, 2006), whereas practical activities require a similar but distinct coordination of life, time, and roles – even meeting for coffee or to complete the minor tasks of the workplace. The organization of meetings and conference calls, for example, obviously requires coordination of time frames and places and understandings with other people and relationships (Mokros, 2006). However, this does not simply happen at work but is necessary in couples, marriages, or long-term partnerships. Couples may be deeply in love but may nevertheless fail in the task of setting up an effective relationship in this way (Parks, 2006). Also increasingly clear is that couples who embed themselves firmly in strong and stable networks will experience greater consistency in their growth towards a more lasting marriage (Milardo & Allan, 2000; Parks & Eggert, 1991). The trick for us is to begin to realize more clearly how such reorganization or management of conflict, and so on, are actually connected to the network, perhaps directly through effects on the other people, or indirectly through the expectations that the network creates.

Hammering out such issues as 'who does what' will involve discussion perhaps with other people who know the rules that work well in relationships of the same type (Baxter et al., 2001), but also will involve significant amounts of conflict between the partners themselves (Veroff et al., 2000), and some of that causes emotional fallout in addition to the struggles involved in making things work. For example, Weger (2005) reports that both husbands and wives feel less verified by their partner when the partner withdraws from such conflict.

More broadly, there are in any case, good and bad kinds of conflict to have during courtship and 'organizational' rather than purely 'emotional' conflict is actually useful, because that kind of conflict seems to help the relationship to become organized (Kurdek, 1994). The differentiating feature of 'good' conflicts is that they target roles and routines and involve negotiation of tasks, activities or duties in the relationship. Couples may expect to argue about who does what, who goes where how often, what I shall do for you if you do this for me, who decides who does what, and the like. By sorting out role and relational organizational issues, even if it causes a few arguments at first, the couple is actually binding itself together more effectively as the two separate individuals start to function as a social unit (McCall, 1988). So those kinds of conflict (and their resolution) can be helpful.

The kinds of conflict that are not helpful are about incongruent goals or inconsistency of desired outcome in the relationship. If we argue about the nature of the relationship (e.g., whether it is to be a marriage or just a friendship) rather than who does what in it and how it should be organized, then we are in trouble. If partners handle these stresses and organizational aspects of their early relationship successfully, then they lay the foundations for handling them successfully in the later committed partnership where tasks and duties shift and new problems occur (e.g., during the transition to parenthood; Kayser & Rao, 2006). The effects of conflicts or unresolved negotiations at this stage do not always show up until later into the relationship (Notarius, 1996). Even serious conflicts in a courtship do not necessarily prevent couples from carrying on and getting married, but these conflicts do predict dissatisfaction with the marriage five years later.

However, Klein & Johnson (2000: 80) also note that 'similar conflict issues may play out differently in different family "types"', with traditional male-breadwinner families discussing the issues of household chores differently from spouses in peer marriages or lesbian partnerships. In the latter, Otis, Rostosky, Riggle & Hamrin (2006) note that LGBT (Lesbian Gay Bisexual Transgender) relationships often struggle to survive at all in a climate of lack of *social* support and the couple is affected by the stresses involved in maintaining relationship quality in that network climate.

Network opinion is also relevant, not only in reality, but also in partners' minds. Sprecher & Felmlee (2000) showed that people tend to perceive their network's views about their relationship as concordant with their own, to change with time (also concordantly with the subjective experience of the relationship), and to be connected with the state of the relationship at a later time. The study successfully shows that the couple's *perceptions* of network views are consistent with their relational experience, but we need other evidence to show that the network itself has *causal* impact on personal relationships like courtship. Such evidence is of course available from many sources. La Gaipa (1981) noted the effects of social networks on adolescents' likelihood of selecting particular dating partners, and adolescents tend to ditch partners that the network clique does not approve or recommend. Foster and Campbell (2005) conducted three studies that showed how the difficulties of keeping a relationship secret from the network tend to affect its perceived quality. Baxter et al. (2001) showed that network members told one another about the rules of relationships and also enforced their enactment, so relational choices and stability are not simply private or personal efforts, but involve reference to and awareness of the likely reaction of network members outside the relational pair itself.

TRY THIS OUT: ROCKY ROADS

Consider a relationship you have had with someone, whether in the family or a romance, and draw a turning point graph of its ups and downs over time. Indicate where the relationship got suddenly better and where it got suddenly worse on a graph. Label the turning points. Pick the two most important up turns and the two most important down turns and identify the main things that changed as a result (topics of talk, feelings, actions, routines, and so forth). After you have done that, write on it a note of any talks or other input that you had *from network members* at any point in the graph and whether/how it affected the relationship.

The important lesson for us readers, then, is that the steady establishment of a stable relationship is to do with the manner of constructing properly interwoven daily lives, communicating about the issues and routines there, and interactively conducting the relationship within a network context of support and also of expectation.

Getting the relationship organized for outsiders

Outsiders in the network have a say about the ways in which our relationships turn out and are continued. Society at large also serves to enforce the forms of such relationships, declaring that certain forms of partnership are not 'marriage' and that others are not 'family' and so do not qualify for benefits or welfare. But let's also think about the ways in which the same relationships can get labelled differently over time and receive different levels of outside support of different forms of internal organization. The family, the committed long-term relationship, and the courtship involve at least two of the same persons even though their relationship itself is differently organized and so is labelled differently as a result of the organizational changes and modifications that have taken place along the way. The different labels that are applied to that pair of people ('courtship', 'lovers', 'marriage') mean that only some aspects of the relationship are new or different. The partners are the same and live life in many of the same old ways throughout the period from falling in love to long-term commitment and legal recognition, if available. For this reason, many of the same sorts of issues and problems recur for the couple throughout that interconnected history from courtship to commitment (and, perhaps, to separation). Thus many researchers look at early relational organization as the best predictor of divorce five years later (Rodrigues, Hall & Fincham, 2006). We will do the same but will also look at the ways in which relationships are organized in the context of other outside, practical aspects of life (for example, how work affects relationships and the fact that even at the bureaucratic level certain relational formats are problematic: for example, there used to be no space on school information forms for the nontraditional parent or 'blended'/adoptive parent to be reported as a child's caretaker; Fine & Demo, 2000).

As we saw in Chapters 2 and 3, relationships become internally organized in several ways – for example, distribution of responsibility, power structure, time organization, development of idiomatic forms of language, even establishment of routines of daily life. In this respect they take on many of the properties and qualities of other organizations, such as shared history, private jokes and languages, and a sense of belonging (McCall, 1988). These are additional to the feelings that the partners have for one another, but they are just as important since they provide predictability and stability (Allan, 1995). Relationships can succeed or fail as much because they become disorganized as because the partners stop liking one another as people. Suitor (1991), for example, reported that arguments over distribution of household labour were significantly disruptive of marital satisfaction. These arguments are as likely to create disaffection as is the simple decrease in emotional attachment to the partner. In perhaps unwitting ways that we have not connected together yet, we have all heard people complain about relational organization, and it is about chores or division of labour even though people complain that 'The relationship was too intense' or 'The relationship wasn't going anywhere' or 'We liked one another, but the *relationship* just didn't work out'. These sound like comments on the internal dynamics alone, but they actually reflect social/normative expectations about the way a relationship *should* look and be arranged. It thus incidentally reflects the indirect effects of outsiders and their social/normative influence. Even when people create stories about the relationship (Koenig Kellas, 2005), such stories are only partly for internal consumption and may also be made available to outsiders in a way similar to that discussed in the previous chapter concerning breakdown (Grave-dressing processes).

These organizational predictabilities help to explain why breakdown, development and repair of relationships are disruptive, not only to individuals but also to other people outside the pairing (a divorcing couple's kids, parents, networks). The routine organization of a relationship necessarily also involves other people, who may play a part in various social activities or relational formats that we enjoy. 'The family', for example, connects in multiple ways with other folks; the parents and children who form a nuclear family also work with other people and are therefore necessarily connected with an extended family network, as well as with other parents, and such organizations as schools, as well as neighbourhoods and society as a whole.

Recognizing two people as 'a couple'

One required element of relational organization is making it consistent with available social forms that these other people recognize, for example, acting like 'a couple', and of course this is another way of saying that 'the personal is the social' or that we derive our experience of a relationship in part from the fact that other people can recognize and support its form (Milardo & Wellman, 1992). The couple's attempt to 'become a socially recognized unit' is not an automatic consequence of their liking one another, and the couple has to do work in the network and in the social context in order to be recognized and accepted by other people as possessing a relationship of a particular type (as the recent arguments about 'gay marriage' are all too obviously indicating at gale force; if a society takes the view that gay partners cannot 'marry', then the couple's own personal preferences run into that social brick wall). For instance, as a courtship becomes more intense, so the couple will withdraw from contact with friends to some extent (Milardo, Johnson & Huston, 1983). If the friends know about the courtship then the withdrawal is unlikely to cause offence, though sometimes such withdrawals are secretive at first or at least not very obvious (Baxter & Widenmann, 1993).

Even the honeymoon has this kind of role in helping the couple to withdraw from society in order to carry out a role transition from unwed to married (Hagestad & Smyer, 1982): the honeymoon helps the couple make the important transition from one role or couple type (engaged) to another (married) by having them pull away from their normal range of associates for a while and go somewhere special. When they return, they come back in a different status (as a coupled marital pair). We might think of this honeymoon ritual as having just the function of allowing the couple to enjoy one another in private for a while, but sociologists have interpreted it as serving a social reorganizational function also. Immediately after being formally joined by the marriage ceremony, the couple go away from all the friends and relatives who knew them as 'unjoined' individuals. When they return, they return as a socially recognized couple and the absence created by the honeymoon period gives everyone else the chance to adjust to the transformation.

Of course, for gay and lesbian couples such transitions have not been socially approved and so this network/social context presents the couple with an extra emotional issue to resolve (Huston & Schwartz, 1995). For instance, Weston (1991) indicates that homosexual couples may be estranged from their 'blood family', who reject the couple's orientation, and for this reason homosexual unions are often celebrated with family-of-choice present but the 'blood family' absent. The recent recognition of same-sex marriages in some countries now allows this same status transition to people who have previously been denied it (Lannutti, 2005).

LOOK OUT FOR THIS IN THE MEDIA

Find a quiz or a TV discussion on relationships where your total at the end is used to tell you whether your relationship is 'good' or 'bad'. Consider whether this is a social force on the way in which you understand your relationship. Is your relationship really good enough? Did you make that decision or did somebody else?

Other factors that influence a couple's satisfaction also depend on socially recognized standards for internal organization of the relationship. Such factors could be, for instance, knowledge of the average statistics for frequency of sexual intercourse, which may affect the partners' views of whether they are behaving 'normally' (Simmel, 1950). Other examples come from societal definitions of the 'proper' distribution of labour in marriage, good relationship conduct as contained, for example, in magazine agony columns or articles about relationships whether in men's magazines or women's magazines (Duran & Prusank, 1997). These forces in society essentially instruct or guide people on the ways in which relationships may (or even must) be 'properly' conducted.

If a society generally promotes the view of gender that supposes that the 'good husband' carries out certain duties whereas the 'good wife' performs other quite distinct duties, then the couple who arrange things in that differentiated way will feel that their marriage is ideal in that respect (Allen & Walker, 2000). But, if the society generally expects both partners to share all duties equally, then the same couple (or one member of it) will feel aggrieved and dissatisfied. The difference in the two cases is not the actual work or duties carried out but the context of attitudes in which they are carried out (Allan, 1993). Furthermore, what counts as a perfectly acceptable distribution of labour in the twenty-first century bears very little resemblance to that in the ideal marriage in the nineteenth century. Couples from the two times who felt perfectly contented would probably look on each other's marriages with disbelief and even shock.

Also in recent times, the issues of dual earning couples have become very significant (Allan & Gerstner, 2006; Crouter & Helms-Erickson, 2000) and marital satisfaction must be understood in terms of its connection to the experience of work 'outside' the relationship as well as in terms of the experiences 'inside' the marriage on its own. Clearly daily experience of work spills over into the home life twice as often when both spouses bring home their concerns from work and when a society (via email and mobile phones, for example) makes that so much more possible than it used to be (and in some cases, companies now expect more or less constant availability from their managers and executives, not excluding weekends and vacations). 'Spillover' effects are partly the responsibility of the individual who brings the work home, and partly may be assigned to the way in which society creates expectations about individuals and the relationship of their work to home life, especially now that mobile phones, the Internet, telephone answering machines, and instant messaging make such spillover more likely (see Chapter 6). Bad effects of spillover are thus only partly attributable to the internal dynamic nature of a relationship and must also be assigned in part to the nature of society in modern times.

Social norms and expectations

Thus part of the feeling that a marriage is working well depends on what the partners *expect* relative to social norms established by other people rather than just on what they actually do, and expectations come partly from the beliefs that society has about marriages. Zimmer (1986), for example, indicates that the very prospect of marriage causes strong anxieties about the stability and success of the marriage, with partners getting cold feet and going through a turbulent phase just at, or after, the point where they have decided to get married. Often couples doubt the possibility of being able to have both security and excitement in the same relationship. Yet partners can see how their marriage matches up to society's ideals for the relationship. If they see themselves carrying out their roles well, then they will be satisfied. Dissatisfaction can be created by partners' feelings that their relationship does not live up to the societal ideal. Most of us are guided in our feelings and behaviour by such influences, but some people actually take the lead strongly from social norms. Norms show people where they stand and increase their satisfaction with the relationship since norms make it easier for people to know what is required of them, but this is another way of saying that our embeddedness in a social network gives us guidelines for our own expectations. Once more, the personal is social (Milardo & Wellman, 1992).

Such *exogenous* (or external) factors as social norms matter as much as the factors we usually assume to be significant (i.e., the endogenous or emotional factors) in marital satisfaction. The partners' feelings for one another, their communication style, and their relative power are examples of *endogenous* (or internal) factors. The three (feeling, communication, and power) really represent one and the same thing: expression of affection is done through communication, and power is a communicative concept, too. When we talk of power in a relationship, we are describing partly the way in which one person's communications affect the other person and partly the way in which that other person responds. As Kelvin (1977) points out, power does not 'reside in' a person: you do not have power unless someone else treats you as if you do. Power is thus a *relational* concept and depends on the acceptance of a person's power ploys by the person to whom they are directed or by others with some institutional authority. In the case of violent abuse, for example, the abused partner may be quietly constrained to accept whatever the abuser does because institutions like the church encourage the view that one must accept both the 'for better' and the 'for worse' aspects of a marriage (West, 1995). Thus a lack of social support translates into a force that deprives a woman of real choice and becomes ultimately one extra source of the abuser's power (Foley, 2006b). In part, these factors reflect the way in which any new couple is organized within a network context of expectations and social norms for behaviour in certain types of relationships.

LISTEN IN ON YOUR OWN LIFE

What rituals do you have in your family? For example, what particular rituals/routines does your family adopt at religious or social holidays? Take a close look at what you actually do and how any practical activities or rituals sustain your relationship. How do these differ

(Continued)

(Continued)

from the rituals of your friends' families and how do you think they may serve to build your sense of specialness or community member-ship in your own family? (Notice that your knowledge of these rituals acts as a boundary to outsiders who do not know what they are or how to do them.)

Do you have routines of (daily/weekly/regular) contact with family members? Which family members do you contact most often, and which ones contact you most often? How do you find out what is going on in the family? Who is the 'kin-keeper' who brings you up-to-date on everyone else's life?

Take a look at Bruess & Hoefs (2006) on family Christmas rituals and Sahlstein (2006a) on kin-keeping and then reflect on how other people's behaviour influences your sense of what sort of relationship you have with a target individual.

Organizing the couple's new connections

External norms and forms of relationships tend in most societies to favour mar-riage as an institution that fits a formally recognized rule structure, and as a cou-ple enters that state the above organizational changes are matched by the ways that the relationship is treated by other people.

Once a couple is committed long-term, the partners effectively join together two previously unconnected families and acquire themselves a set of in-laws, not just restricted to fathers-, mothers-, brothers-, and sisters-in-law but a whole bunch of other associated relatives of various extents of unfamiliarity, not to say oddity. Although you now have a degree of choice over the partner whom you marry, you don't have any choice at all about the rich variety of other souls and genetic deviants that come along with the partner in this way and filmmakers have found many ways to draw comedy from the situation with such films as *Meet the Fokkers* (2004) and *Guess Who* (2005). Serious social points have also been made about the joining of families in such old classic films as *Guess Who's Coming To Dinner* (1967).

Morr-Serewicz (2006) has carefully analysed the nature of the in-law relation-ship but the topic has been surprisingly under-investigated so far, with other ram-ifications of role changes as you become an involuntary aunt- or uncle-in-law, acquire a new set of grandparents, and are adopted into the – probably quite strange – rituals and styles of this second, acquired, family, and appears to be a rich area for future study. What we do know about the in-law relationship is that it is usually perceived as a relatively awkward one in a typical case, and when people get along well with the in-laws they usually brag about it or at least remark on the fact as if it is noteworthy and arrestingly unusual, at least in Western culture. As Morr-Serewicz (2006) points out, there are some cultures where a person is not so much adopted by the spouse's family as actually becoming one of its members, and gives away the rights of membership of the previous family of origin. Thus in some parts of India, the bride is literally given away by her original family to become a full member of her husband's family from thenceforward.

LOOK OUT FOR THIS IN THE MEDIA

Go and see a movie representation of network or cultural influences/ other relational influences on the dyad. Some examples of this are *Boys Don't Cry*; *Meet the Parents*; *Meet the Fockers*; *Guess Who*; *Guess Who's Coming To Dinner*; *Bend it like Beckham*.

In the West, the in-laws, especially the mother-in-law, have historically been regarded with apprehension and as the butt of jokes. With the in-laws – sometimes quite reasonably regarded as 'outlaws' – comes a host of organizational and hierarchical problems: with which set of parents (and therefore of in-laws, for one partner) does the couple spend Thanksgiving, holidays, or Christmas? What does the couple do when it receives entirely contradictory advice from the two sets of parents/in-laws about houses, vacation places, jobs, marriage and the raising of children? Although these dilemmas are of course resolvable, they do put the couple in at least a momentary bind because they triangulate two partners: they place one person or both people in the couple between two other sources of influence that are pushing or pulling in different directions. The awkwardness of the in-law relationship comes in part from this – and triangulation is a source of other relating difficulty to which we will devote Chapter 7.

Overlooked so far in the exploration of the in-law relationships acquired by marriage are the other roles that can be likewise acquired at the same time. For example, you can become an aunt- or uncle-in-law and can develop fondness for, and closeness with, the children of a spouse's siblings. Pleasure and role in these forms can be a further loss arising from any later divorce, in that someone may have enjoyed being an aunt to the children of her husband's brother and may have particularly enjoyed gift-giving at Christmas and birthdays and may subsequently regret the loss of that role once their own marriage is dissolved (Rollie, 2005).

Adding children to the relationship

At marriage, the members of the couple immediately acquire these new relationships and roles but in the course of time, their own dyad could be modified by the addition of their own children – and in some cases marriage later in life brings along the pre-existing children of a partner who has been in a committed relationship previously. The presence of children is a significant influence on couple satisfaction. Many married couples eventually have children and more and more same-sex partnerships choose to adopt or have children too (Allen & Walker, 2000; Suter, 2006). Whereas we think of children as 'bundles of joy', the transition to parenthood is one of the greatest stressors of a relationship. Satisfaction with marriage declines sharply after this transition and conflict equally sharply increases (Veroff et al., 2000). In part this may be due to the disruption of sleep that occurs as a result of infant care but is also partly because of the extra *relational organizational* problems associated with the project of becoming a family. The couple will need to alter many of its previous routines including sleep patterns and availability to deal with illness or (later) school commitments for the child, also, which may disrupt – but will certainly impinge upon – work commitments, time and responsibility, requiring adjustment of the organization of life and giving a whole new dimension to the 'spillover' effects of work and home life previously discussed (Crouter &Helms-Erickson, 2000).

In addition, as has been pointed out by researchers in several different places (e.g. Powell & Afifi, 2005), the recent social trend towards adoptions, remarriage and blending of previously separate families has created a kind of relationship which people have found immediate difficulties in performing or in having accepted by outsiders and institutions such as schools. The topic of such blending is a whole issue in its own right (Ganong, Coleman & Hans, 2006) and this book can only mention it briefly. Its effects and difficulties, however, evidently reflect the general principles I've been introducing here and are in very many ways routine and organizational in nature, not only dealing with internal organization of the relationship but its organized connection with exterior network forces also. Powell & Afifi (2005) focus on the adjustment issues that adoptees experience, but there are also issues of 'loss' felt by adoptees as they reach adulthood and wish to know more about their biological origin. The adoptive role involves uncertainty management and ambiguous loss because adoptees experience uncertainty about their own identity and there are emotional responses that are shaped by the familial, perceptual, and situational factors that compose them.

Adoptees and parents both need to organize their lives to confront these extra ambiguities and uncertainties and also to develop stories that project an identity as a family to both members and outsiders (Koenig Kellas, 2005). As Koenig Kellas (2005) and Koenig Kellas & Trees (2006) have noted, the process of family storytelling is important to the creation of a sense of family identity (which in terms of the present chapter is an identity told to others in the network also, as well as within the family itself). The communication – both between family members and between the family as an entity and the outside world – is an important element of a family's sense of identity and acceptance by other people (Koenig Kellas, 2005). There is important sense-making occurring in any narration of family history as well as the fact that family stories involve particular people known to everyone in the audience, namely family characters. Koenig Kellas & Trees (2006) demonstrate that narratives are particularly helpful for people trying to make sense of difficult or traumatic experiences. During storytelling, families engage in joint sense-making about the family and the meaning of a family experience, such as adoption of children or divorce. Of course in doing this they also share separate versions of the story and the individual conclusions that they have reached about the meaning of the story.

A similar set of issues arises for stepfamilies, though the focus here is usually on the current childhood experience. Afifi (2003) examined the communication patterns that foster and ameliorate triangulation in stepfamilies. She found that children feel caught between their custodial and noncustodial parents and the parents and/or stepparents feel caught between the children in the stepfamily. The author discusses triangulation, and the greater complexity of relationship organization that is required when family members negotiate new role status and membership outside of the family of origin. The author notes that the cohesiveness of the parent–child bond is related to permeability of communication boundaries and rule management systems.

People experience some difficulty in deciding what is appropriate and inappropriate for communication in this setting, and it seems to come down to the question of whether they regard their stepfamily as part of their immediate group or not. Basically, the report confirms that when you get into a new relationship you have to work out privacy barriers and that people will experience anxiety levels around the difficulties of making those decisions. Again, then, in these particular sets of circumstances, the relationship becomes an organizational problem for the people in it and does so partly because of the triangulation noted previously, where other sources of pressure impinge on a specific dyad within the family and partly because the addition of descendent children transforms the couple into a different sort of organizational structure. However, it is now attached to other groups and families, is a family of its own, and the family is a microcosmic network of the sort just discussed: it consists of lots of relationships that affect the conduct of other relationships. So we will now look at 'families' next.

FAMILIES AND NETWORKS

A family is a set of relationships determined by biology, adoption, marriage, and, in some societies, social designation and existing even in the absence of contact or effective involvement and, in some cases, even after the death of certain members. This implies that the boundaries of a family cannot be described by an observer: one must ask the respondent because family, according to this definition, is subjective' (Bedford & Blieszner, 1997: 256). In 2000, the same authors (page 158) indicated that 'the term "marriage" includes intimate relationships between gay and lesbian couples and between common law heterosexual couples.

Actually, 'the family' (defining that more or less how you like, since, as the above quotation observes, researchers cannot agree on the definition) represents an intriguing collection of interacting networks and mini-networks. Although 'a family' sounds like an entity with its own will and energy, actually it is a label given to a collection of individuals with lots of separate connections. In a family, every member has some sort of personal relationship with every other member and so in a paradigmatic, advertisers' dream family of two attractive parents with two attractive kids of complementary sexes, each person has three individual dyadic relationships (e.g., Child 1–Father, Child 1–Mother, Child 1–Child 2; Father–Child 1, Father–Child 2, Father–Mother; etc.) and all of these occur very often in the sight of, and with the knowledge of, the other folks. Siblings may talk to their parents about each other, or may conspire with one another against the parents themselves (Nicholson, 2006), and parents may disagree about how to educate a particular child.

TRY THIS OUT

Before you read the rest of this chapter think about the ways in which:

- a family is 'organized' by its routines (how does your family 'do dinner'; 'do vacations'; 'do birthdays'?);
- a family is like a network (how does your relationship with one parent affect that parent's relationship with the other parent?);
- a family intersects with other sorts of relationships (neighbours, schools, other families and so on);
- family interior life is responsive to outside forces.

What sort of picture comes to mind when you imagine a *typical* family? Two youngish, attractive, well-groomed, smiling parents with 2.4 happy children driving in an average-sized shiny new car to an ordinary supermarket to buy their lo-carb health-food, right? The advertisers and politicians love to represent families that way, even though some estimates are that only 10 per cent of families are actually like that (Demo, Allen & Fine, 2000). Even average people in ordinary families like to think of families as typified that way.

There are many aspects to family functioning that fascinate researchers, too. Relationships in families (particularly as they form the basis for a child's beliefs about self or about relationships with other people in general: DeHart, Pelham & Tennen, 2006; Feeney, 2006; Kitzmann & Cohen, 2003) raise a number of particularly interesting issues for us. Not least is the recent reconceptualization of the notion of 'family' away from the above myth to include single-parent families (Aquilino, 1996; Booth, 2006), co-parenting after divorce (Adamson & Pasley, 2006), families where one parent lives elsewhere and is not involved in child custody (Rollie, 2005, 2006), families where both parents are the same sex (Suter, 2006), and families where parents do not marry but instead decide to cohabit (Sher, 1996). Many people also choose to stay single or create blended families that combine persons previously in other marriages (Coleman & Ganong, 1995; Ganong et al., 2006) or may adopt (actually a pretty huge number of adoptions takes place every year: http://www.calib.com/naic/statistics.htm cited in Powell & Afifi, 2005).

Thus the idea of 'a family' can be represented in different ways and scholars still argue about the best way (Galvin, 2004). Fisher (1996) differentiates between the *traditional nuclear family* (two married parents and their kids); *single parent family* (an unmarried, separated, divorced, or widowed parent with kids); and *extended family* (consisting of three generations in the same household, usually grandparents, parents, children). The extended family is a family style that is very commonly found in the same household in some cultures. *Kin networks* are particularly common in African-American communities where families are 'organized around large informal networks of blood relatives and also may be long-term friends but who are considered family members' (Fisher, 1996: 314). *Blended families* are formed where a single parent joins a household with another adult who may already be a parent or might be child-free.

Thus, in case it is not clear from the above, the defining characteristic of 'a family' comes down to only one thing: it is a transgenerational concept that involves the presence of at least one child who is the responsibility of at least one adult. This, however, is a limiting concept because we should not forget that as time passes so children take over responsibility for care of their ageing parents (Bedford & Blieszner, 2000), and this reformulation of family *structure* is enormously important in the middle and later years of the lives of adult children and one that changes both power dynamics and sense of self (of all parties) in significant ways, especially if a grown up 'child' has to become the representative of an ageing 'parent' in medical encounters – for example, taking over the discussion of the patient's personal and private details because the parent has become incapable of understanding medical instructions or gets easily confused about the details of a medical regimen (Petronio, Sargent, Andea, Reganis & Cichocki, 2004).

A general point that is clear enough from the above is well recognized by family experts: that a family – however it is made up – is not a simple unit but a complex of relationships between individuals (Fisher, 1996) and that these individuals have many types of relational experiences outside their family, also. These other, external forces can be equally influential on all sorts of things, such as attitudes to self or the way one behaves in connection with drugs or sexuality. In seeking to understand the family we need to see 'it' as both a context for personal relationships (e.g., family atmosphere provides a context for a child's growth of self-esteem or sense of gender; Allen & Walker, 2000) *and* as a set of relationships that all impinge on the individual *and* as something that functions in a variety of social networks and cultural contexts. As with other relationships involving people who are growing, learning, developing, changing or ageing the relationships in a family change over time. Babies become children, children become adolescents, adolescents become adults, parents become grandparents, and adult children may take over the role of caring for those who once took the role of caring for them (Cooney, 2000).

In particular it is short-sighted to view the parent–child relationship from a point that sees the parent and child as independent and different when in fact they are mutually interdependent and increasingly similar as time goes by (Blieszner, 2006). Only in a trivial sense is the relationship between these relatives the same across time; in the non-trivial sense the relationship is mightily different as a result of the changes in age, and concurrent changes in responsibility and style (Pearson, 1996). Thus families are essentially entities that are dynamically *changing all the time* and are not fixed entities. If families could never change then there would not be any family therapists, yet families can not only be dysfunctional but they can even create problems for their individual members. To illustrate the network of interdependencies and before we look at more extensive cases, consider how families support their members in dysfunctionality.

Systemic interdependence

Relationships are not all good for people all the time and families can cause people problems. When we observe such problems as alcoholism or drug abuse then it is a pretty natural assumption that this is a problem of an individual – and we are at best likely to see the family as the unfortunate people who have to deal with this person. However, some therapists see such problems as alcoholism and drug abuse as *family* problems, or individual psychoses as generated by bad relationships with parents or see problem individuals as representing and acting out symptoms of the family's distress (Wright & Wright, 1995). The Systems Theory approach to families sees these groups as interacting units that keep one another functioning in the ways that they do, even suggesting that 'individuals with problems' are symptoms produced by the interaction of that system. For example, a troubled adolescent is not a troubled *person* but a signal of trouble in the family as a whole. Some students immediately see this as a really interesting idea and some see it as ridiculous. Make up your mind as you read on.

LOOK OUT FOR THIS IN THE MEDIA

Watch for stories in the media that indicate a systemic interdependence of family members, either as a unit dealing with problems such as alcohol or drug abuse or as a 'community' coping together with a serious chronic health problem suffered by one particular member. In what ways do these stories represent the difficulties of one person alone as being essentially 'shared problems'? What do you make of the idea that coping is essentially *a communal* process rather than just being an individual one? Discuss this question and your examples in class.

How can an individual's alcoholism or drug abuse possibly have anything to do with family process? The heavy (problem) drinker may not merely be an individual who happens to have impact on a family (i.e., it is not adequate simply to see the drinker as 'the problem'). Although obviously there are such one-way impacts (e.g., on children of parents who drink excessively, or a dysfunctional child who 'drives a parent to drink'; Orford, 2001), there are some problems with this kind of interpretation. For one, a large proportion of families are quite resistant to improvements in the family member with the problem. Spouses themselves sometimes break down when their partner's drinking problem is cured (Orford & O'Reilly, 1981). Also partners sometimes describe 'the other person when drunk' in terms more favourable than they describe 'the other person when sober'. In particular, wives often describe their 'drunk husbands' as more masculine and dominant (which they happen to regard as attractive characteristics) than they describe their 'sober husbands'. Orford, Oppenheimer, Egert, Hensman & Guthrie (1976) even found that unfavourable 'when sober' perceptions of a spouse were predictive of poor outcome for the drinking problem over the subsequent twelve months. If we prefer the behaviour of our partners when they are drunk (for example, they may be extremely funny when drunk but very depressed and withdrawn when sober), it is very unlikely we shall truly support their attempts to stay sober.

The feelings of one family member towards another who has a problem can help to sustain the problem and interfere with attempts to solve it. This kind of systemic interdependence essentially comes down to a relational process that 'influences individuals' self-definitions and conduct in interpersonal contexts' (Wright & Wright, 1995: 128). One feature of the situation where a parent is alcoholic is that the spouse often employs a variety of tactics for denying or minimizing the problem or concealing it from others. This typically involves the discouragement of children from acknowledging or responding to the problem, whether by parents passively modelling denial and overlooking or joking about 'Daddy's Little Lapses', or actively by instructing the children to adjust to the alcoholic parent ('Leave her be', 'Deal with it', 'He's had a bad day and needs to unwind'). When one parent is incapable and the other is pretending nothing is wrong, the children are soon discouraged from talking about the problem and can become convinced that nothing really is wrong, or if it is, that the problem is something to do with *them* or is somehow 'their fault'. Such children can lose their trust of other people, do not talk openly to others and often lose the ability to express emotion clearly. In short the children are pulled into a complex family game and become altered themselves as a result of the roles that they adopt to keep the family functioning. Once again, then, this makes the point of the present chapter that individual pairings and relationships work only in a context of other relationships and this network affects the pairings on top of any internal dynamics that occur in the partnership.

Another example of a general systemic interdependence in relational processes has been observed in people who have problems with drugs (Lewis & McAvoy, 1984). Partners and children of opiate abusers, such as heroin addicts, are frequently called on to structure their lives in a way that, as it were, depends on the addiction of a family member. For example, the partner and children may spend the day routinely stealing money to pay for the drug. As I have been pointing out, routines of life are important to us as frameworks in which to conduct ourselves. Suppose the addiction is treated. How does that alter the way in which the addict's partner and children need to spend their routine day, and does that change their attitudes to themselves? In a sense, they are no longer needed: their functions have become redundant. As we might predict, these people frequently resist the therapeutic exercise and lead the addict back to the addiction, thus re-establishing their own routine usefulness to the addicted family member (Lewis & McAvoy, 1984). In such cases, treatment for opiate abuse often needs to include treatment for the abuser's family. Treatments strive to provide some alternative structure and routine for the abuser's family so that the addict's return to normality does not simply empty their lives together (Lewis & McAvoy, 1984). Wright & Wright (1995) conclude their review of the evidence by seeing such systemic interdependence as a relational activity that does not necessarily imply any underlying individual pathology – it is, instead, an adaptive means of making sense of what is going on and keeping life stable for those in the unhappy situation. In brief, the participants adapt and play out 'situated identities' based on the context provided by their human relationships in the family. Thus Wright & Wright conclude: 'relationship processes influence individuals' self-definition and conduct in interpersonal contexts' (1995: 128).

   As another set of examples of the ways in which the personal is social, this line of work could hardly be more compelling and in later chapters we will also consider more fully the ways in which an acquired disability or chronic illness becomes a family matter and is not merely an issue for the individual to cope with. For the moment I will just point out, for you to reflect on, the fact that important recent scholarship has drawn the attention to the value of looking at coping as a shared activity and not as primarily an individual psychological or unidirectional phenomenon, that is to say towards an interdependent process that is also relational (Lyons, Mickelson, Sullivan & Coyne, 1998). Lyons et al. (1998: 580) note the ways in which coping with illness involves 'the pooling of resources and efforts of several individuals (e.g., couples, families, or communities) to confront adversity'. Accordingly, the difficulties are evaluated and treated as 'our problem and our responsibility' (Lyons et al., 1998). Management of stress, therefore, becomes a family matter and can be distinguished from *social support* and *individual coping*.

KEEP A JOURNAL: FAMILY LIFE WHEN AWAY FROM HOME

Keep a journal that records the number of times that you are in contact with members of your family and the level of interest that you have in the material which is discussed during such contact. Make a specific record of how much of the time is spent talking about other family members. Also, keep a note of the specific members of the family with whom you communicate, and the relative frequency of each one.

   When you have drawn up your list, look over it and reflect on what it illustrates about the 'control' of family information, and the ways in which your relationships with different family members are constituted or constructed. How different is the present pattern of communication and information flow from the patterns that pre-existed the time when you left home?

Happy families?

A cosy myth in our culture is that most families are enjoyable and safe environments in which to live or grow up or learn about gender (Allen & Walker, 2000).

Our adherence to the pastime of keeping family albums and tracing family trees testifies to most people's wish to belong to and remain in a family and the fact is that all people take part of their identity from seeing themselves as a part of a larger (family) community through their life. Yet, surprising as it sounds, outside of the armed forces, the family is the most physically violent group or institution that a typical person is likely to encounter (Straus, 1985)! The term 'intimate terrorism' has been used to describe some husband–wife relationships (Foley, 2006b), and we are more likely to see, commit, or be a victim of violence within the family than in any other setting (Eiskovits, Edelson, Gettmann & Sela-Amit, 1991). Indeed, it has long been recognized that we are more likely to be murdered, beaten, or physically abused by our spouse, mother, father, or siblings than by a random stranger (Straus, 1990; Straus & Gelles, 1986), and sexual abuse by a family member is the primary instance of such abuse in most relevant statistics (Coleman & May-Chahal, 2003).

Equally, families are not particularly stable. At least 50 per cent of all first marriages end in divorce and about a quarter of those who marry today will be divorced before their seventh anniversary (Notarius, 1996). There now seems to be a trend away from long-term commitment and towards serial monogamy (Vanzetti & Duck, 1996), but in fact, divorce is now doing the work that death did 200 years ago (Duck, in press SAGE CA, see refs): before recent times, most marriages were ended by the death of one spouse before the 15th anniversary (Stone, 1979). By the time they are 18 years old, one out of every two children will experience some of their upbringing in a single parent household (Cherlin, 1992; Glick, 1989). Furthermore, it is now much more common than previously for spouses to live apart in commuter relationships (Rohlfing, 1995; Sahlstein, 2006b).

Lastly, while the Victorian family was something of an emotional iceberg, modern families are mythologized as emotional refuges and strongholds. These shifting demands couple with new economic and social conditions to place new strains on the family as a unit (Bass & Stein, 1997). Spouses are now asked to be satisfying lovers, caring friends, medical superintendents, financial providers, and even mutual therapists. Many are also faced with managing the stresses of family and two careers in the same household (Crouter & Helms-Erickson, 2000). At first, we might see all this as a welcome development, but the increased importance of these competing roles has the paradoxical effect of making it more likely that the members of the family will fall short of the emotional demands placed upon them (Sher, 1996). Some scholars have presented a radical critique of the family that argues that when it functions best, the family is the ultimate destroyer of people by social means (Braverman, 1991). It draws people together through a sense of their own incompleteness, it impedes the development of an individual's identity, it exerts too strong a social control over children and it indoctrinates family members with elaborate and unnecessary taboos (Fisher, 1996). Obviously other views of the family exist in the face of these opinions, and the family could still buy whole-grain breakfast cereals, watch DVDs together and talk to one another often on mobile phones, and help to develop one another's well-being (Segrin, 2006).

However, from all the above, we should recognize that because a 'family' is made up of many interacting and reacting systems and subsystems the members do not interact in equivalent ways. For example, one parent may prefer Child A and treat Child B less well; that difference in itself may influence the behaviour of each child as a growing individual and of each child towards the other. It may have impact upon the development of each child's self-esteem as well as its inter-actions with each parent. If one child in a family has a disability (Lyons & Meade, 1995), then this may cause the parents to behave differently towards the several children in the family, and if the disability is severe then the other children may get very little attention at all.

Finally, parents are obviously not the only models for children; children are exposed also to the behaviours of grandparents, aunts and uncles, teachers and neighbours, to say nothing of friends' parents and the children's own friends (Parke & O'Neil, 1997). Thus a family is more than a pair of parents, and as a child develops, so the social world is increasingly made up of more than just the imme-diate family anyway. Nonetheless, the family remains a major source of the child's learning about human relationships, both through the child's experiences in the family and its observation of the family. Indeed Lindsey, Colwell, Frabutt & Mackinnon-Lewis (2006) concluded from an investigation of family antecedents of children's friendship, that characteristics of family relationships have implications for the impact of the family on children's development. No understanding of indi-vidual behaviour can be divorced from relationships shared with others outside of the family or from the interconnections within the family that develop between parent and child.

Parents and peers as influences on kids

There are other issues in human relationships in the family that are worth attend-ing to beyond the way the adults relate to one another in a couple or deal with the ways in which they relate together or separately to the children. Some issues here are the ways in which children perceive parental affection (everyone seems to feel that the parents preferred their sibling!) but also illustrate the ways in which par-ents' relationships with children affect what the children learn, not only about their self-image but also about such things as drugs, tobacco, alcohol and sex.

Floyd & Morman (2005) investigated the naïve theory of affection that many children hold assuming that parents' affection is something for which they must compete against their siblings, even though naturally enough, parents do not view their own affection this way. Sons tended to see their father's affection distributed unequally and as favouring other siblings, whereas the fathers themselves reported being more affectionate with their sons than their sons reported them being. Similar results are found for mothers and daughters (Miller-Day, 2004) with several daughters reporting resentment of the selective way they were treated by their mother. More broadly, Repinski & Zook (2005) compared the significance of closeness in adolescents' relationships with parents and friends and found that although the type of closeness in the two cases is different, both sorts of relationship are influential on self-esteem. All in all, though parents seem to be roughly treated in children's recollections, with the notable tendency to be recalled as favouring one child or another, the parents do not typically agree with that perception.

However, self-esteem is not all that is learned in childhood and adolescence. Both families and other peer relationships influence much other learning. Heisler (2005) examined young adult student–mother–father reports about their conversations concerning sexuality. Although most people reported discussing sexuality with their parent or child, the topics discussed between parents and offspring were most usually restricted to relationships, morals, and pregnancy, and most people relied on friends as their main source of experiential (and personally more important) sexual information (the 'how to?' and 'what's it like?' stuff).

In related fashion, Miller-Day & Dodd (2004) explored parent–offspring talk about drugs and tobacco and found that the most common sorts of topics were moral ones, and also that, if they were specifically targeted towards the topic alone, then such conversations tended to be less effective than discussions of the topic which were more naturally embedded in everyday discourse. Miller-Day (2002) also found that significantly more adolescents felt closest to and preferred talking with their mothers about risky topics than with other family members. Even elsewhere within the family, Milevsky (2005) shows, not surprisingly, that siblings are a source of information about self and other topics, and that there is a compensatory effect of social support received from siblings relative to psychological adjustment in emerging adulthood. Sibling support compensated for low parental and peer support, in particular in relation to depression and self-esteem. In short, then, parents' relationships with their children are differently recalled by the parent and the child, but are in any case recalled, and have their effects, only in the context of other relationships that will also have an influence.

To some parents' concern and regret, they are not the only sources of influence on the children about other matters than self-esteem. Children are increasingly influenced by their peers and friends as they age, and also by sources of information that can be obtained from the Internet, music or radio and TV. Such interactions are sources of self-esteem and self-worth, too. Few teenagers look to their parents for advice on dress or music, for example, and 'hanging out with the wrong crowd' has long been suggested to be a bad influence on adolescent habits. Lloyd & Anthony (2003) conducted a longitudinal study of youths growing up in an urban area in order to discover the relationship between levels of parental supervision and levels of affiliation with delinquent and deviant peers. Although there were major influences from hanging out with delinquent crowds, maintenance of parental supervision created important reductions in association with deviant peers, even in urban and socially disadvantaged communities.

Simons-Morton, Haynie, Crump, Eitel & Saylor (2001) also found that social influences outside the family can promote or discourage substance use and that 'problem behaving friends' (i.e. those who were involved in drugs or tobacco use) exerted an influence on an individual's choices, such that peer influence is associated with substance use. Miller-Day (1998) gave such evidence a more precise relational and communicative edge, when she found that adolescents were often placed in great difficulty when offered drugs or tobacco by peers, because refusals carried strong *relational* implications. Being put into the position of having to refuse can affect people, increase the risks of disappointing a reference group, and lead to a consequent increase in negative responses, resentment and the apparent violation of relational expectancies that assume that adolescents will usually do the same things as their friends: 'The risk of disappointing the reference group carries a threat to the maintenance of the relationship and may violate the norms of the relationship' (Miller-Day, 1998: 363). Once again, then we see the importance of attending to the relational context, and the impact of other network members on a particular individual's behaviour – effects which extend even to the breakup of the basic family structure, also.

LISTEN IN ON YOUR OWN LIFE

How frequently do you discuss with other people such things as health issues, relational standards of behaviour, or decisions about your own personal life? How many of these conversations serve to provide some sort of 'benchmark' for your own behaviour on the topic discussed? In what ways do such conversations affect your future actions?

Give some thought to the question of why you would ask people about these issues of *personal* behaviour.

The disorganizing effects of family breakup and reconstitution

All through this chapter I have written about distressed families that stay together nevertheless. Many couples, however, get divorced (although an increasing trend is for couples to avoid marriage in the first place; Bedford & Blieszner, 2000). What 'causes' divorce? Answers range from demographic factors, like race and religion, to personality factors like achievement motivation and extroversion, to interactional factors and relational processes (Rodrigues et al., 2006). However, divorce is not an event for which a simple cause should be sought but is a transitional process (Chapter 3), and researchers now look for those causal factors which combine to fuel the relentless, unforgiving development of that process. Divorcing often takes a long time because there is more to it than just 'falling out of love' (Fine & Harvey, 2006) – and in line with what I'm proposing in this chapter, I want to build on what I said in Chapter 3 focusing on the organizational issues and the fallout effects on other people when one pair dissolves.

There are at least three parts to marriage that have to be unpicked in divorcing (Hagestad & Smyer, 1982). As we saw in discussing courtship, partners have not only to love one another (one part) but to be successful in meshing their activities and daily routines together (second part). As their relationship becomes well-bonded and the routines, work, or division of labour in the relationship are sorted out, so the partners develop attachment to the role of spouse – the 'being a husband or a wife' (third part). These three things (love for partner, attachment to established routines, attachment to the marital role) all are built up in courtship and marriage. All have to be disassembled during divorcing where the last element (legal commitment) is dissolved (fourth part). There are many types of divorce that have been identified (Hagestad & Smyer, 1982). The first distinction is between orderly and disorderly divorce, but again, this distinction plays to the social expectations for relationships held by other people outside the dyad and concerns the organization of the relationship both internally and for other people.

There is only one form of *orderly divorce*, namely one where the partners detach themselves successfully not only from their feelings for one another but from their attachment to the role of 'husband' or 'wife', from their involvement in an established set of daily routines, and from the legal role. They have to decide that they do not love their partner, do not want to be 'a spouse', do not miss the routines of their daily life together, but do want to be legally divorced.

Disorderly divorces are those where at least one aspect of these disengagements is not successfully completed. For instance, one partner may stay in love with the 'ex', or may find it impossible to adjust to 'not being married'. Hagestad & Smyer (1982) list seven types of disorderly divorce. Given that in an orderly divorce the partners detach from all four of the elements noted above (attachment to partner, attachment to role, shared routine, and legal commitment), the disorderly divorces are made up from the seven remaining possible combinations of scores on the four elements. For example in the first type (divorced in name only) the partners are legally divorced, but still emotionally involved, still invested in the spousal role, and still sharing routines, possibly even living together. Type 2 ('I wish it hadn't happened') is in evidence when partners' daily activities are disconnected from one another and they are legally divorced but one partner still feels love for the other one and still connects with the spousal role. The partners in Type 3 ('I've got you under my skin') share no daily routines, no desire for the spousal role as such and no legal connection, but all the same they are still emotionally attached to their spouse. As one subject put it: 'If we ran into one another it used to just kill me. I used to take the long way home just so I wouldn't see him.' In Type 4 ('the common law arrangement') the partners do not want to be married, as such, and are legally divorced but do feel love for one another and desire to be connected in routine. These couples are essentially cohabiting after divorce instead of before marriage! The fifth type ('why not be roommates') encompasses those who share their lives and like the marital status, even though they do not have a legal marital role and do not have any other emotional attachment to the partner. Type 6 ('marriage has its advantages') includes people who think that the state of marriage is better than singlehood, even though they are not attached to their partner and do not share routines. Type 7 ('business as usual') comprises couples who want to be legally divorced and do not love one another but continue, essentially for convenience, or just for the kids, to stay in the same house and do the same sorts of routines in daily life as they have always done.

Three points about divorce

First, divorce is a stressful process with both physical and psychological side-effects on the individuals. It affects and disrupts the partners' daily lives, routines and sense of identity as well as just making them unhappy but it should be seen as broader than this in its effects on the network. The divorce of two persons has consequences for many more people than just the two persons who are separating. For example, it obviously affects the children of the marriage. Since we are looking at the family as a system, and the parents of the divorcing pair as well as their siblings, we should think about those effects. Less obviously, to become divorced, couples have to separate – that is, to unmake, 'brick by brick', the relationship they have previously painstakingly put together. To do this they have to undo all the things just listed in the previous sections of this chapter, but to do so against a background of family and societal pressures and forces that may want them to stay together. Just as society creates exogenous influences on couple's courtships and marriages, so it creates barriers to the dissolution of marital relationships. Two obvious ones are:

1 'Divorced' is a negatively valued state that people do not like to have to apply to themselves. One adjustment that divorcees have to make is to the sense of shame and failure that often is felt by the person or imposed by outsiders. As noted earlier, in Chapter 3, our society believes that a divorce is a *failed* relationship (rather than, say, a courageous and honest response to an unworkable partnership).

2 Society is organized in a way that 'expects' people to belong to couples, so that it is actually regarded as embarrassing, say, to invite a single person to a dinner party without inviting another 'single' (invariably one of the opposite sex) to balance things out. What may seem right to the hosts, however, can sometimes be embarrassing to the 'single' guests who probably take mild offence at being crudely paired off like that.

However, many divorced people remarry or enter new roles and so reconfigure their family and also their experience of what 'a family' is (Coleman & Ganong, 1995). While the restructuring is not the only thing that happens, it is the element of the whole process that most researchers focus on. One thing to bear in mind also is that about 25 per cent of previously married men and women move into gay or lesbian relationships after divorce, but the most common reconfiguration is a remarriage or a new cohabiting relationship (Ganong et al., 2006). Families reconfigure in a variety of ways, do so quickly after a divorce (which in some cases was presumably precipitated by an affair which then becomes the new, replacement relationship anyway), and reconfigure several times. Remarriage eventually embraces some 60 per cent of divorced men and 40 per cent of divorced women, usually occurring much more quickly (i.e. after a shorter courtship) than the first marriage, and occurs under the watchful eyes of intimate third parties who have an interest in the eventual stability of the new relationship (Ganong et al., 2006). A large part of the process of remarriage is a blending of routines and patterns of behaviour (Coleman & Ganong, 1995). But there are also necessary adjustments to the exterior existence of ex spouses, who may have access to the children included in the newly blended relationship (Rollie, 2006). Just as families develop stories about their family identity (see above and Koenig Kellas, 2005), so there is a need for narrative sense-making – that is to say for some story that 'explains' what happened – to account for both loss and the reconstitution of families (Bosticco & Thompson, 2005; Ganong et al., 2006). The narrative serves both an organizing function for the members but also a valuable explanatory function for outsiders, in that it helps them to understand what happened and how readjustments have been accomplished.

Children and divorce or reconfiguration

Divorce is an extended transition that inevitably 'affects the entire family system and the functioning and interactions of the members within that system' (Hetherington, Cox & Cox, 1982: 233). It does not stop once the marriage is ended but flows on into the people's lives in innumerable ways for years afterwards (e.g., in terms of a legal requirement to pay certain costs of the ex-partner; strains in required discussions about children's future; loss of trust in relational partners; poor relationships with one's own children; Barber & Demo, 2006). The outcome and experience of the divorce affect different members of the family differently, and the problems faced by the divorced parents are likely to be different – and to require different skills – from those faced by the children (Kitson & Morgan, 1990), particularly where there are needs for arrangement of co-parenting or coordination of custody and sharing of responsibilities concerning split living arrangements (Rollie, 2006). There is no such thing as a victimless divorce – that is, one where no member of the family reports any distress or exhibits absolutely non-disrupted behaviour. Even reconfigured families are 'incomplete institutions' that have typically not been recognized by official bodies such as schools (Coleman & Ganong, 1995) when it comes to allocating responsibility for a child or recording the names of those people to be contacted in an emergency. Coleman & Ganong also note that society has an ideology that permits officials and policy-makers to intrude into family life at the point of a legal divorce (e.g., deciding who pays for which of a child's needs) in a way that they rarely feel able to do when a marriage is still intact, even though the relationship involves the same people. Once again, then, the network intrudes itself into the family in ways which make the family more than a simple collection of individuals with personal relationships only to one another.

Children in distressed families, particularly those who experience separation and divorce, develop certain personality styles or views of themselves and also manifest social-behaviour problems when interacting with other children (Amato, 1991). Children experiencing parental divorce tend to suffer from depression and psychological disturbance, such as excessive feelings of their own guilt – they particularly tend to assume that they are in some way responsible for their parents' divorce (Kitson & Morgan, 1990). Hetherington also found that boys do better with their fathers and girls do better with their mothers, although if living with their mother the boys adjust better than girls do to a stepfather (Hetherington, 1979).

In the first year, particularly, of the divorce, children from divorced families are more oppositional and obstructive, more aggressive, lacking in self-control, distractible and demanding than are children from families that are still together. This is true even if the comparison, intact, families are showing high rates of marital distress and discord. The divorce itself is a significant factor, but the children are adjusting to new arrangements that are puzzling and difficult (e.g., 'Why do I spend one weekend at this house and the next weekend at another house?').

Being labelled 'the child of divorced parents' is something that children find difficult to cope with (Amato, 1991). For example, they may get a 'hard time' at school for 'having no mother or no father'. In an attempt to explore this issue, Gottlieb (1983) reports a programme in Canada designed to deal with the aftermath of parental divorce. By introducing children of divorced parents to one another, Gottlieb was able to establish support groups for them. The support group shows that they are not alone in their experience and helps them to develop ways of coping with their problems. This technique makes use of what researchers now have learned about children's friendships outside the family. However,

Segrin, Taylor & Altman (2005) showed the enduring consequences on children of a parental divorce, particularly in connection with relational and attitudinal effects. It is well known that there is a greater risk for divorce among those adult children whose parents were divorced, but there also appears to be higher family conflict, more negative attitudes towards marriage, and a greater likelihood of marriage to a previously divorced person (which could equally be due to the fact that the person is more willing to accept others with similar background or to the fact that the affair between the two persons led to both of their respective divorces in the first place). A child's experience of parental divorce may lead it to be more willing to contemplate divorce, more likely to divorce, and more likely to marry someone who has previously been divorced. Children of divorce may simply acquire negative attitudes towards marriage, rather than suffering any direct effects of parental divorce by itself.

The relationships of children to their parents also change somewhat predictably after divorce, however. For one thing only 33 per cent of children have at least monthly contact with the non-residential father (Furstenberg, Nord, Peterson & Zill, 1983), and 44 per cent of 12–16 year olds had not seen their father in the previous 12 months. Part of this may be due to the fact that only 16 per cent of children are involved in *joint* custody of any type (Donnelly & Finkelhor, 1993), but in part it is supported by the fact that absent fathers stay in contact with daughters more than with sons after a divorce. Rollie (2006) noted that some of the difficulties experienced by such children and their fathers may stem from the complexities of the non-residential parent (NRP) role in the first place and from the fact that at the social cultural level the NRP–child relationship is shrouded in ambiguity. Non-residential parents have many difficulties to contend with, not least being the difficulty of understanding what their role may be in relation to the child's upbringing and having no formally recognized place in that. At the practical and routine level in interacting with the child, there is also a constant need to prepare for both the occasional and usually short meetings that they have with their child but also the constant need to prepare for being separated once again afterwards. A number of communicative devices are used by the non-residential parent to deal with this situation, including conversational reminders of their place in the child's life and attempts to re-establish routines and rituals to reflect the basis of the life which the parents once lived with their children (Rollie, 2006), but the emotional toll is significant on both parent and child.

In addressing this kind of issue more broadly, Coleman & Ganong (1995) apply the above Hagestad & Smyer (1982) model to the issues of family reconfiguration and look at the processes by which parents become disattached from their roles as parents, whereas Hagestad & Smyer originally looked at the ways in which people became disattached from their roles of married persons. The process of relationship loss is made up in this model by a complex of different features and most are experienced as loss of control and hence are enormously stressful. In reconfiguring families, the emotional attachment to children, attachment to the role of parent, and attachment to the routines of daily family life are all affected. If a father has no custodial rights then an uncontrollable loss of the role of 'father' (as normally understood and as enacted through routines) will be experienced. Accompanying this sense of loss, according to many divorced fathers is a sense of reduced masculinity and loss of rights as either a head or a participant in a house-hold (Arendell, 1993). Many fathers respond to such senses of loss by becoming as absent from the other roles as possible also, whereas those who retain some cus-todial rights do not (Umberson & Williams, 1993). Coleman & Ganong (1995: 90) suggest that 'the ambiguity of the non-residential father role may be too uncom-fortable for some men, so they withdraw from their children, essentially aban-doning the role rather than continually face situations in which they feel awkward and unsure of how to continue fathering'. If you have time to discuss this idea in class, you might find it interesting to do so.

SUMMARY

The basic point of the chapter has been a simple one: that dyads do not work in isolation from other relationships and hence that internal or dyadic psychological dynamics are not all that characterizes the workings of relationships. The people in a pairing are always connected to other people outside of that relationship and so their particular relationship exists in the context of members of larger net-works, the rest of society and other members of a family. Complex interrelation-ships with outside third parties and society at large affect our social behaviour, even in the apparently private context of our behaviour in dyadic couples. Relationships, like people, have a history and have come from somewhere, often taking a long time to emerge and develop in detailed and organized ways but we also have many relationships with other people outside of the dyad itself and these are influential on our personal and private thinking and behaviour in many ways discussed here. A marriage can be affected by the style of the preceding courtship adopted by the partners; a family, as a whole, can be influenced by the kind of marital interaction between the two spouses in particular; the child at school can be affected by the quality of previous interaction in the family home. The learning that the child gathers about relationships from being in the family environment can carry over and influence the child's approach or avoidance with other children in the neighbourhood or at school and vice versa. The parent–child relationships, like other pairs of relationship in the family and the relationship of the family itself to outsiders, also are bidirectional. It is too simple to say that par-ents influence or direct children or that families are not affected by networks and vice versa: instead there is a two-way street of influence where each element acts with and responds to the other. Even very young children have their own ability to interpret and understand – and hence to react to or even resist – what another person does or says to them. Hence relationships are created by reciprocity with the persons involved, and with outsiders, and with contexts surrounding the relationship. We looked in this chapter at the ways in which these forces and factors are also relevant and powerful influences on thinking and processing of relational status, especially in decline, divorce or reconfiguration of family.

As a result of reading this chapter you should now be able to recognize exogenous, exterior forces on the form and conduct of relationships, to see how routines and the expectations of other people serve to guide both the feelings and the conduct that arise in our personal relationships and also to assess the occasions when you are inadvertently responding to or being guided by such exogenous forces. In thinking about family forms and stress you should now also be able to recognize some of the ways in which these arise outside of the relationship and to see the complex nature of things that are arranged and rearranged when divorce occurs. Finally, you should be able to comprehend a significant set of ways in which both the children and adults involved in divorce may need to rethink their roles, feelings, routines and behaviours.

SELF QUESTIONS

- Look at The Rocky Roads Report that you did earlier in the chapter. What principles do you now see at work here? For example, did you originally write down anything about the relevance of routines or roles, the impact of others' expectations, or comparison with social norms or others' behaviour, and if not, would you be inclined to rethink that now?
- What sorts of things do you notice other people doing differently as they fall in love? Reflect on changes that you have observed in the structure of their behaviour (how they organize their time, for example) rather than simple stuff like how often they touch or whether they look one another in the eye (as in Chapter 1).
- If you have experience of divorce or blended families, or if you know people who have, then you may want to consider the degree to which the reformulation of the family involves significant restructuring of routines, roles, and the opinions and behaviours of other people outside the family.

FURTHER READING

Demo, D., Allen, K.R. & Fine, M.A. (Eds.). (2000). *Handbook of family diversity*. New York: Oxford.

Duncombe, J., Harrison, K., Allan, G.A. and Marsden, D. (2004). *The state of affairs*. Mahwah, NJ: Lawrence Erlbaum.

Fine, M.A., & Harvey, J.H. (Eds.). (2006). *Handbook of divorce and relationship dissolution*. Mahwah, NJ: Lawrence Erlbaum.

Milardo, R.M., & Duck, S.W. (Eds.). (2000). *Families as relationships*. Chichester, UK: Wiley.

Parks, M. (2006). *Communication and social networks*. Mahwah, NJ: Lawrence Erlbaum.

PRACTICAL MATTERS

- What advice would you give a couple who have already decided to divorce (so you're not attempting to persuade them not to do so), concerning the issues that they should give their closest attention?
- Can you think of ways to use network interconnectedness to develop a media campaign to discourage alcohol use during pregnancy? (For example, can you think of ways to stimulate a network to discuss the topic in a manner that could significantly affect a target population of pregnant women?)
- How would you modify such a campaign to make it relevant to reduction of tobacco consumption in general or in getting teenagers to think about drug use, safe sex and other health issues?
- In short, how could you employ the relational network principles in this chapter in order to affect individual health behaviours?

5

Influencing Strangers, Acquaintances and Friends

[R]elationships are the engine of much that is of concern in understanding communities, such as interpersonal influence, media influences, impact of health messages, group decision making, and the proliferation of innovations or the impact of gossip and opinion. The relational interactions that constitute daily life experience are the unexamined basis of many processes that have hitherto been explained by use of specific theories of communication and community about the above topics. (Carl & Duck, 2004: p. 3)

Focus points for note taking when reading this chapter:

- How much of what you do is the result of your relationships and the role they have in monitoring your behaviour in various ways (for example your concern about what your partner might think if you were discovered doing what you are doing)?
- How might we be influenced by our close relationships in our personal decision making or our thinking more generally?
- Are relationships persuasive and is persuasion a relational activity?
- Does it matter if the target of a persuasion attempt is a friend or not? How? Why?
- Does it matter if the source of a persuasion attempt is a friend or not? How? Why?
- How might the routines of life act as hidden persuaders in what we do?

The preceding chapter dealt with the influence of others on relationships and the present one continues that theme with a twist, by looking at the ways in which relationships influence others. *All* communication involves persuasion, brings cultural and social baggage to interactions, and carries relational outcomes. The converse is also true: that relationships influence us and provide a context for all forms of persuasion, whether this comes from parental authority style (Chapter 2), routines of relational practices (Chapter 3), or the social networks that intersect with personal decisions (Chapter 4). Even politeness and facework (essentially, attention to one's own and other people's dignity in an interaction) are simply examples of the overall fact that persuasion is inherently and inescapably relational, not only because we are used to thinking about proper ways to talk to people without simply bullying them or ordering them about, but also because when we frame persuasive requests, we take account of relationship factors and 'face needs' (Kunkel, Wilson, Olufowote & Robson, 2003).

In this chapter, then, the context that I bring out for relationships is the relationships themselves. We will look at how persuasion relies on relationships and vice versa. Even when we are just chatting with friends we may do so in ways that happen to give us new ideas for facing a problem, or to reinforce our view of self, or our feeling of being generally supported and having reliable alliances available (Leatham & Duck, 1990). Even everyday chat about apparently trivial matters can therefore serve to inform or enlighten us in unintended ways. Everyday talk becomes important because it provides a continuous background for much else that we do that *is* deliberately persuasive: it creates a long-term context for bigger moves, such as the seeking of specific support in a time of crisis, when we turn first to those from whom we have learned through routine everyday interaction that we may expect a positive response. So although many situations are obviously 'persuasive' (e.g., asking someone to lend us a car, come on a date, or break off a relationship) they are special instances built on a general truth: communication is *always* indirectly persuasive – always setting something out that has a relevance to influence.

All relational activity involves support for an aspect of the world (for instance, every interaction supports a view of the relationship of one's self to the partner, of the importance of topics discussed and also of the meaning frameworks in which their evaluation is embedded, for starters). Talk represents the speaker's view of the situation, audience, own identity, and way of understanding things, for which we invite our audience's acceptance (Carl & Duck, 2004; Duck, 1994). Since relational partners already endorse many of our attitudes (Chapter 3), their presence is encouraging and hence persuasively supportive. Accordingly, I do not regard situations specifically labelled as 'attitude change' – where someone attempts to bend our will, to win an argument, or to sell us a car – as the only places where persuasion occurs. The present chapter shows deeper structural connections between 'persuasion' and 'relationships', even in the familiar everyday experiences where we deal with others who face us with predicaments or difficulties.

LISTEN IN ON YOUR OWN LIFE

Notice times and ways in which you talk to friends to encourage or address their personal competence or see themselves as good people, or sustain their self-esteem. In what ways may this sort of conversation persuade them to see their power to make good decisions? How does encouragement or discouragement *persuade* people? What is it you are effectively persuading them *about* and how might it connect to relational concerns?

Daily experience occasionally involves preventing, coping with, or digging ourselves out of predicaments, and Miller (1996) discusses the sorts of public embarrassment that are horribly familiar, when our performance fails to present a competent image in the face of other people's attention. When we go about daily business, we are occasionally confronted with unexpected situations that force us to deal with awkward strangers – strangers who light a cigarette in a No Smoking area, jump ahead of us in a queue, irritate us in launderettes, or may even sexually harass us. On other occasions, the problem is to deal with people whom we know a little, but not very well, and ask them to do something for us that they may be inclined to resist. Our regular bus driver may have to be persuaded to change a large banknote; we may want someone to turn off their mobile phone during a movie; we may have to ask our class instructor to extend a deadline; or a person in our dormitory may need to turn down the music system. Sometimes we may even want to persuade a friend to do us a troublesome favour or to bring a partner round to our way of thinking about key decisions, like buying a car or deciding whether to take a job offer. There may be relational matters that we do not typically even see as 'persuasion' at all, such as when we invite a classmate on a date, or (persuade someone to) end a relationship, or (persuade someone to) have sex, or to (persuade someone to) heed our advice or accept an offer of help. Even 'education' is a persuasive process – having students (agree to) do something in a way different from before (García-Pastor, 2005).

All such situations involve us in changing someone's mind, influencing them, their behaviour, beliefs, impressions of us, or getting them to do things for us. Daily life brings us into contact with many different sorts of people, some of whom we know, and some of whom we do not. Sometimes we may do things for people easily because we like them. Sometimes we may resist an easy request because we *don't* like the person, however good the structure of their message or persuasive argument. I believe the relational judgement usually precedes the one about the value of the argument: first we decide whether or not we like someone and *then* we evaluate their request.

RELATING IS PERSUASIVE AND VICE VERSA

Because of this, the chapter has two goals: first, to show how persuasion is tied up with *relationship* processes, connecting daily relational activity to persuasion more widely than may appear; second, to show how relationships affect persuasion and make it relationally specific (Carl & Duck, 2004). Even car salespeople and advertisers try to mimic relational activity to establish friendly relationships with customers as part of playing not to logic but to feelings of acceptance. Also our relationship obligations or willingness to do things for people 'because it's you' represent another instance of 'persuasion by relationship'. How often have you heard someone say 'I don't do this for everyone but I will do it for you because you are a friend'? We also use relationships persuasively to suggest a moral obligation to do what we want: 'You're my friend, so do me this favour' and even 'Buddy, can you spare a dime?'. Most often the relationship does not need to be spoken in this way. The very fact that it is your boss or your best friend who is asking you to do something is sufficient for you to feel the implicit relational force of the request.

Most everyday uses of power are actually informal, and make power an inherently relational force, not a structural one, although of course raw force can be used by dictators, bullies and incompetent managers. Hepburn & Crepin (1984) demonstrated that prison guards have less power over prisoners than we would assume and in fact are dependent upon them in many ways, both physical and career-related. Because the guards are outnumbered by the prisoners they are at constant physical risk, but also their access to promotion and favourable job evaluations depends on them being able to make the prisoners cooperate with them. Therefore guards who are unable to create persuasive relationships with the prisoners tend to be unsuccessful at their jobs, and are noted as such by their superiors.

This chapter proposes that 'persuasion' gets more interesting and informative once we look at it *as* relating. It is true that in the cases of strangers, acquaintances and friends, the issues are somewhat different, despite the underlying similarities of the persuasive processes, but we should look at both similarities and differences.

Persuading strangers, acquaintances and friends

When dealing with strangers, we necessarily assume that they are average, sensible members of society about whom we know only what we can see: they will be influenced by the usual things, such as power and logic, and have average, normal attitudes unless something about the outward appearance or behaviour suggests otherwise. (Do they look rich? Are they drunk? Do they have lots of body piercings, scars, or strange tics? Are they dressed officially in uniform that suggests a duty to assist or oppress others?) Since we have no relationship with them except as one anonymous human being to another, they are contextless for us and we have no special knowledge of their personal characteristics, even if we can construct reasonable guesses on the basis of appearance. Such cues nevertheless affect their credibility as a source of opinions and Seiter & Dunn (2000) showed how a female's physical attractiveness affected an audience's beliefs in the credibility of her claims about sexual harassment, an unattractive model being rated on physical appearance alone as deceptive and dishonest about such a claim.

By contrast, with acquaintances we attempt persuasion in a different relational context: we probably do want to emphasize that they know us a little and that they should consequently treat us as persons with individual characteristics. We can claim special treatment: we are not 'just another person who wants something done in a hurry', but someone to whom they have a minor obligation to grant special treatment. Also, we do know about the attitudes and beliefs systems that they have (Chapter 3). So we know a little about whether a particular request has even a remote chance of being agreeable to them. We may know enough about them to know how to put them in a good mood and raise our chances of a positive outcome just a little bit.

With friends, we use whatever special knowledge we have about them, but we are probably also concerned to preserve the relationship in the long term over and above any desired immediate outcome of our specific request. However, friendship is a source of obligations: part of the role of 'friend' involves willing acceptance of unwelcome chores, inconvenient duties, and obligations to do favours (Wiseman, 1986). Part of the 'voluntary contract' of friendship involves us tacitly agreeing to support our friends in times of need, to take time away from our own business in order to attend to *their* business, and to engage their demands upon our resources.

On my own limited reading of work on persuasion it seems that these relational differences are elided as scholars search for *absolutely* effective ways of persuading based in part on the structure of messages (such as the ways in which a speaker adapts the *structure* of a message to reflect the context or audience; Meyer, 2000), partly on the sequence of messages (such as foot in the door or door in the face – discussed below). Such literature typically pays little attention to the everyday smallness of tasks like persuading someone to come on a date, have sex, tidy their bedroom, or leave us alone. Issues usually addressed are very rare events such as agreeing to put up a political poster or to make a donation to a charity. Too little heed is also paid to the broader relational context for persuasion, and the role of relationship knowledge or the fear of relational consequences. You'll do something for your boss, because you know that otherwise she will make your life more hellish, not because you think she is right: you know she is a bully and your short-term compliance will make life easier than will principled opposition.

LOOK OUT FOR THIS IN THE MEDIA

Look out for the numbers of ways in which the media and especially advertising sources use relationships in order to persuade people. Pay particular attention to word-of-mouth marketing and the emphasis in advertisements on relationships and inclusion, the idea that after you purchase a particular product, you will gain membership of a privileged group. Think what such methods indicate about relationships as persuasive tools?

Everyday persuasion

In keeping with my own emphasis on daily life in this book, I believe that large-scale decisions and attitudes occupy much less of people's time than the work on Big Issue Persuasion might lead us to imagine. Partners spend longer arguing about decorating the living room, which car to purchase, or where to go for a meal or holiday than they do confronting partners about political issues or prejudice towards racial groups. I do not mean that the latter issues are not important; they are (Seiter & Gass, 2004), but we must not misrepresent the contours of social life. Big Issue discussions are less frequent than a thousand other minor trivial squabbles or arguments and a psychology of human experience should address experience representatively.

Classical rhetorical theory assume three basic means of persuasion (O'Keefe, 2004): logic (*logos*); emotions (*pathos*); character (*ethos*). Traditional approaches to attitude change in social psychology and communication have focused on all three and I will try to sketch each of them before showing that in everyday life. *Ethos* – the identity, personality, and character of a speaker – is the most influential in everyday relationships. (Indeed I'd introduce a new fourth term *philos* to separate out that part of *ethos* that comes from the personal relationship of the person to the audience rather than from general 'character' or credibility). It is 'who you are' more than 'what you say' that matters in persuading friends, in most cases. *Logos* is essentially the component of persuasion that relies on the well organized argument, the well spun tale, the well prepared case. Arguments are persuasive because they are well structured, attentive to the issue, follow accepted rules of logic, evidence and proof, and deal with points raised by the other side. Classic debate is largely about *logos*. By contrast, *pathos* is that element of persuasion that appeals to emotions such as patriotism, guilt, fear or love. The messages that rely on *pathos* are rarely completely separable from other elements of persuasion, but you can nevertheless listen out for them in political speeches, especially, since politicians routinely talk about 'what people want' and make implicit appeals to fear of chaos, of terrorists, of other racial groups, or even of the collapse of civilization as a basis for adopting an argument they wish to press forward. *Ethos* is the appeal to the character of the speaker as a source of persuasion. References to a speaker's position or experience are references to *ethos* and the introduction of public speakers usually plays to *ethos*. Such references usually play up the person's suitability to be the speaker and point to expert knowledge, but may simply indicate that the speaker is the President, Prime Minister, or CEO. In everyday life, *ethos* takes the special form that people do not always do things because they believe them to be right, but because they think that *other* people believe them to be right, and they care about the opinions of those other people who are friends or relatives or are otherwise significant to them (e.g., teenagers smoking to look cool to other teenagers; Pechman, Zhao, Goldberg & Reibling, 2003).

Therefore, though *logos*, *pathos* and *ethos* are separable concepts on paper, it is rarely the case that they are separate in practice when persuasion takes place in relationships. In everyday life, a person persuades partly by logic or message structure, but also by reason of the person they are in relation to the 'audience' (even an audience of one). *Ethos* is the major persuader in everyday relational life on top of anything created by *logos*.

KEEP A JOURNAL

Keep a list of the types of persuasion that you overhear in everyday life and try to categorize them in terms of their reliance on logos, ethos or pathos. Try to discover whether it matters whether the audience is a stranger, an acquaintance or friend and try to differentiate whether particular attempts are made to use one of the three methods in each case, predominantly.

INFLUENCING STRANGERS

In dealing with strangers, we lack knowledge about their particular characteristics as people and they lack such knowledge about us. What we both see on the surface is almost all we have to go on (plus knowledge of social norms of behaviour) and although we may be affected by surface appearance in judging someone's credibility (Seiter & Sandry, 2003), we cannot safely deduce their psychological structure from appearance (Berscheid & Walster [Hatfield], 1974). Accordingly, we are likely to balance the persuasive context differently from when we persuade acquaintances or persuade friends. We need to be especially attentive to our own *ethos* – others' perceptions of our character – in the setting, especially if outside observers view the episode. If a stranger 'causes a scene', we may be concerned about our assessment by other people present whereas when dealing with friends, we probably take positivity for granted and have *their* feelings and interests in mind as much as our own along with concerns about the relationship itself (García-Pastor, 2005).

Strangers on the train

When I was working on the first edition of the book, I had to go to London to record a television programme on 'social skills' with a man who specialized in assertiveness training. The journey back involved a three-hour train ride, which, on this occasion, took more than four hours because of poor weather. I always choose a non-smoking section, which is clearly marked with a red circular notice on every window, showing a cigarette crossed out, the words 'No Smoking', and a statement of the penalty for violating the rule. The carriage filled with another 31 passengers, and we departed. I looked around at the strangers who were my fellow passengers. Directly opposite was a young woman who looked like a student and a young man who was stapling together leaflets about solvent abuse, warning teenagers about the disadvantages of glue sniffing. He soon started chatting to the student and it turned out that he was a vegetarian who jogged every day and helped to run a youth sports centre. I began to see why he had chosen a non-smoking section: he cared about health. Across the central corridor of the open-plan compartment was a table occupied by two large and hungry people who began tucking vigorously into a pile of 'junk food' bags. I sat reading a paper about loneliness in college students whilst I listened to *The Lark Ascending* by Vaughan Williams on my personal music system. I could keep an eye on things by 'looking out of the window' since it was a dark winter's evening and the carriage lights reflected the carriage events clearly. These cameos continued amiably enough along their own paths for some hour and a half, as the train lurched on its journey, interspersed with announcements from the guard/conductor and bar steward.

Then one of the Big Eaters lit a cigarette.

I drew his attention to the fact that it was a non-smoking section and asked him to go to a different section. He replied that someone further down the train was smoking but, as a computer manager from Manchester pointed out to him, that did not actually contradict my point that he was sitting in a non-smoking section. Out of the other 30 passengers just that one man joined in the argument and supported my request whilst the others looked on with a mixture of amusement, embarrassment and British reserve.

When the smoker would neither put out his cigarette nor move there flashed across my mind one of the points from the television programme I had just finished recording: stick to your guns. However, it was with something of a sense of failure that I went looking for the guard/conductor who asked the man to move, which he then did, flashing in my direction one of those looks that would kill a toad: as far as he was concerned, it was I who was in the wrong.

What we had here was a 'social confrontation episode'. As Newell & Stutman (1988) pointed out, the key feature of such an episode is that one actor in the situation points out to another actor 'that his or her behaviour has violated a rule or expectation for appropriate conduct within the relationship or situation'. Key elements are: the legitimacy of the invoked rule; the legitimacy of any other rule that might supersede the first rule; whether or not the person actually performed the illegitimate behaviour; whether the behaviour actually amounts to a violation of the rule; whether or not the accused accepts responsibility. If we analyse the present problem and the ways in which it unfolded we can see that all of these elements were silent fellow travellers in that railway carriage on that dark and stormy night!

What about the other passengers? The solvent/health man later left the section for a while and as he returned to his seat placed a pack of cigarettes and a lighter in front of him. He had said nothing, I assume, because he felt divided loyalties. On the one hand, he smoked, but on the other hand he recognized the need to consider other people's rights while doing so and had himself left the non-smoking carriage when he wanted to smoke. Or perhaps he didn't want to be involved in another scene where he would be asked not to smoke. His behaviour did raise an interesting issue, though, since his other actions and statements pointed to a concern over health and a care for others: so why did he smoke? The student was a non-smoker who had earlier told the veggie health guy that she always chose non-smoking compartments, so why did she say nothing?

Some researchers would point to the first smoker's attitude structure: his beliefs about smoking, his beliefs about the legitimacy of his action, and, given that he could see others smoking, his consequent belief that he was being unfairly singled out for criticism. Some would argue that he felt his freedom was being constrained and so he reacted against the constraint. Others would look at the internal, logical structure of my request and its evident ineffectiveness. Some would point to other circumstances, such as the passivity of the others in the compartment: that provided a context for the support of rule-breaking and no support for me. Some of these ideas have been applied generally to all persuasive contexts, but some are more likely to be important in this setting and others elsewhere. Some matter in dealing with strangers and some do not; some are more important in dealing with friends, for instance, and whether a challenged behaviour threatens the relationship itself. The common element for me is the relationships that are either expressed or implied in the relevant conversations: The Veggie-Health-Smoker was apparently interested in chatting up The Student; The Conductor/Guard had an official relationship with all of the passengers and with his employing organization and therefore had a duty to act in a particular way; the Computer Manager was a manager, used to being obeyed by others in his organization; nobody else knew the Big Eater or me.

Being noticed

Yet, even when dealing with strangers, a first requirement is *credibility,* that is, a basis to be noticed and have them pay attention to our request, so we have to present ourselves in a way that makes clear that we have the right to have our request dealt with. By contrast, when dealing with friends, our right to be heard and noticed is built into our relationship: friends heed us because they know us and because we have some common history, shared interests, knowledge of one another's needs, strengths, and flashpoints, and a degree of desire to preserve the relationship between us. With strangers, however, we might need to use some guile and devices that at best will attempt to mimic or substitute for these other things.

Attention to a persuasive message is well established as a critical factor for persuasion to occur (Hovland, Janis & Kelley, 1953). People attend more closely to a *credible source*, one that appears to justify our attention, has authority and can be trusted. In the 1950s, when Hovland's studies were conducted, it was found, for instance, that Robert Oppenheimer, who headed the team that had just created the atom bomb, was more readily believed by a US audience than was *Pravda*, the Russian newspaper, whether or not the topic was nuclear bombs.

Source credibility is freely manipulated in advertisements. Advertisers like to say 'Doctors recommend' or 'As used in hospitals' as a way of tying their product to credible sources. Other symbols of credibility are also used. For instance, when persons are shown recommending drugs or pharmaceuticals, they are frequently in white coats ('scientists') or smart business clothes ('executives') – with greying hair if they are male ('authority'). They usually wear glasses ('intelligent'), carry clipboards ('data'), are seen giving other people directions ('power') against a background of test tubes ('science'), and they use fountain pens ('class'). The same person saying the same thing about pharmaceuticals on a football field in sports gear would appear less credible even if the message, the words, the claims, were all the same. We respond to cues in context, all carefully prepared to suggest credibility within our culture. Here credibility is produced by symbols of expertise.

TRY THIS OUT: MANIPULATE YOUR CREDIBILITY

Spend a day dressed in a manner which is intended to increase your credibility. Record your experiences in a log/blog. Then think about the following questions.

(Continued)

(Continued)

- How did people treat you differently and how do you yourself feel?
- How will you dress for your job interview and what will it accomplish to do so? What persuasive symbols are you altering for this purpose, and how do they work – i.e., what do they effect in terms of an audience's perceptions (Authority? Knowledge? Confidence? Comfort? Accessibility? Political affiliation? Sexual orientation?).

Research has found credibility to depend on expertise, trustworthiness, attractiveness and similarity to the target audience, arguing against one's personal interest or 'expected' lines, and status. Take these things into account when planning your interview.

LOOK OUT FOR THIS IN THE MEDIA

Look out for TV ads that manipulate source credibility. How do they do this? What kind of model is used to advertise such different things as household products, diarrhoea medicines, electronics, vacations, insurance? What sex is the model in each case, and what race? What aspects of NVC or speech codes (see Chapter 1) are made relevant to this credibility?

How is credibility 'done' on the radio, where obviously the visual cues are not available? By what means do you hear the credibility of the source being established? Is the voice recognizable from some other context (e.g., a person famous for something else) and how is that context relevant to the advertised product?

In dealings with strangers, source credibility is one of the most important factors, but source credibility alone is not enough to explain persuasion nor is it always a helpful guide. We are quite often thrown into persuasive contexts quite unexpectedly by the unpredictable actions of other people, and we need to influence them then and there: 'Please serve me next, I was here before this person'; 'Please move your car, you're blocking my exit'; 'Please stop smoking, you're in a No Smoking section'; 'Why don't you turn down your music, I'm trying to work'. Everyday life is not always conveniently arranged, and yet we have to deal with the actual context in which we find ourselves. If we happen to be nicely turned out, and wearing spectacles then we may have the credibility to influence them but we may happen to be in running gear or a bathrobe or to have just (been) woken up. In any case, appearance alone does not guarantee persuasive success.

When dealing with familiar people, however, what about source credibility then? After all, it is not created by clothes or appearance but is transportable: it moves with us when we interact with people we already know. Credibility comes not from the usual cues of clothing and the rest, but from what we know about the person, relevant competencies, and how we feel about him or her. Since I know my brother is a professor of economics, I am more likely to credit his statements on economics. Also I am more likely to credit the arguments of someone I love or respect, even if he or she does not dress well. Those I know as irritatingly incompetent probably will not persuade me, however they dress up, or even if they pay careful attention to the structure of their messages. People I regard as enemies will hardly ever be able to persuade me to do things, even if they sweeten the deal with gifts and promises (as Virgil, the Roman poet put it, 'I am wary of the Greeks even when they are bearing gifts'). Relative power positions in the network are also well known in our everyday encounters and are significant in this context. Over a period of time, we get to know who has authority or credibility and who has not; we learn which friend is the group leader or gives reliable advice; we know which student in class is bright and is good to work with on class projects; we have ideas about which colleague carries authority or has a strong political base in the organization as opposed to those who are regarded as 'losers'.

Real-life cues based on personal knowledge affect perceptions of credibility in everyday life much more than business clothes, glasses or well structured messages. A friend is credible because I know and trust him or her, not because of the clothes. In everyday life, power, credibility, and trust are based on vibrant, familiar relationships, on everyday talk, and on built-up trust, not on the fripperies of the advertising image. It is only when that deeper familiarity is lacking that we cannot rely on inherent source credibility and we need other strategies, like choosing words carefully and taking great thought over the structure of our persuasive message.

The apathetic context

Our predicaments in social life – even among strangers – often involve us in taking a stand on some matter when other people are there to see, like other people standing in the queue that someone tries to 'jump'. Awareness of the reactions of strangers or friends, whether physically or only psychologically present, often guides our action ('What would the neighbours think?' or 'What do these other people think of all this?'). These powerful social concerns are influential on the ways in which we act and they connect with Chapter 4 (embeddedness in social networks).

In the non-smoking compartment I found myself in a public situation: my request to the smoker was uttered before an audience of other people who were also affected by the smoker's behaviour but evidently cared less. No one else did anything and no one else (bar one) took my side. Twenty-eight people sat around saying and doing nothing whilst the two-act melodrama went on in their midst. This meant that the smoker was not being made to defend himself nor being socially pressured, an important psychological context for my persuasive attempt. In terms of the Newell & Stutman (1988) analysis above, this apathetic context tacitly suggests the unimportance or illegitimacy of the rule that I invoked.

It is an important fact, not just a coincidence, that we live as members of communities which provide contexts against which to evaluate our actions, thoughts and beliefs. We are strongly affected by the views and actions of relevant other people, and we habitually compare our behaviour, dress, attitudes and beliefs to other people's. Festinger's (1954) 'social comparison theory' observes that we assess ourselves against a relevant group of other persons to see if we compare equally, if not favourably, and we prefer to be liked and accepted rather than disliked and rejected. Have you had the experience of turning up to a party dressed in the 'wrong' kind of clothes? Then you have experienced the consequences of social comparison. Festinger indicates that we compare our attitudes, opinions and emotions also: when we want to know if we are acting or thinking in an acceptable manner or making a sensible emotional response we compare ourselves with other people to see how they react. If they do as we do, then we are 'OK'.

Festinger points to a common part of human life: we are *always* comparing ourselves to other people and we want to be acceptable. As students, you often want to know what sorts of exam/test/essay grades everyone else earned, so that you can evaluate your own performance more thoroughly. Just knowing your own score may not be sufficiently reassuring. Whenever we compare our own jogging times, test grades, body weight or salary against average figures, we are doing social comparison. It guides us as we attempt to find out if we are normal or right and can even be used as an argument in persuasion, as any parent of an adolescent has heard: 'Can I stay at the party until 12.00? Everyone else will.'

If we look at what happened – or, rather, what did not happen – in the non-smoking section of the train, we can see social comparison at work, silently telling me I'm wrong. For one thing, the smoker's response was to indicate a comparison group elsewhere to 'make his behaviour right' (i.e. others were smoking in the train). Second, a more subtle comparison was that only one person was concerned about the smoking and no one else reacted. The smoker may look round and think, 'This smoke doesn't bother anyone else or they'd be reacting. I'm "doing OK". The guy here is overreacting'. I look round and think, 'I'm upset by the smoking but no one else is saying anything. Perhaps my reaction is inappropriate'. Since people tend to assume that others are similar to them, a non-reaction is equivalent to support for the status quo rather than for a new proposal. Through apathy, the others are supporting the 'smokus quo' rather than the proposal that it should stop. The message from the comparison group to me, then, is 'You care and we don't, so you're wrong'. In terms of the Newell & Stutman (1988) analysis, they passively deny that the smoker is violating a rule, or implicitly suggest that the rule written on the window (i.e. No Smoking) can be superseded by another rule (i.e. No Smoking Unless Other People Are Not Very Bothered By It In Which Case You Can Do It Anyway).

Could I have reinterpreted their indifference so that it becomes supportive of me and provides a comparison group? A careful piece of oratory directed at the apathetic bystanders might have energized support and changed the balance of opinion for comparison. The stratagem would be to interpret the apathy as something positive and supportive of me. For instance, I could have tried suggesting that they were all too nice to speak up as I had done. ('These other people are too polite to say so but they are offended too'.) If they are *really* apathetic, then they will not contradict and say 'No, I'm not just being polite; I'm really not offended' but, they *might* and then my position would be lame. In dealing with friends we have two different sorts of direct help available: (1) friends are similar to ourselves and so provide useful social comparisons and support for our behaviour (Byrne, 1997; Duck, 1994) (2) we have known friends a long time and understand the sorts of behaviours they will tolerate, so the social comparisons and judgemental standards are built into the relational context and we can assume that our friends are generally supportive.

The dog owner's dilemma

Another fascinating incident showed me the power of comparison with other people's behaviour and also how fate can intervene to correct bystander apathy. I took Christina (then aged nine) and Jamie (then aged four) to the children's playground where a special section for the under-fives was fenced off and had a sign: 'Dogs not allowed in this area'. There were about 20 parents there, each with at least one child, when one turned up with two small children and a dog, which he brought in and allowed to run strenuously around. Apathetically, the rest of the parents looked from one to another, raised our eyebrows, muttered to one another in general terms about 'dogs' and made social comparisons: no one else did anything directly, so why should I be the first? We all said nothing, all expecting someone else to take the initiative, and all unwilling to risk the dog owner's reactions, since he had a generally uninviting look about him. We were all rapidly transformed into non-apathetic good citizens, however, when the dog started to chase one of the children, then several of us heroically united to draw the dog owner's attention to the sign. His response was one of those staggering real-life retorts (it is given below) that no one ever expects. The dog's sudden refocusing of energy made an extra contribution to the incident that forced us from feeling good about ourselves in one way (we are tolerant, open-minded, unofficious) to feeling good in another way (we are good citizens protecting children from danger). That was the crucial change that led to our intervention.

What did the dog owner say when we pointed his good eye at the notice? With marvellous aplomb, he said 'It's only a small dog; they don't count'. This points to something that is missing from the accounts of predicaments given so far: any reference to the fact that the *target* of our persuasion has a mind – in this case quite an inventive one. He probably felt about himself, as most people do, that he was a normal, rational human being, who is basically all right, acts in a reasonable way, and has an above-average sense of humour. How might this have affected his actions and accounted for his beliefs about the dog?

Dissonance

Another model, Festinger's (1957) dissonance theory (different from his social comparison theory), focuses on the attitudes-plus-behaviour of one person. In brief, it argues that when the person holds two attitudes which lead to psychologically inconsistent conclusions or when the person's behaviour and attitude about it do not accord, they will be motivated to restore 'consonance'. Thus, if we disapprove of smoking but find that we have just lit a cigarette or have a dog in a 'no dog' area, then we ought to experience dissonance and be motivated to change something and get back to consonance.

Dissonance was probably felt by the solvent/health man in the non-smoking section. It takes two forms: (1) I am a health enthusiast, but I smoke; (2) I am a smoker, but I am sitting in a non-smoking section. We know how he resolved the second simple instance: he moved elsewhere when he wanted to smoke and thereby removed that particular bit of dissonance. As to the first case, it is much more interesting. It would have *created* or increased dissonance for the health enthusiast both to support me (he would be thinking 'I am a smoker telling someone else to stop') and also to support the smoker ('I am a smoker advocating smoking in a non-smoking section when I care about other people's rights'). Hence his silence.

How would dissonance work with the dog owner, though? To get him to change his behaviour, we have to create dissonance in him somehow. Our blatant attempt to do that ('You have a dog here', 'You're in an area where dogs are prohibited') failed because he found a way to deny the applicability of the rule ('Small dogs do not count'). We could have tried to affect other attitudes of his, for example, the positive attitude that he probably holds about himself. We could have tried to make his positive view of himself inconsistent with his actions. As it turned out, in another brilliant stroke of human ingenuity, he picked up the dog and put it inside his coat, thus stopping it running around (that keeps us happy), but not moving it from the play area (that kept him happy).

PROBLEMS WITH THESE IDEAS

Even though I give these approaches sketchy coverage here because you can read them more fully in a book devoted to persuasion such as Seiter & Gass (2004), you can see that there are problems. To use their principles, we must know in advance just what would be 'consistent' for the target, and, therefore, how to inject enough uncomfortable inconsistency into a personal situation for the person to be sufficiently disturbed to want to remove it. When dealing with strangers, this is precisely the kind of knowledge about them that we never have. On the other hand, if we know the other person well, we can take account of individual personal styles and we need to talk to them differently based on that personal knowledge. We have to know people better before we know how to create specific feelings of inconsistency without having them simply decide to dislike and ignore us. Thus we are likely to rely on well known, generally effective means of organizing speech to persuade (the *logos* that I mentioned earlier).

Logos: messages and persuasion

In any situation, the pattern of the messages that we choose is fundamental but the extent to which the pattern is based on personal knowledge of target is quite varied (O'Keefe, 2004). Some message structures are more persuasive than others as has been recognized since the time of Aristotle, and we'll look at a selection.

'Foot in the door'

Door-to-door salespeople used to use a method of trying to put a foot in the door – literally or figuratively – and getting the prospective client to make a very small and harmless-looking commitment initially (e.g., a commitment to approving the format of a series of books). Once that is made, the commitment is increased gradually (e.g., to taking the first volume of the series on approval, then to agreeing to have a few volumes in the home to see how the set looks, and so on up to the seller's original aim: getting you to pay for 26 volumes). The technique is based on small increments of commitment at each stage so that the client really feels that each step is a logical and hardly noticeable progression from the previous step, until lo and behold, the client owns a fine, extremely expensive encyclopaedia. When you buy a car, watch carefully for this technique being used on you.

LOOK OUT FOR THIS IN THE MEDIA

Watch the car buying/selling sequence in the movie *Fargo* concerning the under seal and the way the salesman (William H. Macy) 'has to go and speak with his boss' about it.

One explanation is that the foot in the door works because the initial compliance allows the persons to feel good about themselves. Kraut (1973) finds that if people are 'labelled' positively when they give to one charity they give more to a second one also. The method of labelling is simple: 'You are really a generous person. I wish more people were as charitable as you.' For such an effect to work, however, the labelled action must be seen by the actor as resulting from 'internal' factors – those under the actor's own control – otherwise there is no credit for having acted that way. External causal factors – those not under the person's own control – often cause people to do things, so the positive label would probably not work if the actor felt that the actions were brought about by other than their personal free choice (Dillard, Hunter & Burgoon, 1984). Also don't forget that your attachment style (Chapter 2) may affect whether you readily accept or tend to be suspicious of such evaluations by strangers.

Intelligent, generous and discerning readers like you who have made a thoughtful choice in buying this book will obviously find many ways of using this method in predicaments with strangers and friends. The technique is useful only if we have control over the circumstances or can choose the precise timing of the requests. Also, a useful relationship can be established even by some very small expression of commitment to help – and that can then be exploited. For instance, Cook (1977) notes that some seducers first attempt to get a partner to do a small favour for them before they make any explicit sexual 'move', and they take willingness as an encouraging sign. Then, they increase the scale of the requests and begin to steer to sexual themes.

'Door in the face'

Will persons who refuse a big demand be more likely to agree to a small one (the so-called door-in-the-face technique)? In the original study of this possibility (Cialdini, Vincent, Lewis, Catalan, Wheeler & Darby, 1975), subjects were first asked to serve as voluntary counsellors at a county juvenile detention centre for two years. Almost everyone turned this 'opportunity' down. When they were subsequently asked to agree to a much smaller request – that is, to chaperone some juveniles on a trip to the zoo – many did so. Again, though, you have to ask whether this sort of thing happens much in everyday life. It's true that friends might ask you to take their kids to the zoo if you're going anyway, but otherwise the connection of this sort of request to real life is pretty remote.

The method seems to work if the initial request is almost ridiculously large, so that the person does not even entertain it as reasonable, and so does not feel negative about himself or herself when turning it down. It also works when the second request is made by the same person who makes the first one – possibly because we would feel bad about ourselves if we turn the same person down twice in a row. It would make us feel mean or unhelpful if we do this. The method is also more successful if the second, smaller request is related to the first, such as completing a small insurance-company survey after declining to complete a much longer one (Mowen & Cialdini, 1980).

'Low ball'

The low-ball technique (Cialdini, Cacioppo, Bassett & Miller, 1978) consists of raising the cost of doing something, once the target (client) agrees to do it in ignorance of the true full costs. For instance, if you consent to show up for an experiment you will be more likely to agree to come before dawn if I hold off on information about the time it starts until after you agreed in principle to participate. This technique differs from the foot in the door only insofar as it involves initial commitment to the *same* behaviour that is ultimately requested, while foot in the door involves initial commitment to a *different* smaller request. It is useful in some circumstances (e.g., selling a car) and even more useful for prospective customers to be aware of. It really depends on there being little or no personal relationship between the people. It loses its effectiveness once we come to realize that someone might use it quite constantly. It is also an extremely offensive and exploitative approach, and will lose more friends than it will persuade, so it is typically a technique that does not work for (and is not normally chosen by) friends to use on one another.

Reflections

There is one odd implication in the material sketched so far. It mostly assumes that persuasiveness 'resides' in the external characteristics of the persuader (e.g., we are persuasive because we dress well or look good); in the internal psychological structure of the target (e.g., people generally change their attitudes in the direction of consistency); or in the broad relationship of parts of the message to other messages that have recently been sent and received (e.g., persuasion follows recent rejection of other persuasion attempts). The effects are largely assumed to be absolute. The strategies are presumed to work irrespective of the personal relationship between participants, though Pechman et al. (2003) note the relative importance to teenagers of appearing 'cool' to their peer cohort and that this relational concern can override the persuasive effects of well structured messages against smoking.

Also, the previous work assumes that our only goal is to persuade the other person, but in most predicaments we actually have multiple goals (O'Keefe, 2004). For instance, we want to ensure no smoking in No Smoking areas, but we do not want to feel bad about ourselves; we want to stop someone letting their small dog into a kids' playground, but we do not want to look to other people as if we are overreacting or officious; we want to get friends to do us a favour, but we certainly do not want to leave them feeling exploited or feel that we are abusing them or that we are 'bad people'. What is needed, then, is to recognize these multiple goals and explain the ways in which *relational* goals might affect the shape of requests that we make on top of other purely persuasive goals.

Social and relational face: Was it something I said?

Let us assume that we all have a range of persuasive strategies to choose from in any set of circumstances: we choose different methods in different encounters, with different people, or on different occasions with the same person, or from circumstances that grow from our relationship to the listener or to the interaction. For instance, one thing we may give particular attention when trying to persuade friends or acquaintances is their social face and their sense of identity as good people. We want them to feel good as well as to do what we ask; we want them to continue to understand that we respect them even if we request their help with something personally inconvenient to them at this precise moment; we want them to appreciate the obligations of friendship but not to feel too obligated; we want to feel we are good people who are not too dependent or needy, even when we have difficulties with which we need help.

Forms of a request

What are the factors that particularly influence the form of a request when one takes particular account of the way the other person feels? Two influences are variously called 'dominance and intimacy' (Cody, Woelfel & Jordan, 1983), or 'status and familiarity' (Tracy, Craig, Smith & Spisak, 1984). These focus on the amount of liking that exists between the two actors (or the degree to which they know one another) and on their relative status. The third factor that influences choice of message type is, rather naturally and predictably, the size of the request or the amount of inconvenience or imposition that will result for the target of the request. The larger the request or favour is, the more the requester takes account of 'felicity conditions' and 'face wants' (Tracy et al., 1984). 'Felicity conditions' refer to two elements of messages: (1) the speaker makes clear why the request is being made and hence establishes that there are legitimate needs for making it; (2) the speaker enquires about the hearer's willingness to perform the requested act (in other words, the person establishes that he or she is making a request rather than giving an order or asking for fulfilment of an obligation or relies on the fact that certain sorts of things are acceptable as persuasive attempts in any particular culture – 'cultural persuadables'; Fitch, 2003). 'Face wants' refer to the concern that the speaker has for presenting a positive image of self and partner (Tracy et al., 1984). There are three elements to this:

1 Messages differ in the degree to which they acknowledge the hearer's desire to be liked and appreciated ('I really appreciate your help on this; you're being such a good friend').
2 Messages differ in relation to the negative face wants of the hearer (i.e. the person's desires for autonomy, freedom of action and freedom from imposition). Speakers acknowledge this need by showing reluctance to impose on the hearer

or by showing uncertainty in their request ('I hate to ask you this, but ... Would it be at all possible for you to ... ?').

3 Messages differ in the attention they give to the speaker's own positive face (e.g., when we ask to borrow money we might make it clear that we have saved some already, but not enough). Note that attention to face wants directly relates to something that we have found here to be vital – making the other person feel good about himself or herself – and that felicity conditions do so less directly but still could help do so.

In their own ways, all of these attend to a relational element of everyday persuasion: caring about someone else's 'face' is in itself a relational act (García-Pastor, 2005), but in the minor persuasions of everyday life between friends, the relationship is more important than other goals. People want to maintain a relationship and keep a friend more than they want to achieve a particular persuasive goal.

Strategy selection

What strategies do we see ourselves having available to us and why do we make particular selections? Certain 'types' of person may habitually choose certain types of strategy or certain types of situation may lead to certain types of strategy-selections by more or less everyone. For instance, powerful people may regularly choose punitive strategies, and people who want to be seen as powerful may think that those strategies are the ones to use – bullies for instance. Men and women may also choose typically different strategies; women are found to prefer to start with reward-based strategies, but their reaction to reluctance or noncompliance depends on the type and strength of the relationship between the two parties and the consequences for it (deTurck, 1985). When persuading *acquaintances* (as distinct from friends), we do choose persuasive strategies that do not 'give *us* a bad time' if things go wrong (Miller, 1982). Our first thought is 'What are the consequences for me if I do not succeed here or things go wrong?' On the other hand, when attempting to persuade *friends*, we avoid strategies that the target could resist only with a feeling of resented obligation or a sense of too unreasonable a demand being made by friendship to do something for us that he or she would really much prefer not to (Miller, 1982). We ask 'What are the consequences for the friend and *for our relationship* if things go wrong?'. Roloff, Janiszewski, McGrath, Burns & Manrai (1988) also show that the more intimate a person is with the target of the request, the less likely is any elaborate explanation of the request or any form of inducement – in short, but importantly, people put the long-term continuance of the relationship above any immediate attempt at persuasion. However, if the request is turned down, then intimates are more likely to come back with a less polite message than are people who are less intimate. The relationship between us and the target influences both the strategies and the messages that we choose.

KEEP A JOURNAL: LIST YOUR OWN PERSUASIVE ATTEMPTS

Your previous journal listed the things you overheard in everyday life. Now start to note the differences between the way you phrase requests to friends, family and strangers. Give some thought to what the request actually is and whether you can find instances where you are persuading or requesting things from other people that you have never really thought of as persuasive in this way. Is a loving glance towards a long-term partner a persuasive request (for sex, for example)? Is the 'Skype me' or the MSN Messenger Sign-in sign a persuasive request? Is the 'no parking' sign a persuasive request?

EVERYDAY TALK AS PERSUASIVE

How do relationships act as a persuasive device? There are two levels to look at here: the subtle one where we use relationships in unexpected ways to persuade, and the less subtle, but still overlooked, point that we do things because other people we care about do them and we often find ourselves doing things that friends, parents, or peers have recommended or modelled for us. I'll start with that, because it has a more obvious intuitive appeal and I will then move on to the issue of ways in which relationships do things for us, more generally, and how messages generally are understood in an environment where you are persuaded by people not necessarily just by arguments. My colleagues and I have recently been looking at a number of ways in which relationships act persuasively (Carl & Duck, 2004; Chang, 2003; Duck & McMahan, forthcoming). Carl & Duck (2004) have noted that the basic function of all communication is to *seek a sense of* control of the environment and of the rightness of one's views of it. Other functions of communication are subordinate to this goal and depend upon it but connect very significantly with matters of interpersonal influence. Carl & Duck argued that these goals are achieved through relationships with other people and through their influence on us and our influence on them. We argued also that relational contexts do things for people in ways that are not necessarily recognized as a part of the conscious or intentional matrix of interpersonal communication.

From this point of view, some underlying themes of the interpersonal communication research clearly show the ways in which interpersonal influence works in everyday encounters through relationship processes rather than just through persuasive logic (i.e., through *ethos* rather than *logos*). Everyday network activity is involved in relationships in ways that give partners a sense of their location in reality and the validity of their ideas. Several different strands of communication research on persuasion and attitude change have an underlying relational dynamic, where relationships are the engine of much that is of concern to communication studies, such as interpersonal influence (friends influence one another's ideas and behaviour relationally), media influences (friends talk about TV programmes, news items, messages and advertisement, and political campaigns in ways that might modify the expected effects of those campaigns when viewed from a strictly logical point of view), impact of health messages (friends talk about health issues and in so doing can be more persuasive than direct advertising, but they can also undermine the effects of health campaigns by mocking the ads or criticizing their message), group decision making, and the proliferation of innovations or the impact of gossip and opinion. The relational interactions that constitute daily life experience are the unexamined basis of many processes that have hitherto been explained by use of specific theories of communication about the above topics.

Let us now explore some of the preceding issues from three new relational vantage points: *first*, from the assumption that, in everyday relational contexts, the two related parties are concerned about the preservation of their long-term relationship at least as much as they are concerned about persuading one another; *second*, from the point of view of the discussion in Chapter 4 that all relationships and all persuasion occur in a network of other relationships to which the partners are also attentive. Just as a person may not be willing to risk losing a good relationship with a partner merely in order to get a particular request fulfilled, so the person may be concerned about the good opinion of *other* close friends or family also and that concern can provide a powerful context for behaviour in persuasion. *Third*, people use relationships and information about them as persuasive and decisive elements in their decision-making. Also, we should think a little more about what that means for human relationships in this topical context. How often does the structure of a message matter less than the relational source from which it comes?

Normally, we think first of persuasion being done verbally. Sahlstein & Duck (2001) suggested that people use such terms as 'friend', 'pal', and 'Mother' as direct attempts to persuade and Sahlstein went further and claimed that there exist Rhetorical Relational Terms by which speakers call out their relationship and make it relevant to whatever else is being said in the interaction. Examples would be 'You're my friend. I need your help here!' or 'What can I expect if even you, my own mother, won't take my side?'. The effect of such appeals is to use the relationship as a persuasive tool to add force to whatever else is said in the attempt at persuasion. Indeed, even prayer tends to invoke relational terms before making a request: consider 'Our Father which art in heaven … give us this day, etc.' The prayer starts with the obvious appeal to a relationship, and specifically one that normally implies a duty of care and concern for the speaker. Finally, Searcy et al. (2005) looked at ways in which group members persuade one another by relational influences and use of collective metaphors that emphasize collaboration, such as 'teamwork', so that people who are not in agreement with the rest of the group can be brought to heel by the implication that they are not acting in ways consistent with their relational obligations. However, not all persuasion attempts in relationships are verbal: putting an arm round a shoulder can be part of a request sequence that stresses a relational element and implies a familiar closeness. Finally we should not overlook the sequential, the chained, or the historical nature of human interaction including interpersonal influence behaviour (Duck, 2002). Instead of studying single utterances or sequences of talk within one interaction, relationships compel us to look at the influence of longer-term conversational or relational history under the assumption that what happened in the past discursively and relationally has an impact on what is going on here and now, which once again affects what will happen in the future. So in other words, no persuasive attempt just comes out of nowhere: it comes out of a pre-existing relationship.

Persuasion and concerns about the relational context

An important everyday fact, then, is the significance of the persuasion attempt in both the here-and-now of the person's social life and also its placement in the context of ongoing relationships with pasts and futures. Persuasion has consequences for me now here, yet a persuasion attempt may be based on something that happened in the relationship some time ago and may also carry consequences for its future. We also often have to make persuasive attempts knowing that we must continue in the same social or relational situation afterwards or that other people will get to hear about it or that a particular outcome today could carry long-term relational consequences. If we try to get a neighbour to turn down the music, we may be making our future life less comfortable since the neighbour may become ill-disposed towards other requests and may become 'difficult', or other people may see us as interfering and troublesome and may start to gossip about how we behaved. Little persuasive attempts in the present can, therefore, have large personal and social consequences in the future. We would be making a big mistake if we regarded everyday 'compliance-gaining' and persuasion as neatly packaged within one interaction itself, done at a distance from insistently helpful friends and friendly advisers, or away from the influence of gossip and group membership; or, if we saw 'compliance-doing' as a pure act of 'information processing' that is relatively rapid and based only on sensible, logical, non-social principles, and is not mentally connected to the relational consequences that could fall out on the participants.

A second point is that compliance-gaining in everyday life might take up a lot of time if it violates friendship norms – we could get into a long discussion about friendship and what it means and might even discuss whether so many norms have been broken that the relationship has to end. Persuasion can be a drawn-out process for other reasons in long-term relationships. It is not usually a simple, once-for-all event. The persuasive target is likely to resist us or challenge us, which will require us to take another shot. Furthermore, some compliance takes time to plan. Attempts to seduce a partner or have an essay grade changed by a familiar professor can be thought about or planned in advance, can be modified, and can be thought about later, too, if they fail the first time. Also, as Christopher & Frandsen (1990) showed, individuals often use clusters of sequential strategies in order to achieve such goals as premarital sexual intercourse and may persist over a longer timespan – say, several encounters.

Thus, selection of persuasive strategies within a friendship or romance is, I think, a developmental and incremental activity rather than an isolated, one-off action. In close personal relationships the structure of messages is modified by the long-term context provided by the relationship and is not a 'pure' act of attitude change or persuasion deprived of that context. Also, topics, attitudes, and behaviours can come up frequently in routine interaction within a family, rather than as just one of persuasive putsch. Avenevoli & Merikangas (2003) note that although definitions of family are inconsistent in research on smoking, for example, it remains true that sibling smoking habits are a reasonable predictor of an adolescent's likelihood of smoking – i.e., teenagers are 'persuaded' by what they routinely observe other valued persons in their family doing in a repeated set of interactions, and not necessarily as a result of directly expressed influence, either. Sometimes giving up a habit like smoking means giving up the friends with whom you share the habit and its rituals and with whom you interact while doing it in the places where you normally meet … so the habit stays (Duck, in press SAGE CA, see refs).

Furthermore, when we look at the routine side of real life we see that our knowledge of one another helps us to plan and gives us some awareness of any likely relational consequences since we know the target quite well. When we have to get a parent to lend us the car, persuade a friend to lend us a valuable book, or obtain an extension of a deadline for an assignment, there are inbuilt relational forces that affect not only the immediate goal, but also the feelings of the target of the persuasion and the reputation of the person attempting to achieve the outcome. For one thing, both parties have a view of themselves and the nature of their relationship – and probably wish to preserve it.

Sometimes, we would rather give up on an argument than risk losing a friendship. For this reason, we shall most probably be unwilling to act in a way that threatens the relationship, and we may make this fact a key element in our persuasion attempt. If we make a request that we recognize is too demanding, we might choose to accompany it by some relational preservative like an appeal to the person's good nature, an offer to restore the balance one day, a reminder of a past occasion when the positions were reversed, or a reference to our over-whelming need and the role requirements of friendship. In other circumstances when the relationship is more formal, such as between teacher and pupil, such relational references will refer to the demands of the *role* and the participants are unlikely to persuade by trying to even suggest that there might be a close personal friendship.

Once we recognize that most persuasions occur in such a context of living relationships – not only in partnerships but in networks – and in real social lives and within our long-term goals or projects, not just our short-term persuasive objectives, we see that we need to look carefully into the impact of such contexts on our attempts to gain compliance, including the moral context provided by our close associates (De Santis, 2002). A very important fact that I have repeatedly alluded to in the course of this chapter has been the fact that relationships quite simply legitimate certain sorts of persuasion by their very existence: I may ask you to do something difficult for me simply by virtue of the fact that we are friends. Your friendship obliges you to perform certain kinds of supportive actions and the persuasion to perform them is inherent in the acceptance of the role of friendship (Carl & Duck, 2004). I may structure my request in a way that reminds you that you are a friend and that friends have to help one another: basically we both accept that friendship means that each of us should do things for the other's good and that's that (Sahlstein & Duck, 2001). It would be quite ridiculous for us to spend a long time structuring persuasive arguments, getting our feet in the door or our doors in the faces of friends and parents and relatives in quite the way that some of the old research might lead us to expect to be necessary.

The relational network as a *morally* persuasive context

One of the comments that I made earlier about classical research on attitude change is that it used to strip persuasion out of these everyday relational contexts that direct the way influence actually proceeds. We have now spent some time looking at the ways in which relationships themselves provide a context for persuasive attempts but I have not yet returned to a point I made at the start of this chapter concerning the importance of the network and social context in which any individual persuasive attempt occurs.

When we persuade a single individual our behaviour is still open to the scrutiny of others either directly or as a result of the reports of either party to third parties. If someone tries to bully me, I may tell friends or family and the word could soon reach many other ears when each person tells their own friends and allies that 'X is a bully'. On top of that, the moral context provided by membership of a community also exposes our behaviour to the persuasive influence of social accountability: what I mean by that is that our own behaviour can be shaped and moulded not only by the influence of media or magazine ideals or cultural norms and prescriptives (as discussed in Chapter 4) but by the fact that our own behaviour is subject to the moral scrutiny of our specific community of acquaintances and our network of friends and relatives. When we deviate from agreed and desired goals, we may become the subject of gossip or other more direct forms of social pressure (Foster & Rosnow, 2006).

LISTEN IN ON YOUR OWN LIFE: GOSSIP AND THE SOCIAL ORDER

- We often learn about other people from gossip and – let's be honest – daily communication is often gossipy. Learn to recognize how significant this activity is in social life in relationships, not only as an (unreliable) source of information about other people, but as a way for a speaker to gain status in a group.
- Gossip is usually about other people's private behaviour about which we can really actually know very little except though inference or speculation so listen for moral judgements and narratives that spin the story for us.
- Gossip is often represented by the gossips as 'only trivial' or 'only a bit of fun' or something they are really 'not doing' ('I don't want to be a gossip but ...', 'Don't think I'm prying but ...'), since gossip per se is typically seen as a negative thing to be caught doing. However, listen out for ways in which it enforces moral codes informally, by subjecting people to (the fear of) third-party ridicule or censure (Bergmann, 1993).

Gossip has long intrigued psychologists (Foster & Rosnow, 2006; Suls, 1977), but it is only recently that scholars have begun to look at gossip not simply as a phenomenon of message transmission or social comparison (see above) but as a mechanism for social sanctioning, moral *persuasion*, and relational structuring (Bergmann, 1993; Duck & VanderVoort, 2002). When a person becomes the subject of gossip, the person is essentially being subjected to the moral judgement of the gossipers and the person's behaviour is made the subject matter of these persons' social persuasions. Recognizing this, people very often hold back from doing something just because they fear this consequence: that the neighbours or the family might find out and disapprove. Thus there is a hidden persuader in society that prevents activities that, if discovered, are likely to attract censure from others such as affairs or cheating on partners (Duck & VanderVoort, 2002; Duncombe et al., 2004). Even relational behaviour itself is subject to the direct evaluation of third parties who may intervene and persuade the partners to behave differently, using the moral persuasive force of their position as representatives of the wider society in which the behaviour takes place (Klein & Milardo, 1993) or the right to comment on relationships that is conferred by their social position (in-laws do this a lot!; Morr-Serewicz, 2006). The tools for handling relational conflict itself also include the censure of outsiders' comments on the behaviour as a means of persuading people to cease and desist from the conflict (Klein & Johnson, 2000).

As Bergmann (1993) notes, gossip is therefore a form of persuasion both actively and passively: fear of becoming the subject of gossip passively persuades people not to engage in some forms of behaviour and the comments of other people can actively dissuade a person from some courses of action. Thus when we place persuasion in the everyday context of lived experience in relationships within a culture and its attendant expectations, we can see yet another side of it which is not reached by classic analyses of attitude change and persuasion: the moral and interactive relational context in which the persuasion is carried out. This needs to be included in thoughts about persuasion, just as do our personal evaluations of the others in our network who are sources for any information we collect that is relevant to the decision.

The moral context is also easily recognized in cases where one person gives advice to another, since advice is often directly about choices and consequences of actions and so is very clearly morally loaded. Equally advice is often the same thing as social support – as when it helps a person to solve a problem, supports their way of acting, or validates an alternative that they have proposed (Sarason et al., 2001). However, the moral overtones of advice taken or given are also relational in their consequences and the rejection of advice can strain a relationship into the bargain.

Furthermore, in long-term relationships the advice given to one person on a small matter may provide a basis for the two people to set up expectations of support and assistance in other contexts. For example by finding frequently that Person X helps me with little tasks or talks constructively and encouragingly about daily trivia, I can form the impression that the person is a supportive and helpful friend. Thus, when there comes a need for some big help with something hugely disastrous or significant, it is this person rather than another person in my network to whom I would turn for support (Leatham & Duck, 1990). Daily conversations thus provide a subtle building of context for the provision of social support that merits more research attention. Such conversations also serve to structure networks for us mentally in the sense that from the experiences obtained in these trivial conversations we can build up some sense of the organization of our network (Milardo, 1992) into those who are best helpers, those who help under protest, and those who never help at all. Thus we build up a sense of the relative difficulty of persuading such persons to come in and make an effort for us when we need it (Leatham & Duck, 1990).

Relationships as hidden persuaders

Let's face it, when I talk to other people about something seeking advice, it is not because I can see the arguments and make up my own mind, but precisely because I cannot. I want relevant help, and I want useful personally-tuned guidance, so I will pay account to the reliability and credibility of the source as much as to things such as topic relevance. Relationships are very important to such information flow, and also to the evaluation of information, even information from government sources. Such commentary, advice, and guidance can come up at any moment during the course of everyday routines in long-term relationships. Bricker et al. (2003), for example, showed that when both parents quit smoking, children's odds of daily smoking were reduced by 39 per cent compared to when both parents were current smokers. It seems that the behaviour of influential others in relationships all around you leads not only to you being persuaded through observation, but also, I guess, from the fact that the family as a whole discusses the value of their new actions and so influences the children along the way. This is a much smarter connection of relationships to persuasion than assuming a blanket influence of 'family' or 'siblings' on such things as smoking, as Darling & Cumsille (2003) point out, and I'd suggest that the mechanism is relationally-based talk, such that programmes which stimulate discussion of a topic in a network are likely to create persuasive influences. For example, Simons-Morton et al. (2001) showed that social networks can promote or discourage substance abuse and that peer activity was positively associated with drinking for girls but not for boys. Having problem friends was positively associated with drinking for both boys and girls. Although associating with deviant peers promotes, and authoritative parenting protects against, smoking and drinking, it is of course the talk in practice, rather than 'the association' in the abstract, that has this effect: the 'association' leads to relational activity focused on discussion of the topic in the normal course of everyday talk, and we tend to care about what 'associates' say to us.

In a stunning demonstration of the potential effects of talk amongst friends, De Santis (2002) showed how groups of friends and acquaintances in a cigar shop routinely supported one another in denigrating Government health warnings about the risks of smoking and collectively upheld resistance to information that attacks their habit. The daily conversation of the customers who smoked at the shop indicated six different sorts of argument to which they all subscribed. The first argument was that there can be nothing wrong with an action if it is done only in moderation (and lo and behold, they all saw themselves as only moderate smokers); the second argument was that health benefits from smoking are not given enough credence (for example, its role in stress reduction); third, it was pointed out that cigars are not cigarettes (and so people do not inhale and it is the inhalation rather than the smoke itself which is dangerous); fourth, they used a 'flawed research' argument that essentially suggested a fashionable capriciousness in science (What's bad today is good tomorrow and vice versa; research doesn't reach Truth only today's truth); fifth, they suggested life is altogether dangerous anyway and that smoking is no more dangerous than many other things that people do (for example, there is much else in life that is dangerous, such as food additives or excess alcohol or lack of exercise, and cigars are relatively *less* dangerous). The sixth argument was perhaps the most striking and was labelled by De Santis as 'The Greg argument'. Greg, a former member of the group, had died from heart failure and the smokers' group took the position that he did not die from smoking but from a weak heart and alcohol over-use instead. By this means they convinced themselves that the causal relationship between smoking and heart problems was not only not established but was even refuted by their own close up experience! This study is thus a spectacular demonstration of the point I'm making here that friends filter information for one another and adjust its persuasive impact.

Accordingly, Figure 5.1 indicates the relative value that we attach to input from different members of our social networks and the extent to which we are shaped by the social network to act in particular ways in a given set of circumstances. The middle rows of Figure 5.1 deal with incoming 'information' from the media and which of course may be discussed with other people and accepted or rejected as a result of such discussion. Information has no direct, and unmediated effects on a person in the model I am proposing: everything is filtered through both one's own judgement and also through discussion with people who may influence that judgement to different degrees. I believe that Figure 5.1 represents the flow of persuasive information as modified by the relational forces that I have pointed out in this chapter. The role of history of the relationship, alluded to earlier, affects not only the top left-hand box, but also moderates the third column.

Although Figure 5.1 is derived from the comments I have made throughout the chapter concerning the persuasive effects of relationships, my main point has been that the most important forms of persuasion and the information processing

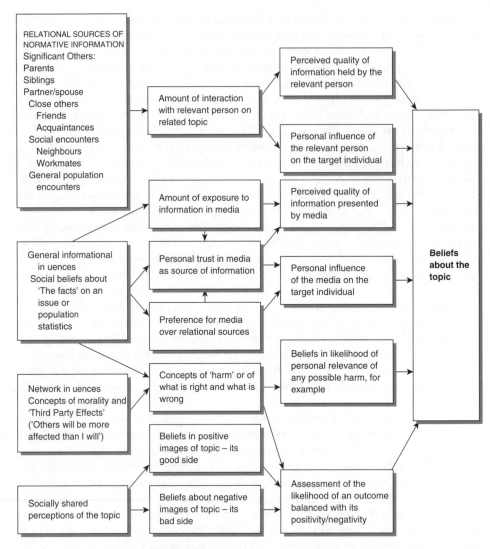

Figure 5.1 Interpersonal model of message processing

connected thereto are inextricable from the relationships in which we all embed ourselves. The two should not be separated in the study of human relationships, because in everyday life they are rarely separate either. Even when we are talking with friends about TV shows, such persuasion is occurring and the balance of opinions and ideas is being rhetorically processed.

SUMMARY

We have looked at some real-life examples where one person chose to try to stop a stranger from doing something he wanted to do. Relationships operate to persuade in everyday life and the relationship between speaker and target modifies what happens there. In everyday real life, the nature of the relationship between the persuader and the target is a significant influence on persuasion and also on processing of information. However small many of our persuasions are in real life, many of them can be drawn out and anxiety-provoking in ways not true of persuasion about 'big' attitudes (for example, about nuclear power or the environment or politics). Decision-making and persuasion in the context of our everyday life involve us in thinking about the consequences for our relationships with partners, friends and colleagues as well as in simply assessing the merits or demerits of two sides of an argument or of two alternatives that lie open to us. I discussed the role of gossip in indirectly, but firmly, persuading people to do moral things, and I looked at a number of interpersonal and relational activities that are inherently persuasive. My main points were that such activities are ones that we slither into during everyday life without special signposts; they happen as a routine part of everyday life and emerge seamlessly from it. Persuasion cannot be explained merely in terms of the psychological features of individuals that take no account of important hidden persuaders like relational context, social network, and a person's experience of the society.

You should now be able to notice persuasion occurring in life at some finer levels and should be able to see such things as advice, support, ordinary discourse and even gossip as inherently persuasive in effect but also as based on relationship forces in complex ways.

SELF QUESTIONS

- How much persuasion takes place in life through routines? What practices in your daily relational life amount to persuasive influence?
- Do you argue with people about politics and nuclear weapons or other things more often? How does either type of argument reflect the principles discussed in this chapter?
- Reflect on Attachment Style from Chapter 2 and see if you could find any ways in which attachment patterns might be relevant to strategy choice in persuasion.
- Have you ever bought something on the recommendation of a friend? How important is word of mouth in your decision whether to see a movie?

FURTHER READING

Bergmann, J. (1993). *Discreet indiscretions*. New York : Aldine deGruyter.

Billig, M. (1991). *Ideology and opinions: Studies in rhetorical psychology.* London: SAGE.

Bohner, G., & Wanke, M. (2002). *Attitudes and attitude change.* London: Psychology Press.

Carl, W.J. (2006). What's all the buzz about?: everyday communication and the relational basis of word-of-mouth and buzz marketing practices. *Management Communication Quarterly, 19,* 601–634.

Gass, R.H., & Seiter, J.S. (2006). *Persuasion, social influence, and compliance gaining, 3rd ed.* Boston, MA: Allyn & Bacon/Longman.

PRACTICAL MATTERS

- How do you think advertising campaigns could be used to 'tweak' networks for informational purposes or for marketing purposes (e.g. how would you get a network to talk about a topic, rather like the 'talk to your kids about drugs' campaign)? What might be the drawbacks?
- Note the growth of WOM (word of mouth) and 'Buzz' marketing and try to find some websites that advocate it. Apply what you have learned in this chapter to the processes that they discuss. (Try www.bzzagent.com, for example.)
- What practical suggestions would you make to a Government agency about the relational context as influences on the processing of information about smoking, drugs or alcohol?
- The chapter noted that Education is a kind of persuasive activity. In what ways might this be a wrong idea?

6

Technology and the Boundaries of Relationships: It's all Geek to me

It is not the consciousness of men which determines their existence but on the contrary it is their social existence which determines their consciousness. (Karl Marx 1932: 4)

Focus points for note taking when reading this chapter:

- How does new technology affect relational life?
- Is new technology essentially about the reorganization of *relational* life?
- What boundaries are there around your relationships? How does new technology force you to spill over from one boundaried area to another?
- Are your relationships portable and as mobile as your phone?
- What rules govern the ways in which you can use your relationship accessibility in social situations?
- Is the need to communicate really a need to relate?
- If you were to invent a GPS for your relationships what would you have in it?
- Are etiquette rules about use of mobile phones really about *relationship* boundaries?

Some of the biggest cultural and lifestyle changes in recent years have been focused on 'relational websites' such as eHarmony.com and directdating.com. The largest amount of spam that I get every day is offering me all sorts of relational experiences, from opportunities for casual sex to chances to extend my network of 'friends' in the local area, or to find long-lost friends and ex-lovers. My teenage sons are concerned about their social networks on the Net and my students display their relationship status on facebook.com and myspace.com with astonishing dedication. In addition e-mail and instant messaging connect people together electronically and the effect has been that the so-called 'information technology' takes an emphatically relational spin.

This relational spin was not foreseen by its inventors, who focused instead on the *educational* value of both new technology and the World Wide Web (remember the emphasis on 'The *Information* Superhighway'?). The relational effects were even missed by the mobile phone industry which in the mid-1980s estimated that by the year 2000 there would be about 900,000 mobile phones worldwide, used exclusively for business operations (http://news.bbc.co.uk/1/hi/technology/5019394.stm). In fact by 2000 there were 450,000,000 mobile phones in the world and they were being used by young people rather than old business moguls and mostly for *relational* purposes. The industry got it 46,000 per cent wrong because it thought only in terms of business and completely overlooked the fact that human beings are first and foremost social animals.

I believe we gain more by looking at 'technology' as a *fundamentally* relational implement than just as mere electronics that happen to get used in relationships. It is astonishing how people relentlessly bend every new technological development to relational uses, despite the fact that each one was often developed for other purposes originally, whether writing (developed originally for accounting purposes), the telephone (once dismissed by a potential investor as having no use beyond a mere curiosity value), and the Internet, as mentioned above, foreseen as a reserve of information, and now used relationally by almost everyone who uses it, whatever else they do with it.

Human relationships are all too often overlooked as a significant driving force of modern life where descriptions are more usually termed in exciting and shiny technological language. But does the modern behaviour represent something new or is it merely an extension of a much broader human need for recognition, acceptance and relationships and merely uses electronic methods to do it? Hold those thoughts for the rest of the chapter while I now show how technology crosses many boundaries including continents.

KEEP A JOURNAL

- How often do you check such sites as facebook.com and my space.com?
- Do you check your own page or look at other people's?
- Keep a record of how you use the sites and navigate around them.

(Continued)

(Continued)

- Start to think about what you're trying to find out and how it connects to relational networks of the kind that we discussed in Chapter 4. What do you think people are doing in terms of face work when they present themselves on the sites?
- How often do people in everyday life face-to-face conversations discuss the things that they freely reveal on facebook.com such as cheating on tests or on other people? How different from or similar to your everyday communication are the topic lists laid out on any myspace.com site?

CROSSING RELATIONAL SPACES

So here I am sitting in Amsterdam, enjoying an essentially interconnected world that now crosses multiple boundaries in many different ways, real, national, technical and relational. I am an Englishman who lives and works in America, but on this occasion am in the Netherlands, relaxing on the bank of a rather pleasant canal in springtime instead of huddling indoors against the Iowa windchill. I am in an outdoor café reading the English newspapers and carrying my laptop. On my belt is an iPod equivalent, my characteristic Swiss Army knife, and my mobile/cellular phone. I'm aware of being able to call friends and family in the USA any time I want, though this situation is imbalanced because only a few of them know my European number and are able to contact me. I like being able to call them when I choose, which in Amsterdam is, frankly, not particularly often. I like that balance of choice, so that I limit touch from people whose electronic touch is as unwelcome as other sorts of touch.

Shift scenes to a bar in Amsterdam, which I happened to find at random in my ceaseless search for new experiences. Having read the newspaper first, and without my laptop, but with a mobile phone still predictably attached to my belt, I started to read through this book manuscript. There were a few other people (all Dutch) and – a clue I should've recognized but had not interpreted at the time – the bar served beer only in 300 ml glasses, which in the UK amounts to about half a pint, and is thus about half the standard measure by which beer is usually ordered in the UK. I have since noticed that other bars in Amsterdam that do so have only Dutch people in them, no English, and I suspect without proof that this is an informal mechanism for keeping out the famous British 'lager louts' who drink lager beer by the pint and usually have too much of it. It might conceivably be a signal about the owner's attitude towards the English. When I went back to the bar to top up, the bar woman noted in pretty good English, 'So you think this is your office'. At the time I took this as simply an observation, I made a suitable but unmemorable reply, paid for the beer and returned to the writing of my masterpiece, regrettably not a Dutch masterpiece. The next time I went back to the bar the barwoman asked me to leave on the grounds that this was not in fact an office, whether mine or anyone else's. It had been unproblematic for her when I read an English newspaper, but once I started reading other sorts of papers I evidently offended her sensibilities about behaviour that is suitable in a bar. In this case, then, the disjunctions between different types of space and uses of space indicated that I was not in a truly interconnected world.

Let's start by analysing that bar in Amsterdam as a relational space. While I was reading newspapers I was evidently doing something regarded as social and acceptable in that space. Once I began reading other kinds of papers, I elicited in the barwoman the observation that her bar was not an office, essentially a comment about the use of a particular space for a particular type of function. At a deeper level of analysis of the situation her comment was also about an abstract concept of what it means to be in an office and what it means to be in a social space like a bar where the few other people were talking and laughing together. From her point of view an office is a place at which one does certain kinds of work and a bar is a place for social relationships. But what if I had been in my office and a friend called me on the phone? Do the limits on use of space go in only one direction? Why would relationship spaces be diodes?

What other information does this interaction tell us about the way in which we regard life as being bracketed and segmented into particular roles and performance areas? In terms of social orders and understandings there might be further overlays to the analysis of the bar which are relevant to discussion of relationships and such performances too. It was rather obvious that the other people in that particular bar were not office workers and my performance of 'office behaviour' might have carried social and stratification messages to the barwoman and to them. Class is not just an abstract concept but means something in terms of social orders and understandings and the actual *performance* of behaviours. That is to say, social structures come down to interaction and talk and behaviour – not merely to membership of a classification (Allan, 1998; Duck, in press SAGE CA, see refs). Patterns of belief and consciousness are enacted in talk and identities and 'world orders' are projected through activities. What threat to the barwoman's world order would my reading of research papers offer? Was her response an enactment of anti-intellectualism or a rejection of 'doing work other than that done by the other people in the bar'? Or was I in fact at fault in breaking a relational rule by reading certain sorts of formal material in an informal relational space?

I have no idea whether my assessment of the situation is correct, but it has been possible to analyse this interesting event in terms that are relevant to the things we will discuss in this chapter. These concern the bleeding over of lines of privacy, the segmentation of space for specific purposes, and the interconnection of people through media and other sources that have invaded our world in recent years.

These are ultimately *relational* questions: privacy is about keeping other people away/out; spaces used for some purposes rather than others (as we saw in Chapter 1) are most often separated and differentiated according to rules of intimacy or relational function (Duck, in press SAGE CA, see refs); mediated connection is a relational event that does not recognize or adhere to those same rules about functions of spaces.

In particular, the chapter will make us think about the ways in which the relational space bleeds into other kinds of space and the way in which technological advances are encouraging and facilitating that to happen. So what is the space where 'relationship work' can be done and how is that modified by accessibilities afforded through technology? Think for example, about the placing of computers within the household. Should they be in public or in private parts of the home? What difference does it make? Bear in mind also that there is now a large growth in the effort to have households acquire wireless routing systems. Such wireless systems make it possible for people with laptops to move them around the house and use them in almost any place anyway, so this further breaks down the barriers that are implied in the specific allocation of space to one particular use, whether social or work-related, or even cooking and food consumption, because a wireless laptop could (theoretically, even if impolitely) enable somebody to both work and also eat a relatively formal meal at the same time in the same place.

Researchers do not yet agree on whether communication patterns in families connected to the Internet differ from those who are not connected, for example. Some scholars believe that the family is strengthened through the collection of separate family activities such as working, learning, and shopping that were previously spread across different times and places for accomplishment. Other scholars are not optimistic and believe that use of the Internet fosters reduced interaction between parents and children. Mesch (2006) examined the effects of introduction of the Internet into the household and suggested that it can negatively affect the spending of family time. Believe me, it certainly increases the amount of time that parents spend doing their kids' homework! It can also be a force for the increase of family conflicts, yielding a low overall perception of family cohesion when family members argue about whose turn it is on a computer and about the uses to which the computer and the Internet may be put. Mesch suggested that frequency of adolescent Internet use is associated with a decline in family cohesion, even if a researcher controls for personality characteristics that might lead to more frequent Internet use, such as shyness. The suggestion of the study was that Internet use can be beneficial in some contexts, insofar as it strengthens boundaries and creates memories that help to develop collective identity within the family, but that it also has very negative effects on family life. So this research does not answer the question about the effects of the Internet on family cohesion and we could call this basically a draw, though not a particularly surprising one!

Although we know that some spaces, places and times are specifically for relationships (e.g., a candlelit dinner), how do we keep the boundaries around such special things when all the other boundaries are made so easily permeable by technology? I ask because I just saw a couple having a candlelit dinner holding hands across the table, the man holding his wine glass in the other hand while his date was using her other hand to talk to someone else on her cell phone. For reasons we can look at later in the chapter it often appears that relational activity on the cell phone takes precedence over face-to-face interaction, although there are increasing pressures to consider the etiquette rules that apply to such usages. The etiquette is often spelled out with respect to space. Some railway carriages in the UK are designated as 'quiet areas' where mobile phones may not be used, and one such quiet area exists in the NWA WorldClub in Detroit, though, for reasons best known to the management it is the area where CNN is left on continuously on the television. So the space is not exactly quiet space, just space where no one should use a cell phone. What is done by designating spaces in this way as places where you may or may not bring or talk with your friends telephonically but may do so in person? When the technology makes our relationships portable, why can we take them into some spaces and not others?

The mobile phone allows the public to intrude into the private, the formal into the informal, and the distant into the intimate but at some point people obviously find this as inappropriate as the barwoman found it for me to read a book manuscript (but not perhaps a book) in her bar. The issue then is where and how boundaries are drawn around relationships when technology would otherwise smudge the lines for us. Should we analyse the technological territory and the technological invasion in the same terms that we used for nonverbal territory and nonverbal invasion in Chapter 1? (I'm not going to be able to cover all of these issues here so you could reserve them for class discussion.)

The Internet as problematic relating

Lots of recent research suggests that Internet technology represents a new way of relating but I broadly disagree. Has technology altered our relational lives or merely given us much greater opportunities for conducting them whenever we want? Whereas people who wanted to contact their friends in 1773 had to write letters and wait weeks or months for a reply, we get instantaneous access to them, for good or ill, but are we really doing anything terribly different in terms of the role of human communication in the human condition?

In a different café in Amsterdam (my favourite, the Café Corso) I was sitting and reading *The Guardian*, a British newspaper, and there was an article by a philosopher who wrote a book on email with someone he'd never met. He asks some interesting questions, one of which is whether anything happens over Computer-Mediated Communication (CMC) that doesn't happen in face-to-face – which tradition obliges me to refer to henceforth as 'F2F'.

> Humans have different kinds of relationships, all of which have different needs. Some kinds of working relationships clearly are well suited to being conducted online. Before too long, perhaps it will be usual to hear people say that the most trusted and liked colleagues are the ones they have never met. ...Contrast this with the common experience people have of falling out with friends who become business associates. Knowing someone in the flesh does not seem to make us reliable judges of how well we would work with them.
> (Julian Baggini, *The Guardian*, 6 January 2005: 17)

CMC now of course comes in many forms, some of which were not available when the first research on it was reported in the early 1990s. Types of CMC are now changing and expanding as companies such as Skype and Logitech combine to offer video as well as VOIP (Voice Over Internet Protocol) and more complex interconnections of types of technology are clearly being foreshadowed, all of which seem destined to bring CMC into closer connection with, and lack of differentiation from, F2F interaction. Very recently large cable TV providers, music/media groups, Internet providers, phone companies and others have been merging in ways that suggest 'fourplay' as Virgin's CEO Richard Branson calls it, suggesting an important convergence of four different forms of technology into one device – possibly even available by the time this book is read – that receives TV, email, and Net content and also works as a phone, as well as making it possible to download movies and music. Let's hope they are working on ways to download tunes to your pacemaker for when you get old.

Much that was written about the risks of CMC when it took a very basic form (see Lea & Spears, 1995) might now not apply in the same way, although some risks clearly still exist. In particular, it is often stated that there are particular risks of CMC for conveying mistaken understandings, 'flaming' and doing disinhibited interaction, even though the same sorts of things can happen elsewhere in life. However, once the distinctions are eroded between public and private space, then our whole codes for understanding behaviour are also eroded because there are several intimate things, like conducting personal relationships, that are normally regarded as suitable for doing only in 'private places' (Duck, in press SAGE CA, see refs), but if there is no firm boundary nowadays between public and private relational spaces then these differences likewise evaporate. Another important difference in CMC, however, is that information is not dealt with through slow and organized reciprocation (as we saw in Chapter 3), but merely through individualized disclosure or discovery at one's own chosen speed and pace. You should consider whether 'normal' rules about reciprocity in information flow are actually a help or hindrance in face-to-face relationship building.

LOOK OUT FOR THIS IN THE MEDIA

Watch out for stories reporting instances of uses of Internet, mobile phones, or even the iPod and iTunes in *relational* ways. In particular, you could look for stories about the use of photographs on mobile phones in gang-related incidents, where part of the purpose of using the pictures is to identify with a particular gang and its activities or to brag about its activities to other people (a relational activity at its root). You could also consider how the sharing of music and ring tones or music downloads or digital photographs, or even jokes broadcast to a network of friends might be used as relational bonding activity, creation of membership or recognition of mutuality and shared meaning as discussed in Chapter 3.

In CMC we can form impressions, work with people, conceal facts about ourselves, promote aspects of self that we want people to believe, and generally do the business of human relationships, although some models strongly suggest that CMC requires specific sorts of compensation in the processing of information (for example, reading words carefully rather than just listening to them. The Internet usually presumes an ability to read that F2F does not – in fact one site offers to send a leaflet to people with reading difficulties!). Many researchers take a negative view of the Internet and fear its effects. In their SIDE (Social Identity of Deindividuation Effects) model Lea & Spears (1995) proposed a way of seeing the social self in general as more than simple physical presence, based on the observation that individuals using the Internet are able to both make and also to counter significant misrepresentations of their self in a standard email or instant messaging format. The SIDE model pays attention not only to social and personal identity but also to the social categories that a person identifies with. That is to say, it looks not only at the fact that you are who you are as a person in your own right but also at the fact that you belong to social groupings that contribute to your identity too (such as religious groups, racial groups, biological groups – male/female for example – a socioeconomic grouping, a geographical and national grouping and so forth). It is evident that CMC users employ both the self-evident and the implied cultural, social, and psychological groups to which they or another person may belong in order to convey social information or manage impressions, for example by directly referencing their sex, race, nationality or other groupings. We can also claim an identity just by means of the cues that give it away, as revealed by the things that we write about, the words we use and the things that we take for granted or directly by representing ourselves as having particular musical preferences, for example, on myspace.com. However, search engines organize racial and ethnic information and people of mixed origins are forced to rank order or at least to separate themselves into identity parts by the very way that these engines organize their content, themselves, and the people who use them.

In short we can present ourselves quite effectively using standard or available categories on CMC but users may change a self-presentation technique when they understand the ways in which other people are able to recognize the social categories to which they belong. That is to say, they can alter their ways of expressing and presenting themselves by manipulating the cues that create those impressions. This appears to me to be done much as people do in everyday F2F also, for example by adopting normative behaviour that appears to be consistent with the categories that they present (like you do when you show up to an interview wearing business clothes in order to look as if you belong to the 'professional' group). Even in a medium that relies primarily on the written word, it is possible to use such things as linguistic style, politeness strategies, name usage, and emoticons in order to transmit social information that can affect the impressions that another person forms. According to the SIDE model therefore, individuals are not restricted only to the written word, but pay attention to the social categories which are conveyed by the words and forms that are used (Lea & Spears, 1995).

The effects of anonymity on social identity processes can, however, occur in CMC in ways that seriously affect not only intergroup relations but also the development of trust and liking and indeed any sort of judgements about the performance of partners who do not see each other. Walther & Bunz (2005) considered how trust develops for people who do not see one another given that geographic distance can create a number of disruptive effects. They point out that relational communication is necessary between team members even in a virtual environment, but can be harder in CMC environments that are asynchronous and where messages can be delivered but unread for hours or more and hence are not in a timeframe where immediacy of response is always relationally possible. Trust is something that is particularly difficult to establish in asynchronous environments and in the absence of the visual contact which is normally relied on very heavily to detect deception (see Chapter 1).

However, virtual contact does not render people completely impotent in respect of relational dynamics, trust or other relevant information; it's just different and occasionally harder to establish such things, but not impossible. In most groups, whether those who are working through face-to-face interaction or by means of CMC, some trust is built through collective/synergistic action. Walther & Bunz (2005) indicate that reliance on procedural rules is often a substitute for other sorts of informal trust. CMC can make it take longer to establish the sort of trust that occurs much more easily face to face, but it is not, nowadays (when people are much more familiar with CMC, to the point of spending all their life familiar with it) as big an ogre as it used to be seen to be. Walther & Bunz (2005) discuss the use of rules in CMC group functioning and how they help such collectives to work together in a trusting way. Six rules that they suggest are: (1) get started right away; (2) communicate frequently; (3) multitask getting organized and doing *substantive* work simultaneously; (4) overtly acknowledge that you've read another's messages; (5) be explicit about what you're thinking and doing; (6) set deadlines and stick to them. Their study shows that these kinds of rules are effective in increasing trust over CMC, although they also note that a cynic could assume that following *any* rule tends to decrease uncertainty and increase trust. However, at least one of these rules (#4) has quite explicit relational functions, while two others (#2and#5) are implicitly relational directives, too, because frequent communication and openness are a widely recognized part of proper relational building.

Research on CMC tends to believe that the strategies used there are atypical and something almost new to human experience, but in fact I cannot think of much that you could do on CMC that isn't also possible F2F except that you can touch someone literally and physically in F2F but not CMC. The presentation of information is quite similar on the Net, although there people lay it out in linear and direct ways that are quite open and list-like, and hence in ways that do not occur so freely and in such complete fashion F2F. In everyday conversation people have to show initiative to find things out about one another and they also have to do active detective work to find out the sorts of information that are quite often freely and openly offered on the Net without such effort or detective work being necessary – as for example in myspace.com where people are often daringly revealing about sexual orientation, favourite colour, whether they've ever cheated on anyone, and whether they can still remember their first love. It is all a bit indiscreet, really, and some of it is information that a reasonable person might not tell even a best friend or spouse, let alone all the perfect strangers out there reading this stuff on the screen.

A key difference appears to be that such information is offered in a way that does not pace itself, but arrives in a rush and without any prompting from questions, reciprocal exchanges, or the detective work normally required in F2F interaction. This raises interesting relational issues not only about access to other people but access to oneself opened up by publication on the Net of private information directly, given the normal relational effects of such things (see Chapter 3).

Sometimes such detective work F2F is face threatening and very difficult not only in itself but because of norms of reciprocity that mean you should tell things back to people who tell you things, a norm so strong that therapists receive training in how *not* to do it. When people offer it freely on the Net then they remove face threats otherwise inherent in both its detection and its revelation F2F. It is far more difficult to ask personal questions F2F than it is to read the information on the Net, and also far less threatening to put it up on the relatively anonymous-looking screen than it is to tell someone in person, when you may unintentionally blush or otherwise look awkward about the revealed information.

Hence online, one collects more, more organized, and deeper information, rather quickly, which serves to shorten the time spent self-promoting (you just put upon your webpage things that promote the self you want people to believe to be the real you and so you don't have to wait for chances to bring it up in conversation) nor do you have to wait for them to ask. The same is true for other self-presentation and for self-disclosure, and the open declaration of self on a webpage immediately decreases the sense of distance between people. The shortening of all of these social processes tends to create a sense of proximity and fosters an impression of immediate connectedness. In F2F of course, this is normally based on only *gradual* acquisition of such knowledge face-to-face. In CMC, then, technology and relationships co-constitute one another; that is to say, the open use of the technology as a self-disclosing or self-presentational device shortcuts the usual deliberate slowness and the typically reciprocal nature of these processes in F2F settings as well as removing some of the personal embarrassment of F2F shyness. All the same, people lie, self-present, manipulate others, express themselves, lust after one another, and engage in fantasy in both forms of communication, F2F and CMC.

TRY THIS OUT

If you have a page on myspace.com/facebook.com/bebo.com, then write down any three of the things that you have revealed there and see how easy or hard you find it to reveal those same three things to a random stranger out of the blue by going up to them and just saying it. (If you do not have a page on these sources, then look at someone else's page and write your own answers to the questions on their profile and then do the same exercise.)

The things to note here as you do this exercise are: (1) how does it feel to do this face-to-face? (2) what are the responses of the other person? and (3) does this kind of disclosure create distance or closeness face to face?

Discuss your reactions and findings in class.

So what's different? Don't forget the comments in Chapters 1 and 2 about communication carrying both content and relational elements. On email, the awkwardness of relying on content only has led to the attempt to enrich the relational and paralinguistic aspects of an otherwise content-only based narrative by introducing emoticons and development of a whole set of coded language in order to make much more subtle distinctions than the basic :) versus ;) or the ☺ and ☹ distinction. We all know that writing things in full capitals on email is now regarded as shouting and so as disrespectful or as angry, but, lacking the poetic narratives skills of novel authors, most people are confined to the immediate response of text and things just don't always come out how you meant them to do. However, the opposite can also be true, namely that CMC gives you more time to craft a careful message before it is sent out, just as has always been true of letter writing. One difference is that since the words are written up there on screen and can be created and sent without a great deal of mature reflection, there can be less corrective work done on them before they are embedded in the other person's experience. One further important element of CMC that is also shared with letter writing but is not available in normal, unrecorded, F2F interaction is that under some conditions every word of an interaction can be retained and recalled – even searched – at will and can be taken to other contexts when desired, thus giving to the transitory ephemerality of most interactions a kind of permanence that may be either useful or entirely undesirable, depending on circumstances.

If communication were simply about the sending of messages then we'd all know that it had happened and what the right interpretation of the message was. As indicated in Chapter 1, it normally takes two channels and two sets of codes/language to accomplish this, the NVC and the verbal, but on email, the only available code is language, nowadays possibly accompanied by some emoticons that serve to provide a kind of nonverbal relief. One difference between F2F and email then is the restriction on the number of available channels, and although the visual channel is also absent on the phone, there we do not also limit paralanguage, chronemics and so on – you can pause, laugh, change tone and speed of speech on the phone in ways that are not possible on email. In text chat the letters come out at a constant speed, and without tonality or paralinguistic variation, or any immediate reaction from the other end to which you can respond promptly or even interruptively.

Another supposed difference between CMC and F2F, at least until the widespread use of the webcam, is that communicators are invisible to one another, except through what they write. Even instant messages and chats or Skype VOIP can be carried out without the sorts of visual contact that provide not only feedback on synchronous interaction in normal F2F contexts but also serve to identify us as the people we claim to be. However, the same is also true of telephone usage and always has been. People can lie on the phone or claim to be someone they are not there too and we can also judge or ignore information that people tell us F2F just as we can ignore or judge what they tell us about themselves on screen.

Furthermore, researchers often write as if Net interaction is the only form of interaction that occurs between people who use it, whereas many people establish contact first of all on the Internet and then follow up with telephone or even face-to-face meetings. In CMC however, as Lea & Spears (1995) noted, people can quite easily misrepresent their identity, and even now that webcams are more common it is still possible to manipulate some elements of one's appearance or situation. This feature is of course shared with telephones or written communication and is not confined to CMC. When you think about it, it is even – and has always been – possible F2F for people to be deceptive. In 2005, a man was convicted in the UK for representing himself as a member of the aristocracy to everyone he met over a period of some 20 years, before being found out. Even after conviction and imprisonment, he declined to reveal his true identity, and neither the police nor his wife of many years have yet properly identified who he 'really' is.

LIST SOME DIFFERENCES BETWEEN CMC AND F2F AND GIVE EXAMPLES.

Consider the following possible elements: copresence; visual contact; speed of presentation of material; reciprocity of disclosure; depth of disclosure; range of information available; politeness norms; possibility of misunderstanding; complexity of messages; self-presentation; the rules for relating in the different settings; the order of discovery of information; the model presented in Chapter 3 concerning a revelation of information. This list is not exhaustive, merely illustrative.

Discuss your findings in class.

Some relational downsides of the technology

The saturated and surveilled self

One of the problems of access via the Internet is that other people can get hold of your address and send you stuff. I don't just mean spammers or stalkers or the porn pimps, but the people who might think that they have a right to connect and that you would be glad to hear from them, such as former classmates, old dates and long lost loves or colleagues from work over the weekend. We are nowadays saturated by contacts and superficial encounters, something observed by Gergen well before the Internet and mobile phones got such a grip on our lives, but which has rapidly increased since he first made the observation (Gergen, 1990).

There are other problems of technology, too, particularly concerning surveillance at work, which can take many forms, from video cameras to the reading of employee emails and checking into the types of websites that they visit. From the employer's point of view (and also from the point of view of some workers who feel cheated by their co-workers otherwise) the problem is workers who are playing with the computer instead of working. Misuse of employer resources and time is a serious problem and the issue is actually a relational one. Zweig (2005) studied the ways in which surveillance and electronic performance monitoring bleed across the basic psychological spaces and boundaries between the employer and employee – and hence create a different representation of the type of relationship between them. Zweig explored the consequences of the violations of such boundaries and their implications, which ran the gamut from simple dissatisfaction and resentment to stress right through to dramatic resistance and deviance ('withdrawal of effort') or complete non-performance of required work. Although there is not just one (useful) boundary between the employer and employee but several, the bleeding over from 'legitimated' to 'illegitimate' areas is part of the problem. There are clearly some boundaries and limitations of usage which are 'reasonable', for example the right of the employer not to have goods stolen from the workplace and to expect that a person who enters into a legal agreement to get paid a certain sum per hour and work eight hours a day will work as agreed. That person is stealing something from the company when not working and if John is calling his partner about family matters during work hours then much the same is true. It's not all right if I sleep during work hours or read a book or write entirely personal emails with no connection to the business in hand, especially when the content of an email is personal but is written on company property and on company time using company resources and facilities. It is at least comparable to working hourly manual labour jobs where you work incredibly hard while others are just messing around. It is not only unfair to the company; it is unfair to co-workers, and hence once again is a relational issue.

Zweig (2005) indicates that people are inclined to see some supervision as violations (opening of the employees' postal mail or unreasonable searching of wallets and clothing) and yet employees expect and tolerate other forms of supervision, much of which are regarded as entirely legitimate and as predictable duties or binds of the job, such as being timed and observed and told what to do or moved from one task to another at the will of the manager. In short, some forms of 'intrusion' are regarded as acceptable, even if not desirable, within the parameters of the relationship. One thing you might like to think about is what it is that we dislike about this kind of observation when it is not F2F. If my boss is looking over my shoulder and I get caught writing private emails during company time then I see it as my fault. If they are monitoring my email electronically, I see it as an invasion. Why? Rethink NVC from Chapter 1 and compare NV violations to these. Discuss the differences in class.

The argument comes over the question of which areas may be supervised, how much supervision of legitimate areas is tolerable, and whether we are aware that it is being done. As with nonverbal intrusions dealt with in Chapter 1, it appears to be more reasonable for a boundary violation to occur when it is known about in advance and hence permitted to occur. Perceptions of fairness are essentially about acceptance of a violation or redefinition of violations as acceptable. It is important for something to be labelled as a 'violation' that it is done without one's knowledge or intent and hence/or else without one's express or implicit permission, although that is not the only relevant criterion for something to be a violation (as in undesired intrusions into one's personal space).

Privacy and fairness appear to need greater definition in terms of more than simple relational boundaries, particularly in environments where there are multiplex boundaries and non-boundaries that are possible. We all have several personal boundaries concerning different aspects of our life (for example, our home life and our different roles at work, some of which may be based on friendship and some based on hierarchical position) and the problem is that they are different and indeed may conflict. For example, once a person at work is promoted over a friend, then is it all right to make use of private information acquired during the course of the friendship but relevant to the performance of the role of boss (Zorn, 1995)? Even at work, some boundary violation is accepted as legitimate, and in many relational settings it is even desired (for example, consensual sex involves violating physical boundaries in ways not otherwise acceptable). The questions you should think about here involve the extent to which electronic violations feel different from physical violations and the degree to which they depend on the amount of 'ourselves' which is made available on the Net or through our interactions with technology, and hence the extent to which they amount to *relational* violations.

In addressing this kind of issue for the workplace, Zweig & Webster (2002) point to the fact that privacy is defined in terms of control over information rather than in terms of the type of information itself and indeed the 'ownership' of information that is created in a relationship is a matter of some dispute (Petronio, 2002). What is it about 'the individual' that is *or is expected to be* 'respected', given that much of the basis of our individuality is voluntarily shared with friends in the first place? The availability of electronic technology makes it possible for us to display more of our 'selves' in public, even if we may choose fairly carefully the sorts of things that we reveal. In essence, we are revealing what we choose, but we are doing so to a wider audience about whom we do not necessarily know anything in return. In the workplace, the relevance of a violation to the task that is being performed as part of work increases the perception of the reasonableness of any such invasion. Zweig & Webster (2002) use the term 'spying' when discussing electronic intervention and of course this automatically implies illegitimate, subversive and underhand use against the person's best interest. The authors also talk of procedural justice, which implies that the person may at some point 'give permission' for any form of surveillance at work, and such permission is obviously implicit in any voluntary revelation of personal material on the Net.

In the case of surveillance at work, however, Zweig & Webster (2002) note that respecting of 'privacy' is essentially an acknowledgement of individual dignity, and although one may question whether some of the people revealing the information that is displayed on myspace.com are particularly concerned about their own dignity, they do in fact have a choice that the workplace surveillance may not afford them. The usefulness of a technology in the workplace and the fairness of its use are balanced by people and we evidently have relative positioning for the importance of 'respect' against the acknowledgement that the intrusion is occurring (Zweig & Webster, 2002). The authors are clear that the invasion of psychological barriers is the key issue in the workplace.

> It appears that a technology that removes control over the type and scope of information we share with others, changes the fundamental nature of interpersonal relationships, and drives people to question their own and others' behavior, will trigger strong at the negative reactions. (Zweig & Webster, 2002: 627)

In our ordinary use of the Internet for relational activity, that control is essentially retained by our choices whether to reveal or not to reveal certain information. The alleged and real risks of the Internet come when that choice is lost (or not used wisely).

The problems of human computer interfaces: the annoying and socially unskilled office assistant

There is one more side to CMC in connection with relationships and social behaviour. Many office applications and other programs on computers are now designed to be 'user-friendly' (notice the *relational* term). There are even assistant devices that are supposed to help us in times of difficulty, whether these come in the shape of a computer animated dog, an animated paperclip, or the friendly computer-generated old guy. Bickmore and his colleagues (Bickmore, 2003, 2004; Bickmore & Picard, 2005) have looked at these devices ('relational agents') in terms of some of the social skills which are discussed in Chapter 1. Rather interestingly, relational agents turn out to be markedly deficient in social and relational skills, mostly because they don't pay the slightest bit of attention to what we are doing. They are programmed to just show up whether we have requested their attention or not. Imagine how that would be treated in social situations where an annoying person continually turns up and freely offers advice about whatever you are doing at the time. See the problem? The people who have animated the software have not taken account of the rules of relational behaviour that are built into the giving and receiving of advice. They have simply treated the problem as a technical one, where advice is required, and therefore they assume that it is sought. The manner of engagement of these computer-generated devices is gauche and unskilled, so that they are extremely annoying to deal with and most people apparently turn them off at the first opportunity.

The people who are inventing these devices are assuming that they can create artificial relationships between the uses of a computer and the computer itself. Computers do not really fulfil the role of a relational partner, especially if you specify that people have relationships with people they designate and the object doesn't perform an act of psychological involvement. So the idea is that the relational agents mimic relationship behaviour without any of the underlying basis for those exhibitions of the behaviour. Bickmore & Picard (2005) note that one of the problems with computers is that they do not check in regularly with the user and certainly do not act as a result of anything the user says; feedback appears simply to be ignored or to be given the boilerplate ('your call is important to us') treatment. You should immediately start thinking about ways to remedy this problem, since it will come up in 'Practical Matters' at the end of the chapter.

> ## TRY THIS OUT
>
> - Find ways to connect intrusions or failures on help lines as *relational* violations.
> - Compare the help and advice-seeking and advice-giving amongst friends with help offered on help lines or web-based interaction sources.
> - What annoys you about the impersonal stuff? Try to think of ways you could make use of the principles in this book to improve such sources.

Part of the importance of real relationships is positivity, ritual and strategies of maintenance, as we have already seen in Chapters 2 and 3. Also the nature of any task relates to the sort of behaviour which is appropriate to completing it. When the programmers try to establish some sort of 'emotional connection' to a robot they mean only 'positive feelings' rather than anything more complicated and they rarely program in the opportunity for a machine to make us feel good about ourselves in any meaningful way. Since most of us regard 'a computer' as a logical and no-nonsense device, it would be likely that people would see it as 'uninterested' in chitchat. However, it might be worth you asking yourself the fundamental question as to why the computer programmers believe that mimicking a human relationship by means of a CGI (computer-generated image) object with 'lovable' human characteristics is a good idea in the first place. Why not just make a computer helpful in its own right, rather than pretending it to be human?

THE INTERNET AS A RELATIONAL ACQUISITION AND DEVELOPMENT TOOL

Whatever else the Internet does, it certainly facilitates acquisition and development of relationships, and such sites as directdating.com claim more than 3 million members. In fact for many adults the acquisition and development of relationships represent one of the primary functions of the Internet these days. Too often, in focusing on the parallels with everyday life or on asynchrony, the research on CMC has merely noted the increasingly relational nature of the uses of computers and yet has paid relatively little attention to the ways in which relational activity actually unfolds or is sustained there. In a redress of this oversight, Ramirez & Burgoon (2004) observed that even in computer-mediated channels there is tremendous importance on initial interactions. Because of the fact that there are now multiple forms of communication, such as audio and video modalities that supplement text-only formats in relationally focused websites, they are often included in the websites' processing of relationship initiation. The authors investigated the effects of these additional aural and visual modalities on the way in which initial interaction processes proceeded and also on how outcomes were achieved online. The ready availability of access to nonverbal cues, especially if they were positive, had a marked effect on interaction involvement and the key variable of mutuality – that is, 'the character of unit relationship between sender and receiver as a function of the interaction. This manifests itself in terms of, for example, how well partners connect to each other as well as the extent to which perceptions of receptivity, similarity, and understanding are engendered' (Ramirez & Burgoon, 2004: 426–427). This is particularly important since mutuality is a marker of intimacy and interactivity and serves to increase evaluations of future relationship potential. In many of the studies that we considered in Chapter 3, the presumed *future* of the relationship is a key variable in its ultimate development. It is important, therefore, that this study shows that a desire for future contact is independent of the medium, since in real life such continuities are assumed to develop. In lots of early studies of initial attraction, the studied partnership was an artefact of the experimental design and therefore had zero future, although it was zero *history* that was always emphasized in the settings, as is presently still the case in studies of artificial problem-solving group interaction.

Finally, in this context it is worth referring once again to the study by Caplan (2005), who made the attempts to integrate research on social skill and self-presentation into the study of generalized problematic Internet use. The basic idea is that people who are deficient in self-presentational skills are especially likely to prefer to use the Internet for social interaction instead of face-to-face communication. Broadly speaking, the study supports this conclusion, and is supportive of the general point I have been making in this chapter here that technology is essentially a relational instrument rather than a purely informational one, and that it serves to break down boundaries – relational boundaries – in the interconnected world. The previous references to the ways in which people use facebook.com etc. as relational preservatives and declaratives ('Here's who I know') also support this general position.

To underline the point that technology is a relationship device and that technology bleeds over from relational space into other spaces through its use, consider the point made elsewhere in the context of learning.

> [L]earning is mobile in terms of space, i.e. it happens at the workplace, at home, and at places of leisure; it is mobile between different areas of life, i.e. it may relate to work demands, self-improvement, or leisure; and it is mobile with respect to time, i.e. it happens at different times during the day, on working days or on weekends. (Vavoula & Sharples, 2002: 152)

By contrast with this latter declaration, my point is that it is *relationships* which become mobile through the use of technology, and that the new technology acts as a relational transport, something which is extremely clear when we look at mobile phones and their uses and surrounding issues.

KEEP A JOURNAL

- Keep a record of any misuses of mobile phones that you observe in the course of your everyday life. How are you defining 'misuse'?
- What rules are being broken? Think in terms of privacy, boundaries, exclusivity, attention to task, and time usage.
- Who breaks the rules? Do you detect any differences between men, women, younger and older people?
- How explicit are the broken rules? For example, if someone uses a mobile phone right under a notice declaring that they should not be used, then that is different from somebody using a mobile phone in a restaurant, where there are other people at the table. How do you know what the rules are?

OH GIVE ME A PHONE WHERE THE CHARGES DON'T ROAM ...: MOBILE PHONES AND PERPETUAL AVAILABILITY

Let me here note that the term 'mobile phone' or 'handy' is the preferred term in the UK and Europe while the term 'cell (or cellular) phone' is the more common term in the USA. Does 'cell' make you think of a living cell or of a prison? 'Mobile' emphasizes freedom and portability and 'handy' emphasizes convenience and usefulness. A rhetorical analysis of the metaphorical implications of the terms is instructive, with the freedom and liberation of 'mobility' contrasted with the imprisoning and confining effect of 'cells'. Likewise the advertising in the two continents/cultures was initially framed in different ways (Duck, 2000). Advertising for such phones in the USA originally stressed and explicitly depicted both photographically and verbally the uses of cell phones for business purposes. Availability to seal a deal, maintain contact with clients even when one was away from the office on the golf course ('Don't miss that call, even on the green'), and the ability for the astute business professional to close contract deals at any time were all stressed in such advertising. People in business suits were depicted consulting, and presumably conferring about, pie charts and sales reports while talking in airports, cars or hotel lobbies. The earliest advertisements showed golfer Arnold Palmer sealing business deals on the golf course, a clever advertising artifice neatly concealing the fact that in the late 1980s when the advertisements began to run, you needed a golf cart to haul around the battery.

By contrast, advertising in the UK focused on relational situations, and the Orange network leaflets in 1999 did not show a single phone in any of their advertising brochures: instead they showed people in social predicaments or in social connectivity with other people or just out and about enjoying their life; even Orange's business advertising shows bicyclists, hot air balloons and Chinese lanterns (Duck, 2000). The implied message of the latter advertising is that phones are for relating and relaxing, not just for doing business. Interestingly, saturation for mobile phones runs between 77 per cent (for teenage males) and 87 per cent (for teenage females) in the UK, and at only 66 per cent in the USA (Pew Report data for October 2004, http://www.pewinternet.org/PPF/r/179/report_display.asp). Only more recently, as US advertisers have also switched to the emphasis on relationships, so has saturation there increased also, with the largest demographic for cell phones (the term has stuck) being teenagers and young adults now.

Igarashi, Takai & Yoshida (2005) looked at the ways in which F2F social networks and mobile/cell phone text messages (MPTM)-mediated social networks evolved and how they were affected by sex differences. For the most part MPTM social networks consisted of dyadic relationships between pairs of associates so they tended to grow more slowly than F2F social networks. Intimacy levels between friends who communicate via both F2F and text messaging were considerably higher than between those who just communicated F2F, which is worth bearing in mind in light of what we have previously been reading and since it suggests that those people who are closest use multiple channels of communication in order to continue their relationship. Another interesting finding of the study is that women tended to expand their text-based mobile phone social networks more than men, possibly indicating that men and women place different reliance on the mobile phone for relational functions.

As I noted at the opening of the chapter in a different way, technological innovation needs to be understood as connected to basic processes of interpersonal yearning and the present growth of mobile phone usage resonates very strongly with propositions derived from the study of personal relationships, particularly as covered here in this chapter on the smudging of relational boundaries. The societal impact of mobile/cell phones is best understood as based on principles previously uncovered by such research on personal relationships rather than those based on business practices. The *need to communicate* is quite simply a yearning *to relate* and this analysis bears on market penetration, demographics of use, and symbolic forms socially available in deployment of mobile phones (Duck, 2000). For instance, mobile phones not only allow you to connect with other people but they allow you to be *seen* (and since they are not in a phone box connected to a fixed place, they also allow you to be *heard*) communicating with other people. That's an important difference between hearing and seeing. You can't unobtrusively eavesdrop on a sign language conversation because you have to stare right at people but you can eavesdrop on spoken language because sound is omnidirectional.

As we have already discussed in Chapters 1 and 3, when communication occurs in the presence of others, it also becomes diversified in meaning: it sends out meta-messages about that act of communication taking place between the two major participants and says 'We are relating to one another and you can keep out of it'. For example, the style of communication between two persons conveys information to eavesdroppers concerning the level of intimacy and familiarity between them. In Chapter 1, we discussed the studies by Planalp & Garvin-Doxas (1994) which showed that observers clearly and reliably differentiate the content and style of speech between mere acquaintances and close friends and correctly identify each. However, when speech occurs in the presence of other people, it also conveys to them meta-messages about the partners' relationships to and differentiation from those observers. As Hopper, Knapp & Scott (1981) showed, communication between close partners contains code that draws boundaries around the relationship and not only makes partners feel exclusive but also keeps out the outsiders. Such codes are usually in the form of nicknames, shared references or hypertext as discussed in Chapter 1. For purposes of this chapter, communication serves important functions of indicating to observers the centrality (in a communicative network) and the (social or relational) nature of the two primary communicators (or of the one of them who can be observed at the time). Using a mobile phone is thus not only connecting to another person, but showing to everyone else that you are connected to somebody, rather as I pointed out in connection with facebook.com or myspace.com. The parading of one's connectedness is a very important aspect of social life and is the same motive which encourages us to display received Christmas cards and birthday cards in obvious places rather than simply putting them in a private drawer (Duck, 1991). That is to say, when you are seen using a mobile phone, you are demonstrating that you know someone else, a small point with larger ramifications once we come to understand the importance of demonstrating popularity.

Use of mobile phones thus demonstrates relationships, to outsiders, and various types of relationships such as mother–child, grandparent–grandchild, husband–wife, same-sex friends, opposite-sex friends, romantic partners of the same sex, dating and co-workers have some things in common, but also their own subtleties (Hinde, 1981). In using each term to position a person relative to some other person on a given occasion (e.g., in 'calling out' the mother–child relationship) we draw attention to that relationship in preference to others to which the parties also simultaneously belong (e.g., husband–wife, sibling, grandchild) and we highlight for the purposes of the moment that particular relationship out of all those to which the parties belong. We parade their particular dyadic relationship as central only at the time the speaker names and parades the relationship. Although such 'calling out' can be done by naming the relationship, as above, or by referring to the type by some indicator during a mediated communication (for example, 'Hi Dad'), the sort of relationship may often be inferred by those overhearing a (mediated) exchange or may be directly implied by the speaker. So the nature and style of talk overheard by the public – who hear one end of the mobile phone conversation – send some signals about the kind of person who is doing the talking, and the centrality of that person in some network of other people. When we hear people talking on the mobile phone then we are getting some messages about their social identity, or at least the one they hope we will accept.

Each relationship between two people actually occurs in a social environment that contains many other people also, some of whom have their own relationships with one or other of the two partners and some who do not know them at all. Such real or generalized observers are not neutral but they affect the conduct of relationships as we saw in Chapter 4, often being called upon directly to comment on relationships (Klein & Johnson, 2000) or else being tacitly referenced in a couple's composition of its behaviours or its expectancies about behaviour (Simmel, 1950). In the real course of events participants too must carry out that relationship not for themselves alone but in the eyes of others who may make comments upon it and its conduct or appropriateness, since, in the real social world, all people are part of a broader network with many different components (compare Chapter 4). For example, someone giving instructions to the person on the other end of the line is implying a superior–subordinate relationship and observers party to the one end of the call can draw their own inferences or be presented with strong hints by the speaker.

When a relationship is conducted in public in either of the above senses, this publishes the relationship. The conduct of a dyadic relationship, while often studied at the dyadic level, is very often a public performance (Carl & Duck, 2004). Although the uses of mobile phones to conduct relationship business are one aspect of their importance, the fact that they blur boundaries of public and private demarcation and so bleed the conduct of intimate activity into the public sphere is also as important as the bleeding of 'office' into 'relational' space in the bar in Amsterdam. This latter aspect is often accentuated by use of mobile phones in public places, and is quite a relevant point when thinking about the ways in which mobile phones are used. Conversation, especially everyday conversation, is a fundamental form of social and emotional life (cf. Duck et al., 1991), but also serves, in the absence of partners, to publicize and demonstrate that social life to other people.

The evidence of belonging to a group is sometimes a thing that people like to make plain ('member', 'in group', 'friend'). The use of mobile phones is an example of a subtle performance of membership and belonging that makes the user look connected to other people and often the loud use of the device is apparently done in order to help the surrounding people understand just how important the speaker is and how often his or her orders are both given and obeyed.

The mobile self and its mobile relationships

Mobile phones introduce one new element, however, since they are by definition portable – which always means not just able to be carried but actually carried *with* you – and hence render the carrier 'constantly available for relational activity' while simultaneously rendering it possible that private talk will be conducted by chance in public places. In the NWA WorldClub in Detroit, once, for example, I entered the men's room for reasons that we can skate over, and there in one of the stalls was a man talking on his mobile phone to a business partner. As a practising social psychologist my first thought was to try to evaluate how many rules of privacy were being violated by such an interaction, of course, but the fact that we can now conduct conversations with other people when both of us are more or less anywhere is an intriguing development of relational life in itself (Katz & Aakhus, 2002) and further smudges the boundaries that are the topic of this chapter.

TRY THIS OUT

Stand in front of a mirror and note all the things about you that 'transport' your relationships. You could note your T-shirt logos, baseball caps, rings, emblems of membership like tattoos and piercings or pop group emblems, religious symbols and so forth.

(Continued)

(Continued)

Did you describe your clothing as indicating membership of a student group, a particular sex, or socioeconomic group?

Having made that list, now make a note of people on your phone list. How are these relationships identified in the other things on your list?

Does the carrying of a phone change anything about your memberships and their identification?

Some mobile phones ask you to place your contacts into mutually exclusive categories of friends, relatives, colleagues and so on. Sometimes you might like to put someone in more than one group but what does this tell you about the categories that exist for relationships and the ways in which they are 'supposed' to be kept separate?

The essence of mobility in this case is not just the portability of both 'self' and time but of all your relationships so that the time gets shifted and the occasions for personal relationships bleed into other times and spheres of daily life (you can call a friend as you walk from one class to another, and without a mobile phone you could not connect to them at that time and place). The mobile phone thus modifies both the space and time localizations of human interactions that are normally taken for granted as being separated. The phone itself, however, modifies, and therefore displaces, the relational access that is normally restricted by these other localizations. In other words, if you have your phone with you, then you have your network with you as well wherever you are! This may be one reason why parents first buy phones for younger teenagers, as safety devices. Indeed mobile phones are often advertised and reported in news stories as search and rescue devices, which people can use when they get lost, after accidents, or when they feel that they are in danger and desire social network members to assist them. In fact as I was reviewing this chapter for final submission, my son called on his mobile phone to have me check the weather forecast on the Internet for the area he was driving through, so that I could advise him whether to deviate from his chosen route or just keep on going. Mobile phone, Internet, The Weather Channel and instant answers. A lot better than the old bit of seaweed hanging by the door to tell you what weather to expect.

Smudging the time boundary

A less obvious point about mobile phone usage is that it does time shifting for you. It shifts temporality and the typical organizational structure of the day in ways that are reflected in the episode in the bar in Amsterdam, or the candlelit dinner I mentioned earlier. Since people who carry mobile phones are *ex hypothesi* never away from them, then it follows that they are perpetually available for communication with those people who know their number. Until I realized that people assume that anyone calling their mobile number must be someone who has been given explicit permission to use it and hence might be calling in an emergency or for a very important reason, it always struck me as weird that the mobile phone ring is regarded as an undeniable imperative: actually it still does strike me as weird of all you other people, and when I give out my number I am only giving it to people to use at times that suit me! I was once almost naked on a massage table and my mobile phone rang amidst the pile of clothes on the chair, when the therapist stopped and asked if I wanted to get the call. Why would I? I came in for a massage and was halfway through it. How could a call from anyone possibly top that?

For many reasons discussed above, the mobile phone deprives the day of the time and relationship brackets that divide it into work time and social time, family meal time and desk time, in-office or out-of-office time (Duck, Cirstea & VanderVoort, 2000). For these sorts of reasons, mobile phones have important influences on social and relational structure, not merely on ease of communication. The phones do not merely make life easier but also have effects on relationships and the restructuring or separation of relationships from other aspects of life from which they were previously marked off as private (Kelvin, 1977). This means not only that 'private talk' is able to be done in public but the other side of the coin is also true: that relating also loses some of its privacy and separation from the rest of life. If you can be on the phone to a third friend when having a candlelit dinner with your lover, then the phone is bringing other people to the romance as surely as if they were sitting off to the side of the table listening in on the romance.

LISTEN IN ON YOUR OWN LIFE: MOBILE PHONE ETIQUETTE

Relational abuses of the mobile phone are legion. Use of phones interrupts other activity. Also it changes the sorts of questions that we ask (e.g., if one sees X sitting on the sofa then one can say 'What are you reading?' but on a mobile phone it would first be '*Where* are you reading?').

Revisit your earlier list of mobile phone 'misuses'. Now look at the list specifically from the point of view of the question of 'social queuing'. Who gets precedence when two people demand your attention at once? Is it any different when one of them is on the telephone?

(Continued)

> *(Continued)*
>
> Have you ever lied to anyone about your whereabouts when using a mobile phone?
> Do you ever make calls from a mobile phone just because you can or just to fill time?

Let's put this in the context of some observations made in Chapter 3. You recall that traditional studies of relationships tend to take it as a given that people seek relationships and such studies have looked for differential influences that sort relationships into those likely to succeed and those likely to fail (Byrne, 1997; Gottman, 1994). In this search, however, the embedding of relational activity in its everyday practical contexts is often a casualty of the analysis. The focus of research is often on initial selection of relationships or the specific internal dynamics of known relationships rather than on the practical contexts in which they are routinely carried out (Milardo & Allan, 2000). Yet it is routine Every-Day-Life behaviour where much of the performative elements of the emotions and attitudes presumed to drive the relationship are really enacted (Wood & Duck, 2006) and this is especially relevant when treating mobile phones or other technological innovations as relationship devices. Therefore, relationship research risks dissociating relational activity from other routine activity and instead focuses on special instances of behaviour that unambiguously signify relating.

Traditional research studies have then examined the significant observable disclosures or important acts of intimacy, turning points, or major conflicts that lead to changes in intimacy levels in relationships, often assuming that once a relationship reaches a particular level of intimacy it stays there until another major event occurs. However, recent research has suggested that the availability of *daily, routine, mundane and even trivial* communication is much more important in cementing relationships than is significant, Big Moment communication. Studies of relationships now claim that everyday talk helps to sustain the relationships under study (Duck, 1994; Wood, 2006). Indeed I have already commented in an earlier chapter on the fact that most daily communication even with friends and close partners is routine, mundane, trivial and gossipy: yet the absence of such trivial and routine talk is noticed and missed by partners in a relationship when that talk does not occur, so although it might sound unimportant at one level, nevertheless at another level it must be doing some important work. Since talk and co-presence are confounded in typical analyses, the mobile phone presents an interesting way to help differentiate the relative importance of interaction from physical co-presence. At least one function of talk in daily experience is therefore to embody and perform the relationship rather than to develop it.

Recall that Duck & Pond (1989) suggested that talk in relationships can serve any or all of three functions and see if we can apply that to the analysis given here about mobile phones. Duck & Pond (1989) proposed:

- Indexical functions are served when the talk indicates that the relationship exists at a certain level of intimacy (thus talk between strangers is recognizably different in tone and style from talk between close friends as above and in Planalp & Garvin-Doxas (1994));
- Instrumental functions are performed in talk which does something to change or effectuate the relationship, for example a proposal of marriage, a request for a discussion of relationship status, and the asking of someone out on a date;
- Essential functions of talk are the ones discussed above, where the mere occurrence of the talk establishes and maintains the existence of the relationship at its present level of functioning.

From application of this proposal, I have been trying to get you to think about usage of mobile phones from three different perspectives: (1) from the speaker's relational needs and perspectives; (2) from the point of view of the recipient of the call and his or her interpretation of its receipt; and (3) from the point of view of the outsiders to the conversation and their assessments of the relational persona of the speaker whom they can actually see. Although these represent boundaries between different parts of the process of making phone calls, they all bleed over to relational processes in ways you should now understand in a different light.

The importance of the mobile phone is not that it produces constant contact but that it renders such contact possible. The stress on perpetual accessibility is a cue to the importance of the person and the need to be accessible so that others can order their lives satisfactorily. Speaker and receiver benefit from the indication of the speaker's location, distance from a destination, or other relatively trivial looking information, all of which serves to polish the existence of a relationship and to reaffirm the centrality of a caller in the life and business of the call recipient. Outsiders can observe the involvement of the speaker in others' lives and may even be treated to exhibitions of others' importance in such settings or in decision-making hierarchies. In these cases, usage of mobile phones serves an essential function for relationships: frequent trivial calls embody and sustain the existence of the relationship for both parties. At the same time reiteration of the relationship serves to index the relationships for onlookers and to manage, whether the onlookers care or not, the image that the person at the other end of the transmission regards the speaker as a familiar, important and integral to their own relational and social experience.

In part the value of the routine everyday exchanges of daily conversation is to offer implicit support or acceptance for the visions encoded in a conversation by those with whom a person talks, as we saw in earlier chapters. However, when such things are done in public the speaker is charged with the added responsibility of managing her or his 'face' in front of the audiences of the public (Goffman,

1959; Metts, 2000). Whereas public phone booths are demarcated spaces for the conduct of essentially private business, hedged around with physical markers of privacy and exclusion, only *psychological* boundaries are present for the mobile phone user, whose interactions take place sometimes in densely populated public spaces, and occasionally unexpectedly, inconveniently, or in undesired or embarrassing ways. What is spoken into the mouthpiece and heard in the earpiece may be private but the fact that the conversation is not physically demarcated as occurring in a private zone represents an interesting feature of their use and bleeding of private conversations into public spaces.

This is rather similar to the way in which I bled 'office' into the bar in Amsterdam.

This chapter has turned on the question of boundaries and the crossing between one place, whether national, real or metaphorical, and another. It has been a key point that new technology crosses relational boundaries for us, and essentially renders them non-existent under certain circumstances discussed in the chapter. The key change brought to relational life by technology is not to change how we do relationships, or even where we do them, but to blur any differentiation between doing them in public places and in our own heads. Essentially, the thinking that we do about relationships does a lot to make them what they are (Duck, 1990; Duck & Sants, 1983). When our thinking about relationships can be conveyed to someone else more or less at any time then the previous differences between thinking and doing, especially in a face-to-face context, are removed and that makes a fundamental difference in our appreciation of what human relationships may be.

So the message of the chapter is both deep and superficial: you are your relationships, and wherever you are, so also are your relationships, but technology now allows us to share that fact. An 'interconnected world' is also one where boundaries get smudged and in the case of relational technology, the accessibility of people for relationships is significantly enhanced. We could ask ourselves, then, whether our use of the technology or merely its presence is the driving force behind relational permeability of the kind discussed at the start of this chapter. Perhaps the emphasis on relational life on the Net is just telling us how very important it is to people to be in human relationships.

SUMMARY

This chapter has considered the various recent technological innovations which have had an impact on relational life. One of the main themes of the chapter has been that all such technological advances ultimately get bent towards relational goals and are used in the service of human relational needs and my basic proposition has been that technology simply activates a communicative need that is deeply concerned with the human desire for *membership*, community and inclusion. We have looked at computer-mediated communication, the use of the Internet, mobile phones, a number of other issues concerning messaging and the constant availability that is expected of us in the present day. Wherever we go, we can usually gain access to other people pretty freely if they have mobile phones or access to computers, and we are allowed access to their numbers. The 'need to communicate' is really a 'need to relate' – not in the sense of 'telling' or 'narrating', but in the sense of having relationships and connecting with other people. Thus mobile phones are less importantly a technology of communication than a technology of yearning. This fact helps us understand the rapid market penetration of mobile phones and their rapid appeal to the youth demographic. The chapter gave a lot of consideration to the relational implications of this.

After reading this chapter, you should be able to identify relational spaces and the ways in which they are eroded by mobile technologies or fixed technologies that can be accessed from many different places such as servers that can be reached from computer terminals in different towns or countries. You should also be more alert to the ways in which the availability of other people is dependent less on place, and more on their psychological accessibility. You should be thinking more astutely about the reasons why etiquette and ethics are both large concerns in the world where such boundaries are smudged, and you should have thought carefully about issues of surveillance as connected to the relational transportability that I have been discussing.

SELF QUESTIONS

Make a list of the major differences between CMC and F2F. communication.

1 What social and relational issues are unique to mobile phones (what does a mobile phone do or create socially)? For instance the complaint that use of a mobile phone is socially disruptive in restaurants and other public places is not unique to mobile phone usage but applies equally to any other form of intrusion. As much disruption is created in public places by boomboxes, or use of a portable TV, or loud speech. Also in terms of relational implications and the management of 'face', a standard telephone with call waiting can be equally insulting and face threatening to others, since a present caller is effectively made to take second place to someone who has made a later call but nevertheless makes an immediate claim on the attention of the receiving party. It is

(Continued)

(Continued)

socially acceptable to 'jump a queue' by calling up on the phone and so getting attention before the others lined up ahead, but not to do this by pressing past everyone else standing in line. Why do you think this is?

2 How do mobile phones facilitate rituals of relational maintenance? Intimacy can be 'performed' in many ways, and the actual *content* of talk is only one of them, both in mobile phones and in other conversations but relational maintenance can be done at any time with a mobile phone and hence one has less excuse for not doing it.

3 Is it a mobile or a displacement technology? As our experience of the use of mobile phones has increased, so we have got more used to developing strategies to deal with consequent social diffi-culties, breaches of etiquette, problems of having phones ring unexpectedly, badly chosen ring tones, and so forth, while also increasing opportunity for doing things that would be regarded as ill-suited to face-to-face interaction (for example, one is not sup-posed to conduct business meetings on a toilet or while naked but can do so on either a mobile phone or a land-line. However, a mobile phone allows one not only to make, but also to receive calls in these circumstances and in ways and inappropriate places much less likely in the case of land-lines). Mobile phones also 'dis-place' an important aspect of human life, namely the likelihood of consideration and reflection, and they replace such reflective thought with opportunities for impulse.

As you reflect on your usage of these technologies, what do you see as the major problems and advantages of our continual access to relationships?

Discuss your answers in class

FURTHER READING

Katz, J.E. (2006). *Magic in the air: Mobile communication and the transformation of social life.* New Brunswick, NJ: Transaction Publishers.

http://www.pewinternet.org/PPF/r/179/report_display.asp is a report on the use of cell phones in the USA.

(Continued)

(Continued)

http://www.pewinternet.org/pdfs/PIP_Internet_ties.pdf considers how people use the Internet to maintain social networks and build ties when making big decisions.

http://www.pewinternet.org/PPF/c/1/topics.asp reviews the ways in which people use the Internet for relational connectivity.

PRACTICAL MATTERS

- What would you do in designing a relational agent for a computer company? What principles drawn from this book as a whole could you make particularly important?
- How would you make use of mobile phones to encourage children to eat more sensibly?
- What uses of the Internet could be made to establish relationships in teaching courses about relationships? What about iPods?

7

The Management of Relationship Difficulty

For who would bear the whips and scorns of time, the oppressor's wrong, the proud man's contumely [scornful arrogance], the pangs o' despised love, the law's delay, the insolence of office, and the spurns that patient merit o' the unworthy takes ... who would these fardels bear to grunt and sweat under a weary life?

(Shakespeare's HAMLET, Act Three [just before the balcony scene])

Focus points for note taking when reading this chapter:

- What makes a relationship difficult?
- Are there difficult people?
- What routine obligations of relationships do we accept as just part of being in a relationship?
- What sorts of trouble in a relationship go beyond the pale? What makes them different from the things that we are prepared to just put up with?
- What sorts of choices and dilemmas do we accept just to stay in a relationship (e.g., what are the acceptable difficulties, not just the rewards, of getting close to someone)?
- what situations create relationship difficulties because they spill over from one sphere of life to another?
- Think about the difficulties in a relationship that might arise as a result of illness, particularly chronic illness or disability.
- What are the dark sides of relationships and what makes them that way?
- What relationship difficulties might in–laws face? What ones might they create?

Hamlet asks some interesting questions and places them right in the middle of the human relationship mélange and in the context of an experience of life that we can all recognize. Yes, our major hassles are about other people: we have all met upsets in life, all seen arrogance in action, been rejected by people we like, run into people who enjoy doing the details of their job and abusing their power. The routine insults of minor events and small-minded people are a continual experience of life. I had to look up 'fardels' to see if I had borne any, but yes I have: burdens, anything cumbersome or irksome. You got it Hamlet, baby: life sucks quite a lot of the time and it is oppressors and proud people and officers and ex-lovers and unworthy people who are on the other end of the hose pipe. People: you can't live *with* 'em and you can't shoot 'em. So what is a book on relationships doing making it sound as if relating is all routine, useful and even fun?

People come in all shapes and sizes and so does difficulty in relating. Some of it is very minor and temporary — the effects of such small events as bad moods, poorly chosen words, or inept actions, for example – but some of it feels less transitory in nature and importance, more endemic and (rather importantly) more typical of the person in whose presence it is experienced. In short some difficulty is attributed to people *as people*. Whether we are dealing with difficult neighbours, power struggles, the in-laws, the problems of handling long–distance relationships, the regrettable consequences of using our beer goggles and later enduring the walk of shame after a hookup, gossip, enemies, the dark side of relationships, stalkers, violence, or just those irritating little buggers who make life difficult from time to time, we often report that we are dealing with difficult people. But this is short sighted and although quite a commonly held belief is evidence of the fundamental attribution error in action (Ross, 1977), that we blame other people's behaviour on their personality and our own bad acts on circumstances alone.

Any sort of analysis of the perils of relating and the ways in which relationships impinge upon our lives when they go wrong must be able to parse out a number of different elements. Since relationships interweave with our lives in so many ways, it must follow that problems with relationships will interweave with our lives in at least the same numbers of ways. Sometimes the very fact that a relationship is not going well can make us feel bad about something else and, of course, vice versa. Sometimes a partner can cause us to feel bad about ourselves and that transfers to other aspects of life for the time being, or some difficulty elsewhere in our life spills over into a relationship (as, for example, when people bring work problems home). And of course, sometimes we encounter people who would simply be more valuably disposed of in a vat of boiling sulphur.

FOUR DEGREES OF ... SEPARATION

In analysing the different levels of contribution that such people make to the negative side of our lives we must start to ask ourselves some questions of definition, so that we can use Figure 7.1 to distinguish between at least four different degrees of difficulty in relationships (inherent tensions/balancing acts; dealing with

---

Hamlet's Fardels: Inherent 'routine rubs' of humdrum life as we know it:

- Bond-Bind (acceptable downsides of relating, such as duties and obligations of partnership)
- Dialectical tensions (pushes and pulls of mutually contradictory but equally desirable things)
- Spurns and patient merit (competing obligations; relational dilemmas)

Whips and scorns: unpredictable events and unwelcome minor stresses/rough patches:

- Predicaments (facework and momentary pratfalls or embarrassments; insolence of office/petty bureaucracy; nastiness; impoliteness)
- Spillovers (work/home; friend/boss; flare ups with colleagues; disorganization of routines)
- Boundary disputes: (involuntary relationships; cross-sex non-romantic relationships; premarital Post-dissolution relationships; friends with benefits; hookups; interfaith issues)

Oppressors' wrongs: serious turbulence (that might [not] get resolved or dealt with):

- Major life adjustments (chronic illness, aging/development)
- Pangs of despised love (breakdown of desired relationships; rejection by prospective partner)
- Negative relationships (bullies, enemies, stalkers and the general dark side)

Slings, arrows and outrageous fortune: devastating, finalized relational events

- Jilting (rejection by established partner);
- Death, grief and adjustment
- Loss or Death of partner
- Divorce

Figure 7.1   Four degrees of ... relating difficulty

unpredictable minor disruptions; serious and persistent turbulence; devastating relational catastrophe). We can then differentiate the regular tensions that make daily life a rich experience with good and bad, which we happily consume without complaint; the more startling, but nevertheless mundane upsets of daily life that arise in predictable and accepted ways without causing us to foresee the end of the world; the more dangerous, serious and impactful turbulence in relationships which may mean something serious, lasting and critical; and the devastating or catastrophic effects on life, which necessarily occur only once or at least very infrequently, such as death of a spouse, death of a parent, divorce, or the calling off of an engagement or a wedding, although these singular events can have permanently disfiguring effects on a person's psychology (cf. Miss Havisham in Dickens's *Great Expectations*, whose experience of being jilted at the altar moulded the rest of her life).

If we ever imagined that relationships are all smoothness and joy, and that the difficulties of relationships can be bracketed off to one side, then, we have seriously misunderstood the nature of relating (Kirkpatrick et al., 2006). Everyday life confronts us with many tensions and difficulties in relationships which are entirely common and natural elements of the whole process. However, they are not all major issues. In considering the negative side of relationships, it is important to recognize that there are some minor but inherently distressing routine rubs that necessarily balance the delight which is felt in the company of loved other people. These can unexpectedly involve us in obligations to perform duties for partners or to carry out favours that may cause us personal inconvenience. This is not the same thing as noting that some types of relationships are always distressing and seem to carry few benefits, or that any relationship can go through very rough but temporally extended patches where the essence of the enterprise is more negative than positive (conflict episodes with a partner, momentary disputes with neighbours, or faculty meetings, for example). Rather, it recognizes that much relationship conduct is actually a management or balancing of a complex set of elements, some of which can be good and some bad, and that *two* people, not just one, contribute to the outcomes – sometimes one person must make reasonable but inconvenient demands on the other person ('Please drive me to the airport').

That's just how relationships are: they have good and bad stuff in them, even the good relationships. The experience of everyday life relationships is surely one where challenges are managed against balancing positivities or rewards: not even in a Disney world are all our experiences unremittingly positive. For the most part, we do not notice the management that we do day-to-day in our ongoing relationships, because we know that that is how the cookie crumbles and we are not dumb enough to expect everything to go well all the time. However, the forms of this management can, as noted above, be various.

KEEP A JOURNAL

Keep the record of those aspects of life in your relationships which appear to make it more difficult.

You should keep a list not only of 'difficult people', and major events, but also minor hassles and predicaments which occur in the everyday course of events. Do not focus only on major catastrophes but try to become more aware of other smaller things that can happen, too, but which are still intrusive and disruptive and cause irritations that require management.

We all know that even our friends can present us with temporary predicaments from time to time and that the very nature of human relationships is fraught with immediate or obvious management 'issues', where we must balance out good and evil or positive and negative consequences of our desire to be connected to other people (Duck & Wood, 1995). Even the most well-run relationships have their moments of challenge and yet we do not fold up our tents and leave in disgust. We expect there to be rough and smooth, better and worse, good days and bad days. It is therefore important as we consider the management of relationship difficulty in a way that recognizes that quite a large part of what we experience in everyday life is a balance of the problematic and the straightforward. Any simple-minded classification of relationships into positive and negative is most likely to be naïve in the first place – although of course we can all tell horror stories about relationships which were all bad from the beginning and never changed, just as we may carry around beliefs about the overall positive nature of relationships and the blissful mythic expectations of relational happiness and satisfaction that our culture usually tends to push in our direction in the form of various Cinderella stories (Wood, 2004).

Thus when we consider the nature of difficulty in human relationships we should recognize that it is most sensibly separated into several different components, styles, and elements of different magnitudes. Just taking Hamlet's 'fardels', the inherent and broadly acceptable difficulties of everyday relationships (Figure 7.1), we can split them into three sorts. First, there are the inevitable downsides to relationships noted above, and which come with the plus side and every relationship brings with it occasional obligations, duties and constraints, which we willingly accept as part of the role of being a friend, acquaintance, or lover; second, there are the natural dialectical tensions, which are the concurrent elements of any relationship process (for example, the fact that we always in any relationship, seek a certain degree of interconnectedness with other people and yet also a certain degree of autonomy so that we are not completely smothered by the relationship, and that from time to time we'll need to balance these two things out); third, there are the occasional dilemmas in relationships that must be managed from time to time, where there are unexpectedly competing obligations (such as work conflicting with home life at a particularly awkward moment) or inopportune but simultaneous requests from two equally desirable people to whom we are equally committed (for example, two different friends inviting us to their separate weddings on the same day).

Beyond this three-part level of tolerable and manageable difficulty, there are to be found increasingly difficult cases ranging from the 'whips and scorns' and temporary embarrassments that create hiccups in experience, but from which we just turn and get on with life, putting them behind us. Then there are examples of the 'oppressors' wrongs', the nastiness and horror that come from our placement among the rich range of the human condition and different styles of behaviour that would fit in third place in Figure 7.1. There are stalkers, unwanted ex-lovers, permanently hostile neighbours, bullying bosses, violent partners, and generally hurtful and oppressive, obnoxious and obstreperous people who persistently and irremovably inhabit the same world space that we do. Enemies exist in most people's experience (Wiseman & Duck, 1995), and there are those who would do us ill but we have to continue to relate with them anyway because of the circumstances (for example, she might be our boss, our neighbour or our colleague at work) and so we try to adapt or bear it. Lastly, there are the just plain awful 'slings and arrows' of outrageous fortune that create such relating difficulty that they end relational life as we know it, permanently and perhaps unexpectedly, such as death of a partner or loved one and the irretrievable breakdown of a long-term relationship that ends in separation and divorce.

This chapter will consider these various degrees of difficulty, and their management, which come with any style of human relationship. In discussing difficulty in relating, though, it is essential that we recognize the range of things that can be discussed and not focus only on the extremes of those relationships which are inherently bad, or just the rough patches which occur in every relationship, whether as part of the nature of the bonds and binds that come with the territory of relating (Wiseman, 1986), or because partners have entered a different phase of their character and are perhaps entering a descending or disintegrating pattern of the sorts discussed in Chapter 3.

LISTEN IN ON YOUR OWN LIFE

- Are you ever deliberately difficult? In what ways may other people see you as difficult and in what circumstances does such a feeling arise?
- If you encounter other people as difficult, what is it that they are doing that makes you see them that way? Is it things they say or things they do or a mixture? How far is a sense of blame involved?
- What are the social situations that can make anyone a difficult person, and what do you see as the main elements?
- What are the main difficulties that you have to deal with day-to-day in relationships?
- Keep this list and review it at the end of the chapter so that you can see how you may want then to alter it.

Hamlet's fardels: the daily binds of relating

Although there are major health catastrophes that have both indirect and direct relational effects and there are also such relationally relevant things as the difficulties of dealing with grief after loss of a long-term relationship (Harvey & Fine, 2004), it is nevertheless the daily challenges, which confront most of us most often

(Duck & Wood, 1995), and which require such unremarkable handling that we may not notice that *we do it all the time*. Consult your responses to the 'Listen in' box here and consider how often you listed such things as working out who will cook tonight, deciding what to do for the weekend, which movie to rent, where to eat, when, where, and how to have sex, who will drive, where to park, whose fault it is that you have run out of milk, and so on. If you did not list such things, then take a moment to reflect on the frequency with which they do actually enter relational discussions and the effects that they have on relational satisfaction and your sense that things are 'going well'. Once you have recognized the fact that these little hassles occur quite frequently, we should now consider what they mean.

The Humdrum

Wiseman (1986) very sagely noted that all relationships, even the very good ones, have another side to them that essentially consists of the undesired things that we just accept and put up with. Wiseman wittily designated this as the bond–bind issue – the drawbacks and binds that come with the coupling bonds of affection or love. With joys come duties, with support provided by others comes an expectation that we will provide support to them in our turn when they need it, however inconvenient it may be at the time when they need to ask us. The sense of reliable alliance (Weiss, 1974) that makes relationships feel safe and desirable cuts both ways, and we are supposed to be reliable to our friends, just as we expect reliability from them. This is an inherent characteristic of relationships and reliable alliances, namely that they work in both directions and a person cannot just take the advantages without any of the responsibilities and still be acceptable in the partner role. (As Sandra Bullock discovers in a shocking personal moment in the film *Crash*, her 'best friend' cannot be relied on to drive her to the emergency room when she sprains her ankle, falling down the stairs, since the urgent obligation unfortunately conflicts with the friend's appointment for a massage! This is, for Sandra Bullock's character, a defining moment in her life as she realizes the nature of the friends to whom she has been committing herself and begins to appreciate more fully those who have in fact been loyal to her and have been 'doing friendship' without her noticing before.)

Accordingly, whenever we enter relationships we do so in light of the double-sided nature of the bond–bind issue (Wiseman, 1986), that we get the benefits of couplehood bonds in exchange for the duties and requirements that come with it (binds). The nature of relationships is thus inherently obliging and inescapably involves ups and downs, which we must be prepared to accept if we are willing to enter the relationship in the first place. It is important, therefore, to place this type of 'difficulty' in the context of other difficulties that we will discuss, and to recognize that many of them are so routine and fundamental to the existence of relationships that we do not even dignify them with the title of 'difficulty'. Rather we take them as part of the package and as the humdrum and predictable or taken-for-granted existence of daily life. For example, the need to feed your child, take a turn doing the dishes, tidying family rooms, looking after sick partners, taking time to help a friend clean up after a party, listening to a friend's continual anxieties and offering comfort – all of these are inconveniences of relating but aren't really Big Deals. They are just some of the dutiful 'stuff' that occurs in relationships that we describe on the questionnaires where we say we are 'friends' or 'in love' or 'married'.

Dialectics

At a more minute and routine level this duality of good and bad coexists in our daily activities and humdrum communications in other ways, too. An extremely influential approach to relationships has been provided by a focus on the dialectical tensions that we all face in our interactions, that is to say, the push–pull tensions that play one force against another (Baxter & Montgomery, 1996). Indeed, some recent theory suggests that relationships are always and absolutely subject to dialectical tension (Baxter & Montgomery, 2000) and that we are continually playing one pressure against another in all relationships. Rather than this being a tension between one desired thing (freedom from obligation, for instance) playing out against another *un*desired thing (duties of relating, for instance) as above in Wiseman's examples, dialectical tensions are instead experienced between things which are *equally desired but mutually incompatible*. For example, everyone voluntarily entering a romantic relationship wants to become attached to the new partner and so experiences a pull towards closeness, but at the same time has a sense of autonomy and independence and a desire to retain some individuality. In entering a relationship there is therefore a natural tension between autonomy and connection and part of the creation of a stable relationship depends on negotiation of the amount of connection and amount of autonomy which each individual partner can tolerate: nobody wants to give up all of their autonomy just so they can be in a relationship, but few people wish to keep all their autonomy if that means they will never have any relationships at all. Likewise, there is a tension between closedness and openness, with most people wanting to retain a certain amount of privacy about some of their own personal business despite the fact that entry into a relationship requires us to be open and honest with our partner. The privacy–openness dialectic is therefore another one which is readily experienced in all relationships.

Baxter & Montgomery (2000) identify several other important tensions in relationships, such as stability/novelty, where a relationship manoeuvres between changes in form and style that make it interesting and exciting while also retaining enough of the stable and predictable forms of its previous existence that made it comfortable and recognizable to the partners. Dramatic change may be too disruptive for partners, but too much stability on the other hand becomes tediously boring. Hence the stability/novelty dialectic is a process that involves partners in modification that nevertheless retains enough of the central character of the relationship for it to be recognizably 'the same' and yet still enjoyably 'different'. Baxter and her colleagues have successfully demonstrated the applicability of this dialogical approach to such areas as renewal of marriage vows (Braithwaite & Baxter, 1995), the conduct of closeness and distance in long-distance relationships (Sahlstein, 2004), rules for relational communication in social networks (Baxter et al., 2001), the management of conflict (Erbert, 2000) and stepchildren's communication with their stepparents (Baxter et al., 2004). These are simply a subset of the possibilities and the general point is that management of such inherent dialectical tensions is a routine and far–reaching aspect of all relational life.

This approach to relationships essentially depicts some of the things that I'm calling 'difficulty' as inherent in all relationships and not as something specially problematic or disruptive. Although not all such management issues are bonds–binds or dialectics, all relationships are stories of the management of competing forces, the daily challenges that partners experience in coordinating the little constituent interactions of their lives are not necessarily disruptive so much as soluble and essential (Duck & Wood, 1995). For example, the necessary accommodations to one's timetable that are required to make it possible to meet for lunch at a specific time on a specific day with a friend are not Big Issues, but working them out satisfactorily could still well make the relationship ultimately feel more comfortable and enjoyable, while also being, at the time, tricky to accomplish.

In brief, then, there are management issues in relationships that are not so much 'difficulties' as 'normalities' and they are the sorts of things that we handle in constructive and routine ways to make relationships work at all. However, although that point provides context for much that follows in the rest of the chapter, it does not mean that all relational difficulties are trivial, routine or mundane nor does it mean that they should be overlooked even if most of such activity is inherent to the conduct, maintenance and development of relationships.

TRY THIS OUT

Next time you have an experience of irritation with a relational partner, try to reframe it in terms of a dialectical tension. Instead of focusing on what is irritating about the event or about the other person's behaviour during the event, pause, think hard and recast the whole thing in terms of *what it denies you*. Having specified what you are denied, give some sort of label to the opposite of that. Have you got yourself a dialectic that represents a tension between two things that are equally desirable under different circumstances?

If that is how things turn out then what sort of label would characterize the dialectic?

Whips and scorns: unpredictable events and unwelcome minor stresses/rough patches

Facework

In the everyday round of conversation between friends there is a large amount of routine validation of one another's desired social identity or 'face'. Facework involves the prevention of face loss by either party and, in short, is about helping people to look good. As we saw in Chapter 5, people have positive face wants (they want to look good) and negative face wants (they don't want to be imposed upon unduly) and lots that we do in daily life deals with these important aspects of keeping everyone looking good. It is rude, even if it is true, just to say 'You're late again', and so we can preserve the other person's face by saying something less direct, such as 'I hope you didn't have too much trouble getting here' or 'I was worried whether you were OK'. Alternatively, the other person could get in first and save your face by taking the blame entirely and openly, saying 'I'm so sorry I am late, and I apologize for holding you up', and then might offer an excuse such as 'There was a traffic accident and I got delayed' (which also saves the speaker's face by placing the responsibility somewhere else) or 'I am such a bad person. I completely let you down' (which is an unabashed apology that preserves the listener's face by damaging the speaker's face).

The need to be aware of 'face' and to retain politeness is an ever present routine of relationships, that fits into Level 1 (Fardels) in Figure 7.1 most of the time and hardly amounts to a 'relating difficulty'. However it bleeds over into Level 2 in Figure 7.1 (Whips and scorns) once somebody burps loudly, trips on the step or drops coffee on your lap. At this point the routine rubs and responsibilities can become intensified by a need to deal with one of the occasional, often amusing, but sufficiently disconcerting predicaments in friendship that arise from minor pickles in interpersonal interaction – the accidentally spilled water, the bumped head, the inconsiderate but instantly regretted remarks, the unwise email, the nonverbal mistake. These exceptions to normal routine create temporary difficulty, but this is usually a literal or metaphorical hiccup that gets pardoned and dealt with. However, it is an example of a ramping up of the 'facework' that is normally just a low level requirement in daily relational life (Metts, 2000) until things cross over the boundary of the routine stuff and spill over into 'emergency'.

Spillover

Some similar problems also occur as a result of increased facework needs that develop around upswings and downswings in human moods and the fact that there are days when things go well and days when things go badly, sometimes leading to carelessness about the other person's feelings, rudeness and irritability. To the extent that relationship scholars have noted these fluctuations in emotions and experiences, they often tended to focus on specific instances that, for example, connect problems in the workplace to the emotional tone that is brought home (Crouter & Helms-Erickson, 2000), or to note that certain days of the week generate more conflict in relationships than others (Alberts et al., 2005; Duck et al., 1991), or they have focused on conflict as a topic in its own right (Hocker & Wilmot, 2006). There has been remarkably little recognition of the fact that life itself is a corrugated experience and that it is hardly surprising if relationships are a reflection of those ups and downs themselves.

Part of the problem both for researchers and for people in relationships is that the spillover of effects of one realm of life on another depends on the drawing of boundaries that can be spilled over in the first place, and these can be not only across situations, but also across roles, or across aspects of self. We presently see work and home as different spheres of activity, even though Chapter 6 has challenged the blackness of the lines between one set of relational areas and others. Such spillover can occur in many ways other than just those that arise when concerns from work or school are brought into the home, and Chapter 6 has already discussed the spillover of one relational activity into another when one person in face-to-face conversation willingly interrupts it to answer the mobile phone and talk to a third person who is not present face to face. This type of action spills over one relationship experience into another and creates relational difficulty, just as it can when a partner or colleague changes mood or loses their temper and so spills over from the role of reasonable person into an agitated performance. This predicament requires you to deal with the crossing of the boundaries between the person's different presentations of self.

In all of these cases, what has happened is not simply the confusion between places, such as the home and work, but the spilling of one aspect of relational or personal life into another. It is this that creates the difficulty and can create role strain, that is to say a difficulty of performance of one role created by the presence of a need to perform another role also. The separation of work and home is normally recognized not only through the difference in the places, but also through the performance of different roles in each place, and the separation of friendship and non-friendship is normally recognizable in the different behaviours that go with each role (as we saw in Chapter 1). Hence the difficulty that is experienced is one that is not simply created by differentiation of places, but is a specific example of more general principles that occur from the spilling over of performance needs from one sphere of life to another, that is normally separated from it by a particular kind of boundary (role performance).

Boundary disputes

Although Chapter 6 noted the permeability of some such boundaries, there are many other boundaries around relationships, whose crossing creates relating difficulties at Level 2 (Figure 7.1). For example when politeness and facework require us to be nice to people we are forced to work with but do not really enjoy being with, there is an extra difficulty created by the work involved in maintaining the boundary between 'freedom of association based on liking' and 'involuntary association'. The very politeness of our behaviour actually serves to deny that any boundary exists between *in*voluntary relationship and liking, and our nonverbal behaviour is designed to conceal the boundary with smiles.

In addition to the extra effort involved in keeping up politeness in this situation, these sorts of boundary disputes can create difficulties at work, most obviously if we do not really like a colleague but have to work with him or her all the same or come have our intentions misunderstood as overly inviting and personal. Hess (2000) looked at relationships with disliked others and found five strategies that included: (1) ignoring the person or the person's human qualities; (2) detaching psychologically from the person; (3), decreasing involvement with the person; (4) depersonalizing interactions with the person (that is to say, treating them more or less as objects); (5) showing explicit antagonism. Obviously all of these strategies involve effort and social or role strains to maintain distance across boundaries, in particular, any detachment from the person psychologically. It can sometimes require quite a lot of work to create this kind of psychological detachment or masking of true feelings so as not to get upset by someone you do not want to be involved with. Kramer & Tan (2006) also showed that at work people specifically reported that generation of negative feelings is created by inappropriate behaviour, but that these emotions are typically masked in the interaction and so the relationship stays negative and effortful.

Normally of course, we would expect that friendships at work reduce effort and negativity and can enhance individuals' work experiences and their work effectiveness. An unexpected complexity arises when one of two friends is promoted above the other at work (Zorn, 1995) and this tends to create problems for the partners as the boundary between 'friendship' and 'superior–subordinate' has to be kept in place. Restating this, it changes the roles which are required in the persons' performances and de-emphasizes the performance of the friendship role relative to the performance of the subordinate/superior role. For example, a boss is not supposed to give favours to friends that friends normally expect to receive and so the promotion raises a kind of boundary dispute between the roles.

However, when good relationships at work dissolve then both individuals and organizations suffer both pain and stress. Sias, Heath, Perry, Silva & Fix (2004) looked at employees' narrative accounts of their bad or deteriorating relationship experiences at work and found five primary causes of workplace friendship deterioration: (1) personality clashes; (2) distracting life events or personal experiences from other parts of life that flowed over into the workplace role performance; (3) conflicting expectations about the roles of friendship and workplace performance; (4) promotion of one party over the other in a way which renders the relationship no longer viable as a friendship; (5) betrayal, usually in the workplace, of the friendship norms. This last item, of course, represents a crossing of the boundaries from friendship to non-friendship as well as creating a boundary problem between workspace and personal/relational space, and many of the others also represent crossing of boundaries in the ways that we have discussed.

So what can you do about it? Sias & Perry (2004) rated the sorts of techniques that people use to disengage from a workplace relationship that was unpleasant, whether with a supervisor, a peer co-worker, or a subordinate employee, and found that individuals were most likely to use de-personalization/de-humanization and least likely to use cost escalation to decrease closeness in a workplace relationship. It was quite unlikely that people would talk to the person to 'have it out' (see the Self Question Box at the end of this chapter for a poem by William Blake about this tendency in human nature). We all tend to dismiss minor negative experiences with liked other people and to just let them go (compare Chapter 5 on how the first assessment is always about liking and the following assessments are then made of acts). With disliked others on the other hand, the negativity is more often both less likely to be permitted to escape attention and also more likely to generate deeper feelings of negativity, and this can lead to increased likelihood of a deterioration in the relationship (Sias, 2006).

These sorts of situations are very distressing given the amount of time we spend each day with people we must work with, and according to Omdahl & Harden Fritz (2006) such stress can create burnout that leads to ulcers, insomnia, anger, paranoia, alcohol abuse, and depression, amongst other things. However, it is clear, as analysed above, that all of these changes and problems result from some form of boundary cross-over between one kind of relationship performance and another and this particular point can be generalized to other relational situations that cause tension and difficulty.

Another boundary that creates relational difficulty is between friendship and romance. We know that the two are (supposed to be) separate but sometimes 'friends' become 'lovers' and many organizations have found it necessary to try to draw a boundary line between work relationships and sexual relationships, developing policies on sexual harassment and consensual relationships. Essentially, the rule is that you can't enact any romantic role and have sex with people who are in your power in some other role, such as teacher–student or boss–worker, so the romantic role must be separated from the power relationships existing between the two people when the relationship is viewed from a different and non-romantic perspective. The boundaries between these roles and spheres of relational lives are therefore very important, especially as they serve to protect the weaker person from the power of the stronger and hence to stop them being abused in one (sexual) role on the basis of a person's power in another (work) role.

Similar boundary issues arise elsewhere too, as, for example, when the different actions in different sorts of relationship are called to account as boundary issues by such things as the relationships for which we are typically unable to come up with a quick and handy name, such as cross-sex non-romantic friendship, friends with benefits, or premarital post-dissolution relationships (that is to say, premarital romantic relationships which have turned simply to friendship). In all of these cases, the relationships take a form which society has previously not recognized, and members of the group and network are often guilty of suspicion that the relationship is not exactly as it has been described, namely 'just friends'.

Werking (2000) explored the problems that non-romantic cross-sex friends have when explaining to others that they are 'just' friends, since people tend to assume that cross-sex implies just sex. Likewise, Masuda (2006) showed how aware and careful premarital ex-romantic partners are to differentiate sex and ex: that is to say when premarital partners break up and end their romantic/sexual involvement but remain friends, they face an immediate problem that other people do not believe that their sexual relationship has actually finished. This presents the partners with several relating difficulties, especially as they become romantically involved with some third party and want to retain both the romance with their new partner and the friendship with the old partner.

On the other side of the boundary dispute are the deliberate crossing of some boundaries while maintaining others, and friends with benefits relationships (FWBRs) are obviously crossing the sex line, while intending to keep the relationship as essentially labelled a friendship and not as a romance, following the popularization of the idea by *Seinfeld* and *Sex in the City*. Hughes et al. (2005) found that people are quite open about their FWBR activities and generally receive network support, suggesting that the new relational form is increasingly accepted. However, the attempt to get the 'benefits' without any friendship, has led to a growth in casual hookups, where different boundary issues arise, and the attempt to enjoy sexual intercourse without any affectional tie at all presents a relational difficulty when the two partners do not previously know one another well, and so do not receive network support in the way that FWBRs do. Paul (2006) looked at casual hookups on college campuses, where sexual activity with a previously unknown partner (or at least a partner with whom there is no present or intended romantic involvement) was the only object and it was pretty much explicit that no strings would be attached afterwards. The difficulties experienced here follow from the way that the network reacts as well as from the persons' own experiences of themselves afterwards. A person who becomes well known for frequent casual hookups starts to attract a negative reputation from the network that ultimately damages his (or especially it seems, her) likelihood of finding lasting romantic partnerships. The relating difficulty here is therefore presented by third parties rather than by the hookup relationship itself.

The boundary issues also appear to involve the network, then, so that relating difficulty is not simply about what happens within the dyad, something to which we will return. All the same, the daily hassles of living are not, then, what we typically perceive to be the major difficulties of relating, even though we actually spend rather more of our time dealing with them, and like underground guerrillas, they slipped under the radar and do quiet but persistent damage, rather than showing up in one mighty face-to-face pitched battle or confrontation. When we think of relationship problems, we normally think of the big stuff (Levels 3 and 4 in Figure 7.1), so before we move on to considering how relating difficulty most often really works, let's look at more unusual problems and get a bit of dark relief from all these small predicaments, and turn to the Darkside, where things are much more sweepingly serious. Clearly we have to think about this extreme, too, before we can make general pronouncements about difficulty in general.

LOOK OUT FOR THIS IN THE MEDIA

- Look for stories in the media that present a double standard, in which men are expected to pursue sex for its own sake, whereas women are expected to pursue sex for the sake of a relationship. First of all how easy was it to find such examples, and second, are they consistent with your experience of both men and women?
- Do you think there is a sexual double standard and that men can 'get away' with things in relationships that women cannot, and vice versa? What are the differences you can see? Discuss this issue in class. It is often interesting not only to see the differences that people claim between men and women, but also to note how differently the men and women report what is different between them. See if the men and women in your class notice different things.

Oppressors' Wrongs 1: some more unusual problems with relationships

As noted above, relationships routinely involve some kind of duty of reciprocation and care for one another, and although in most cases this is pretty undemanding, in other cases, such as parent–child, it is a substantial commitment especially when the children are very young. In the case of parents and children the direction of care is usually one way until later in life, at least. For many years, research has been conducted on the nature of social support, and its importance in the maintenance of people's happiness and even in the sustenance of life is thoroughly well established (Sarason & Duck, 2001). People with large and dense networks tend to live longer and have more fulfilling lives and the more closely people are embedded in a social network, the more likely they are to avoid health problems and negative life events (Heller & Rook, 2001). It is altogether satisfying to be part of the community, to belong, and to be a member of a group where one knows that there is care and love (Weiss, 1974). A lot of books have been devoted to this topic, and I gave it more coverage in the third edition of this book (Duck, 1998) so I will not be covering it in such detail here and you are referred to the Further Reading list at the end of this chapter.

What I want to mention briefly here is the other side of social support and embeddedness and the fact that the providing of support to other people is exacting and difficult. Provision of any support, such as comforting, reassurance, friend-therapy, or emotional buttressing during grief is very demanding on the provider. For example, comforting requires the use of certain interpersonal and diplomatic skills (Burleson et al., 2005), and it can be as draining to use them as it is disconcerting to find that they are not working effectively and as intended or desired (Burleson, 1990). The kindness that kills and the well-intentioned-but-failed effort at assistance are both in their own ways personally and relationally draining. Equally, not all friends are prepared for the stresses that attach to witnessing and managing someone else's grief where a need to be emotionally available can be an unwelcome demand on both time and psychological energy. A sobbing and distraught friend can be an enervating sight, and we are often all too aware of our own inability to say and do the right thing (Barbee, 1990), especially when someone is grieving a death or has just had their house smashed by a tornado (which happened to one of my friends just as I was writing this chapter! What do you say to someone whose house was – just two hours ago – fully functional and expected to be there for ever, but is now a pile of rubble?).

Specifically in connection with provision of support in illness, Lyons & Meade (1995: 210) observed, 'We are just beginning to scratch the surface of relationship functioning in illness and realizing that chronic health problems are, in essence, a relationship issue'. Whether one is caring for a sick relative or adjusting family patterns and routines to the fact that one of the adults has a chronic disease, both individuals and families experience such things as very stressful (Lyons et al., 2006). Not only this, but the person on the receiving end of the support also experiences relational difficulties and several problems follow from the presence of chronic diseases, because these very often have an impact on the way in which social life is carried out, and some of them may have 'invisible' or non-obvious effects on behaviour or concentration and social participation. For example, people with certain diseases quite often need to withdraw from social interaction in order to carry out medical procedures such as injections or the cleaning of wounds, may not be able to stand being in bright sun light (and hence cannot take part in or watch any community sporting or social activities that require being out of doors), or may be unable to tolerate noisy or smoky social environments.

Illness also makes people less energetic and hence less available for social interaction at times when other people may expect them to be ready (Lyons et al., 2006). Disability may lead to a necessary restructuring of social life, which precludes certain kinds of relational activities such as dancing, and even in some cases it makes it very difficult to be in public places or may even require that the person is positioned in such a way as to have rapid access to toilet facilities or requires other socially restrictive care and attention to layout of the social space (see for example Grewe's (2006) discussion of the need for people in wheelchairs to deal with the physical conduct of relationships; e.g., to locate themselves in special places in restaurants, cinemas and other social areas that basically limit their choices and so also restrict any companions' choices about where to sit).

This might not seem like a relationship activity or constraint, but there are relational and social limitations that follow from such restrictions on mobility, such as the effects on spontaneity to conduct relationships. If you have to be continually aware of such physical facilities then you cannot unthinkingly agree to meet people wherever they are, or you may not be able to join social events, because you know that the timing of them conflicts with your need to rest for a fixed period each day. However, there are also significant social effects of which other people are all too often insensitively unaware and this creates a relational and social difficulty for the persons with a disability. People are curious and intrusive, wanting to know 'what happened to you?' or in some cases feeling completely free to ask spinal cord injury patients personal relational questions such as whether they still have sex and how they do it (Grewe, 2006).

In other ways, too, adjustments to relationship activity are very significant when chronic illness and disability take hold. Sick parents are less able to look after their children in ways that they feel should be possible, and they may also be less able to be spontaneously playful with the children or with their other friends, in the sense that they cannot necessarily drop whatever they're doing when a child needs attention or when a friend comes round. Furthermore, they may be able to take fewer trips and have a generally less deep involvement in any social activity within a network (Lyons et al., 2006). Hence illness and chronic disability constitute relational problems as well as physical ones.

Furthermore, even the *receipt* of social support can be a nuisance, if the offer of help reawakens in a person their awareness of their physical or social impairment and many people with disabilities are very sensitive to the fact that other people offer more help than they wish to receive (Reinhardt, Boerner & Horowitz, 2006). Hence again the illness turns itself into a relational difficulty or a social predicament, and the very existence of a disability can become problematic for someone who is being introduced to new friends or acquaintances. Braithwaite & Koenig-Kellas (2006) reported a complex interaction between two able-bodied persons and a person in a wheelchair, indicating the subtle ways in which people have to adjust and do face-work in the context of social stigmas, not because of the way the persons with disabilities experience themselves, but the fact that many people they meet are evidently uncomfortable around them, and hence make relationships problematic, or are fussily attentive to the interaction as they go out of their way to attempt not to raise touchy subjects or try hard to avoid using – or apologize for using – metaphors that refer to able–bodiedness (such as 'running to the store', 'take a hike', 'this project has legs', even 'stand up for yourself' cf. Braithwaite & Koenig-Kellas, 2006).

On the positive side, however, Haas (2001) explored the far-reaching kinds of social support offered not only to the target individual but also to the couple, in the form of relational maintenance for gay couples where one member or both members had HIV or AIDS. Although the partners themselves were the main sources of support for each other, family members and friends were also major providers of support. As we might assume from the discussion in Chapter 4, network members served to assist the couple to maintain their relationship as well as sustaining a specific target individual who had the greatest need for personal support. This suggests that support which addresses illness also serves to address unseen relationship issues, and so helps the partners to cope not only with their personal struggles, but also with their relational interdependence. This is a particularly interesting finding in that it connects the experience of network help in coping with disease to the sorts of relational maintenance that have previously been studied independently. Haas's research thus shows how social support and relational maintenance co-occur – perhaps somewhat fortuitously or perhaps as evidence of a more complex underlying dynamic connection between particular support needs and *relationship* maintenance.

KEEP A JOURNAL

Start noticing the interactions that you have with people who have a visible disability and pay particular attention to the way in which these interactions are conducted in public. In what ways do other people respond to people with disabilities? Start taking notes based on what you have read in this chapter.

You could write down some indications that you notice concerning the way in which people regard persons with disabilities as 'non-persons' (for example asking someone else in the party to make decisions for the person in the wheelchair).

Notice the ways in which your interactions with people are affected by their visible disability.

You may want to discuss in class the kinds of conclusions that you have reached and compare notes about the way in which communities cope, manage facework, and generally deal with persons who have disabilities.

You could also consider what your journal tells you about the way in which relational and public life may be experienced from the point of view of the person with a disability.

Oppressors' Wrongs 2: the darker side of relationships

For the first 10 or 15 years of the life of the field of personal relationships, most research was devoted to the good stuff and studies would focus on issues of attraction (whether physical attraction or just a liking for somebody else) and love (Berscheid & Walster [Hatfield], 1978). Researchers were struggling to understand the ways in which the positive side of relationships had supportive and good effects on health and sense of well-being (Klinger, 1977), the life extending value of social support (Sarason, Sarason & Gurung, 2001), and the regenerative effects of the experiences of intimacy (Reis & Shaver, 1988). Along similar lines, many studies were conducted about relationship development, pathways to marriage (Huston et al., 1981), the joys of self–disclosure in relationships (Sprecher, 1987), and the undoubted benefits of being embedded in large social networks (Gottlieb, 1985). While all of this work reported observations which are rarely disputed today – in that people recognize the positive advantages of human relationships, and even their central role in the creation of happiness (Argyle, 1987) – the picture was quite one-sided, despite some early attention to breakdown and disordering of relationships as a general part of the discovery of relational dynamics (Duck, 1982; Duck & Gilmour, 1981).

That changed with the milestone publication of a book by Cupach & Spitzberg (1994) on the dark side of interpersonal communication although, for example, some research on the positive side of social support had already begun to be balanced with comments about the difficulties of providing it and the effects of caregiver burnout (La Gaipa, 1990). Also, in 1997, Kowalski discussed the underbelly of social interaction in a book on aversive interpersonal behaviours, covering such topics as the purposeful induction of a partner's guilt, intentional embarrassment, making of complaints, excessive egotism and non-direct aggression. By 1998, Spitzberg & Cupach were able to produce a whole book focused specifically on the dark side of close relationships and the chapter listing makes grim reading, with whole sections devoted to seducing, confusing, bruising, abusing, and losing relationships. Sexual coercion, unrequited love, the mental health problems that follow from interpersonal relationship disruption, fatal attraction, jealousy and envy, conflict in relationships, and obsessional stalking were only some of the topics covered in that book (see 'Further Reading' section).

Since there are so many possibilities, listed and discussed in the Further Reading or noted in passing elsewhere as we considered divorce or chronic illness in this and other chapters, I will focus here on only a couple of special instances namely violence in relationships and sexual harassment/stalking (ORI, obsessive relational intrusions, Cupach, Spitzberg & Carson, 2000). Let us hope that these will be outside most readers' experiences of relational difficulty.

In a paper that makes for difficult emotional reading, Wood (2004) looked at male felons' accounts of intimate partner violence. She was interested in the ways in which men's accounts of intimate partner violence could be classified and understood, especially, as they may reveal some underlying assumptions about the nature of manhood. Wood found three sorts of themes in the felons' accounts of violence: justifications ('She disrespected me as a man'; 'A man has a right to control his woman'; 'She provoked me'; 'She took it'); dissociations ('I'm not the abusive type'; 'My violence was limited and abusers don't limit their abuse'); and remorse ('I regret I abused her'), and she reports two different sorts of views of manhood: *men as dominant and superior*; and *men as protectors of women*. Wood offers an actor-focused interpretation of men's intimate partner violence, that is to say, one that is based on their perceptions of causes for their actions, and notes that certain types of justifications predominate in accounts of men's intimate violence, as they attempt to connect the causes of their actions to some broader overarching social narratives. Basically the men attempt to put their violence into the context of cultural stories of manhood more broadly, where there are cultural myths and fairy tales about the relationships between men and women and what is permitted or expected there.

Foley (2006b) has looked at this problem from the women's point of view and pointed out that abused women often do not regard the level of violence in a relationship as odd, unusual, or unacceptable until it is pointed out as such by an outsider. There are not only broad cultural stories, but also actual institutional pressures on women to 'just accept it' or to be 'dutiful' to a husband, and so the reframing of the violence as unacceptable is occasionally something to which the women need to make a greater psychological adjustment than we would expect. On the other hand, rape myths often attach to male sexuality, and Willan & Pollard (2003) indicate that the perception that women really always want sex and actually consent to it in contradictory or ambiguous ways actually fuels a man's likelihood of acquaintance rape.

Although not focused specifically on such myths and behaviour, Cupach et al. (2000) looked at sexual harassment/stalking, noting that this is a relationship which breaks the usual assumptions of the research in the personal relationship field that relationships will be mutual and voluntary, and one party clearly wants a level of intimacy in a relationship and the other party does not. Instead of the familiar term, stalking, they prefer to use the term obsessive relational intrusion (ORI), which is the 'repeated and unwanted pursuit and invasion of one's sense of physical or symbolic privacy by another person, either stranger or acquaintance, who desires and/or presumes an intimate relationship' (Spitzberg & Cupach, 1998: 234–235). So in addition to the fact that the ORI relationship is characterized by the strong desires of one person being unmatched by the preferences of the other, there is a crossing of symbolic boundary lines between areas which are marked off as unavailable to one person by another. That is to say, one person crosses over the privacy boundaries or personal boundaries or choice boundaries of another person and in doing so transgresses into the realm of the unacceptable relating difficulty.

However, a further difference is that ORIs involve activities which would be perfectly suitable in some circumstances but do not apply under the above conditions. For example, pursuit and attentiveness are acceptable forms of behaviour in romantic relationships which are desired by both parties. These forms of behaviour become unacceptable only when one party does not wish them to occur. Since this often involves a value judgement by one person, it is rather difficult to establish when normal practice crosses over the boundary into obsessive activity. However, like obscenity, when it happens, you can see it even if you can't define it, and most of us would know what stalking/ORI is. However, an extremely interesting point that is relevant from the perspective taken in this book is this possibility that obsessive pursuit is firmly fixed in the ordinary, routine, and mundane activities involved in managing personal relationships (Cupach et al., 2000). It is the transference of these routine behaviours into the realm of the obsessive that makes the boundary transition from normal processes into abnormal ones that count as relating difficulty.

THE GREYER SIDE OF REGULAR RELATING DIFFICULTY

It is clear by this time that the honeymoon is over, and that the field of personal relationships is becoming more realistic in recognizing that there are both good and bad sides to our relational experiences. The trick, however, is not to go overboard in wallowing in the negative, but to recognize the balancing acts that we all perform and to try to comprehend these miraculous performances in some broader framework. Although the above discussion of the different levels of relating difficulty, especially the really dark side of relationships, should not be underestimated in importance, the rest of this chapter will try to put them all, including the more mundane and routine aspects of difficulty in relationships, into a unifying framework that proposes a particular way of understanding how relating difficulty should be characterized.

Are there difficult people?

Are there difficult people? Yes, of course there are, if we mean by that, people whose style and habits generate many judgements that they are invariably tough to be around, and that this awkwardness is also relatively independent of circumstances. There are Grinches and Hitlers and Scrooges and evil psychopaths and all the rest, but much more common are the other sorts of *Person × Situation* or *Person × Person* interactions that should make us reconsider what 'a difficult person' really is. ('*Person × Situation* or *Person × Person* interactions' are used in the technical sense to mean that any effects that are observed come not just from the person or just from the situation but from the interaction of the two of them

[Dragon & Duck, 2005]. For example, I may not be an anxious person and a wedding may not be a situation that creates anxiety in guests, but if I am due to give a speech there, then the interaction of person and situation in this case may create anxiety. It works in the same way for *Person × Person interactions.* Person A and Person B may be perfectly fine on their own but when you get them together, the sparks fly.)

Most of the time when we think of difficulties in relationships we tend to think of 'difficult people' – a concept that suggests that difficulty in relationships resides with the nature of an individual or perhaps at best with both people in the relationship. It is true, of course, that there are conflicts which are caused by the battering of one person's principles against another or by the untimely intervention of some circumstances into the run of life by a particular person turning up drunk or in a bad mood. However, this does not necessarily mean that they are difficult people, but could mean simply that they have imported difficult interactive tendencies to the situations in which they are found and might need to read the Chapter 1 discussion of social skills.

While it can sometimes take outstanding personal effort to be really obnoxious, obnoxiousness in itself is not necessarily a characteristic of persons, as Davis & Schmidt (1977) first demonstrated. These authors pointed out that many characteristics which we regard as personal and individual characteristics of specific persons are actually social in character and derive from the fact that we are social beings who make social judgements about other people in social context. For example, the description that somebody is 'an introvert' or 'a lonely person' appears to be describing a person's individual characteristics and yet the characteristics are both defined only – *only* – in terms of sociality: that is to say, somebody could not be described either as introverted or as lonely without a concept of the existence and relevance of other people against which their lack of sociability is in fact defined. Loneliness describes the absence of other people and introversion describes the rejection of, or lack of interest in, other people. Likewise, hostility is a reference to the way in which an individual interacts with other people, as are such terms as 'kind', 'nice', 'shy' and 'polite'. In essence then, these terms presume relational activity, and not describe individuals without that implicit social reference point.

In the discussion of difficulty in relating it is important to bear this kind of point in mind, since most descriptions of the difficulty that we observe in other people are actually descriptions of social relationships rather than individual characteristics. Many of the circumstances which generate shame or guilt (Retzinger, 1995) are also relational rather than individual and depend on the presumed existence of other people observing our behaviour or on the occurrence of our behaviour in a public setting in which other people may make judgements about what we have done.

The next time you describe somebody as 'difficult' therefore, you need to reflect on whether in fact you're describing an individual characteristic or some connection of them to your own circumstances and behaviours. In this light the present chapter will consider a number of difficult relationships (or is it difficulties in relating?). I will try to demonstrate some ways in which relating difficulties are actually situational and circumstantial as much as they are part of an individual's own personal makeup. Thus, for example, any criticism of in-laws needs to take account of the fact that they are in a difficult relational situation, which inherently creates ambiguities about their role relative to the major parties in another relationship (Morr-Serewicz, 2006). That is, in-laws are brought into contact with the other person in a sort of parent role, but they aren't actually the parent, so they have a sort of authority, but they also do not. Likewise, the difficulties of conducting long-distance relationships are not necessarily characteristic of the individuals involved so much as of the relationship itself: long-distance relationships are tough on anyone (Rohlfing, 1995). More than this, the sense that the relationship is a difficult one to carry out in the first place comes in part from recognition of the ease with which other relationships can be conducted face-to-face. The trouble with distance, therefore, is in part a result of one's experience of other relationships which are proximal and easy to conduct and the fact that these construct a comparison point for judging the outcomes of a long-distance relationship (Sahlstein, 2006b).

TRY THIS OUT

Keep account of any difficult interactions that you have with people during the course of the next week. Start taking notes about the extent to which any difficulties are the result of situations or people specifically and if you think in terms of 'difficult people'. Now try to see if you can somehow re-describe the situation of the difficulty in terms of, say, a *Person* × *Situation* or *Person* × *Person* interaction (see the text above), where the behaviour of the person is influenced by the situation in which they find themselves, or is a consequence of normative expectations. (Is the police officer really unpleasant or 'simply doing her job'?)

Another thing to bear in mind, and which makes the notion of 'relating difficulty' a better label than assigning a problem to 'difficult people', is that judgements of difficulty in a relationship are often temporary, time bound, or context dependent: for example, someone who gives you 'the silent treatment' may be seen as *momentarily* hostile rather than perpetually negative and the perception may prompt us to look for an immediate explanation of their behaviour or for a way to create redress and relief. Likewise a person who is difficult at work may be known to be a fine parent, kind spouse, or excellent neighbour, and the decision to call someone 'a difficult person' may be derived from a variety of circumstances, rather than single (or even repeated) circumstances.

Other situational and contextual elements to bear in mind are norms of appropriateness. It is all right in a Western culture for a 25-year-old and a 23-year-old to marry, but it is odd and will excite comment if a 75-year-old and a 23-year-old do so, and it is actually forbidden in Western society for 75-year-old and a 13-year-old to do so. The likelihood of a relationship being seen as 'difficult' thus depends on how a society views the nature of relationships permitted by circumstances between people of different ages. Also, CEOs are permitted greater latitude in their behaviour than ordinary workers, because they attract 'idiosyncrasy credits' from their position (Hollander, 1958) and are therefore judged differently for the same behaviours as compared to others in their organization. The judgement that the relationship is 'difficult' is a culturally nuanced assessment (Duck & VanderVoort, 2002).

Triangulation

In considering the nature of difficulty in relationships therefore it is important to bear in mind the fact that 'relating difficulty' is often a description of a complex intersection of styles of the two partners, the situational context, time, place, and the social norms that exist concerning such people and relationships. To deal with these variables, Duck, Foley & Kirkpatrick (2006b) introduced the concept of triangulation: that is to say, a feature of all difficulties in relationships is that they involve three terms where the first two terms are represented by the two individuals who have a relationship (Person 1 and Person 2, the *base* in Figure 7.2), whether this is an acquaintanceship or a long-term romantic relationship, a marriage or a relationship at work. The third term in any triangulation is the triangulator and this can take several different forms (Duck et al., 2006b), but is also a term describing two more *relationships*, one with Person 1 and one with Person 2 in the original relationship. For convenience of discussion and in Figure 7.2, Person 1 is designated as the Target and Person 2 is named as the Partner. A triangulator can be a *Framer*, an *Interferer*, a *Linchpin*, or a *Comparison Point*, as we shall see, and the difficulty arises not from the characteristics of any individual particularly, but from the triangulation process as a whole. As a quick example to give you some sense of what will be coming, a third party may intervene or interfere in the conduct of a relationship through gossiping about the Target to the Partner (as Iago did to Othello) and so may sour the relationship between the two partners (in this case the relationship between Othello and Desdemona). Here, then, Iago is the triangulator who creates relating difficulty between Othello and Desdemona.

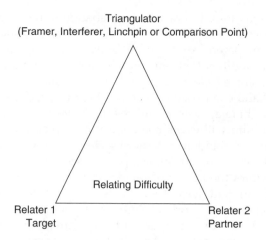

Triangulator
(Framer, Interferer, Linchpin or Comparison Point)

Relating Difficulty

Relater 1
Target

Relater 2
Partner

Figure7.2   Locus of difficulty as triangulation

Note that in the discussion, each **leg** of the triangle also represents a kind of relating (see below) although it is normally the **base** that is seen as representing the
target 'difficult' relationship.
Source: Kirkpatrick et al., 2006

Examples of the other types of triangulation will be given as we proceed, but
you might like to think about the way in which some of your relationships seem
to be better than others and so provide a context that creates negative feelings
about those which are regarded as difficult. As I've indicated in previous chapters,
people very often compare their own relationship dynamics with larger societal
statistics and become dissatisfied with their personal relationships as a result of
such comparisons, rather than because of anything that is going on in the relationship itself. Thus, for example if any popular magazine tells you that everyone
else is having sex 25 times a week, you will be dissatisfied with the 20 times that
you experience it and the *comparison point* which is provided by the popular magazine is a part of the difficulty or lack of satisfaction which you experience in your
own personal relationship. So that is another example of the triangulation I will
now introduce in more detail.

Difficulties with a Framer

A Framer offers triangulation to a relationship by providing a perspective
from which to view the relationship in the dyad and the perspective renders a
relationship problematic when a couple had not previously seen it that way. Thus
if a friend, acquaintance, legal officer, or social worker frames a relationship as

'abusive' (Foley, 2006b), then whether or not the two people in the dyad had previously seen it that way they are now confronted with the difficulty of representing it to others in a more positive light or else coming to see that their previous manner of conducting it needs to be altered. As another example, when talking to other people about a former lover who is now 'just a friend', people tend to give accounts that take heed of the fact that the audience may frame the relationship as if it were (still) a romantic, sexual liaison, especially if the audience happens to be the new romantic partner of one of the people involved (Masuda, 2006). In both of these cases, the relating difficulty is signalled by the fact that an outsider frames the relationship in ways different from the manner in which the two partners (wish to) frame it.

LISTEN IN ON YOUR OWN LIFE

Listen for people framing others' relationships and positioning one of the partners as a source of problem in the relationship itself. Attend carefully to the ways in which they do that. Do they position only one person's behaviour as 'The Problem' or do they discuss the nature of the whole relationship as problematic? Do they make reference to social norms, to 'acceptable standards' or to social expectations as part of their framing of the difficulty?

What seems to you to be the most frequent and habitual way of framing relationship difficulties? Does it involve personalizing the problem? Does it involve blame? Does it involve forgiveness? Does it involve some wider explanation of the nature of human experience?

A similar aspect of relational framing triangulation arises when a person points out to you that you are being taken advantage of by a partner or that you are being inequitably treated by the person in the relationship, have less power than you thought, or are guilty of selecting a 'slutty' hookup partner (one who 'does not deserve you'!). In all cases of such triangulation, one person (Target) is identified as the source of the problem which creates disadvantage for the other person (Partner) in the relationship. The Partner is thereby absolved from responsibility for the relating difficulty and so it is often the case that the Framer has a partisan role in the triangulation process and in identifying the relationship as problematic. Hence, for example, one co-worker may accuse another of being too willing to accept the power plays of the boss, and so frames the other's relationship with the boss as too weak and accommodating (Lovaglia & Lucas, 2006). In short, the framing is not neutral and thus serves to position one of the relaters as in the wrong, while relieving the other of the responsibility.

Difficulties caused by an Interferer

In this case, rather than merely framing or describing the Target in unprepossessing terms, the triangulator is an Interferer who actually enters and disturbs the conduct of the relationship. The residential (custodial) parent of a child of divorce might interrupt the non-residential parent's (NRP) opportunities for seeing the child, can alter schedules, fail to deliver the child as agreed, or may sow negative ideas in the child's mind about the absent parent, such that when the NRP finally does meet the child the parent–child relationship is disrupted or made more difficult to enjoy or may even be resented. The above example of Iago in Othello fits here too and so do people who gossip and spread rumours about other people in relationships, and alleging affairs or making disparaging reports (Foster & Rosnow, 2006). The key result of the Interferer triangulation is to force a choice on the person since the person is now presented with a dilemma and the resulting choice interferes with the good conduct of the relationship, often, in the case of divorced parents, for example, forcing the child to choose between one parent (or one parent's story) and another, or in the case of gossip, forcing the listener to ally with the gossiper and against the Target or to reject the gossip and ally with the Target, thereby perhaps placing oneself out of the loop for future information that could be relevant to the future conduct of the relationship and choices about it. The Interferer specifically attacks one of the people in the partnership, then, rather than reframing the relationship between the two of them as inappropriately conducted from a societal point of view.

Difficulties resulting from a Linchpin

Linchpins are not necessarily as aggressive as Interferers, but nevertheless may place a Target in an awkward position by reason of their very existence. The in-laws are imported willy-nilly into the marriage created by their respective descendents and may have views about a relationship or may be consulted for commentary or advice by one of the partners, simply as a result of their position as elders with experience and with whom the consulting partner has a lasting relationship involving a degree of confidence and trust. The difficulty is created by the fact that relationship to one of the parties is forced by the actions of the other party (for example, one's son marries into another family) but, recognizing the problem, many linchpins work hard to reduce the problems and contain the disadvantages that their presence might otherwise create (Morr-Serewicz, 2006).

Blended families experience this form of difficulty also (Coleman & Ganong, 1995), since the presence of a stepparent necessarily creates new relational structures in the family and possibly affects alliances or creates changes in connections between individuals in the reformed family, as well as with those now outside the previous family arrangement (such as the non–custodial parent or any children who went to live with that parent). As Barber & Demo (2006) and Powell & Afifi (2005) separately demonstrate, the individuals involved in such relationships experience considerable uncertainty in the management of boundaries, not only among themselves within the family setting, but also between themselves and former resident parents/partners, and also a number of important difficulties that result from the emergence of new step-grandparents and step-relatives of various degrees. These new linchpins serve to complicate the relationships within the blended family.

Baxter et al. (2004) examined stepchildren's perceptions of the problematic tensions, contradictions, and dialectics that affect the talk that takes place within a blended family. One of the main problems was that stepchild–stepparent communication was significantly influenced by a dialectic of integration, that represented both closeness and distance. As might be expected, this represents a tension that these previously unconnected people have in accepting one another into their lives in roles that would suggest great intimacy (parent–child), but that is not in fact the actual basis for their own relationship, which is necessarily formed involuntarily by the actions of other people. A second problem in stepchild-stepparent communication was reflected in a problematic view of parental status, where the stepparent both was, and was not, perceived as having any rights to act legitimately in a parent role. A third relating difficulty in stepchild-stepparent communication was that neither party is entirely clear about the extent to which they should be completely candid about their family situation or their feelings for one another, as compared to a need to be discreet, private and contained about such things. In this case, then, the partner/parent brought in to the blended family, the additional relatives who come with the person, and any extra children blended into the new unit represent linchpins to create relating difficulty between people who previously had none, as well as creating difficulties in their own right between adult and child. There is also the possibility here that some of the children's difficulty arises from the fact that they compare this relationship with the previous relationship with their now absent blood parent.

Difficulties created by a Comparison Point

Comparison Points (or comparison levels) are familiar in social psychology through Social Exchange Theory (Thibaut & Kelley, 1959) that assesses 'profit' and 'loss' in relational dynamics. Comparison points are also represented in some of the suggestions I have made earlier in the book about the ways in which we all tend to make reference to other people's relationships in deciding what to make of our own. Comparison Level (CL) in Exchange Theory is the level of advantageous outcome which a person expects to receive from relationships in general, basically what the person thinks relationships will yield, on the whole. Comparison Level for Alternatives (CL_{alt}) is the level of advantageous outcome which a person expects to receive from alternatives to the present relationship specifically.

Someone may perceive the advantages of the present relationship as being below the CL (that is to say below what the person would hope to get from relationships in general) but nevertheless, above the CL_{alt}, that is to say above what the person can get anywhere else. Such a person would be *dependent* on the present relationship because the person does not believe that he or she could do better by leaving the present relationship even despite being dissatisfied with its outcomes. Thus, people sometimes stay in poorly functioning relationships because they do not believe that they could do any better elsewhere. For this reason, someone who is shy may put up with a boring friend, because the shy person does not feel capable of creating a relationship with a more interesting person (Bradshaw, 2006).

LOOK OUT FOR THIS IN THE MEDIA

Watch the film *Love Actually* and pay particular attention to examples of triangulation that occur. For example, you could observe the behaviour of the office secretary (Mia) in relation to the marriage between the characters played by Alan Rickman and Emma Thompson; the behaviour of the US president (Billy Bob Thornton), the British prime minister (Hugh Grant), and the prime minister's PA (Martine McCutcheon); or the effect of the psychologically damaged brother on the relationship between Laura Linney's character and her officemate. There are other good examples in this movie.

These two different anchors for comparison create triangulation points from which we are able to assess whether our own relational achievements are as good as we should be getting or could get elsewhere. As Allan & Gerstner (2006) note, however, relational outcomes assessed this way can extend to money and the bequests made in wills. The relating difficulties created by unequal distribution of goods to one's children, the decision to give a prized ring to one daughter rather than to another, or even to appoint one son as executor of a will rather than both together, and so forth, can create relational difficulties between the children if the action makes the children compare themselves to one another in unfavourable ways or appears to create favoritism. Also, we can understand the processes working in the same sorts of ways in contentious divorce cases, which are often about 'fair' distribution of assets and resources, whether money, houses, or children's time. Such real economic control is an element of relational dynamics that is all too readily overlooked in psychological and communicational research, but nevertheless plays out in relational action all the same in real life.

Some of the difficulties created by chronic illness and ageing are likewise related to Comparison Points also in their own way and the person's unhappy comparison of present social or relational abilities or opportunities with those which they previously experienced. In part, this stems from the ill person's perception of self as a less valuable and engaging partner than previously, as well as from some of the other issues already discussed in relation to spinal cord injury (Grewe, 2006). An ageing person feels less able to reward others in social interaction than previously was the case and many an elderly person refuses to engage in social interaction through fear of being 'a burden' on younger and more active partners (Lyons et al., 2006). Once again in both cases, the difficulty in relating comes from a Comparison Point that was more favourable than the present one.

As a final example, Sahlstein (2006b) notes that one of the problems of conducting long-distance relationships is the awareness that everybody has of the ease with which proximal relationships are normally conducted relative to the distant ones. Long-distance relationships are less spontaneous and more strained, and there is more of a sense that every interaction has to be a good one whenever face-to-face interaction is possible. In part this is because everyone looks forward to their face-to-face interactions with significantly raised expectations, and in part because people are able to forget the fact that their proximal, face–to–face relationships are also difficult from time to time or because these routine difficulties get overlooked and are given lesser significance. In military marriages therefore, where one partner is posted overseas on duty, partners very often experience considerable strain once they are reunited, because they expect every interaction to be a very good one and are constantly aware of the pressure that their meetings must be again curtailed as time advances and the partner is once again recalled to duty.

SUMMARY

This chapter has looked at four different levels of relating difficulty and then attempted to give them an overall framework for being understood. We looked at the low-grade routine bonds and binds of relationships, relationship dialectics, and the various dilemmas which confront individuals who try to protect one another's face. Moving on from these routine activities, we looked at the effects of temporary predicaments and momentary pratfalls or embarrassments as well as the way in which the need to increase and attend to facework could threaten relationship smoothness. The chapter also considered the effects of spillovers from one domain to another and paid particular attention to the crossing of boundaries between relationship types. The serious consequences of other elements of life as they impinge upon relationships led us to consider a number of relational issues for people suffering chronic illness, and we then looked at some of the serious problems that can develop from negative relationships, specifically violence or obsessive stalking.

I then made an attempt to put all of these kinds of difficulty in the same framework, and I introduced the concept of triangulation in order to help us understand the way in which relating difficulty works. Several different kinds of triangulation were identified and applied to the difficulties we have discussed.

After reading this chapter, you should be able to pay more sensitive attention to the kinds of relating difficulty which occur in life, in particular those which are somewhat below the radar for other people, and you should be able to differentiate the kinds of elements that make relationships difficult. In particular, you should be able to analyse whether it is a situation or a role that actually makes somebody 'difficult' and you should be able to explain how the concept of relating difficulty can be broken down into its different parts.

SELF QUESTIONS

Here is a poem from William Blake:

> I was angry with my friend;
> I told my wrath, my wrath did end.
> I was angry with my foe;
> I told it not, my wrath did grow.

This appears to propose a 2 × 2 box involving the two dimensions of (1) friend/enemy; and (2) tell–reveal/not tell–reveal. The friend–reveal box yields a positive outcome while the enemy–not tell box leads to a negative outcome. What would you predict for the other two boxes? Discuss your conclusions in class.

Do we have a whole tendency to 'personalize' difficulty? Comment on this in class, and in particular, consider the question of whether it matters. You might like to think about the role of such a question in the decisions that juries make about court cases for instance.

FURTHER READING

Cupach, W.R. & Spitzberg, B.H. (1994). *The dark side of interpersonal communication.* Hillsdale, NJ: LEA.

Harden Fritz, J.M., & Omdahl, B.L. (2006). *Problematic relationships in the workplace.* New York : Peter Lang.

(Continued)

(Continued)

Kirkpatrick, C.D., Duck, S.W., & Foley, M.K. (2006). *Relating difficulty: The processes of constructing and managing difficult interaction*. Mahwah, NJ: Lawrence Erlbaum and Associates.

Kowalski, R. (1997). *Aversive interpersonal behaviors*. New York: Plenum.

Kowalski, R. (2001). *Behaving badly: Aversive behaviors in interpersonal relationships*. Washington, DC: APA Books.

Lyons, R.F., Sullivan, M.J.L., & Ritvo, P.G. (1996). *Relationships in chronic illness and disability*. Thousand Oaks, CA: SAGE.

Sarason, B.R., & Duck, S.W. (2001). *Personal relationships: Implications for clinical and community psychology*. Chichester, UK: Wiley.

Spitzberg, B.H., & Cupach, W.R. (1998). *The dark side of close relationships*. New York: Erlbaum.

PRACTICAL MATTERS

- How could a mediator or conflict manager use the principles in this chapter to do their work?
- Using the principle of triangulation that is articulated in this chapter, can you make proposals to a large organization about the ways in which it should deal with an employee regarded as difficult by most, but not all, of those people who work in the same office? What sorts of data would you gather before you make a recommendation?
- I didn't write about competing obligations, but you can think about the problem of how you decide what to do when two friends invite you to their weddings on the same day at the same time, or how to handle simultaneous invitations from the in-laws, as well as from your parents to spend Christmas with them.
- What should Hamlet do? How would you advise him to deal particularly with his stepfather/uncle?

8

Some Applications of Relationship Research

Focus points for note taking when reading this chapter:

- In what ways are relationships used to channel and to process information, make decisions, guide our behaviour or steer our lives?
- How do relationships influence purchasing decisions?
- How might relationships influence jurors in their deliberations?
- Does it make sense to reconceive relationships as *ways of knowing the world*?
- How could you use knowledge about relationship processes in spheres of life like business, management, the law, medicine, teaching, advertising or health campaigns?

As we have proceeded through this book, I have on a number of occasions drawn attention to the practical effects both of relationships themselves and also of research on relationships. Relationships connect to, and provide the motive force for, persuasion (Carl & Duck, 2004), for protection from ill health (Sarason et al., 2001), for a general sense of well–being (Lyons et al., 2006), for the spreading of information of both health related and commercial kinds (Carl, 2006b), and for a host of other things from likelihood of smoking (Lloyd & Anthony, 2003), to the use of mobile technology (Chapter 6), to strategies for coping with life's little hassles (Chapter 7) and constructive efforts in the workplace (Dutton & Ragins, 2007). Yet they are also sources of the most intense grief (from loss or divorce, for example; Chapters 4 and 7) and often the cause of lost productivity, reduced commitment to the workplace, and actual conflict there too (Harden Fritz & Omdahl, 2006). Given that our membership of relationships is so powerful and so pervasive a force in our lives, how surprising it is that the relational underpinnings of so much of that life have yet to be brought out in the practical application of research. Yes, of course, we have all read the agony columns about ways to apply relational research to life's dilemmas, and there are often dramatic and exotic claims made about the relevance of specific studies to broad social policies, notwithstanding that results are derived from 18-year-old college students responding to hypothetical scenarios by reporting (no doubt with silent snickers and their tongues in their cheeks yet without any sanctions for false reporting) invented responses that they might conceivably make under hypothetical and imaginary circumstances, given the right sorts of special inducements and peculiar pre-existing conditions. From such studies are nevertheless unselfconscious conclusions drawn about important social issues by researchers with more enthusiasm than balanced awareness of the limitations of their research.

That is not what I mean by 'application'. I am arguing for a broad shift that does not only apply the implications of specific sets of studies, but goes further and rethinks what relationships do for us and the ways in which that function connects with so much else in real life that we have previously seen as different. In this respect, there really is surprisingly little attempt to show how much of life is simply underpinned and driven forward by relationships in ways that alter other processes supposed to happen there. This chapter will take a few steps towards doing this.

I have also pointed out a number of contexts that surround relationships, and emphasized the communication that makes the inner and private and emotions, feelings and attachments public and so helps to make the psychological inner experiences come alive. All communication contains a relational component (Chapter 1). Thus not only is it true that every speech act contains a relational overtone but also so does every leaflet, webpage, office structure and furniture arrangement and many other kinds of nonverbal cues. The business that overlooks such relational dynamics, cues and forces is losing out.

I have, therefore, played up not only the obvious significance of actual communication in relationships, but also the importance of *performance* of relationships in everyday life (that is, not just the psychological states that characterize them, but the way we do relating). This has focused us on the continuities of relationships rather than on their steady states. That is, we have looked at the ways in which their extension through time brings out their variability and turbulence, which in turn faces us all with issues of management of relationships day-to-day and moment-to-moment. Some of the implications of this turbulence were discussed in the previous chapter concerning relating difficulty, but the important fact about the variability of relationships is not that it leads to difficulty but rather that it constitutes their very existence.

Furthermore, I have placed great emphasis on the fact that dyadic relationships do not occur in some magic forest of isolation, but are always inherently connected to other relationships, to other people, to networks, and hence to wider society and its norms, preferences, concerns and impositions. We are never conducting even our most personal and private relational activity at any real distance from the implied or actual gaze or influence of other folk (Milardo & Wellman, 1992). An implication of this fact is that there can be an underlying relational dynamic in many apparently non–relational activities, such as education, marketing, purchasing, decision-making and operation of belief systems, where all of these can be construed as a form of persuasion or attempt to change attitudes about a particular topic in social or relational contexts.

As an extended summary of these points, the book has so far proposed that:

- relationship elements are inherent in all 'messages', whether verbal or nonverbal, and they are the essential substrate of all communication;
- relationships are not simply emotional states, they are dynamic, interactive processes; hence relationships are not consistent experiences but they are constantly modified by specific interactions;
- relationships are managed and performed rather than simply enjoyed;
- relationships manage identity and can be ways in which people validate themselves or in which others (e.g., enemies, gossips, interferers) seek to invalidate them – one source and reason for 'difficulty';
- relationships are conducted in a network of other relationships that influence the way they are experienced even at the personal level;
- relationships are therefore subject to the social control and the real or implied public observation of other people and are often directly influenced significantly by third parties;
- relationships are held to standards beyond the wishes and desires of the participants themselves;
- relationships are bounded and steered (and also liberated and enabled) by social and cultural expectations;
- relationships reflect and are sometimes even controlled by the knowledge that we have about other apparently irrelevant features of society – such as the advice about relationships available in the media and by the general consensus of other people;
- relationships are crucial sources of information and also critical sources for *processing* any information that comes from other sources, even information otherwise held to be true in a given society.

Although these points were introduced separately and innocently throughout the book, they come together in a number of important ways. For one thing, all of these aspects have serious effects on how we *do* relationships and our performances can be influenced not only by skills (such as nonverbal skills dealt with in Chapter 1), but also by (the fear of) gossip (Chapter 4) or by the kinds of relationships that we had with our parents when we were infants (Chapter 2).

Yet relationships can and should be understood in a new way that revises the manner in which we consider practical applications of relationship work, namely that *relationships act as ways of knowing*. Huge and underestimated amounts of relational time are devoted to assessing, comparing, evaluating, sifting and judging information about the world and how to deal with it. Relationships look outward as well as inward and if there is the direction that the field needs to take it is, in my opinion, to discover more about those contacts of relationships with reality, to add to what we are already learning about internal relational processes such as conflict and self-disclosure or attachment styles. The fact is that relationships are used as means of processing information and part of what you lose when you lose a relationship is the shared knowledge that it embodied and which can no longer be relied upon.

KEEP A JOURNAL

Keep a log of the things that you discuss with your friends and associates that make you think or reflect or which introduce you to something that you had not considered previously. How often does discussion of these things change what you know, alter your opinion or make you consider differently what you might do?

RELATIONSHIPS ARE KNOWLEDGE

Human relationships are not simply states, nor are they just affective, inevitably continuous places where we experience our emotions in the context provided by connection to many other people, but they are also places where we check our facts (and also get a lot of our facts), transmit, compare and question information or its sources, and generally form, compose, modify or develop our views of the world and how to confront or ally with other people's take on them. Nobody needs to be reminded that we often ask friends, family or lovers to help us perceive the world. For example, 'He asked me to marry him and I said no. Do you think I was right?', 'She said I was overreacting. What do you think?' We also understand, assess, validate and compare views of much more than just relationships: as Chapters 5 and 6 have suggested, we process information through our relationships and we also select relationships in the first place in ways that take us through processes of information confirmation and validation (take a second look at the serial model of meaning development presented in Chapter 3).

These familiar experiences indicate a very important fact about all sorts of relationships, namely that our connections to other people serve to check our bearings in the world and to help us understand whether we are acting correctly or incorrectly in both specific respects and also in terms of our more general 'philosophy'. These understandings are not things we can develop just on our own so we discuss them with people we trust, but it is all too easy to overlook the important work that everyday talk does in this respect. Relationships serve as sheet anchors for our experience of the world and importantly serve to stabilize, cross-check, and in some cases redirect, the ways in which we think. Arguments and discussions with lovers, friends and acquaintances all serve to clarify for us exactly what we think and whether we are making reasonable reactions to the events that we experience in the world (Duck, in press SAGE CA, see refs Weiss, 1974).

We process information routinely through our acquaintances and our daily performances of social and personal relationships in our everyday interactions. These daily interactions are easily overlooked in importance but are crucial to the way we understand the world and often extremely influential on our subsequent actions. Many people have chosen to frame someone's behaviour by reference to the advice of their friends or have been given ways to look at a complex conflict with their lover by discussing it with someone else. People sometimes take a job decision only after discussing it with acquaintances, and many opinions and attitudes are formed through discussion with these people. It is now widely recognized in marketing that WOM (word-of-mouth marketing; Carl, 2006b) is one of the strongest ways in which movies, TV shows, and other products come to the attention of a wider public. It is also recognized that some of the resistance that teenagers show to health messages about smoking is based on their discussions with peers or their wish to seem 'cool' to other teens and not just on their own personal evaluation of the message itself (Kobus, 2003).

Recall the discussion of the research by De Santis (2002) from Chapter 5. He examined the everyday talk that took place in a cigar shop and found that the people who regularly went there often discussed the evidence about the dangers of smoking. Instead of finding that the clients were continually impressed and persuaded by the weight of evidence that smoking is dangerous, he instead found that the clients invented ways to undercut such reports and to reinterpret them in ways that made their own smoking behaviour more acceptable in one another's eyes. Government figures on the connection between smoking and disease were routinely disputed, challenged, mocked or treated as part of a government conspiracy to mislead people into giving up smoking. The everyday conversations of these clients therefore resulted in the confirmation of their smoking habits rather than the undermining of them. In such a striking case as this, the evidence that friends construct our attitudes and our beliefs about the world is overpowering.

The lesson to draw from this set of considerations is that one of the major functions of relationships is to manage information and help us to evaluate it. This process also serves to support and confirm the speaker's views of the world rather than to challenge them because people with whom we speak tend to agree with us more often than any random set of people would do precisely because we originally selected them, and continue to find them congenial, because they continue to agree with us about the general big issues for the most part, or even if they do not agree with us entirely, they will at least tolerate our position. We do tend, after all, to *select* our relational partners because they are broadly similar to us in the first place and we like the way they see things (Chapter 3).

An important point to notice from this, however, is that discussions with our friends also serve to give precedence to evidence from our friends as preferred sources of information, presented in the model offered in Chapter 5. Although the above evidence from the cigar smoking case may be regarded as extreme and foolish, the general process is still a fundamentally important one that we can all recognize from our own experience: we tend to be confirmed in our opinions and beliefs by friends and lovers, and we tend to prefer friends and lovers who share and support our beliefs.

RELATIONSHIPS ARE KNOWLEDGE MOVERS AND SHAKERS

This exceptionally important – and all too often overlooked – element of relationships can be extended. Not only do relationships establish knowledge but they *change it* through the same processes. The ways in which we interact in everyday life with our relational contacts serve not only to share but also to *shape* our understanding. How many times have you changed your mind about something, or begun to see the importance of something you have not valued before, as a result of comments made by one of your friends or because of some remarks made by another person? (Consult your log from earlier in the chapter.) The range of possible topics here is limitless whether this is a view of your own behaviour or a view of current events or some general impression about the rights and wrongs of a particular political issue, new device on the market, legal question, public event, celebrity activity, government health warning, proposed business strategy, complaint about a co-worker, a rumour about a politician or friend or even the reasonableness of the outcome of a sports event.

Our everyday communication with other people is the major source of our conclusions not only about what is believable but also about what is preferable and acceptable in our society at large. Our preferred 'truth' is established in the course of our everyday performance of relationships; this truth is not an absolute thing that is independent of our social relationships. The things we talk about around the office water–cooler or in the pub, with our partners or with our friends, are given the trust and credibility – and produce consequences – that have important impact on the ways in which we continue to interact with the world. We believe things in part as a result of the people with whom we associate.

This represents an important new way in which relationships should now be understood (Duck, in press SAGE CA, see refs). We know, we believe, we understand, in part because we talk to other people with whom we have relationships based on liking, trust and respect. The sorts of people with whom we associate therefore exert major influences on the knowledge that we have and the opinions that we trust about the world. Information campaigns, corporate advertising messages, and media reports are given credibility not as a matter of fact but are processed as a result of our relational connections. If you have seen the film *V for Vendetta*, then you may note how the daily conversation of people in bars and other social places is portrayed as undermining the totalitarian messages of the government and becomes the force through which a unified resistance is formed. The idea that isolated individuals make decisions about these things on their own is somewhat outdated, then, even if it was ever realistic in the first place. 'Individual choices' may be the result of social interaction, rather than quiet personal reflection alone.

The derivation of knowledge and opinion from relationships is probably the most important – and yet presently underrated and under–represented – fact about relationships. Public opinion results not from the independent judgement of lots of people, but from the interaction and relationships of those people to yield a uniform view by means of focused discussion. The management of knowledge through relationships is more important than feelings, and than the fact that 'relationships' are crucial in organizations (because it tells us what that means – they are not crucial because they are about emotions but because they are about information) and the [in]validation of information, especially about self, generates emotion, especially in a network of other people to whom one's presentation of 'face' matters, even if that network is an involuntary one. The fact is that relationships work differently from the emotional way that we suppose is their unique dynamic, and they shape what we know, believe and adhere to and can sometimes defeat cold logic. For example, we might prefer to ignore a government health warning because we prefer to keep our friends who disagree with it.

LISTEN IN ON YOUR OWN LIFE

Pay attention to the discussions that you have with your relational associates in terms of the effects of the relationship on what you say or do, and the number of times when you may decide to do (or not do) something because of the likely effects of a particular choice on the relationship, rather than because you think the action is wrong or right on your own.

This fact has considerable but unrecognized implications for the conduct of business, the effectiveness of organizational management structures, the creation of information campaigns, and advertising, the production of marketing systems and even the creation of legal arguments based not only on a knowledge of likely ways in which a set of jury members will interact with each other, but also on the ways in which evidence is evaluated both in everyday life (for example, how and where people get and process information about 'the facts') and also in the court-room itself (Duck, in press SAGE CA, see refs).

APPLYING RELATIONAL KNOWLEDGE

This all should have drawn your attention to a particular way of thinking about relationships that should help us now to consider some areas where the importa-tion of 'relationship thinking' can be valuable to the treatment of issues that have previously been seen in other terms: relationships are intimately connected with ways of knowing and experiencing the world ('epistemics'). The task of applying relationship research thus becomes one of translating, so that, for example, busi-ness management is not so much to be seen as the exercise of power as something that works in relational and informational contexts, where face work, relational contracts and information transformation are carried out. Furthermore, the prepa-ration of legal arguments for presentation to a jury should be viewed in a way that facilitates development of some form of interpersonal relationship between its members that will influence the jury's decision-making about the information pre-sented to it. Even matters that affect the everyday handling of professional con-cerns by the police, health professionals or social workers show how the issues of connectivity or daily management of relationships can be fundamental (e.g., deal-ing with conflict or violence between spouses, handling parents concerned about the hospitalization of their children and vice versa, or processing problems of drug abuse that could be the result of family mis-functioning).

Much as I have pointed in Chapter 5 to the value of adding a relational analy-sis to studies of persuasion in addition to those that deal with the structuring of messages, or the sequencing of strategies that can be employed to change attitudes or influence behaviour, so I'll try to bring out some ways in which relationship research could be useful in these other places. This will lead us, for example, to ponder the ways in which advertisers' messages and product information can be influenced by attention to the mechanisms of diffusion and transmission of mes-sages throughout relational networks in addition to continuing research on such things as fear appeals or preparation and structure of the *messages* of advertising alone. This point also connects to the large emphasis on 'relational marketing' these days, the tendency of companies to want to treat their customers as if they were friends and to mimic a friendship relationship in terms of trust, doing dis-closure, and making some intimacy claims.

Speaking to convictions: relationships in legal settings

Given the above general ideas that are in this book, what other specific implications of a 'relational approach' could be applied in the legal setting? Actually, there are huge number of things, from the relational implications of the nonverbal layout of the courtroom, to the processes of relationship formation in juries that may influence their decision-making, to the fact that new forms of relationship such as blended families, cohabiting, POSSLQs (Persons Of Opposite Sex Sharing Living Quarters) and the property-ownership issues arising therefrom, relational implications for legal issues about custody, access and parental rights (and vice versa), and the fact that relationships are subtle sources of informal persuasion at layers several levels further down than overt persuasion attempts (in ways which influence how people learn facts relevant to the dangers of using certain projects, like tobacco or fast food, in the real world – something that may help lawyers in the construction of their cases).

Lawyers know that relationships are important, whether in contract, in mediation, or in family law, divorce and custody issues. Research on many of these issues in the last 25 years has blossomed and breakdown of relationships, the role of relationship problems in criminality, and the place of relationships in jury decision-making are all better understood (Searcy et al., 2005). But recent developments in research in relationships have shown a significant number of ways in which relationships are important in other ways that good lawyers need to know. The most significant developments have been the recognition that the nature of relationships influences the flow of information through networks (Chapter 5); relationships are means by which people gain information and assess its reasonableness; relationships persuade people to do things they would otherwise not do.

However, although we may have assumed that where formal power relations exist, they are exercised formally, we have seen that everyday life realities can confound this clarity of operation. Status and power are managed in relationships in informal ways that do not necessarily represent formal structure. Hepburn & Crepin (1984), for example, showed the informal power of relationships and how prison guards are in fact subject to the control of prisoners in various ways, such as dependency for their physical safety when they are actually outnumbered by the prisoners, and even for promotion, where it is important for them to appear to their superiors as able to control the prisoners effectively. Therefore, many guards strike up informal relationships with the prisoners that make these things possible.

The key point – alongside a lot of discoveries about how people manage identity, carry out trust, disclose things in talk, evaluate evidence, where everyday life is a jury room of sorts (and vice versa) – is that relationships do two unacknowledged things that have far-reaching legal consequences:

1 Relationships represent ways of thinking, so that their structure and performance create personal worlds (including NVC in relationships, and the ways in which disability affects relationships, something bearing on the legal operation of the Americans With Disabilities Act – ADA), presentation to clients, appealing to the jury.

2 Relationships persuade people. That is to say, people do things because of everyday relationships. This occurs not just in the obvious way that people are affected by the attitudes of sources they value, but also that the impact of their consequent behaviour on the relationship is taken into account. People will not necessarily perform a wise action if it would have unwelcome effects on their relationships and they may, for example, choose not to inform on a friend even if it is supposed to be their legal duty to uphold the law rather than to adhere to their personal allegiances.

Think like a lawyer for a moment and notice that although many relationships generate emotions, they are not always based on them from a legal standpoint. Even when relationships originate in love, such as romantic involvement, they can eventually take a legal form (e.g., marriage) where the importance of the emotions of the parties for one another becomes replaced by legal norms of equity and contractual interests. The two people who have sex because they love one another may enter a marriage and then discover that love alone is replaced or superseded by rules about conjugal rights and limits on romantic behaviour, or that they can no longer have sex with *other* people whom they love without also simultaneously committing adultery and hence breaking a legal contract. Two friends who trust one another and enter into business relationships find that their informal trust must be replaced by formal definitions and delineations of the meaning of trust, and how it is to be executed and monitored. The formal and legal representation of the informal assumptions about the basis of relationships may be quite a shock to people, just as it may shock lawyers that in everyday life individuals often trust one another in legally stupid and naïve ways. However, the fact does serve to emphasize the important underlying (in)validating effects of relationships and social interaction and the fact that people prefer to be validated than to be alone.

TRY THIS OUT

How would you prove that you have a close personal relationship with someone? What sort of evidence could be produced to a court in order to demonstrate that it really exists? If you are seeking a permit

(Continued)

(Continued)

for legal residence in a country that accepts marriage to a citizen as a ground for naturalization, then how would you prove that your relationship is legally genuine? Would it be enough to say that you love the partner or might an investigating agency want different kinds of proof? What sorts of evidence, could you use? How would you set about demonstrating that you are genuinely in a relationship with someone else? Incidentally, it might be worth you taking a moment to think about not only how you would prove that you are romantically involved with a person, if you absolutely had to prove it, but more disturbingly, how you would prove who you are if you lost your wallet, your keys to your apartment, and your telephone address list. Would you make use of relational information or other people or what? And what if you lost these things when you were visiting France and had no access to your friends?

From the point of view of a legal investigating agency, what sorts of evidence qualify to demonstrate the existence of a genuine relationship between people? If you are a private detective, what sorts of evidence would you accept to prove that two people were having an affair?

Discuss this in class.

Relationships and the law

Justice attempts to treat people equally and indifferently, but the law does recognize the power of personal relationships in various ways – for instance, in giving parents certain rights to control the future of their own children but not the future of the children of other people at random; allowing tax breaks to couples who are 'married' but not to couples who are not; limiting the extent to which spouses can be forced to testify against one another; or permitting extension of legal liability from one person to another (e.g., making a parent legally liable for the actions committed by the parent's child; Rubin, 1987). This will be particularly true in court since judges really do have power. There are various special relational sanctions and rules which apply in court (e.g., the court has power to deprive you not only of life, property, money, liberty but also of relationships, as in divorce or child custody cases, the issuance of restraining orders, and decisions about taking control over the wardship of children, adoption decisions, and enforcement of restrictions on sexual behaviours between people, such as paedophilia and adultery).

Also the law has recently begun to get interested in whether people in POSSLQs are, to all intents and purposes, rather like spouses as far as the rights to property are concerned after a relationship breakup. In 'palimony' trials, there are sometimes questions about the measurement of love and the extent to which there are different types of love (e.g., whether live-in lovers are in love in the same way as spouses are; see Chapter 2 here), how love should be valued, what it entails, how much an intertwining of daily life routines (Chapter 3) is an indicator of the existence of a 'relationship' and so forth.

The law defines certain sorts of relationships as acceptable and others as not acceptable. For example, it does not accept marriages between people of the age of 5, prohibits incestuous marriages, revolts against sexual relationships between adults and children, widely approves of single serial marriages between adults of different sexes but disapproves of bigamy and adultery, and in many places does not permit marriages between people of the same sex, and recognizes the rights of spouses to inherit one another's property under certain circumstances where a will does not exist. Indeed, the law is per se the only way to establish or end the very existence of certain types of relationship whether these be contractual partnerships or the more routine pairings of life. Marriage, after all, results *only* after a legally recognized ceremony and so does divorce, if you call that a ceremony. Lastly, the legal system is able to break up (by a legal divorce) those families that it formerly recognized as legitimate, to set limits on the kinds of frequency of meetings between children and non–custodial parents, and to regulate the sorts of behaviour that married couples can perform with one another (for example certain kinds of sexual practices, such as sodomy, are illegal in some states in the USA whether or not the partners are married and consenting).

There are many questions about the legal process that interest social scientists and several have a relational substructure that is presently just implicit. For example, although Rubin (1990: 2 [vol 6(2) 1–3]) points out his excitement as a social scientist learning to practise law, he does not mention its obvious relational underpinnings. He says he recalls 'being struck by the central importance of psychological assumptions, not only with regard to such psycho-legal staples as insanity and criminal intent, but also with regard to such commonplace questions as what constitutes "acceptance" of an offer (in contract law), what makes a payment to a former employee a "gift" (in tax law), and what sort of behaviour is "negligent"(in the law of torts)'. Notice how much relationship research has to add to such things as defining gifts between friends, understanding of acceptance of a sexual proposition or a request for a date, or negligence in caring for a friend. In such cases, the record of reciprocity, acceptance of the bond–bind history of performance, and the power relationships between the partners are relevant relational considerations.

I also believe that lawyers should appreciate the ways in which relationship research can feed into their work, through the elaboration of the ways in which relationships are defined in practical daily life and the ways in which acquaintances treat each other (Duck, in press SAGE CA, see refs), the expectations that relationship partners form towards each other or the basis on which they judge the existence of relationships (Chapter 3). In divorce and custody cases, then, the assessment of step-relationship communication quality in the blended family (Baxter et al., 2004) or the role of parental styles of education about relationships (Pettit & Clawson, 1996) could be as important a factor in a decision about suitability for custody, as can the arrangements made for the non-residential parent relationship on the basis of the communicative complexities of such relationships discussed by Rollie (2006) and covered in Chapter 7.

Another thing to consider is how language and relationships influence one another, convey relational information about liking and trust, or indicate power differences, such as we considered in Chapters 1, 3 and 4, so we could look at relational implications of language in the courtroom (Duck, 1998). Relationally-based persuasion goes on in court both in lawyers'speeches and in the jury room and a final set of relational issues concerns the ways in which jurors, as a group, reach their decisions (Searcy et al., 2005). Given the mission of this book, we could ask a relatively new question about the relational underpinnings of jury decisions: how do relationships get formed between jury members and do these relationships influence trial verdicts? Are powerful members of smaller juries more likely to establish the kinds of influence that come from liking than they are in larger groups? We could also look at the ways in which personal contact between jurors influences the manner in which decisions are reached and whether the jurors are likely to consider the detail of evidence in an *interpersonal and relational* context. For example, are the personal dynamics between jurors any more or less influential than the facts of the case? Are jurors likely to be swayed by the evidence or also by the personalities of the other jurors *discussing* that evidence? I will propose that relational principles and processes help us here to deal with such questions.

How do juries make decisions?

After members of the jury have heard the evidence in court without discussing it amongst themselves – i.e., after each of them has formed a supposedly independent judgement – they all retire together to the jury room and expose their views, their thinking, their judgements, their attitudes, and their personalities to the other members of the jury. Such circumstances are exactly those that apply in our everyday relational activity. In giving opinions about other people (witnesses and defendants) the strangers on the jury are actually being encouraged to behave towards one another as friends do: they are self-disclosing about their personal opinions, their judgements and their value system (Chapter 3). They are giving away personal information about the ways in which they think and the attitudes that they hold. In fact it is rather unusual – and therefore is likely to be an interpersonally powerful experience – to be in a roomful of strangers and tell them what personal opinions you have formed about another person and to display your meaning system (Chapter 3) so thoroughly and so personally.

It is also notable then that in long trials the jurors get a relational sense of one other and in complex jury discussions it is likely that relationships between jurors have some bearing on the outcome. What goes on in the jury room? What sort of impact will the shy and lonely jurors make, for instance? Whose views will be given the most credence? What are the effects of having to self-disclose your thinking to a group of strangers and argue with them about your own personal judgements? How do interpersonal relationships affect the decisions in a jury? Can likeability of jurors affect the weight given to their opinions by others?

These questions are all, in one way or another, relational questions based on relational principles and processes. The emphasis of most previous research, however, has been on the decision-making processes alone and the decisions that are reached or on jurors' liking for and attraction to the defendant only, and not on the ways in which relational activities between jurors may predispose jurors to agree or disagree with one another. Thus relational research can add something to the understanding of factors that are prior to the making of group decisions in a jury.

Are juries like other decision-making groups? Do they recall testimony accurately, stick to the correct issues, and reach a verdict felt by others (e.g. judges or trial lawyers) to have been the right one based on the facts? Because research cannot be conducted directly on real juries, simulated ones have to be used for studies on these issues. In some instances subjects are drawn from normal jury rosters and asked to listen to recordings of real trials. When we look at the specific content of speech in simulated jury discussions it has long been known that about 50 per cent is devoted to expression of irrelevant material such as personal opinions about general matters (James, 1959). Only some 15 per cent of talk is actually devoted to the testimony, whilst 25 per cent is devoted to procedural issues in the jury itself (who should speak next, and so on). This could be used as evidence that juries are pretty ineffective and inattentive to the true needs of the court. On the other hand, it could be taken to make a much more interesting point, namely, that people in such a situation need to establish some relational familiarities with each other first and to find out what sorts of people they all are before they get down to the business of making a complex decision about a defendant's life (Searcy et al., 2005). I have already pointed out in the rest of this book many times that humans spend a good deal of their time doing things and accomplishing social effects by talking to other human beings and we have learned how these trivial conversational discussions help to establish and bond relationships together as a basis for getting other life-activities coordinated. Routine and mundane communication serves important relational purposes and establishing a 'trivial' but working relationship first is a good basis for discussing complex evidence, and has been confirmed as a good relational principle for group decision-making over the Internet (Walther & Bunz, 2005).

So some research that seems to show that juries are ineffective may on second thoughts suggest instead – or also – that jurors are merely ordinary human beings who want to establish good working relationships with one another, just like they do everywhere else. And so on. As a lawyer might say, I rest my case.

LOOK OUT FOR THIS IN THE MEDIA

Watch the movie *12 Angry Men* and analyse the relational dynamics. How is the final decision about the defendant influenced by the *ethos* of the jury members and the relationships that form between them? How do facework and other issues of (in)validation of *persona* connect to the ultimate impact of each juror's arguments and opinions?

Relationships in the workplace/marketplace

We spend almost as much time at work as we do asleep (though in favourable circumstances, both objectives can be completed at once). In most jobs, we have interactions with other people and some of these interactions are embedded in relationships of both voluntary and involuntary types, though both follow principles outlined in this book. As Dutton & Ragins (2007) have observed, relationships are '*front and center* in organizational life. Under this view relationships represent not only the essence of meaning in people's lives, but they also reside deep in the core of organizational life; they are the means by which work is done and meaning is found in organizations'. Readers of the present book could hardly disagree, at least the author doesn't! But since I have already discussed some of the issues that affect workplace environments and involuntary relationships in Chapter 7, I'm going to focus on some other issues here that apply relationship work to marketing specifically.

One of the things that struck me in recent years has been the number of ways in which Big Business is realizing the value of a relationship perspective on its endeavours. I have been asked by companies whether they should treat customers as 'friends' and what that would entail – especially in terms of the new buzzword, 'engagement'. There is also growth in relational marketing (i.e., basing the marketing of products on relationship themes, such as membership – always an old staple of advertising – the idea that if you buy a particular product, you will therefore become accepted and popular and that 'membership has its privileges'). A third and growing approach is to try to understand the ways in which networks of friends exchange information and how this may be used to market products, especially by WOM or so-called buzz agents, or influencers (i.e., those in a network who are central enough to affect other members' purchasing preferences for particular goods).

An important point here is the assumption that identifiable features of friendship can be transferred to other sorts of relationships and can serve to change them into friendship without any other processes being gone through. Obviously in everyday life relationships we have a sort of contract with our friends concerning their obligations not to reveal any private information that we disclose to them, but we also have mutual trust, shared respect, a common concern for one another's welfare, and an equal flow of information in both directions, and at the very least ... oh yes, and a shared history of development of a relationship that didn't just arrive out of nowhere. It is clearly going to be tough for business organizations to match all of these elements, especially since they want the relationship to come into effect more or less instantaneously and to mimic not simply superficial acquaintance, but deeper friendship. Particularly where such organizations hold proprietary secret information about their operations that they need to protect, it is unlikely that they will entirely succeed in creating a relationship.

Zweig & Aggarwal (2004) noted that trust of consumers for large organizations is very fragile and in particular consumers are concerned about efforts to record and track their purchasing behaviours, since they regard these transactions as personal and private, and hence as items that they have not intended to be shared with others. The use or distribution of such information could be seen as a violation of privacy (itself a relational violation) or as a breach of a relational or implicit psychological contract between brands and consumers (another level of relational concern). Zweig & Aggarwal (2004) conducted studies to explore, and if necessary differentiate, these possibilities and found that consumers perceived a breach in the psychological contract between the brand and the consumer when information was distributed and were somewhat less concerned with the relevance of information than they were simply and singularly offended by a perceived betrayal of the relational contract, per se. Such a perceived breach in the psychological contract then led to annoyance at the privacy invasion and so changed brand attitudes. The perceived breach in itself is what best predicts thoughts, feelings and intentions towards the brand and so the upholding of an organization's perceived contractual promises can lead to more positive brand evaluations. These results are strikingly consistent with the ways in which people treat friends who appear to violate a relational contract as opposed to those who betray someone, so they represent an important lesson for those organizations wanting customers to believe that the organizational relationship can be like a friendship in the absence of such relational contractual observance.

Engagement

Besides enjoying an implicit relational contract based on trust, looking after the best interests of one another, establishing mutual respect, and ensuring validation of self, friends also engage one another meaningfully through comprehension of one another's meaning systems, as we saw in Chapter 3. Recently, the concept of 'engagement' has begun to appeal to the marketing world. The problem is that the notion of engagement is superficially understood in such a context and needs a better relational basis that can be supplied from current relational research thinking.

What do I mean by engagement? You know that moment when you are telling an interesting and involving story, and you notice that your audience has just glazed over, or has glanced over your shoulder, or has just changed to a fixed and polite stare? That's the moment when you lost them and they were no longer engaged. Of course they're still 'listening' at some level – and 'active listening' has been a big topic in communication texts for years, but we should change it to 'engagement' because there's more to engagement and involvement with a speaker than simply listening carefully to what is being said, even if you listen intently. Tape recorders can do that. Engagement is not just listening, it's caring, trusting, wanting to know more, being excited, feeling enlightened, attached and concerned, in short, the sort of attention that we pay to friends rather than to televisions.

Another familiar set of examples comes from the standard attempt to be friendly and positive on the 'on hold' messages on telephones, boilerplate responses to technical support questions on email, and written apologies from banks/airlines/hotels. All of these start by saying how important we are to them, while at the same time both the form of the message and the rest of their own behaviour send a contrasting message. For example, if our call really is important to them then why did they put us on hold for 20 minutes and why do they *always* tell us that they are experiencing an unusually high volume of calls? Do they really want us to believe that they don't manage their business well enough to adjust to the volume of calls when it increases, if indeed that is what has happened? If they really spend their lives hoping that they can be helpful just to us personally as we wrestle with our technical problem, then why is our name just boiler-plated into text that was already written and looks like it was also sent to thousands of other people? If they really value our particular and special custom on their airline as a very special Platinum Flyer Card holder then how come my son who was due to fly with me on the same cancelled flight, got the same letter, with the 'Platinum Flyer Card' bit missing? Actually he didn't get as many palliative apology miles credited to his account and was very annoyed indeed at the airline concerned. If a friend says 'of course I'm listening' while looking bored and distracted, then we can treat the conflict of messages in a relationally negative way (Chapter 1). Most of us probably do the same with these evidently insincere messages attempting to establish relational connectivity between the organization and ourselves.

In all of these cases, it is the lack of engagement that matters and that puts people off.

Here are the definitions (and differences) for hearing, listening and engagement:

- HEARING: words go in the ear.
- LISTENING: you process and attend to what is said.
- ENGAGEMENT: you attend and also make a personal relational connection with the speaker/source.

What's the difference? Well there are lots of differences, the obvious one is about nonverbal attentiveness that trainee managers are taught how to fake in all the training and coaching courses ('How to look interested: Eye contact and warmth...'). The bad managers learn to do this without ever learning about engagement, however. Then there is the routine conversational approach about 'active listening', summarizing what the other person has said – 'reflecting' it is sometimes called – and making clear that you are attending to what is being uttered. At least you can paraphrase it. But this gets us only to the second part of the list above and doesn't guarantee that you have actually understood the overtones of what is said. For example the gist can be formulated in a reflection (what was actually said) but that is not necessarily the key part (the upshot or importance of what was said): you might have understood and could 'reflect' that when someone said 'As a divorcee I am against the occupation of Iraq' they were stating opposition to the situation in a foreign country but you might have missed the deeper significance of the first three words. Since they are apparently irrelevant to the rest of the sentiment expressed, they were probably uttered because they are central to the *speaker's view of self* and therefore constitute a major part of what the speaker wants to tell the world. If you are *engaged* you will pick up on that, and will validate that aspect of the speaker's self as evidently regarded as relevant to the discourse by the speaker.

In our engagement with others in everyday life relationships, we have expectations of mutuality that can, however, connect to other aspects of life, such as mutual concern over one another's well-being, and it is in the last area that I will expand the connection of people, information, relationships, and understanding to the application of relationship thinking to health.

Relationships and health

The sick role and the social side of illness

I already noted in Chapter 7 that there are connections between health and relationships and also between chronic illness, disability and relationships. The relationship connection to health is not limited to these above topics however.

We may think that people go to the doctor just because they are ill, but the true picture is somewhat more complex. Reporting of illness is not based on absolutes:

for example, we are not just either sick or well. We are often somewhere in between. The health–illness continuum is a continuum, not a dichotomy of absolute health versus absolute illness (Shuval, 1981). What do human relationships have to do with the health–illness continuum, and why, when, and how do we decide we are ill enough to need help? In fact we do not report that we are sick every time we have germs, viruses and physical trauma. Instead our likelihood of reporting sick depends also on how we feel about the experience, on psychological factors based on the perception of symptoms and what they mean, and on the opinions of other people around us as to whether we should be alarmed.

Some symptoms in themselves mean little (indeed physicians tend to look for clusters of symptoms rather than single ones anyway). Accordingly we have to *decide* whether symptoms indicate illness – and, if so, whether it is appropriate to consult a doctor. Jones (1982) points out that pain initiates a search for causes, and people will pin the explanation on any cause that seems both plausible and salient, even if it is actually incorrect. If a recent event seems likely to have caused the symptoms (e.g., if a sudden severe headache follows a blow to the head), then we are likely to attribute the effect to that cause even if, for example, the real cause is actually a spontaneous brain tumour. If a friend advises us to consider alternative information or explanations, then we may weigh up the symptoms in a different way – yet another case where relationships link to knowledge and information processing. Thus psychological or relational processes help to determine what we will make of symptoms.

By contrast, a psychological or relational state can also contribute to the occurrence of certain symptoms. For instance, an extremely anxious person might develop ulcers or headaches and someone whose colleagues at work are 'difficult' may develop such symptoms more than someone whose work relationships are rewarding (Harden Fritz & Omdahl, 2006). Indirectly, also, anxiety about relationships may cause us to change our habits: negative relational experiences may make us careless or prepared to act in a self-destructive manner, for instance, by drinking excessively, eating irregularly, and driving dangerously (see Duck, 1998).

Of course anxiety and stress are often caused by relational experiences themselves such as conflicts or arguments (Sias, 2006). Furthermore, a person can develop symptoms as a result of changes in daily routines or habits, and these can in turn come from psychological changes going on inside or from relational causes. For instance, if we become extremely anxious about relationships or are going through a divorce or a relationship breakup, we may start drinking or smoking and so develop liver or lung ailments, and it is well established that men who are recently divorced start hanging out in dangerous places like red-light districts and are more likely to be the victims of assault or homicides (Bloom, Asher & White, 1978).

This all goes to show that illness is not simply a physically-created state, but one where relational experiences intertwine with physical factors and it runs even deeper than the above. There is more to becoming ill than merely feeling a twinge of pain in the stomach. We decide we are sick when we personally feel that our physical state deserves attention and we receive some sort of relational confirmation that the physical state deserves attention (Heller & Rook, 2001); we are not satisfied with other possible explanations; are willing to accept the consequences of being confirmed sick; and believe that some treatment would be more useful and effective than no treatment. These are psychological, but also relational, factors that link up with our views of ourselves, with our attitudes to pain, physicians and sickness, and with our personal, network, or cultural beliefs about illness. If our culture assumes that illness is a punishment for sin then we may be less likely to tell other people that we feel ill than if we are told it is a reward for doing good or if we assume it is caused by an invasion of viruses over which we have no legitimate, voluntary, personal control. In any case, we may consult our friends or family for advice that will influence what we do next.

The sick role and the social consequences of illness

Being ill is a social as well as a purely physical condition and allows the individual to enter the 'sick role'. To do this, a person must be legitimated by an accepted authority, such as a physician, a caring friend, a concerned colleague, or in the case of a child, by a parent (Parsons, 1951). Second, the illness must normally be beyond the person's responsibility to control (e.g., someone who is staggering and disoriented by reason of intoxication is not regarded in our culture as 'sick whereas someone showing similar symptoms as a result of a blow to the head is accepted in our culture as truly 'sick'). Third, while the sick role legitimately excuses us from certain regular obligations like work, it brings others. A person is obliged to 'get well soon' or to act out the role in a socially acceptable way by, for example, 'bearing pain with cheerfulness and fortitude', being uncomplaining about discomfort, and appearing to be brave in the face of impending death. People who do this in ways that our culture approves have that fact mentioned in their obituaries, whereas those who fail to do so do not have their reactions described at all. You will never see an obituary that says 'When he was told that he was dying he just broke down and cried like a real wimp'(despite the fact that it might be an understandable reaction in the circumstances).

Illness has three further aspects to it (DiMatteo & Friedman, 1982), all with relational overtones: destructive, liberating, and occupational.

First, illness is usually destructive: it causes physical deterioration, pain, disability, and discomfort. This can cause anguish to loved ones, who see a father, mother, partner, child or friend deteriorating before their eyes (Lyons et al., 2006). Insofar as the patient is aware of these feelings or reactions, then psychological pain, including feelings of relational guilt, can also afflict the patient. Equally, the patient has feelings about the destructive side of illness and feels pressure to cope not only with the pain itself but with its social management (e.g., not 'letting it show' to visitors or letting it interfere with relationships; Lyons et al. 1998). Also of course people experience illness as especially troublesome when it does affect their ability to conduct relationships satisfactorily and a large part of the reported distress of diseases such as multiple sclerosis is that it destroys relationships themselves or the opportunity for conducting them (Lyons et al., 2006).These aspects of illness make extra relational demands on the patient, over and above the need to cope with physical discomfort, as we saw in Chapter 7.

Second, illness can also serve a liberating social function. Illness frees people from dull routine, legitimates their non-completion of assignments, and releases them from exams, duties, tasks and obligations (Parsons, 1951). Social, intellectual, and task-related failures can be excused by reference to sickness ('I wasn't concentrating: I have a headache'). These excuses are not damaging to the individual's social *face* (or 'image'): the persons are 'off the hook', it is not their fault, they should not blame themselves, they do not lose their 'social credit'. They can blame the illness, the person is out of sorts and not fully responsible. In this case the illness feeds an excuse into poor relational performance but the link between illness and relationships is still important.

Third, illness can become an occupation that takes over a person's life like a full-time job. The person may need to restructure daily routines like feeding and toilet needs in significantly restrictive ways or go to bed much earlier than usual, cut down on social time, and make much less effort to go out and see people. Although such things are caused by the illness, they nevertheless afflict the person's social life and relationships and are experienced as additionally unpleasant for that reason (Lyons & Meade, 1995).

Social relationships and health

To suggest that our health might be influenced by our relationship and the membership of a network and by the practices that are common in that group is not a new idea. One early example of research on epidemiology is based precisely on this idea. The British researcher Snow (1854/1936) showed that cholera was developed by villagers sharing one particular well more frequently than by others using a different source of water. He also showed that Scots who put water in their whisky were more likely to contract some diseases than was a group of people who drank whisky neat or who boiled their water to make tea instead. The identification of such relational features or network practices as correlates of disease remains one of the primary steps that epidemiologists take. For example, the first step in understanding AIDS in the early 1980s was to discover the *relational* histories and the practices of those persons who contracted it (Vanzetti & Duck, 1996).

In a fundamental and exciting extension of this logic, some researchers have tried to identify specific features of a person's particular groups of friends and family or lifestyle that may relate to the diseases that he or she contracts

(Hooley & Hiller, 2001; Sarason et al., 2001). Other researchers have looked at the relationship styles of the individual. In their classic study, Brown & Harris (1978) show that the presence of a close, confiding relationship with a husband or boyfriend significantly reduced the risk of women developing depression after a major loss or disappointment. Brown & Harris argued that long-term feelings of self-worth or self-esteem are especially significant, that these are provided by important close relationships, and that, to a major extent, these feelings could stave off psychiatric disorder in a crisis. One problem here is that the existence of strong close relationships with very small numbers of friends might be concealed in studies that check just on the numbers of friends that we claim to have (Hobfoll, 1984). If I do a study that seems to show that people are better off with large numbers of friends, I may miss the point that large numbers are made up of several sets of small numbers and the level of intimacy in these small groups – rather than the total number of bodies in our network – may be the key issue. There is certainly evidence that intimate relationships with a small number of persons are what really counts (Heller & Rook, 2001). What may be important is that a minimum level of close relationships is maintained. In other words, within a large group of friends there is at least one subset of one or two very close relationships with one or two special friends. Alternatively regular conversations with specific friends provide the *sense* of support that is important (Leatham & Duck, 1990). Certainly there are features of the transactions of pairs of friends that are significant (Cutrona, Suhr & McFarlane, 1990), such as comforting one another (Burleson, 1990), or cheering one another up (Barbee, 1990). Also people tend to suffer stress and illness when their relationships become disturbed (Duck, 1998) and the presence of strong, close relationships preserves people from the worst effects of stress, whether the presence is just felt to be available or is actually provided (Sarason et al., 2001).

Bertera (2005), for example, looked at not only positive social support but also social negativity and anxiety and mood disorders as they relate to health and illness. Although socially negative experiences tended to be associated with a number of anxiety and mood disorder episodes, positive support did not appear to prevent anxiety and mood disorder episodes. These findings are important in that they showed the significance of negative social interaction on mental ill health, rather than any positive impact of interaction on good health. Lindorff (2005), on the other hand, compared the stresses at work with those elsewhere and found that emotional support is more often received for social stressors (read this as 'relationship problems') than for non-social stressors, especially from relationships outside the workplace as compared with work relationships. Although work relationships provide the most tangible assistance and information for stressors that have occurred at work, non-work relationships provide more generalized forms of support, especially in the form of information, a finding that will not surprise readers of this book.

LISTEN IN ON YOUR OWN LIFE

The next time you or one of your friends/associates looks ill or reports feeling so, then pay attention to discussion that ensues and try to assess the extent to which the relational evaluation of symptoms is relevant to the eventual decision taken about whether the symptoms matter and what they may mean. You may want to reflect on the ways in which 'public information' about the meaning of symptoms threads into such a scenario and may even be able to come up with a recommendation to a health-related organization concerning the ways in which it could help people to identify the symptoms through network processes.

Relationships and the timing of death

There is some evidence that the timing of dying is influenced by relational factors, such as whether spousal anniversaries or significant dates are approaching. For instance, Jewish populations show a marked 'death dip'(a significant decrease in death rate) during the time before their solemn holy day Yom Kippur – the Day of Atonement (Phillips, 1970; 1972). Other research shows that birthdays and anniversaries exert effects on the death of widowed spouses (Bornstein & Clayton, 1972), who tend to die on days close to dates that had significance in the marriage.

Reactions to the death of a close partner have begun to interest social scientists working on relationships. 'Death of a spouse' carries the highest risk on the Life Events Scales, and bereavement brings with it a considerable need for large-scale readjustments to the routines of life. Adults responding to bereavement typically show stress and health problems over an extended period of time (Greenblatt, 1978). They also show a sequence of reactions comparable to, but not identical with, the responses of patients to their terminal diagnosis: first, exhaustion and hollowness, characterized by a sense of emptiness, stress, and overwhelming responsibility; second, a preoccupation with the image of the deceased, even extending to hallucinations or imagining that the person is still alive, has been seen in the street, and the like; third, guilt or a sense of things unsaid, feelings gone unexpressed, time not spent together; fourth, hostility to others or the 'leave me alone' reaction; fifth, changes to daily activity. The fifth reaction can be healthy or unhealthy depending on the nature and extent of the change, of course. Greenblatt's (1978) point, however, is that the psychological reaction to grief is a process that extends over time and is essential to the bereaved person, who naturally enough needs to reconstruct his or her life and identity. In many ways, the reactions of the grieving spouse mark out readjustments and changes to identity, roles and routines as the person comes to grips with the new demands upon them that stem from loss of a partner and makes decisions about the parts, mannerisms, styles, or traits of the lost person they wish to retain in their active life, perhaps by imitation.

Obviously also the death of a loved one and the subsequent sense of loss force a realignment of a person's relationships and so lead on to grieving and individual reactions to the bereavement (Harvey, Barnes, Carlson & Haig, 1995). That person's loss also may lead to losses for others (loss of that person's relationship time for others, willingness to engage in social contact, withdrawal from the network). Lastly, loss causes a person to relive the relationship only in memory – occasionally feeling haunted or chained by such memories.

This last point – that memories become the experience of the relationship – actually leads to an interesting thought. It raises the possibility that *all* relationships are forged largely in memory (since we often reflect about our relationships and think of relationship partners and what to do with them even when they are not present). It also raises the possibility that relationships with someone can *change* even after the person is dead! As I have noted in passing in a couple of places earlier (Duck, 1980, 1998), if we change our feelings towards a person who is not able to be present to make a reply or to be engaged to present their point of view, whether they are dead or simply absent from the scene, we can change a relationship at that point simply by thinking about it and changing our feelings. So are relationships created and maintained largely in thought and the language that we use to describe them? Such an issue is a good one to discuss in class now that you have reached the end of this book.

SUMMARY

This chapter has reviewed a number of ways in which research and thinking about relationships can be incorporated into the practical issues that surround us in everyday life. In particular, I have paid attention to the ways in which new approaches to legal matters in the courtroom, the establishment of relational contracts between a business and its clients, and the connection between relationships and health can become sites for us to evaluate the usefulness of relationship thinking for adding new dimensions to the way in which these issues may be approached. We looked at the way in which the relationships between jurors may affect their decision-making processes, at the way in which a psychological contract established between an organization and its customers could reflect/mimic the nature of friendship, and other consequences that friends may have in the diagnosis and treatment of health-related symptoms.

After reading this chapter (and the book as a whole), you should be able to apply relationship research to a number of different sorts of places in the real world using the idea that relationships are deeply connected to the ways in which we process and understand information about reality. Given that relationships are sources for our assessment about the value and meaning of particular kinds of information, there are huge numbers of areas where the relational underpinnings of other activities can be identified. It has been one of the major themes of this book that the performance of relationships and the processing of information at routine levels in everyday interaction are fundamental aspects is of human relationships.

FURTHER READING

Dutton, J., & Ragins, B. (2007). *Positive relationships at work*. Mahwah, NJ: Lawrence Erlbaum Associates.

http://www.apa.org/journals/releases/fam164381.pdf. is a document from the APA showing how family routines and rituals can contribute to health.

There are various books about relationships and the law but usually looked at from the point of view of how the law deals with such things as broken marriage, contract breach or relationships of dependence and interdependence. These most often take a different stance from the sort offered here but you might be interested in following these up, in which case a web search for 'personal relationships and law' will bring up several different titles about marriage, promises to marry, offers of marriage, divorce and other such issues.

References

Acitelli, L.K. (1988). When spouses talk to each other about their relationship. *Journal of Social and Personal Relationships, 5*, 185–199.

Acitelli, L.K. (1993). You, me, and us: Perspectives on relationship awareness. In S.W. Duck (Ed.), *Individuals in relationships (understanding relationship processes 1)* (pp. 144–174.). Newbury Park: SAGE.

Acitelli, L.K., Duck, S.W., & West, L. (2000). Embracing the social in personal relationships and research. In W. Ickes & S.W. Duck (Eds.), *Social psychology and personal relationships* (pp. 215–227). Chichester: Wiley.

Adams, R., & Blieszner, R. (1996). Midlife friendship patterns. In N. Vanzetti & S.W. Duck (Eds.), *A lifetime of relationships* (pp. 336–363). Pacific Grove: Brooks/Cole.

Adamson, K., & Pasley, K. (2006). Coparenting following divorce and relationship dissolution. In M.A. Fine & J.H. Harvey (Eds.), *Handbook of divorce and relationship dissolution* (pp. 241–261). Mahwah, NJ: Lawrence Erlbaum and Associates.

Afifi, T.D. (2003). 'Feeling caught' in stepfamilies: Managing boundary turbulence through appropriate communication privacy rules. *Journal of Social and Personal Relationships, 20*(6), 729–755.

Afifi, W.A., Falato, W.L., & Weiner, J.L. (2001). Identity concerns following a severe relational transgression: The role of discovery method for the relational outcomes of infidelity. *Journal of Social and Personal Relationships, 18*(2), 291–308.

Alberts, J.K., Yoshimura, C.G., Rabby, M., & Loschiavo, R. (2005). Mapping the topography of couples' daily conversation. *Journal of Social and Personal Relationships, 22*(3), 299–322.

Allan, G.A. (1993). Social structure and relationships. In S.W. Duck (Ed.), *Social contexts of relationships (understanding relationship processes 3)* (pp. 1–25). Newbury Park, CA: SAGE.

Allan, G.A. (1995). Friendship, class, status and identity. Paper to Annual Convention of the International Network on Personal Relationships, Williamsburg, VA, June.

Allan, G.A. (1998). Friendship, sociology and social structure. *Journal of Social and Personal Relationships, 15*, 685–702.

Allan, G.A., & Gerstner, C. (2006). Money and relationship difficulties. In C.D. Kirkpatrick, S.W. Duck & M.K. Foley (Eds.), *Relating difficulty: The processes of constructing and managing difficult interaction* (pp. 81–100). Mahwah, NJ: Lawrence Erlbaum and Associates.

Allen, K.R., & Walker, A.J. (2000). Constructing gender in families. In R.M. Milardo & S.W. Duck (Eds.), *Families as relationships* (pp. 1–17). Chichester, UK: Wiley.

Altman, I., & Taylor, D. (1973). *Social penetration: The development of interpersonal relationships*. New York: Holt, Rinehart & Winston.

Amato, P.R. (1991). The 'child of divorce' as a person prototype: Bias in the recall of information about children in divorced families. *Journal of Marriage and the Family, 53*, 59–70.

Anders, S.L., & Tucker, J.S. (2000). Adult attachment style, interpersonal communication competence, and social support. *Personal Relationships, 7*(4), 379–389.

Antaki, C., & Widdicombe, S. (Eds.). (1998). *Identities in talk*. London: SAGE.

Antaki, C., Barnes, R., & Leudar, I. (2005). Diagnostic formulations in psychotherapy. *Discourse Studies, 7*(6), 627–647.

Aquilino, W. (1996). The life course of children born to unmarried mothers: Childhood living arrangements and young adult outcomes. *Journal of Marriage and the Family, 58*, 293–310.

Arendell, T. (1993). After divorce: Investigations into father absence. *Gender and Society, 6*, 562–586.

Argyle, M. (1967). *The psychology of interpersonal behaviour*. Harmondsworth, UK: Penguin Books.

Argyle, M. (1975). *Bodily communication*. London: Methuen.

Argyle, M. (1983). *The psychology of interpersonal behaviour (4th edn)*. Harmondsworth, UK: Penguin Books.

Argyle, M. (1987). *The psychology of happiness*. Harmondsworth, UK: Penguin.

Argyle, M., & Dean, J. (1965). Eye contact, distance, and affiliation. *Sociometry, 28*, 289–304.

Argyle, M., Salter, V., Nicholson, H., Williams, M., & Burgess, P. (1970). The communication of inferior and superior attitudes by verbal and non-verbal signals. *British Journal of Social and Clinical Psychology, 9*, 222–223.

Aron, A., & Aron, E. (1997). Self-expansion motivation and including other in the self. In S.W. Duck (Ed.), *Handbook of personal relationships*, (2nd edn) (pp. 251–270). Chichester, UK: Wiley.

Aron, A., Dutton, D.G., Aron, E., & Iverson, A. (1989). Experiences of falling in love. *Journal of Social and Personal Relationships, 6*, 243–257.

Asher, S.R. & Parker, J.G. (1989). Significance of peer relationship problems in childhood. In B.H. Schneider, G. Attili, J. Nadel, & R. Weissberg (Eds.), *Social competence in development perspective*. Amsterdam: Kluwer.

Avenevoli, S., & Merikangas, K.R. (2003). Familiar influnces on adolescent smoking. *Addiction, 98* (Suppl 1), 1–20.

Ayres, J. (1989). The impact of communcation apprehension and interaction structure on initial interactions. *Communication Monographs, 56*, 75–88.

Bandura, A. (1977). *Social learning theory*. Englewood Cliffs, NJ: Prentice Hall.

Banse, R. (2004). Adult attachment and marital satisfaction: Evidence for dyadic configuration effects. *Journal of Social and Personal Relationships, 21*(2), 273–282.

Barbee, A.P. (1990). Interactive coping: The cheering up process in close relationships. In S.W. Duck with R.S. Cohen (Eds.), *Personal relationships and social support*. London: SAGE.

Barber, B.L., & Demo, D.H. (2006). The kids are alright (at least most of them): Links between divorce and dissolution and child well-being. In M.A. Fine & J.H. Harvey (Eds.), *Handbook of divorce and relationship dissolution* (pp. 289–311). Mahwah, NJ: Lawrence Erlbaum and Associates.

Bartholomew, K. (1990). Avoidance of intimacy: An attachment perspective. *Journal of Social and Personal Relationships, 7*, 147–178.

Bartholomew, K. (1993). From childhood to adult relationships: Attachment theory and research. In S.W. Duck (Ed.), *Learning about relationships (understanding relationship processes 2).* (pp. 30–62). Thousand Oaks, CA: SAGE.

Bartlett, F. (1932). *Remembering.* Cambridge, UK: Cambridge University Press.

Bass, L.A., & Stein, C.H. (1997). Comparing the structure and stability of network ties using the social support questionnaire and the social network list. *Journal of Social and Personal Relationships, 14*, 123–132.

Baumrind, D. (1972). Socialization and instrumental competence in young children. In W.W. Hartup (Ed.), *The young child: Reviews of research* (Vol. 2). Washington, DC: National Association for the Education of Young Children.

Baxter, L.A. (1992). Root metaphors in accounts of developing romantic relationships. *Journal of Social and Personal Relationships, 9*, 253–275.

Baxter, L.A., & Montgomery, B.M. (1996). *Relating: Dialogs and dialectics.* New York: Guilford Press.

Baxter, L.A., & Montgomery, B.M. (2000). Rethinking communication in personal relationships from a dialectical perspective. In K. Dindia & S.W. Duck (Eds.), *Communication and personal relationships* (pp. 31–54). Chichester: Wiley.

Baxter, L.A., & Widenmann, S. (1993). Revealing and not revealing the status of romantic relationships to social networks. *Journal of Social and Personal Relationships, 10*, 321–338.

Baxter, L.A., & Wilmot, W. (1984). Secret tests: Social strategies for acquiring information about the state of the relationship. *Human Communication Research, 11*, 171–201.

Baxter, L. A., & Wilmot, W. (1985). Taboo topics in close relationships. *Journal of Social and Personal Relationships, 2*, 253–269.

Baxter, L.A., Braithwaite, D.O., Bryant, L., & Wagner, A. (2004). Stepchildren's perceptions of the contradictions in communication with stepparents. *Journal of Social and Personal Relationships, 21*(4), 447–467.

Baxter, L.A., Dun, T.D., & Sahlstein, E.M. (2001). Rules for relating communicated among social network members. *Journal of Social and Personal Relationships, 18*, 173–200.

Baxter, L.A., Mazanec, M., Nicholson, L., Pittman, G., Smith, K., & West, L. (1997). Everyday loyalties and betrayals in personal relationships: A dialectical perspective. *Journal of Social and Personal Relationships, 14*, 655–678.

Beall, A., & Sternberg, R. (1995). The social construction of love. *Journal of Social and Personal Relationships, 12*, 417–438.

Bedford, V.H., & Blieszner, R. (1997). Personal relationships in later life families. In S.W. Duck (Ed.), *Handbook of personal relationships, 2nd edn* (pp. 523–540). Chichester, UK: Wiley.

Bedford, V.H., & Blieszner, R. (2000). Personal relationships in later life families. In R. Milardo & S.W. Duck (Eds.), *Families as relationships* (pp. 157–174). Chichester, UK: Wiley.

Berger, P., & Kellner, H. (1964). Marriage and the construction of reality: An exercise in the microsociology of knowledge. *Diogenes, 46*, 1–24.

Bergmann, J.R. (1993). *Discreet indiscretions: The social organization of gossip.* New York: Aldine de Gruyter.

Berndt, T.J. (1996). Friendship in adolescence, *A lifetime of relationships*. Pacific Grove, CA: Brooks/Cole.

Berscheid, E., & Walster (Hatfield), E. (1974). Physical attractiveness. In L. Berkowitz (Ed.), *Advances in experimental social psychology* (Vol. 7, pp. 158–216). New York: Academic Press.

Berscheid, E., & Walster (Hatfield)., E. (1978). *Interpersonal attraction, second edition*. Reading, MA: Addison Wesley.

Bertera, E.M. (2005). Mental health in us adults: The role of positive social support and social negativity in personal relationships. *Journal of Social and Personal Relationships, 22*(1), 33–48.

Bickmore, T.W. (2003). *Relational agents: Effecting change through human-computer relationships*. Unpublished Ph.D., MIT, Boston, MA.

Bickmore, T.W. (2004). Unspoken rules of spoken interaction. *Communications of the ACM, 47*(4), 38–44.

Bickmore, T.W., & Picard, R.W. (2005). Establishing and maintaining long–term human–computer relationships. *ACM Transaction on Computer Human Interaction, 12*(2), 293–327.

Blieszner, R. (2006). A lifetime of caring: Dimensions and dynamics in late-life close relationships. *Personal Relationships, 13*(1), 1–18.

Bloom, B., Asher, S., & White, S. (1978). Marital disruption as a stressor: A review and analysis. *Psychological Bulletin, 85*, 867–894.

Bochner, A.P. (1991). On the paradigm that would not die. In J. Anderson (Ed.), *Communication yearbook* (Vol. 14, pp. 484–491). Newbury Park: SAGE.

Booth, A. (2006). Proposals for research on the consequences of divorce for children. In M.A. Fine & J.H. Harvey (Eds.), *Handbook of divorce and relationship dissolution* (pp. 619–627). Mahwah, NJ: Lawrence Erlbaum and Associates.

Bornstein, P.E., & Clayton, P. J. (1972). The anniversary reaction. *Diseases of the Nervous System, 33*, 470–472.

Bosticco, C., & Thompson, T. (2005). The role of communication and story telling in the family grieving system. *Journal of Family Communication, 5*(4), 255–278.

Boulton, M., & Smith, P.K. (1996). Liking and peer perceptions among Asian and white British children. *Journal of Social and Personal Relationships, 13*, 163–177.

Bourhis, R.Y., & Giles, H. (1977). The language of intergroup distinctiveness. In H. Giles (Ed.), *Language, ethnicity and intergroup relations*. London: Academic Press.

Bowlby, J. (1969/1982). *Attachment and loss, vol. I. Attachment (2nd edn)*. New York: Basic Books.

Bowlby, J. (1979). *The making and breaking of affectional bonds*. London: Tavistock.

Bradshaw, S. (2006). Shyness and difficult relationships: Formation is just the beginning. In C.D. Kirkpatrick, S.W. Duck & M.K. Foley (Eds.), *Relating difficulty: The processes of contructing and managing difficult interaction* (pp. 15–41). Mahwah, NJ: Lawrence Erlbaum and Associates.

Braithwaite, D.O., & Baxter, L.A. (1995). 'I do' again: The relational dialectics of renewing marriage vows. *Journal of Social and Personal Relationships, 12*, 177–198.

Braithwaite, D.O., & Koenig Kellas, J. (2006). Shopping for and with friends: Everyday communication in the shopping mall. In J.T. Wood & S.W. Duck (Eds.), *Composing relationships: Communication in everyday life* (pp. 86–95). Belmont, CA: Wadsworth.

Braverman, L. (1991). The dilemma of housework. *Journal of Marriage and Family Therapy, 17*, 25–28.

Bricker, J.B., Leroux, B.G., Peterson, A.V., Jr, Kealey, K., Sarason, I.G., Anderson, M.R., & Marek, P.M. (2003). Nine year prospective relationship between parental smoking cessation and children's daily smoking. *Addiction, 98*, 585–593.

Bringle, R.G., & Boebinger, K.L.G. (1990). Jealousy and the third person in the love triangle. *Journal of Social and Personal Relationships, 7*, 119–134.

Brown, G.W., & Harris, T. (1978). *The social origins of depression*. London: Tavistock.

Brown, R. (1965). *Social psychology*. New York: Free Press.

Bruess, C.J.S., & Hoefs, A. (2006). The cat puzzle recovered: Composing relationships through family rituals. In J.T. Wood & S.W. Duck (Eds.), *Composing relationships: Communication in everyday life*. Belmont, CA: Wadsworth.

Bruess, C.J.S., & Pearson, J.C. (1993). 'Sweet pea' and 'pussy cat': An examination of idiom use and marital satisfaction over the life cycle. *Journal of Social and Personal Relationships, 10*, 609–615.

Bugental, D.E., Kaswan, J.E., & Love, L.R. (1970). Perception of contradictory meanings conveyed by verbal and nonverbal channels. *Journal of Personality and Social Psychology, 16*, 647–655.

Burgoon, J.K., & Koper, R.J. (1984). Nonverbal and relational communication associated with reticence. *Human Communication Research, 10*, 601–626.

Burgoon, J.K., Coker, D.A., & Coker, R.A. (1986). Communicative effects of gaze behavior: A test of two contrasting explanations. *Human Communication Research, 12*, 495–524.

Burleson, B.R. (1990). Comforting as social support: Relational consequences of supportive behaviors. In S.W. Duck & W.R.C. Silver (Eds.), *Personal relationships and social support* (pp. 66–82). London: SAGE.

Burleson, B.R., Holmstrom, A.J., & Gilstrap, C.M. (2005). 'Guys can't say that to guys': Four experiments assessing the normative motivation account for deficiencies in the emotional support provided by men. *Communication Monographs, 72*(4), 468–501.

Burleson, B.R., Kunkel, A.W., Samter, W., & Werking, K.J. (1996). Men's and women's evaluations of communication skills in personal relationships: When sex differences make a difference – and when they don't. *Journal of Social and Personal Relationships, 13*, 143–152.

Buss, D.M., & Dedden, L.A. (1990). Derogation of competitors. *Journal of Social and Personal Relationships, 7*, 395–422.

Buunk, A. (1980). Sexually open marriages: Ground rules for countering potential threats to marriage. *Alternative Life Styles, 3*, 312–328.

Buunk, A. (1995). Sex, self-esteem, dependency and extra-dyadic sexual experience as related to jealousy responses. *Journal of Social and Personal Relationships, 12*, 147–153.

Byrne, D. (1971). *The attraction paradigm*. New York: Academic Press.

Byrne, D. (1992). The transition from controlled laboratory experimentation to less controlled settings: Surprise! Additional variables are operative. *Communication Monographs, 59*, 190–198.

Byrne, D. (1997). An overview (and underview) of research and theory within the attraction paradigm. *Journal of Social and Personal Relationships, 14*, 417–431.

Caplan, S.E. (2005). A social skill account of problematic internet use. *Journal of Communication, 55*(4), 721–736.

Cappella, J.N. (1991). Mutual adaptation and relativity of measurement. In B.M. Montgomery & S.W. Duck (Eds.), *Studying interpersonal interaction* (pp. 103–117). New York: Guilford.

Carl, W.J. (2006a). <where r u?><here u?>: Everyday communication with relational technologies. In J.T. Wood & S.W. Duck (Eds.), *Composing relationships: Communication in everyday life* (pp. 96–109). Belmont, CA: Wadsworth.

Carl, W.J. (2006b). What's all the buzz about? Everyday communication and the relational basis of word-of-mouth and buzz marketing practices. *Management Communication Quarterly, 19*(4), 601–634.

Carl, W.J., & Duck, S.W. (2004). How to do things with relationships. In P. Kalbfleisch (Ed.), *Communication yearbook* (Vol. 28, pp. 1–35). Thousand Oaks, CA: SAGE.

Carr, S.E., & Dabbs, J.M., Jr (1974). The effects of lighting, distance and intimacy of topic on verbal and visual behaviour. *Sociometry,* 37: 592–600.

Caughlin, J.P., & Afifi, T.D. (2004). When is topic avoidance unsatisfying? Examining the moderators of the association between avoidance and dissatisfaction. *Human Communication Research, 30*(4), 479–513.

Caughlin, J.P., Afifi, W.A., Carpenter-Theune, K.E., & Miller, L.E. (2005). Reasons for, and consequences of, revealing personal secrets in close relationships: A longitudinal study. *Personal Relationships, 12*(1), 43–59.

Chan, D.K.-S., & Cheng, G.H.-L. (2004). A comparison of off-line and online friendship qualities at different stages of relationship development. *Journal of Social and Personal Relationships, 21*(3), 305–320.

Chang, Y. (2002). *Culture and communication: An ethnographic study of Chinese criminal courtroom communication.* Unpublished Ph.D., University of Iowa, Iowa City, IA.

Chang, Y. (2003). *Who speaks next? Discourse structure as persuasion in Chinese criminal courtrooms.* Paper presented at the National Communication Association, November, Miami Beach, Florida.

Cherlin, A. (1992). *Marriage, divorce, and remarriage.* Cambridge, MA: Harvard University Press.

Chornet-Roses, D. (2006). *'I could say I am "dating" but that could mean a lot of different things': Dating in the us as dialogical realtional process.* Iowa City, IA: University of Iowa.

Christoper, F.S., & Frandsen, M.M (1990). Strategies of influence in sex and dating. *Journal of Social and Personal Relationships,* 7: 89–105.

Cialdini, R.B., Cacioppo, J.T., Bassett, R., & Miller, J.A. (1978). Lowball procedure for producing compliance: Commitment then cost. *Journal of Personality and Social Psychology, 36*, 463–476.

Cialdini, R.B., Vincent, J.E., Lewis, S.K., Catalan, J., Wheeler, D., & Darby, B.L. (1975). A reciprocal concessions procedure for inducing compliance: The door-in-the-face technique. *Journal of Personality and Social Psychology, 21*, 206–215.

Cockburn-Wootten, C., & Zorn, T. (2006). Cabbages and headache cures: Work stories within the family. In J.T. Wood & S.W. Duck (Eds.), *Composing relaionships: Communication in everyday life* (pp. 137–144). Belmont, CA: Wadsworth.

Cody, M.J., Woelfel, M.L., & Jordan, W.J. (1983). Dimensions of compliance-gaining situations. *Human Communication Research,* 9, 99–113.

Cohan, C.L., Cole, S., & Davila, J. (2005). Marital transitions among Vietnam era repatriated prisoners of war. *Journal of Social and Personal Relationships, 22*(6), 777–795.

Cohen, J. (2004). Para-social breakup from favorite television characters: The role of attachment styles and relationship intensity. *Journal of Social and Personal Relationships, 21*(2), 187–202.

Coker, D.A., & Burgoon, J.K. (1987). The nature of conversational involvement and nonverbal encoding patterns. *Human Communication Research, 13*, 463–494.

Coleman, M., & Ganong, L.H. (1995). Family reconfiguring following divorce. In S.W. Duck & J.T. Wood (Eds.), *Confronting relationship challenges (understanding relationship processes 5)* (pp. 73–108). Thousand Oaks, CA: SAGE.

Coleman, S., & May-Chahal, C. (2003). *Safeguarding children and young people*. London: Routledge.

Contarello, A., & Volpato, C. (1991). Images of friendship: Literary depictions through the ages. *Journal of Social and Personal Relationships, 8*, 49–75.

Cook, M. (1977). Social skills and attraction. In S.W. Duck (Ed.), *Theory and practice in interpersonal attraction*. London & New York: Academic Press.

Cooney, T.M. (2000). Parent child relations across adulthood. In R.M. Milardo & S. W. Duck (Eds.), *Families as relationships* (pp. 39–58). Chichester, UK: Wiley.

Crouter, A., & Helms-Erikson, H. (2000). Work and family from a dyadic perspective: Variations in inequality. In R.M. Milardo & S.W. Duck (Eds.), *Families as relationships* (pp. 99–115). Chichester, UK: Wiley.

Cunningham, M.R., Shamblen, S.R., Barbee, A.P., & Ault, L.K. (2005). Social allergies in romantic relationships: Behavioral repetition, emotional sensitization, and dissatisfaction in dating couples. *Personal Relationships, 12*(2), 273–295.

Cupach, W.R., & Canary, D.J. (2000). *Competence in interpersonal conflict*. Propsect Heights, IL: Waveland Press.

Cupach, W.R., & Spitzberg, B.H. (Eds.). (1994). *The dark side of interpersonal communication*. Hillsdale, NJ: LEA.

Cupach, W.R., Spitzberg, B.H., & Carson, C.L. (2000). Toward a theory of obsessive relational intrusion and stalking. In K. Dindia & S.W. Duck (Eds.), *Communication and personal relationships* (pp. 131–146). Chichester, UK: Wiley.

Cutrona, C.E., Suhr, J., & McFarlane, R. (1990). Interpersonal transactions and the psychological sense of support. In S.W. Duck with RC. Silver (Eds.), *Personal relationships and social support*. London: SAGE.

Dailey, R.M., & Palomares, N.A. (2004). Strategic topic avoidance: An investigation of topic avoidance frequency, strategies used, and relational correlates. *Communication Monographs, 71*(4), 471–496.

Dainton, M. (2000). Maintenance behaviors, expectations for maintenance, and satisfaction: Linking comparison levels to relational maintenance strategies. *Journal of Social and Personal Relationships, 17*(6), 827–842.

Daly, J.A., & Vangelisti, A.L. (2003). Skillfully informing others: How communicators effectively convey messages. In B.R. Burleson & J.O. Greene (Eds.), *Handbook of communication and social interaction skills* (pp. 871–908). Hillsdale, NJ: Lawrence Erlbaum and Associates.

Darling, N., & Cumsille, P. (2003). Theory, measurement and methods in the study of family influences on adolescent smoking. *Addiction, 98*(Suppl 1), 21–36.

Darwin, C. (1859 (1985 edition)). *On the origin of species by means of natural selection*. Harmondsworth, UK: Penguin Books.

Davis, J.D., & Sloan, M. (1974). The basis of interviewee matching of interviewer self disclosure. *British Journal of Social and Clinical Psychology, 13,* 359–367.

Davis, M.S. (1983). *Smut: Erotic reality/obscene ideology.* Chicago: University of Chicago Press.

Davis, M.S., & Schmidt, C.J. (1977). The obnoxious and the nice: Some sociological consequences of two psychological types. *Sociometry, 40*(3), 201–213.

De Santis, A.D. (2002). Smoke screen: An ethnographic study of a cigar shop's collective rationalization. *Health Communication, 14*(2), 167–198.

DeHart, T., Pelham, B.W., & Tennen, H. (2006). What lies beneath: Parenting style and implicit self-esteem. *Journal of Experimental Social Psychology, 42*(1), 1–17.

Delia, J.G. (1980). Some tentative thoughts concerning the study of interpersonal relationships and their development. *Western Journal of Speech Communication, 44,* 97–103.

Demo, D., Allen, K.R., & Fine, M.A. (Eds.). (2000). *Handbook of family diversity.* New York: Oxford.

DeTurck, M.A. (1985). A transactional analysis of compliance-gaining behavior: The effects of noncompliance, relational contexts and actors' gender. *Human Communication Research, 12,* 54–78.

Dickens, W.J., & Perlman, D. (1981). Friendship over the life cycle. In S.W. Duck & R. Gilmour (Eds.), *Personal relationships 2: Developing personal relationships.* London: Academic Press.

Dickson, F.C., Hughes, P.C., & Walker, K.L. (2005). An exploratory investigation into dating among later-life women. *Western Journal of Communication, 69*(1), 67–82.

Dijkstra, P., Groothof, H.A.K., Poel, G.A., Laverman, E.T.G., Schrier, M., & Buunk, A.P. (2001). Sex differences in the events that elicit jealousy among homosexuals. *Personal Relationships, 8*(1), 41–54.

Dillard, J.P., Hunter, J.E., & Burgoon, M. (1984). Sequential-request persuasive strategies: Meta-analysis of foot-in-the-door and door-in-the face. *Human Communication Research, 10,* 461–488.

DiMatteo, M.R., & Friedman, H.S. (1982). *Social psychology and medicine.* Cambridge, MA: Oelgeschlager.

Dindia, K. (1994). The intrapersonal–interpersonal dialectical process of self-disclosure. In S.W. Duck (Ed.), *Understanding relationship processes 4: Dynamics of relationships* (pp. 27–57). Newbury Park, CA: SAGE.

Dindia, K., Timmerman, L., Langan, E., Sahlstein, E.M., & Quandt, J. (2004). The function of holiday greetings in maintaining relationships. *Journal of Social and Personal Relationships, 21*(5), 577–593.

Dixson, M.D., & Duck, S.W. (1993). Understanding relationship processes: Uncovering the human search for meaning. In S.W. Duck (Ed.), *Individuals in relationships (Understanding relationship processes 1)* (pp. 175–206). Newbury Park, CA: SAGE.

Donnelly, D., & Finkelhor, D. (1993). Who has joint custody? Class differences in the determination of custody arrangements. *Journal of Family Relations, 42*(1), 57–60.

Doucet, J., & Aseltine, R.H., Jr. (2003). Childhood family adversity and the quality of marital relationships in young adulthood. *Journal of Social and Personal Relationships, 20*(6), 818–842.

Douglas, W. (1987). Affinity testing in initial interaction. *Journal of Social Personal Relationships, 4:* 3–16.

Dovidio, J.F., Ellyson, S.L., Keating, C.F., Heltman, K., & Brown, C.E. (1988). The relationship of social power to visual displays of dominance between men and women. *Journal of Personality and Social Psychology, 54*, 232–242.

Dragon, W., & Duck, S.W. (Eds.). (2005). *Understanding research in personal relationships: A text with readings*. London: SAGE.

Duck, S.W. (1980). Personal relationships research in the 1980s: Towards an understanding of complex human sociality. *Western Journal of Speech Communication, 44*, 114–119.

Duck, S.W. (1982). A topography of relationship disengagement and dissolution. In S.W. Duck (Ed.), *Personal relationships 4: Dissolving personal relationships* (pp. 1–30). London: Academic Press.

Duck, S.W. (1984) 'A perspective on the repair of personal relationship: repair of what, when?', in S.W. Duck (Ed.), *Personal Relationships 5: Repairing Personal Relationship*. London: Academic Press

Duck, S.W. (1990). Relationships as unfinished business: Out of the frying pan and into the 1990s. *Journal of Social and Personal Relationships, 7*, 5–29.

Duck, S.W. (1991). *Friends, for life, second edition, (in UK) (understanding personal relationships, in USA)*. Hemel Hempstead, UK/New York, USA: Harvester-Wheatsheaf/ Guilford.

Duck, S.W. (1994). *Meaningful relationships: Talking, sense, and relating*. Thousand Oaks, CA: SAGE.

Duck, S.W. (1998). *Human relationships, third edition*. London: SAGE.

Duck, S.W. (1999). *Relating to others second ed*. London: Open University Press.

Duck, S.W. (2000). *Oh give me a phone where the charges don't roam but my peers and relating hopes stray: Cell phones as relationship devices*. Paper presented at the National Communication Association, Seattle, WA.

Duck, S.W. (2002). Hypertext in the key of g: Three types of 'history' as influences on conversational structure and flow. *Communication Theory, 12*(1), 41–62.

Duck, S.W. (2006). The play, playfulness and the players: Everyday interaction as improvised rehearsal of relationships. In J.T. Wood & S.W. Duck (Eds.), *Composing relationships: Communication in everyday life* (pp. 15–23). Belmont, CA: Wadsworth.

Duck, S.W. (in press). *The relationship book*. Thousand Oaks, CA: SAGE.

Duck, S.W., & Gilmour, R. (Eds.). (1981). *Personal relationships 3: Personal relationships in disorder*. London & New York: Academic Press.

Duck, S.W., & McMahan, D.T. (forthcoming). *Basics of communication: A relational approach*. Thousand Oaks, CA: SAGE.

Duck, S.W., & Pond, K. (1989). Friends, Romans, countrymen; lend me your retrospective data: Rhetoric and reality in personal relationships. In C. Hendrick (Ed.), *Close relationships* (Vol. 10, pp. 17–38). Newbury Park, CA: Sage Publications.

Duck, S.W., & Sants, H.K.A. (1983). On the origin of the specious: Are personal relationships really interpersonal states? *Journal of Social and Clinical Psychology, 1*, 27–41.

Duck, S.W., & VanderVoort, L.A. (2002). Scarlet letters and whited sepulchres: The social marking of relationships as 'inappropriate'. In R. Goodwin & D. Cramer (Eds.), *Inappropriate relationships: The unconventional, the disapproved, and the forbidden*. (pp. 3–24). Mahwah, NJ: Erlbaum.

Duck, S.W., & Wood, J.T. (1995). For better for worse, for richer for poorer: The rough and the smooth of relationships. In S.W. Duck & J.T. Wood (Eds.), *Confronting relationship challenges (understanding relationship processes 5)* (pp. 1–21). Thousand Oaks, CA: SAGE.

Duck, S.W., Cirstea, L., & VanderVoort, L.A. (2000) *Variation in communication accross the course of a day : Assessing influences of time of day*. Paper presented at the Amercian Academy of Management, Toronto, Canada.

Duck, S.W., Foley, M.K., & Kirkpatrick, C.D. (2006a). Uncovering the complex roles behind the 'difficult' co-worker. In J. M. Harden Fritz & B.L. Omdahl (Eds.), *Problematic relationships in the workplace* (pp. 3–19). New York: Peter Lang.

Duck, S.W., Foley, M.K., & Kirkpatrick, C.D. (2006b). Relating difficulty in a triangular world. In C.D. Kirkpatrick, S.W. Duck & M.K. Foley (Eds.), *Relating difficulty: Processes of constructing and managing difficult interaction.* (pp. 225–232). Mahwah, NJ: Lawrence Erlbaum and Associates.

Duck, S.W., Pond. K., & Leatham, G.B. (1994). Loneliness and the evaluation of relational events. *Journal of Social and Personal Relationships, 11*, 235–260.

Duck, S.W., Rutt, D.J., Hurst, M., & Strejc, H. (1991). Some evident truths about conversations in everyday relationships: All communication is not created equal. *Human Communication Research, 18*, 228–267.

Duncombe, J., Harrison, K., Allan, G.A., & Marsden, D. (2004). *The state of affairs*. Mahwah, NJ: Lawrence Erlbaum and Associates.

Dunkel-Schetter, C., & Skokan, L.A. (1990). Determinants of social support provision in personal relationships. *Journal of Social and Personal Relationships, 7*, 437–450.

Dunn, J. (1996). Siblings: The first society. In N. Vanzetti & S.W. Duck. (Eds.), *A lifetime of relationships* (pp. 105–124). Pacific Grove, CA: Brooks/Cole.

Dunn, J. (1997). Lessons from the study of bi-directional effects. *Journal of Social and Personal Relationships, 14*, 565–573.

Duran, R., & Prusank, D.T. (1997). Relational themes in men's and women's popular non-fiction magazine articles. *Journal of Social and Personal Relationships, 14*, 165–189.

Dutton, J., & Ragins, B. (Eds.). (2007). *Positive relationships at work*. Mahwah, NJ: Lawrence Erlbaum Associates.

Eiskovits, Z.C., Edelson, J.L., Guttmann, E., & Sela-Amit, M. (1991). Cognitive styles and socialized attitudes of men who batter. *Family Relations*, 72–77.

Ellsworth, P.C., Carlsmith, J.M., & Henson, A. (1972). The stare as a stimulus to flight in human subjects: A series of field experiments. *Journal of Personality and Social Psychology, 21*, 302–311.

Emmers-Sommer, T. (2004). The effect of communication quality and quantity indicators on intimacy and relational satisfaction. *Journal of Social and Personal Relationships, 21*(3), 399–411.

Erbert, L.A. (2000). Conflict and dialectics: Perceptions of dialectical contradictions in marital conflict. *Journal of Social and Personal Relationships, 17*, 638–659.

Feeney, J.A. (2004). Hurt feelings in couple relationships: Towards integrated models of the negative effects of hurtful events. *Journal of Social and Personal Relationships, 21*(4), 487–508.

Feeney, J.A. (2005). Hurt feelings in couple relationships: Exploring the role of attachment and perceptions of personal injury. *Personal Relationships, 12*(2), 253–271.

Feeney, J.A. (2006). Parental attachment and conflict behaviour: Implication for offspring's attachment, loneliness, and relationship satisfaction. *Personal Relationships, 13*(1), 19–36.

Feeney, J.A., Noller, P., & Roberts, N. (2000). Attachment and close relationships. In C. Hendrick & S.S. Hendrick (Eds.), *Close relationships: A sourcebook* (pp. 185–201). Thousand Oaks, CA: SAGE.

Felmlee, D.H. (1995). Fatal attractions: Affection and disaffection in intimate relationships. *Journal of Social and Personal Relationships, 12*, 295–311.

Festinger, L. (1954). A theory of social comparison processes. *Human Relations, 7*, 117–140.

Festinger, L. (1957). *A theory of cognitive dissonance.* Stanford, CA: Stanford University Press.

Fine, M.A., & Demo, D. (2000). Divorce: Societal ill or normative transition? In R.M. Milardo & S.W. Duck (Eds.), *Families as relationships* (pp. 135–156). Chichester, UK: Wiley.

Fine, M.A., & Harvey, J.H. (2006). *Handbook of divorce and relationship dissolution.* Mahwah, NJ: Lawrence Erlbaum and Associates.

Fisher, S.W. (1996). *The family and the individual: Reciprocal influences.* In N. Vanzetti & S.W. Duck (Eds.), *A lifetime of relationships* (pp. 311–335). Pacific Grove, CA: Brooks/Cole.

Fitch, K.L. (1998). *Speaking relationally: Culture, communication, and interpersonal connection.* New York: Guilford.

Fitch, K.L. (2003). Cultural persuadables. *Communication Theory, 13*(1), 100–123.

Fleischmann, A.A., Spitzberg, B.H., Andersen, P.A., & Roesch, S.C. (2005). Tickling the monster: Jealousy induction in relationships. *Journal of Social and Personal Relationships, 22*(1), 49–73.

Floyd, K. (2004). Introduction to the uses and potential uses of physiological measurement in the study of family communication. *Journal of Family Communication, 4*(3,4), 295–317.

Floyd, K., & Morman, M.T. (2005). Fathers' and sons' reports of fathers' affectionate communication: The implications of a naïve theory of affection. *Journal of Social and Personal Relationships, 22*(1), 99–109.

Foley, M.K. (2006a). Sorority sisters speaking social support. In J.T. Wood & S.W. Duck (Eds.), *Composing relationships: Communication in everyday life* (pp. 128–136). Belmont, CA: Thomson Wadsworth.

Foley, M.K. (2006b). Locating 'difficulty': A multi-site model of intimate terrorism. In C.D. Kirkpatrick, S.W. Duck & M.K. Foley (Eds.), *Relating difficulty: The processes of constructing and managing difficult interaction* (pp. 43–59). Mahwah, NJ: Lawrence Erlbaum and Associates.

Foster, C.A., & Campbell, W.K. (2005). The adversity of secret relationships. *Personal Relationships, 12*(1), 125–143.

Foster, E.K., & Rosnow, R.L. (2006). Gossip and network relationships. In C.D. Kirkpatrick, S.W. Duck & M.K. Foley (Eds.), *Relating difficulty: The processes of constructing and managing difficult interaction* (pp. 161–180). Mahwah, NJ: Lawrence Erlbaum and Associates.

Furstenberg, F.F., Nord, C.W., Peterson, J.L., & Zill, N. (1983). The life course of children of divorce: Marital disruption and parental conflict. *American Sociological Review, 48*, 656–668.

Gaines, S., & Ickes, W. (2000). Perspectives on interracial relationship. In W. Ickes & S.W. Duck (Eds.). *The social psychology of personal relationships* (pp. 55–78). Chichester, UK: Wiley.

Galvin, K.S. (2004). The family of the future: What do we face? In A. Vangelisti (Ed.), *Handbook of family communication* (pp. 675–697). Mahwah, NJ: Lawrence Erlbaum and Associates.

Ganong, L.H., Coleman, M., & Hans, J. (2006). Divorce as prelude to stepfamily living and the consequences of redivorce. In M.A. Fine & J.H. Harvey (Eds.), *Handbook of divorce and relationship dissolution* (pp. 409–434). Mahwah, NJ: Lawrence Erlbaum and Associates.

García-Pastor, M.D. (2005). *A politeness based proposal on persuasion in ordinary ESL conversatoinal exchanges.*Unpublished manuscript, Valencia, Spain.

Gatewood, J.B., & Rosenwein, R. (1981). Interactional synchrony: genuine or spurious? A critique of recent research, *Journal of Nonverbal Behaviour*, 6: 12–29.

Gergen, K.J. (1990). *The saturated self: Dilemmas of identity in contemporary life.* New York: Basic Books.

Giles, H. (1978). Linguistic differentiation in ethnic groups. In H. Tajfel (Ed.), *Differentiation between social groups.* London: Academic Press.

Giles, H., & Powesland, P.F. (1975). *Speech style and social evaluation.* London: Academic Press.

Giles, H., Taylor, D.M., & Bourhis, R.Y. (1973). Towards a theory of interpersonal accommodation through language use. *Language in Society, 2*, 177–192.

Glick, P.C. (1989). Remarried families, stepfamilies and stepchildren: A brief demographic analysis. *Family Relations, 38*, 24–27.

Goffman, E. (1959). *Behaviour in public places.* Harmondsworth, UK: Penguin.

Goldsmith, D.J., & Baxter, L.A. (1996). Constituting relationships in talk: A taxonomy of speech events in social and personal relationships. *Human Communication Research, 23*, 87–114.

Goodwin, R., & Cramer, L. (Eds.). (2002). *Inappropriate relationships: The unconventional, the disapproved, and the forbidden.* Mahwah, NJ: Lawrence Erlbaum and Associates.

Gore, J.S., Cross, S.E., & Morris, M.L. (2006). Let's be friends: Relational self-construal and the development of intimacy. *Personal Relationships, 13*(1), 83–102.

Gotlib, I.H., & Hooley, J.M. (1988). Depression and marital distress: Current and future directions. In S.W. Duck (Ed.), *Handbook of personal relationships.* Chichester, UK: Wiley.

Gottlieb, B.H. (1983). *Social support strategies: Guidelines for mental health practice.* London: Sage.

Gottlieb, B.H. (1985). Social support and the study of personal relationships. *Journal of Social and Personal Relationships, 2*, 351–375.

Gottman, J.M. (1994). *What predicts divorce?* Hillsdale, NJ: Erlbaum.

Greenblatt, M. (1978). The grieving spouse. *American Journal of Psychiatry, 135*, 43–47.

Greene, J.O., O'Hair, H.D., Cody, M.J., & Yen, C. (1985). Planning and control of behavior during deception. *Human Communication Research, 11*, 335–364.

Grewe, B. (2006). Relationships on the rocks: How a relationship changes after a person acquires physical disability, *Central States Communication Association Annual Convention.* Indianapolis, IN.

Guerrero, L.K., & Andersen, P.A. (1991). The waxing and waning of relational intimacy: Touch as a function of relational stage, gender and touch avoidance. *Journal of Social and Personal Relationships, 8*, 147–165.

Guerrero, L.K., & Floyd, K. (2006). *Nonverbal communication in relationships.* Mahwah, NJ: Lawrence Erlbaum and Associates.

Guerrero, L.K., Trost, M.R., & Yoshimura, S.M. (2005). Romantic jealousy: Emotions and communicative responses. *Personal Relationships, 12*(2), 233–252.

Haas, S.M. (2001). Social support as relationship maintenance in gay male couples coping with HIV. *Journal of Social and Personal Relationships, 19,* 87–111.

Haas, S.M., & Stafford, L. (2005). Maintenance behaviors in same-sex and marital relationships: A matched sample comparison. *Journal of Family Communication, 5*(1), 43–60.

Hadar, U. (1989). Two types of gesture and their role in speech production. *Journal of Language and Social Psychology, 8,* 221–228.

Hagestad, G.O., & Smyer, M.A. (1982). Dissolving long-term relationships: Patterns of divorcing in middle age, *Personal Relationships 4: Dissolving Personal Relationships* (pp. 155–187). London: Academic Press.

Hall, E.T. (1966). *The hidden dimension.* New York: Doubleday/Anchor.

Harden Fritz, J.M., & Omdahl, B.L. (Eds.). (2007). *Problematic relationships in the workplace.* New York: Peter Lang.

Harvey, J.H., & Fine, M.A. (2004). *Children of divorce: Stories of loss and growth.* Mahwah, NJ: Lawrence Erlbaum and Associates.

Harvey, J.H., Barnes, M.K., Carlson, H.R., & Haig, J. (1995). Held captive by their memories: managing grief in relationships. In S.W. Duck, & J.T Wood (Eds.), *Confronting relationship challenges.* (Vol. 5) *Understanding Relationship Processes.* (pp. 181–210). Thousand Oaks, CA: SAGE.

Hatfield, E., & Walster, G.W. (1978). *A new look at love.* Lanham, MD: University Press of America.

Hays, R., & DiMatteo, R. (1984). Towards a more therapeutic physician patient relationship. In S.W. Duck (Ed.), *Personal relationships 5: Repairing personal relationships.* London & New York: Academic Press.

Hazan, C., & Shaver, P. (1987). Romantic love conceptualized as an attachment process. *Journal of Personality and Social Psychology, 52,* 511–524.

Hecht, M., Marston, P.J., & Larkey, L.K. (1994). Love ways and relationships quality. *Journal of Social and Personal Relationships, 11,* 25–43.

Heisler, J.M. (2005). Family communication about sex: Parents and college-aged offspring recall discussion topics, satisfaction, and parental involvement. *Journal of Family Communication, 5*(4), 295–312.

Heller, K., & Rook, K.S. (2001). Distinguishing the theoretical functions of social ties: Implications of support interventions. In B.R. Sarason & S.W. Duck (Eds.), *Personal relationships: Implications for clinical and community psychology.* (pp. 119–140). Chichester, UK: Wiley.

Hendrick, C., & Hendrick, S.S. (1988). Lovers wear rose colored glasses. *Journal of Social and Personal Relationships, 5,* 161–183.

Hendrick, C., & Hendrick, S.S. (1990). A relationship-specific version of the love attitudes scale. *Journal of Social Behavior and Personality, 5,* 239–254.

Hendrick, C., Hendrick, S.S., Foote, F., & Slapion-Foote, M. (1984). Do men and women love differently? *Journal of Social and Personal Relationships, 1,* 177–196.

Hendrick, S.S., & Hendrick, C. (2000). Romantic love. In C. Hendrick & S.S. Hendrick (Eds.), *Close relationships: A sourcebook* (pp. 203–215). Thousand Oaks, CA: SAGE.

Hepburn, J.R., & Crepin, A.E. (1984). Relationship strategies in a coercive institution: A study of dependence among prison guards. *Journal of Social and Personal Relationships, 1,* 139–158.

Hess, J.A. (2000). Maintaining a nonvoluntary relationship with disliked partners: An investigation into the use of distancing behaviors. *Human Communication Research, 26,* 458–488.

Hess, J.A. (2002). Maintaining unwanted relationships. In D.J. Canary & M. Dainton (Eds.), *Maintaining relationships through communication: Relational, contextual and cultural variations* (pp. 103–124). Mahwah, NJ: Lawrence Erlbaum and Associates.

Hetherington, E.M. (1979). Divorce: A child's perspective. *American Psychologist, 34,* 851–858.

Hetherington, E.M., Cox, M., & Cox, R. (1982). Effects of divorce on parents and children. In M. Lamb (Ed.), *Nontraditional families.* Hillsdale, NJ: Erlbaum.

Hewes, D.E., Graham, M.L., Doelger, J., & Pavitt, C. (1985). 'Second-guessing': Message interpretation in social networks. *Human Communication Research, 11,* 299–334.

Hinde, R.A. (1981). The bases of a science of interpersonal relationships. In S.W. Duck & R. Gilmour (Eds.), *Personal relationships I: studying personal relationships* (pp. 1–22). London, New York, San Francisco: Academic Press.

Hobfoll, S.E. (1984). *Limitations of social support in the stress process.* Paper presented at the NATO Advances Study Seminar on Social Support, Bonas, France.

Hocker, J., & Wilmot, W. (2006). *Interpersonal conflict, 7th edn.* Dubuque, IA: Wm. C. Brown & Co Publishers.

Hollander, E.P. (1958). Conformity, status and idiosyncrasy credit. *Psychological Review, 65,* 117–127.

Honeycutt, J.M. (1993). Memory structures for the rise and fall of personal relationships. In S.W. Duck (Ed.), *Individuals in relationships (understanding relationship processes 1)* (pp. 60–86). Newbury Park, CA: SAGE.

Hooley, J.M., & Hiller, J.B. (2001). Family relationships and major mental disorder: Risk factors and preventive strategies. In B. R. Sarason & S.W. Duck (Eds.), *Personal relationships: Implications for clinical and community psychology* (pp. 61–87). Chichester, UK: Wiley.

Hopper, R., Knapp, M.L., & Scott, L. (1981). Couples' personal idioms: Exploring intimate talk. *Journal of Communication, 31,* 23–33.

Hovland, C., Janis, I., & Kelley, H.H. (1953). *Communication and persuasion.* New Haven, CT: Yale University Press.

Howells, K. (1981). Social relationships in violent offenders. In S.W. Duck & R. Gilmour (Eds.), *Personal Relationships 3: Personal Relationships in Disorder.* London: Academic Press.

Hughes, G. (1991). *Swearing: A social history of foul language, oaths and profanity in English.* Blackwell: Oxford.

Hughes, M., Morrison, K., & Asada, K.-J.K. (2005). What's love got to do with it? Exploring the impact of maintenance rules, the attitudes, and network support on friends-with-benefits relationships. *Western Journal of Communication, 69*(1), 49–66.

Huston, M., & Schwartz, P. (1995). Lesbian and gay male relationships. In J.T. Wood & S. W. Duck (Eds.), *Under-studied relationships: Off the beaten track (understanding relationship processes 6)* (pp. 89–121). Thousand Oaks, CA: Sage.

Huston, T.L., Surra, C.A., Fitzgerald, N.M. & Cate, R.M. (1981) From courtship to marriage: Mate selection as an interpersonal process. In S.W. Duck & R. Gilmour (Eds.), *Personal relationship 2: Developing personal relationships* (pp. 53–88). London & New York: Academic Press.

Igarashi, T., Takai, J., & Yoshida, T. (2005). Gender differences in social network development via mobile phone text messages: A longitudinal study. *Journal of Social and Personal Relationships, 22*(5), 691–713.

James, R.M. (1959). Status and competence of jurors. *American Journal of Sociology, 64,* 563–570.

James, W. (1890). *Principles of psychology.* London: Macmillan.

Jones, R.A. (1982). *Expectations and illness.* In H. S. Friedman & M. DiMatteo. R. (Eds.), *Interpersonal issues in health care.* London & New York: Academic Press.

Jones, S.M. (2005). Attachment style differences and similarities in evaluations of affective communication skills and person centered comforting messages. *Western Journal of Communication, 69*(3), 233–249.

Jones, W.H., Hansson, R.O & Cutrona, C. (1984). Helping the lonely: issues of intervention with young and older adults. In S.W Duck (Eds.), *Personal relationship 5: Repairing personal relationships.* London: Academic Press.

Katz, J., & Aakhus, M. (Eds.). (2002). *Perpetual contact: Mobile communication, private talk, public performance.* Cambridge: Cambridge University Press.

Kayser, K., & Rao, S.S. (2006). Process of disaffection in relationship breakdown. In M.A. Fine & J.H. Harvey (Eds.), *Handbook of divorce and relationship dissolution* (pp. 201–221). Mahwah, NJ: Lawrence Erlbaum and Associates.

Keeley, M., & Hart, A. (1994). Nonverbal behavior in dyadic interaction. In S.W. Duck (Ed.), *Dynamics of relationships (understanding relationships 4)* (pp. 135–162). Thousand Oaks, CA: SAGE.

Kelly, L. (1982). A rose by any other name is still a rose: A comparative analysis of reticence, communication apprehension, unwillingness to communicate and shyness. *Human Communication Research, 8,* 99–113.

Kelvin, P. (1977). Predictability, power, and vulnerablity in interpersonal attraction. In S.W. Duck (Ed.), *Theory and practice in interpersonal attraction* (pp. 355–378). London: Academic Press.

Kemper, T.D., & Bologh, R.W. (1981). What do you get when you fall in love? Some health status effects. *Sociology of Health and Illness, 3,* 72–88.

Kendon, A. (1967). Some functions of gaze direction in social interaction. *Acta Psychologica, 26,* 22–63.

Kenrick, D.T., & Trost, M.R. (2000). An evolutionary perspective on human relationships. In W. Ickes & S.W. Duck (Eds.), *The social psychology of personal relationships* (pp. 9–35). Chichester, UK: Wiley.

Kephart, W.M. (1967). Some correlates of romantic love. *Journal of Marriage and the Family, 29,* 470–474.

Kirkpatrick, C.D., Duck, S.W., & Foley, M.K. (Eds.). (2006). *Relating difficulty: The processes of constructing and managing difficult interaction.* Mahwah, NJ: Lawrence Erlbaum and Associates.

Kitson, G.C., & Morgan, L.A. (1990). The multiple consequences of divorce: A decade review. *Journal of Marriage and the Family, 52,* 913–924.

Kitzmann, K.M., & Cohen, R. (2003). Parents' versus children's perceptions of interparental conflict as predictors of children's friendship quality. *Journal of Social and Personal Relationships, 20*(5), 689–700.

Klein, R.C.A., & Johnson, M.P. (2000). Strategies of couple conflict. In R. Milardo & S.W. Duck (Eds.), *Families as relationships* (pp. 79–98). Chichester: Wiley.

Klein, R.C.A., & Milardo, R. (1993). Third-party influences on the development and maintenance of personal relationships. In S.W. Duck (Ed.), *Social contexts of relationships (understanding relationship processes: Vol. 3)* (pp. 55–77). Newbury Park, CA: SAGE.

Klinger, E. (1977). *Meaning and void: Inner experience and the incentives in people's lives.* Minneapolis: University of Minnesota Press.

Knapp, M.L., & Hall, J.A. (2002). *Nonverbal communication in human interaction (5th edn.).* New York: Holt, Rinehart and Winston, Inc.

Knapp, M.L., & Vangelisti, A. (2004). *Interpersonal communication and human relationships (5th edn.).* Boston: Allyn and Bacon.

Knee, C.R. (1998). Implicit theories of relationships: Assessment and prediction of romantic relationship initiation, coping, and longevity. *Journal of Personality and Social Psychology, 74*(2), 360–370.

Knobloch, L.K., & Haunani Solomon, D. (2003). Manifestations of relationship conceptualizations in conversation. *Human Communication Research, 29*(4), 482–515.

Kobus, K. (2003). Peers and adolescent smoking. *ADDICTION, 98*, 37–55.

Koenig Kellas, J. (2005). Family ties: Communicating identity through jointly told family stories. *Communication Monographs, 72*(4), 365–389.

Koenig Kellas, J., & Trees, A.R. (2006). Finding meaning in difficult family experiences: Sense making and interaction processes during joint family storytelling. *Journal of Family Communication, 6*(1), 49–76.

Kovecses, Z. (1991). A linguist's quest for love. *Journal of Social and Personal Relationships, 8*, 77–98.

Kowalski, R. (1997). Aversive interpersonal behaviour. New York: Plenum.

Kramer, L., & Baron, L.A. (1995). Intergenerational linkages: How experiences with siblings relate to parenting of siblings. *Journal of Social and Personal Relationships, 12*, 67–87.

Kramer, M.W., & Tan, C.L. (2006). Emotion management in dealing with difficult people. In J.M. Harden Fritz & B.L. Omdahl (Eds.), *Problematic relationships in the workplace* (pp. 153–176). New York: Peter Lang.

Kraut, R.E. (1973). Effects of social labelling on giving to charity. *Journal of Experimental Social Psychology, 9*, 551–562.

Kunkel, A.W., Wilson, S.R., Olufowote, J., & Robson, S. (2003). Identity implications of influence goals: Initiating, intensifying, and ending romantic relationships. *Western Journal of Communication, 67*(4), 382–412.

Kurdek, L.A. (1994). Conflict resolution styles in gay, lesbian, heterosexual nonparent, and heterosexual parent couples. *Journal of Marriage and the Family, 56*, 705–722.

La Gaipa, J.J. (1981). A systems approach to personal relationships. In S.W. Duck & R. Gilmour (Eds.), *Personal relationships 1: Studying personal relationships* (pp. 67–90). London: Academic Press.

La Gaipa, J.J. (1982). Rules and rituals in disengaging from relationships. In S.W. Duck (Ed.), *Personal relationships 4: Dissolving personal relationships* (pp. 189–209). London: Academic Press.

La Gaipa, J.J. (1990). The negative effects of informal support systems. In S.W. Duck & W.R.C. Silver (Eds.), *Personal relationships and social support* (pp. 122–140). London: SAGE.

Ladd, G.W., LeSieur, K., & Profilet, S. (1993). Direct parental influences on young children's peer relations. In S.W. Duck (Ed.), *Learning about relationships (Understanding relationship processes 2)* (pp. 152–183). Thousand Oaks, CA: SAGE.

Lakoff, G., & Johnson, M. (1980). *Metaphors we live by*. Chicago: Chicago University Press.

Lakoff, R. (1973). Language and women's place. *Language in Society, 2*, 45–79.

Lannutti, P.J. (2005). For better or worse: Exploring the meanings of same-sex marriage within the lesbian, gay, bisexual, and transgendered community. *Journal of Social and Personal Relationships, 22*(1), 5–18.

Lea, M., & Spears, R. (1995). Love at first byte: Relationships conducted over electronic systems. In J.T. Wood & S.W. Duck (Eds.), *Under-studied relationships: Off the beaten track (understanding relationship processes: Vol. 6). (pp. 197–233). Newbury Park, CA: SAGE.

Leatham, G.B., & Duck, S.W. (1990). Conversations with friends and the dynamics of social support. In S.W. Duck with R.C. Silver (Eds.), *Personal relationships and social support* (pp. 1–29). London: SAGE.

Lee, J.A. (1973). *The colors of love: An exploration of the ways of loving*. Ontario: New Press.

Levitt, M., Silver, M.E., & Franco, N. (1996). Troublesome relationships: A part of the human experience. *Journal of Social and Personal Relationships, 13*, 523–536.

Lewis, R.A., & McAvoy, P. (1984). Improving the quality of relationships: Therapeutic interventions with opiate-abusing couples. In S.W. Duck (Ed.), *Personal relationships 5: Repairing personal relationships*. London & New York: Academic Press.

Lindorff, M. (2005). Determinants of received a social support: Who gives what to managers? *Journal of Social and Personal Relationships, 22*(3), 323–337.

Lindsey, E.W., Colwell, M.J., Frabutt, J.M., & Mackinnon-Lewis, C. (2006). Family conflict in divorced and non-divorced families: Potential consequences for boys' friendship status and friendship quality. *Journal of Social and Personal Relationships, 23*(1), 45–63.

Lloyd, J., & Anthony, J. (2003). Hanging out with the wrong crowd: How much difference can parents make in an urban environment? *Journal of Urban Health: Bulletin of the New York Academy of Medicine, 80*(3), 383–399.

Lollis, S., & Kuczynski, L. (1997). Beyond one hand clapping? Seeing bi-directionality in parent–child relationships. *Journal of Social and Personal Relationships, 14*, 441–461.

Lovaglia, M.J., & Lucas, J.W. (2006). Leadership as the management of power in organizations. In C.D. Kirkpatrick, S.W. Duck & M.K. Foley (Eds.), *Relating difficulty: The processes of constructing and managing difficult interaction*. Mahwah, NJ: Lawrence Erlbaum and Associates.

Lyons, R.F., & Meade, D. (1995). Painting a new face on relationships: Relationship remodelling in response to chronic illness. In S.W. Duck & J.T. Wood (Eds.), *Confronting relationship challenges (understanding relationship processes 5)* (pp. 181–210). Thousand Oaks, CA: SAGE.

Lyons, R.F., Langille, L., & Duck, S.W. (2006). Difficult relationships and relationship difficulties: Relationship adaptation and chronic health problems. In C.D. Kirkpatrick, S.W. Duck & M.K. Foley (Eds.), *Relating difficulty: Processes of constructing and managing difficult interaction*. (pp. 203–224). Mahwah, NJ: Lawrence Erlbaum and Associates.

Lyons, R.F., Mickelson, K.D., Sullivan, M.J.L., & Coyne, J.C. (1998). Coping as a communal process. *Journal of Social and Personal Relationships, 15*, 579–605.

Mak, L., & Marshall, S.K. (2004). Perceived mattering in young adults' romantic relationships. *Journal of Social and Personal Relationships, 21*(4), 469–486.

Mamali, C. (1996). Interpersonal communication in totalitarian societies. In W. Gudykunst, S. Ting-Toomey, T. Nishida (Eds.), *Communication in personal relationships across cultures* (pp. 217–34). Thousand Oaks, CA: SAGE.

Manke, B., & Plomin, R. (1997). Adolescent familial interactions: A genetic extension of the social relations model. *Journal of Social and Personal Relationships, 14,* 505–522.

Manusov, V., & Milstein, T. (2005). Interpreting nonverbal behavior: Representation and transformation frames in Israeli and Palestinian media coverage of the 1993 Rabin–Arafat handshake. *Western Journal of Communication, 69*(3), 183–201.

Manusov, V., & Patterson, M.L. (2006). *Handbook of nonverbal communication.* Thousand Oaks, CA: SAGE.

Marston, P.J., Hecht, M., & Robers, T. (1987). 'true love ways': The subjectiove experience and communication of romantic love. *Journal of Social and Personal Relationships, 4,* 387–407.

Masuda, M. (2006). Perspectives on premarital postdissolution relationships: Account-making of friendships between former romantic partners. In M.A. Fine & J.H. Harvey (Eds.), *Handbook of divorce and relationship dissolution* (pp. 113–132). Mahwah, NJ: Lawrence Erlbaum and Associates.

Mazur, R. (1977). Beyond jealousy and pssessiveness. In G. Clanton & L. Smith (Eds.), *Jealousy.* Englewood Cliffs, NJ: Prentice Hall.

Marx, K. (1859). Contributions to the critique of political economy. Cited in R.C. Tucker (1972). *The Marx-Engels Reader.* New York: Norton.

McCall, G.J. (1982). Becoming unrelated: The management of bond dissolution. In S.W. Duck (Ed.), *Personal relationships 4: Dissolving personal relationships* (pp. 211–232). London: Academic Press.

McCall, G.J. (1988). The organizational life cycle of relationships. In S.W. Duck (Ed.), *Handbook of personal relationships* (pp. 467–486). Chichester, UK: Wiley.

McCarthy, B. (1983, November). *Social cognition and personal relationships.* Paper presented at the Lancaster University Relationships Research Group.

Mesch, G.S. (2006). Family relations and the internet: Exploring a family boundaries approach. *Journal of Family Communication, 6*(2), 119–138.

Metts, S.M. (2000). Face and facework: Implications for the study of personal relationships. In K. Dindia & S.W. Duck (Eds.), *Communication and personal relationships* (pp. 72–94). Chichester, UK: Wiley.

Metts, S.M. (2006). Hanging out and doing lunch. In J.T. Wood & S.W. Duck (Eds.), *Composing relationships: Communication in everyday life.* (pp. 76–85). Belmont, CA: Wadsworth.

Metts, S.M., & Planalp, S. (2002). Emotional communication. In M.L. Knapp & J.A. Daly (Eds.), *Handbook of interpersonal communication* (pp. 339–373). Thousand Oaks, CA: SAGE.

Metts, S.M., Cupach, W., & Bejlovec, R.A. (1989). 'I love you too much to ever start liking you'. *Journal of Social and Personal Relationships, 6,* 259–274.

Meyer, J.R. (2000). Cognitive models of message production: Unanswered questions. *Communication Theory, 10,* 176–187.

Miell, D.E. (1984). *Cognitive and communicative strategies in developing relationships.* Paper presented at the Unpublished Doctoral Thesis, University of Lancaster.

Miell, D.E. (1987). Remembering relationship development: Constructing a context for interactions. In R. Burnett, J. McPhee, & D.D. Clarke (Ed.), *Accounting for relationships* (pp. 60–73). London: Methuen.

Milardo, R.M. (1992). Comparative methods for delineating social networks. *Journal of Social and Personal Relationships, 9,* 447–461.

Milardo, R.M., & Allan, G.A. (2000). Social networks and marital relationships. In R.M. Milardo & S.W. Duck (Eds.), *Families as relationships* (pp. 117–133). Chichester, UK: Wiley & Sons.

Milardo, R.M., & Wellman, B. (1992). The personal is social. *Journal of Social and Personal Relationships, 9,* 339–342.

Milardo, R.M., Johnson, M.P., & Huston, T.L. (1983). Developing close relationships: Changing patterns of interaction between pair members and social networks. *Journal of Personality and Social Psychology, 44,* 964–976.

Milevsky, A. (2005). Compensatory patterns of sibling support in emerging adulthood: Variations in loneliness, self-esteem, depression, and life satisfaction. *Journal of Social and Personal Relationships, 22*(2), 743–755.

Miller, G.R., & Parks, M.P. (1982). Communication in dissolving relationships. In S.W. Duck (Ed.), *Personal relationship 4: Dissolving personal relationships.* London: Academic Press.

Miller, K.I., Stiff, J.B., & Ellis, B.H. (1988). Communication and empathy as precursors to burnout among human service workers. *Communication Monographs, 55.*

Miller, M.D. (1982). Friendship, power and the language of compliance gaining. *Journal of Language and Social Behavior, 1,* 111–122.

Miller, R.S. (1996). *Embarrassment: Poise and peril in everyday life.* New York: Guilford.

Miller-Day, M.A. (1998). The social process of drug resistance in a relational context. *Communication Studies, 49,* 358–375.

Miller-Day, M.A. (2002). Parent–adolescent communication about alcohol, tobacco and other drug use. *Journal of Adolescent Research, 17*(6), 604–616.

Miller-Day, M.A. (2004). *Communication among grandmothers, mothers, and adult daughters: A qualitative study of maternal relationships.* Mahwah, NJ: Lawrence Erlbaum and Associates.

Miller-Day, M.A., & Dodd, A.H. (2004). Toward a descriptive model of parent–offspring communication about alcohol and other drugs. *Journal of Social and Personal Relationships, 21*(1), 69–91.

Mokros, H.B. (2006). Composing relationships at work: Three minutes at a wholesale produce market. In J.T. Wood & S.W. Duck (Eds.), *Composing that relationships: A communication in everyday life* (pp. 175–185). Belmont, CA: Thompson Wadsworth.

Montgomery, B.M. (1981). Verbal immediacy as a behavioral indicator of open communication. *Communication Quarterly, 30,* 28–34.

Montgomery, B.M. (1988). Quality communication in personal relationships. In S.W. Duck (Ed.), *Handbook of personal relationships* (pp. 343–362). Chichester, UK: Wiley.

Morr-Serewicz, M.C. (2006). The difficulties of in-law relationships. In C.D. Kirkpatrick, S.W. Duck & M.K. Foley (Eds.), *Relating difficulty: The processes of constructing and managing difficult interaction* (pp. 101–117). Mahwah, NJ: Lawrence Erlbaum and Associates.

Mowen, J.C., & Cialdini, R B. (1980). On implementing the door-in-the-face compliance technique in a business context. *Journal of Marketing Research, 17,* 253–258.

Muehlhoff, T.M. (2006). 'He started it!' Everyday communication in parenting. In J.T. Wood & S.W. Duck (Eds.), *Composing relationships: Communication in everyday life* (pp. 46–54). Belmont, CA: Wadsworth.

Muraco, A. (2005). Heterosexual evaluations of hypothetical friendship behavior based on sex and sexual orientation. *Journal of Social and Personal Relationships,* 22(5), 587–605.

Newell, S., & Stutman, R.K. (1988). The social confrontation episode. *Communication Monographs, 55,* 266–285.

Nicholson, J.H. (2006). 'Them's fightin' words': Naming in everyday talk between siblings. In J.T. Wood & S.W. Duck (Eds.), *Composing relationships: Communication in everyday life* (pp. 55–64). Belmont, CA: Wadsworth.

Noller, P., & Gallois, C. (1988). Understanding and misunderstanding in marriage: Sex and matrital adjustment differences in structured and free interaction. In P. Noller & M.A. Fitzpatrick (Eds.), *Perspectives on marital interaction.* Clevedon, UK & Philadelphia.

Notarius, C. (1996). Marriage: Will I be happy or sad? In N. Vanzetti & S.W. Duck (Eds.), *A lifetime of relationships.* Pacific Grove, CA: Brooks/Cole.

O'Keefe, D.J. (2004). Trends and prospects in persuasion theory and research. In J.S. Seiter & R.H. Gass (Eds.), *Perspectives on persuasion, social influence, and compliance gaining* (pp. 31–43). Boston, MA: Pearson.

Omdahl, B.L., & Harden Fritz, J.M. (2006). Stress, burnout and impaired mental health: Consequences of problematic work relationships. In J.M. Harden Fritz & B.L. Omdahl (Eds.), *Problematic relationships in the workplace* (pp. 109–130). New York: Peter Lang.

Orford, J. (1976). A study of the personalities of excessive drinkers and their wives, using the approaches of Leary and Eysenck. *Journal of Consulting and Clinical Psychology, 44,* 534–545.

Orford, J. (2001). *Excessive appetites: A psychological view of addictions, 2nd edn.* Chichester, UK: Wiley.

Orford, J., & O'Reilly, P. (1981). Disorders in the family. In S.W. Duck & R. Gilmour (Eds.), *Personal relationships 3. Personal relationships in disorder.* London & New York: Academic Press.

Orford, J., Oppenheimer, E., Egert, S., Hensman, C., & Guthrie, S. (1976). The cohesiveness of alcoholism-complicated marriages and its influence on treatment outcome, *British Journal of Psychiatry, 128,* 318–349.

Otis, M.D., Rostosky, S.S., Riggle, E.D.B., & Hamrin, R. (2006). Stress and relationship quality in same-sex couples. *Journal of Social and Personal Relationships, 23(1),* 81–99.

Palmer, M.T. (1990). Controlling conversation: Turns, topics and interpersonal control. *Communication Monographs, 56,* 1–18.

Parke, R.D., & O'Neil, R. (1997). The influence of significant others on learning about relationships. In S.W. Duck (Ed.), *Handbook of personal relationships, 2nd edn* (pp. 29–60). Chichester, UK: Wiley.

Parks, M.R. (2006). *Communication and social networks.* Mahwah, NJ: Lawrence Erlbaum Associates.

Parks, M.R., & Adelman, M. (1983). Communication networks and the development of romantic relationships: An expansion of uncertainty reduction theory. *Human Communication Research, 10,* 55–80.

Parks, M.R., & Eggert, L.L. (1991). The role of social context in the dynamics of personal relationships. In W.H. Jones & D. Perlman (Eds.), *Advances in personal relationships* (Vol. 2, pp. 1–34). London: Jessica Kingsley Publishers Ltd.

Parsons, T. (1951). *The social system*. Glencoe, IL: Free Press.

Patterson, M.L. (1988). Functions of nonverbal behavior in close relationships. In S.W. Duck (Ed.), *Handbook of personal relationships*. Chichester, UK: Wiley.

Patterson, M.L. (1992). A functional approach to nonverbal exchange. In R.S. Feldman & B. Rime (Eds.), *Fundamentals of nonverbal behavior* (pp. 458–495). New York: Cambridge University Press.

Paul, E.L. (2006). Beer goggles, catching feelings and the walk of shame: The myths and realities of the hookup experience. In C.D. Kirkpatrick, S.W. Duck & M.K. Foley (Eds.), *Relating difficulty: Processes of constructing and managing difficult interaction*. (pp. 141–160). Mahwah, NJ: Lawrence Erlbaum and Associates.

Pearson, J.C. (1996). Forty-forever years? In N. Vanzetti & S.W. Duck (Eds.), *A lifetime of relationships* (pp. 383–405). Pacific Grove, CA: Brooks/Cole.

Pechmann, C., Zhao, G., Goldberg, M.E., & Reibling, E.T. (2003). What to convey in antismoking advertisements for adolescents: The use of protection motivation theory to identify effectve message themes. *Journal of Marketing, 67,* 1–18.

Peplau, L.A., & Spalding, L.R. (2000). The close relationships of lesbians, gay men, and bisexuals. In C. Hendrick & S.S. Hendrick (Eds.), *Close relationships: A sourcebook* (pp. 111–123). Thousand Oaks, CA: SAGE.

Perlman, D., & Serbin, R. (1984, July). *A sports report: The effects of racquet matches on loneliness.* Paper presented at the Second International Conference on Personal Relationships, Madison, WI.

Petronio, S. (2002). *Boundaries of privacy*. Albany, NY: SUNY Press.

Petronio, S., Sargent, J.D., Andea, L., Reganis, P., & Cichocki, D. (2004). Family and friends as health-care advocates: Dilemmas of confidentiality and privacy. *Journal of Social and Personal Relationships, 21*(1), 33–52.

Pettit, G.S., & Mize, J. (1993). Substance and style: Understanding the ways in which parents teach children about social relationships. In S.W. Duck (Ed.), *Learning about relationships (understanding relationship processes 2)* (pp. 118–151). Thousand Oaks, CA: SAGE.

Pettit, G., & Clawson, M.A. (1996). Pathways to interpersonal competence: Parenting and children's peer relations. In N. Vanzetti & S.W. Duck (Eds.), *A lifetime of relationships* (pp. 125–154). Pacific Grove, CA: Brooks/Cole.

Phillips, D.P. (1970). *Dying as a form of social behavior*. Ann Arbor, MI. Unpublished PhD Thesis, University of Michigan.

Phillips, D.P. (1972). Deathday and birthday: an unexpected connection. In J.M. Tanur (Ed.), *Statistics: a guide to the unknown*. San Francisco, CA: Holden Day.

Planalp, S. (1993). Friends' and acquaintances' conversations II: Coded differences. *Journal of Social and Personal Relationships, 10,* 339–354.

Planalp, S., & Benson, A. (1992). Friends' and acquaintances' conversations I: Observed differences. *Journal of Social and Personal Relationships, 9,* 483–506.

Planalp, S., & Garvin-Doxas, K. (1994). Using mutual knowledge in conversation: Friends as experts in each other. In S.W. Duck (Ed.), *Dynamics of relationships (understanding relationship processes 4)* (pp. 1–26). Newbury Park, CA: SAGE.

Powell, K.A., & Afifi, T.D. (2005). Uncertainty management and adoptees' ambiguous loss of their birth parents. *Journal of Social and Personal Relationships, 22*(1), 129–151.

Prusank, D., Duran, R., & DeLillo, D.A. (1993). Interpersonal relationships in women's magazines: Dating and relating in the 1970s and 1980s. *Journal of Social and Personal Relationships, 10*, 307–320.

Putallaz, M., Costanzo, P.R., & Klein, T.P. (1993). Parental childhood social experiences and their effects on children's relationships. In S.W. Duck (Ed.), *Learning about relationships (understanding relationship processes 2)* (pp. 63–97). Newbury Park: SAGE.

Qualter, P., & Munn, P. (2005). Friendships and play partners of lonely children. *Journal of Social and Personal Relationships, 22*(3), 379–397.

Ramirez, A., & Burgoon, J.K. (2004). The effects of interactivity on initial interactions: The influence of information valence and modality and information richness on computer mediated interaction. *Communication Monographs, 71*(4), 422–447.

Reinhardt, J.P., Boerner, K., & Horowitz, A. (2006). Good to have but not to use: Differential impact of perceived and received support on well-being. *Journal of Social and Personal Relationships, 23*(1), 117–129.

Reis, H.T., & Shaver, P.R. (1988). Intimacy as an interpersonal process. In S.W. Duck (Ed.), *Handbook of personal relationships: Theory, research and interventions* (pp. 367–390). Chichester & New York: Wiley.

Repinski, D.J., & Zook, J.M. (2005). Three measures of closeness in adolescents' relationships with parents and friends: Variations and developmental significance. *Personal Relationships, 12*(1), 70–102.

Retzinger, S.M. (1995) Shame and anger in personal relationships. In S.W. Duck and J.T. Wood (Eds.), *Confronting relationship challenges.* (Vol. 5) *Understanding relationship processes* (pp. 22–42). Thousands Oaks, CA: SAGE.

Rholes, W.S., Simpson, J.A., & Friedman, M. (2006). Avoidant attachment and the experience of parenting. *Personality and Social Psychology Bulletin, 32*(3), 275–285.

Riggio, R., & Feldman, H. (Eds.). (2005). *Application of non-verbal behaviour.* Mahwah, NJ: Lawrence Erlbaum and Associates.

Rodrigues, A.E., Hall, J.H., & Fincham, F.D. (2006). What predicts divorce and relationship dissolution? In M.A. Fine & J.H. Harvey (Eds.), *Handbook of divorce and relationship dissolution* (pp. 85–112). Mahwah, NJ: LAwrence Erlbaum and Associates.

Rohlfing, M. (1995). 'Doesn't anybody stay in one place any more?' an exploration of the understudied phenomenon of long-distance relationships. In J.T. Wood & S.W. Duck (Eds.), *Under-studied relationships: Off the beaten track (understanding relationship processes: Vol. 6)* (pp. 173–196). Newbury Park, CA: SAGE.

Rollie, S.S. (2005). *MIA (maintenance in absence): Maintaining the nonresidential parent–child relationship.* Unpublished Ph.D., Iowa City: University of Iowa.

Rollie, S.S. (2006). Nonresidential parent–child relationships: Overcoming the challenges of absence. In C.D. Kirkpatrick, S.W. Duck & M.K. Foley (Eds.), *Relating difficulty: Processes of constructing and managing difficult interaction.* (pp. 181–202). Mahwah, NJ: Lawrence Erlbaum and Associates.

Rollie, S.S., & Duck, S.W. (2006). Stage theories of marital breakdown. In J.H. Harvey & M.A. Fine (Eds.), *Handbook of divorce and dissolution of romantic relationships* (pp. 176–193). Mahwah, NJ: Lawrence Erlbaum Associates.

Roloff, M.E., Janiszewski, C.A., McGrath, M.A., Burns, C.S., & Manrai, L.A. (1988). Acquiring resources from intimates: When obligation substitutes for persuasion. *Human Communication Research, 14*, 364–396.

Ross, L. (1977). The intuitive psychologist and his shortcomings: Distortions in the attribution process. In *Advances in experimental social psychology* (Vol. 10, pp. 173–220). New York: Academic Press.

Rowe, A.C., & Carnelley, K.B. (2005). Preliminary support for the use of a hierarchical mapping technique to examine attachment networks. *Personal Relationships, 12*(4), 499–519.

Rubin, Z. (1973). *Liking and loving.* New York: Holt, Rinehart & Winston.

Rubin, Z. (1987). Parent child loyalty and testimonial privilege. *Harvard Law Review, 100,* 910–929.

Rubin, Z. (1990). From love to law: A social psychologist's midlife passage. *ISSPR Bulletin.*

Ryan, R.M., La Guardia, J.G., Solky-Butzel, J., Chirkov, V., & Kim, Y. (2005). On the interpersonal regulation of emotions: Emotional reliance across gender, relationships, and cultures. *Personal Relationships, 12*(1), 145–163.

Sahlstein, E.M. (2004). Relating at a distance: Negotiating being together and being apart in long-distance relationships. *Journal of Social and Personal Relationships, 21*(5), 689–710.

Sahlstein, E.M. (2006a). Relational life in the 21st century: Managing poeple, time and distance. In J.T. Wood & S.W. Duck (Eds.), *Composing relationships: Communication in everyday life* (pp. 110–118). Belmont, CA: Wadsworth.

Sahlstein, E.M. (2006b). The trouble with distance. In C.D. Kirkpatrick, S.W. Duck & M.K. Foley (Eds.), *Relating difficulty: Processes of constructing and managing difficult interaction.* (pp. 119–140). Mahwah, NJ: Lawrence Erlbaum and Associates.

Sahlstein, E.M., & Duck, S.W. (2001). Interpersonal relations. In H. Giles & W. Robinson (Eds.), *Handbook of language and social behavior* (pp. 371–382). Chichester, UK: Wiley.

Sanderson, C.A., Rahm, K.B., & Beigbeder, S.A. (2005). The link between the pursuit of intimacy goals and satisfaction in close the same-sex friendships: An examination of the underlying processes. *Journal of Social and Personal Relationships, 22*(1), 75–98.

Sarason, B.R., & Duck, S.W. (Eds.). (2001). *Personal relationships: Implications for clinical and community psychology.* Chichester, UK: Wiley.

Sarason, B.R., Sarason, I.G., & Gurung, R.A.R. (2001). Close personal relationships and health outcomes: A key to the role of social support. In B.R. Sarason & S.W. Duck (Eds.), *Personal relationships: Implications for clinical and community psychology* (pp. 15–42). Chichester, UK: Wiley.

Schachter, S., & Singer, J.E. (1962). Cognitive, social, and physiological determinants of emotional states. *Psychological Review, 69,* 379–399.

Searcy, M., Duck, S.W., & Blanck, P.D. (2005). The appearance of injustice. In R. Riggio & R. Feldman (Eds.), *Applications of nonverbal behavior* (pp. 41–61). Mahwah, NJ: Lawrence Erlbaum and Associates.

Segrin, C. (2000). Interpersonal relationships and mental health problems. In K. Dindia & S.W. Duck (Eds.), *Communication and personal relationships* (pp. 95–111). Chichester, UK: Wiley.

Segrin, C. (2006). Family interactions and well-being: Integrative perspectives. *Journal of Family Communication, 6*(1), 3–21.

Segrin, C., Taylor, M.E., & Altman, J. (2005). Social cognitive mediators and relational outcomes associated with parental divorce. *Journal of Social and Personal Relationships, 22*(3), 361–377.

Seiter, J.S., & Dunn, D. (2000). Beauty and believability in sexual harassment cases: Does physical attractiveness affect perceptions of veracity and the likelihood of being harassed? *Communication Research Reports, 17*(2), 203–209.

Seiter, J.S., & Gass, R.H. (2004). *Perspectives on persuasion, social influence and compliance gaining.* Boston, MA: Pearson.

Seiter, J.S., & Sandry, A. (2003). Pierced for success? The effects of ear and nose piercing on perceptions of job candidates' credibility, attractiveness, and hirability. *Communication Research Reports, 20*(4), 287–298.

Shackelford, T.K., Goetz, A., Buss, D.M., Euler, H.A., & Hoier, S. (2005). When we hurt the ones we love: Predicting violence against women from men's mate retention. *Personal Relationships, 12*(4), 447–463.

Sher, T.G. (1996). Courtship and marriage: Choosing a primary relationship. In N. Vanzetti & S.W. Duck (Eds.), *A lifetime of relationships* (pp. 243–264). Pacific Grove, CA: Brooks/Cole.

Shuval, J.T. (1981). The contribution of psychological and social phenomena to an understanding of the aetiology of disease and illness. *Social Science and Medicine, 15A*, 337–342.

Sias, P.M. (2006). Workplace friendship the deterioration. In J.M. Harden Fritz & B.L. Omdahl (Eds.), *Problematic relationships in the workplace* (pp. 69–87). New York: Peter Lang.

Sias, P.M., & Perry, T. (2004). Disengaging from workplace relationships: A research note. *Human Communication Research, 30*(4), 589–602.

Sias, P.M., Heath, R.G., Perry, T., Silva, D., & Fix, B. (2004). Narratives of workplace friendship deterioration. *Journal of Social and Personal Relationships, 21*(3), 321–340.

Sigman, S.J. (1991). Handling the discontinuous aspects of continuous social relationships: Toward research on the persistence of social forms. *Communication Theory, 1*, 106–127.

Simmel, G. (1950). *The sociology of Georg Simmel.* New York: Free Press.

Simons-Morton, B., Haynie, D.L., Crump, A.D., Eitel, P., & Saylor, K.E. (2001). Peer and parent infleunces in smoking and drinking among early adolescents. *Health Education and Behavior, 28*(1), 95–107.

Singer, M.A., & Goldin-Meadow, S. (2005). Children learn when their teacher's gestures and speech differ. *Psychological Science, 16*(2), 85–89.

Smith, P.K., Bowers, L., Binney, V., & Cowie, H. (1993). Relationships of children involved in bully/victim problems at school. In S.W. Duck (Ed.), *Learning about relationships (understanding relationship processes 2)* (pp. 184–212). Newbury Park, CA: SAGE.

Snow, J. (1854/1936). On the mode of communication of cholera. In *Snow on cholera (1936).* New York: Commonwealth Fund.

Spencer, E.E. (1994). Transforming relationships through ordinary talk. In S.W. Duck (Ed.), *Understanding relationship processes 4: Dynamics of relationships,* (pp. 58–85). Newbury Park, CA: SAGE.

Spitzberg, B.H., & Cupach, W.R. (2002). Interpersonal skills. In M.L. Knapp & J.A. Daly (Eds.), *Handbook of interpersonal communication, third edn* (pp. 564–611). Thousand Oaks, CA: SAGE.

Spitzberg, B.H., & Cupach, W.R. (Eds.). (1998). *The dark side of close relationships.* New York: Erlbaum.

Sprecher, S. (1987). The effects of self-disclosure given and received on affection for an intimate partner and stability of the relationship. *Journal of Social and Personal Relationships, 4,* 115–127.

Sprecher, S., & Duck, S.W. (1993). Sweet talk: The role of communication in consolidating relationship. *Personality and Social Psychology Bulletin, 20,* 391–400.

Sprecher, S., & Felmlee, D. (2000). Romantic partners' perceptions of social network attributes with the passage of time and relationship transitions. *Personal Relationships, 7*(4), 325–340.

Sprecher, S., Felmlee, D., Schmeeckle, M., & Shu, X. (2006). No breakup occurs on an island: Social networks and relationship dissolution. In M.A. Fine & J.H. Harvey (Eds.), *Handbook of divorce and relationship dissolution* (pp. 457–478). Mahwah, NJ: Lawrence Erlbaum and Associates.

Stang, D.J. (1973). Effect of interaction rate on ratings of leadership and liking. *Journal of Personality and Social Psychology, 27,* 405–408.

Stein, C.H. (1993). Felt obligation in adult family relationships. In S.W Duck (Ed.), *Social contexts of relationship.* (Vol. 3) *Understanding relationship processes* (pp. 78–99). Thousands Oaks, CA: SAGE.

Stiff, J.B., & Miller, G.R. (1984, May). *Deceptive behaviors and behaviors which are interpreted as deceptive: An interactive approach to the study of deception.* Paper presented at the International Communication Association, San Francisco.

Stone, L. (1979). *The family, sex, and marriage in England 1500–1800.* New York: Harper Colophon.

Straus, M.A. (1985). *Family violence.* Paper to HDFR, University of Connecticut, Storrs, April.

Straus, M.A. (1990). Injury and frequency of assaults and the 'representative sample fallacy' in measuring wife beating and child abuse in M.A. Straus and R.J. Gelles (Eds.), *Physical violence in American families: Risk factors and adaptions in 8145 Families.* New Brunswick, NJ: Transaction Books.

Straus, M.A., & Gelles, R.J. (1986). Societal change and change in family violence from 1975 to 1985 as revealed in two nartional surveys. *Journal of Marriage and the Family, 48,* 465–479.

Suitor, J.J. (1991). Marital quality and satisfaction with the division of household labor across the family life cycle. *Journal of Marriage and the Family, 53,* 221–230.

Suls, J. (1977). Gossip as social comparison. *Journal of Communication, 27,* 164–168.

Sunnafrank, M. (1991). Interpersonal attraction and attitude similarity: A communication based assessment. In *Communication yearbook* (Vol. 14, pp. 451–483). Newbury Park, CA: SAGE.

Sunnafrank, M., & Ramirez, A. (2004). At first sight: Persistent relational effects of get-acquainted conversations. *Journal of Social and Personal Relationships, 21*(3), 361–379.

Suter, E.A. (2006). He has two mommies: Constructing lesbian families in social conversation. In J.T. Wood & S.W. Duck (Eds.), *Composing relaionships: Communication in everyday life* (pp. 119–127). Belmont, CA: Wadsworth.

Thibaut, J.W., & Kelley, H.H. (1959). *The social psychology of groups.* New York: Wiley.

Tracy, K., Craig, R.T., Smith, M., & Spisak, F. (1984). The discourse of requests: Assessment of a compliance-gaining approach. *Human Communication Research, 10,* 513–538.

Tuchman, B.W. (1978). *A distant mirror: The calamitous 14th century*. New York: Ballantine Books.

Tyler, J.M., Feldman, R.S., & Reichert, A. (2006). The price of deceptive behavior: Disliking and lying to people who lie to us. *Journal of Experimental Social Psychology, 42*(1), 69–77.

Umberson, D., & Williams, C.L. (1993). Divorced fathers: Parental role strain and psychological distress. *Journal of Family Issues, 14*, 378–400.

VanderVoort, L.A., & Duck, S.W. (2004). In appropriate relationships and out of them: The social paradoxes of normative and non-normative relational forms. In J. Duncombe, K. Harrison, G.A. Allan & D. Marsden (Eds.), *The state of affairs* (pp. 1–14). Mahwah, NJ: Erlbaum.

Vanzetti, N., & Duck, S.W. (Eds.). (1996). *A lifetime of relationships*. Pacific Grove, CA: Brooks/Cole.

Vavoula, G.N. & Sharples, M. (2002). *Kleos: A personal, mobile, knowledge and learning organisation system*. Paper presented at the proceedings of the IEEE International workshop on mobile and wireless Technologies in Education (WMTE 2002), Vaxjo, Sweden, Aug 29-30, pp. 152–156.

Veroff, J., Young, A.M., & Coon, H.M. (2000). The early years of marriage. In S.W. Duck (Ed.), *Handbook of personal relationships, 2nd edn* (pp. 19–38). Chichester, UK: Wiley.

Waldron, V.R., & Kelley, D. (2005). Forgiving communication as a response to relational transgressions. *Journal of Social and Personal Relationships, 22*(6), 723–742.

Walker, M.B., & Trimboli, A. (1989). Communicating affect: The role of verbal and nonverbal content. *Journal of Language and Social Psychology, 8*, 229–248.

Walther, J.B., & Bunz, U. (2005). The rules of virtual groups: Trust, liking, and performance in computer mediated communication. *Journal of Communication, 55*(4), 828–846.

Ward, C., & Tracey, T.J.G. (2004). Relation of shyness with aspects of online relationship involvement. *Journal of Social and Personal Relationships, 21*(5), 611–623.

Watzlawick, P., Beavin, J., & Jackson, D. (1967). *Pragmatics of human communication: A study of interactional patterns, pathologies and paradoxes*. New York: Norton.

Weber, A. (1983, May). *The breakdown of relationships*. Paper presented at the conference on Social Interaction and Relationships, Nags Head, North Carolina.

Weger, H. (2005). Disconfirming communication and self verification in marriage: The associations among the demand/withdrawal interaction pattern, feeling understood, and marital satisfaction. *Journal of Social and Personal Relationships, 22*(1), 19–31.

Weiss, R.S. (1974). The provisions of social relationships. In Z. Rubin (Ed.), *'Doing unto others'* (pp. 17–26). Englewood Cliffs, NJ: Prentice-Hall.

Werking, K.J. (2000). Cross sex friendships as an ideological practice. In K. Dindia & S.W. Duck (Eds.), *Communication and personal relationships* (pp. 113–130). Chichester, UK: Wiley.

West, J. (1995). Understanding how the dynamics of ideology influence violence between intimates. In S.W. Duck & J.T. Wood (Eds.), *Confronting relationship challenges (Understanding relationship processes 5)* (pp. 129–149). Thousand Oaks, CA: SAGE.

West, L. (1994, November). *The importance of what is left unsaid*. Paper presented at the Speech Communication Association Conference, New Orleans, LA.

West, L., & Duck, S.W. (1996, Nov. 1996). *'My sister is a pro-life lesbian tax evader': Self disclosure as social commentary and impression management.* Paper presented at the Speech Communication Association, San Antonio, TX.

West, L., Anderson, J., & Duck, S.W. (1995). Crossing the barriers to friendship between men and women. In J. T. Wood (Ed.), *Gendered relationships* (pp. 111–127). Mountain View, CA: Mayfield Publishing Co.

Weston, K. (1991). *Families we choose.* New York: Columbia University Press.

Wilkinson, J., & Canter, S. (1982). *Social skills training manual.* Chichester, UK: Wiley.

Willan, V.J., & Pollard, P. (2003). Likelihood of acquaintance rape as a function of males' sexual expectations, disappointment, and adherence to rape-conducive attitudes. *Journal of Social and Personal Relationships, 20*(5), 637–661.

Winters, A.M., & Duck, S.W. (2001). You ****! Swearing as an aversive and a relational activity. In R. Kowalski (Ed.), *Behaving badly: Aversive behaviors in interpersonal relationships* (pp. 59–77). Washington, DC: APA Books.

Wiseman, J.P. (1986). Friendship: Bonds and binds in a voluntary relationship. *Journal of Social and Personal Relationships, 3,* 191–211.

Wiseman, J.P., & Duck, S.W. (1995). Having and managing enemies: A very challenging relationship. In S.W. Duck & J.T. Wood (Eds.), *Confronting relationship challenges (understanding relationship processes 5),* (pp. 43–72.). Thousand Oaks, CA: SAGE.

Wood, J.T. (1995). Feminist scholarship and the study of relationships. *Journal of Social and Personal Relationships, 12,* 103–120.

Wood, J.T. (2004). Monsters and victims: Male felons' accounts of intimate partner violence. *Journal of Social and Personal Relationships, 21*(5), 555–576.

Wood, J.T. (2006). Chopping the carrots: Creating intimacy moment by moment. In J.T. Wood & S.W. Duck (Eds.), *Composing relationships: Communication in everyday life* (pp. 24–35). Belmont, CA: Wadsworth.

Wood, J.T., & Duck, S.W. (1995). Off the beaten track: New shores for relationship research. In J.T. Wood & S.W. Duck (Eds.), *Understudied relationships: Off the beaten track (understanding relationship processes 6).* (pp. 1–21). Thousand Oaks, CA: SAGE.

Wood, J.T., & Duck, S.W. (Eds.). (2006). *Composing relationships: Communication in everyday life.* Belmont, CA: Thomson Wadsworth.

Wright, P.H. (1978). Toward a theory of friendship based on a conception of the self. *Human Communication Research, 4,* 196–207.

Wright, P.H., & Wright, K.D. (1995). Co-dependency: Personality syndrome or relational process? In S.W. Duck & J.T. Wood (Eds.), *Confronting relationship challenges: (understanding relationship processes 5)* (pp. 109–128). Thousand Oaks, CA: SAGE.

Zaidel, S.F., & Mehrabian, A. (1969). The ability to communicate and infer positive and negative attitudes facially and vocally. *Journal of Experimental Research in Personality, 3,* 233–241.

Zimmer, T. (1986). Premarital anxieties. *Journal of Social and Personal Relationships, 3,* 149–160.

Zorn, T. (1995). Bosses and buddies: Constructing and performing simultaneously hierarchical and close friendship relationships. In J.T. Wood & S.W. Duck (Eds.), *Under-studied relationships: Off the beaten track (understanding relationship processes 6)* (pp. 122–147). Thousand Oaks, CA: SAGE.

Zweig, D. (2005). Beyond privacy and fairness concerns: Examining psychological boundary violations as a consequence of electronic performance monitoring. In J. Weckert (Ed.), *Electronic monitoring in the workplace: Controversies and solutions* (pp. 95–114). Hershey, PA: Idea Group.

Zweig, D., & Aggarwal, P. (2004). Beyond privacy: The mediating role of psychological contract breach in the relationship between knowledge-based marketing practices and attitudes, Annual Conference of the Association for Consumer Research, Portland, OR.

Zweig, D., & Webster, J. (2002). Where is the line between benign and invasive? An examination of psychological barriers to the acceptance of awareness monitoring systems. *Journal of Organizational Behavior, 23,* 605–622.

Author Index

Subject Index